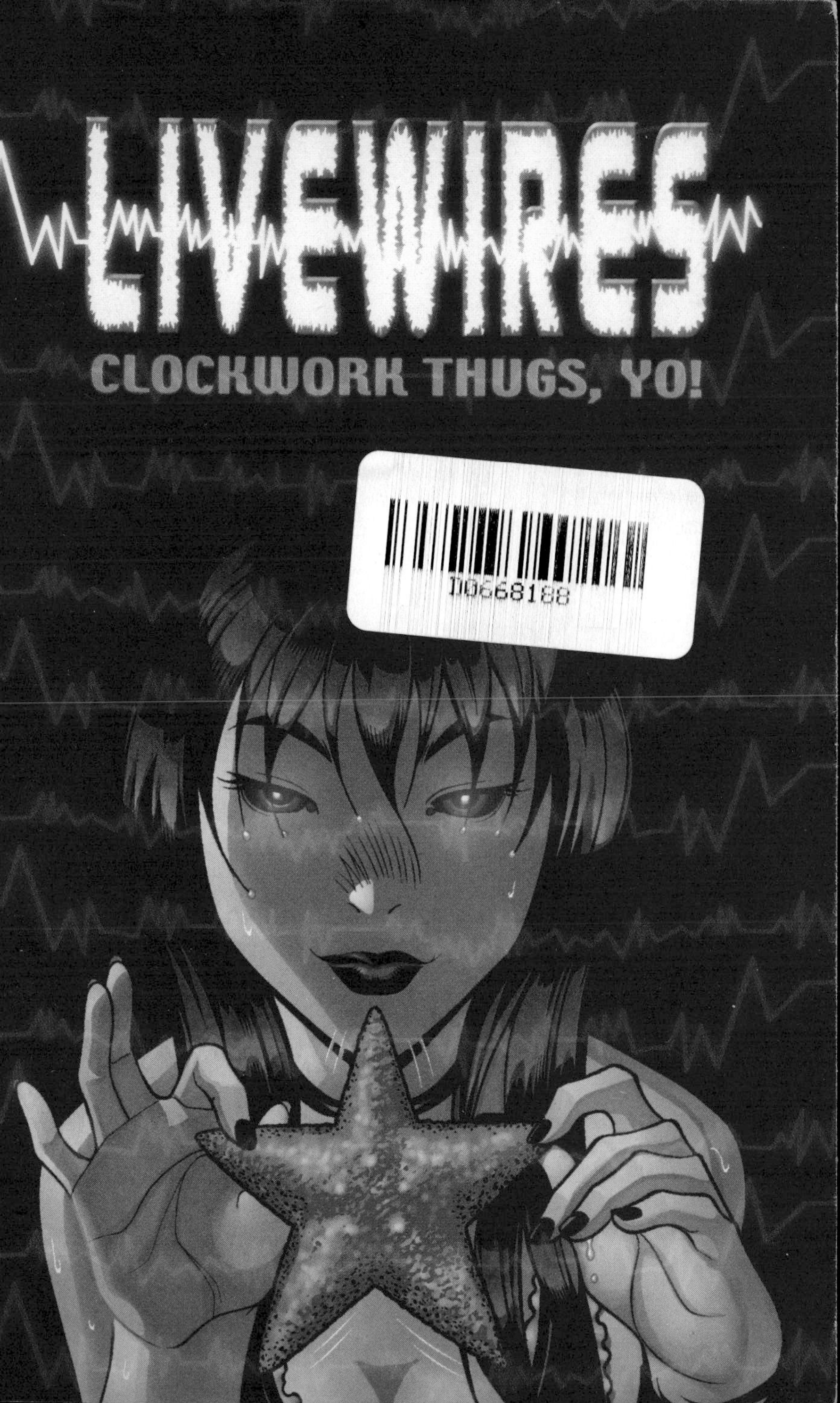
LIVEWIRES
CLOCKWORK THUGS, YO!

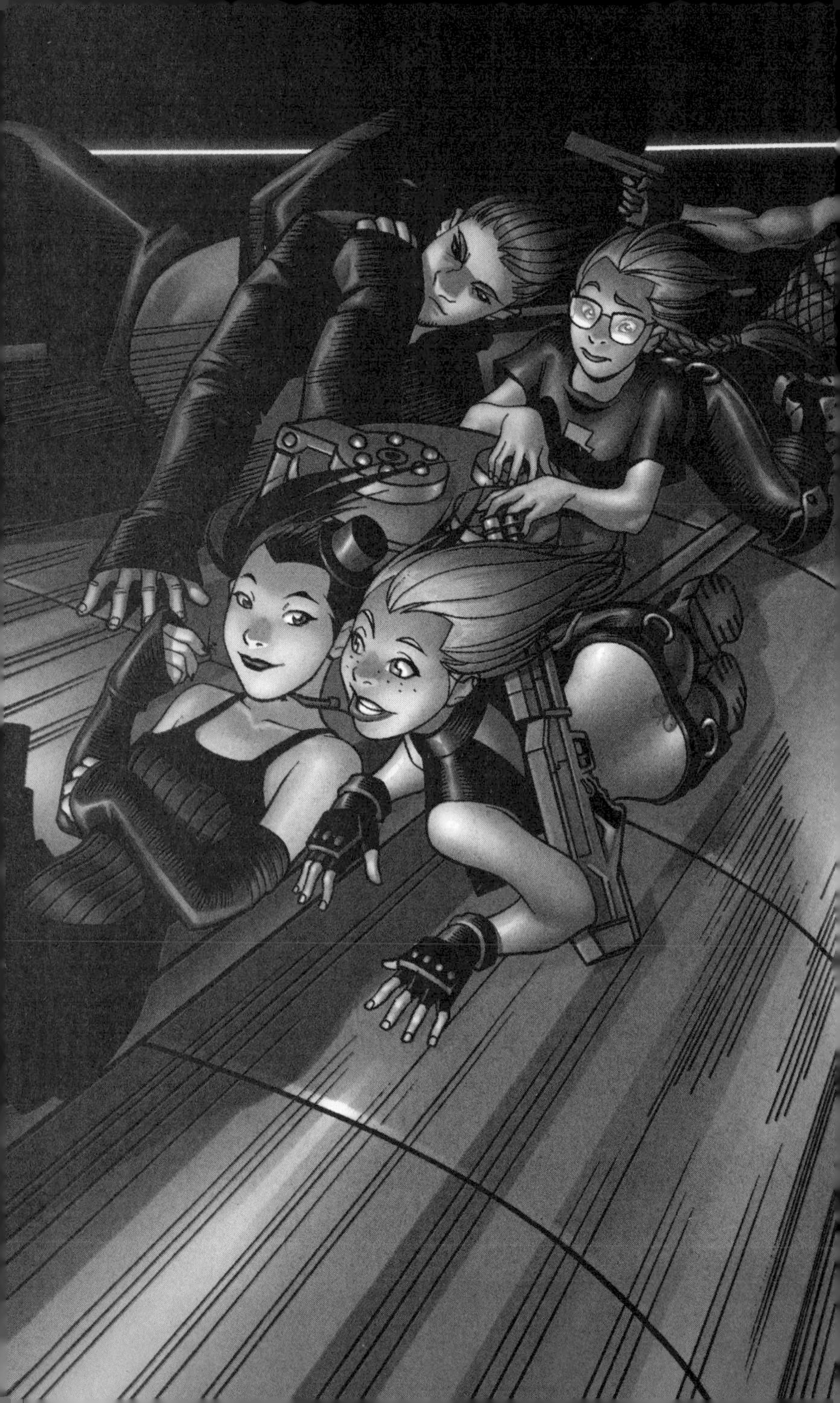

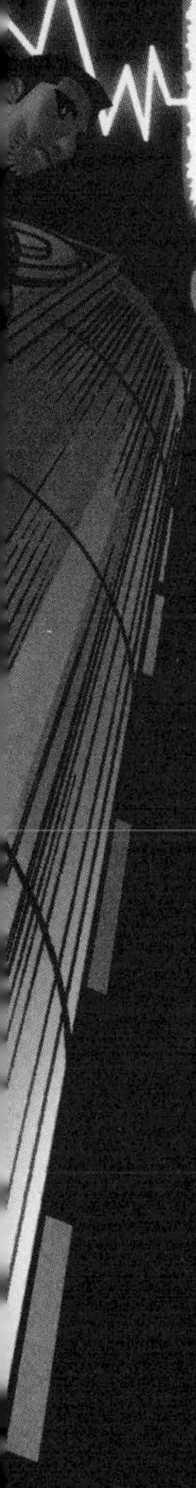

LIVEWIRES

CLOCKWORK THUGS, YO!

Story & Layouts: Adam Warren

Penciler: Rick Mays

Inkers: Jason Martin with Norm Rapmund

Colors: Guru eFX

Letters: Junemoon Studios

Cover Art: Adam Warren

Assistant Editors: Andy Schmidt, Nicole Wiley & Molly Lazer

Editor: Tom Brevoort

Collection Editor: Jennifer Grünwald

Assistant Editor: Michael Short

Senior Editor, Special Projects: Jeff Youngquist

Director of Sales: David Gabriel

Book Designer: Carrie Beadle

Creative Director: Tom Marvelli

Editor in Chief: Joe Quesada

Publisher: Dan Buckley

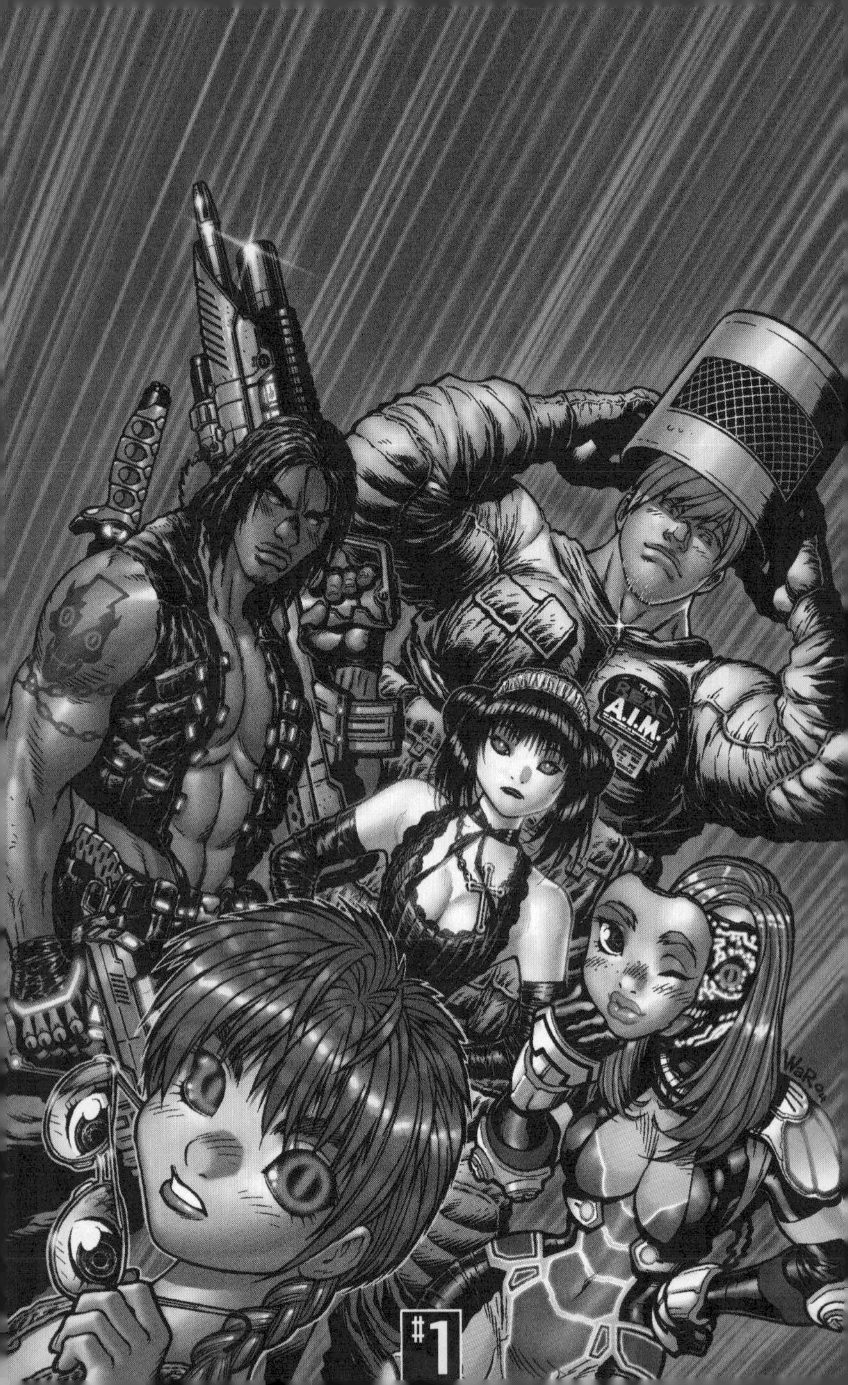
A.I.M.
#1

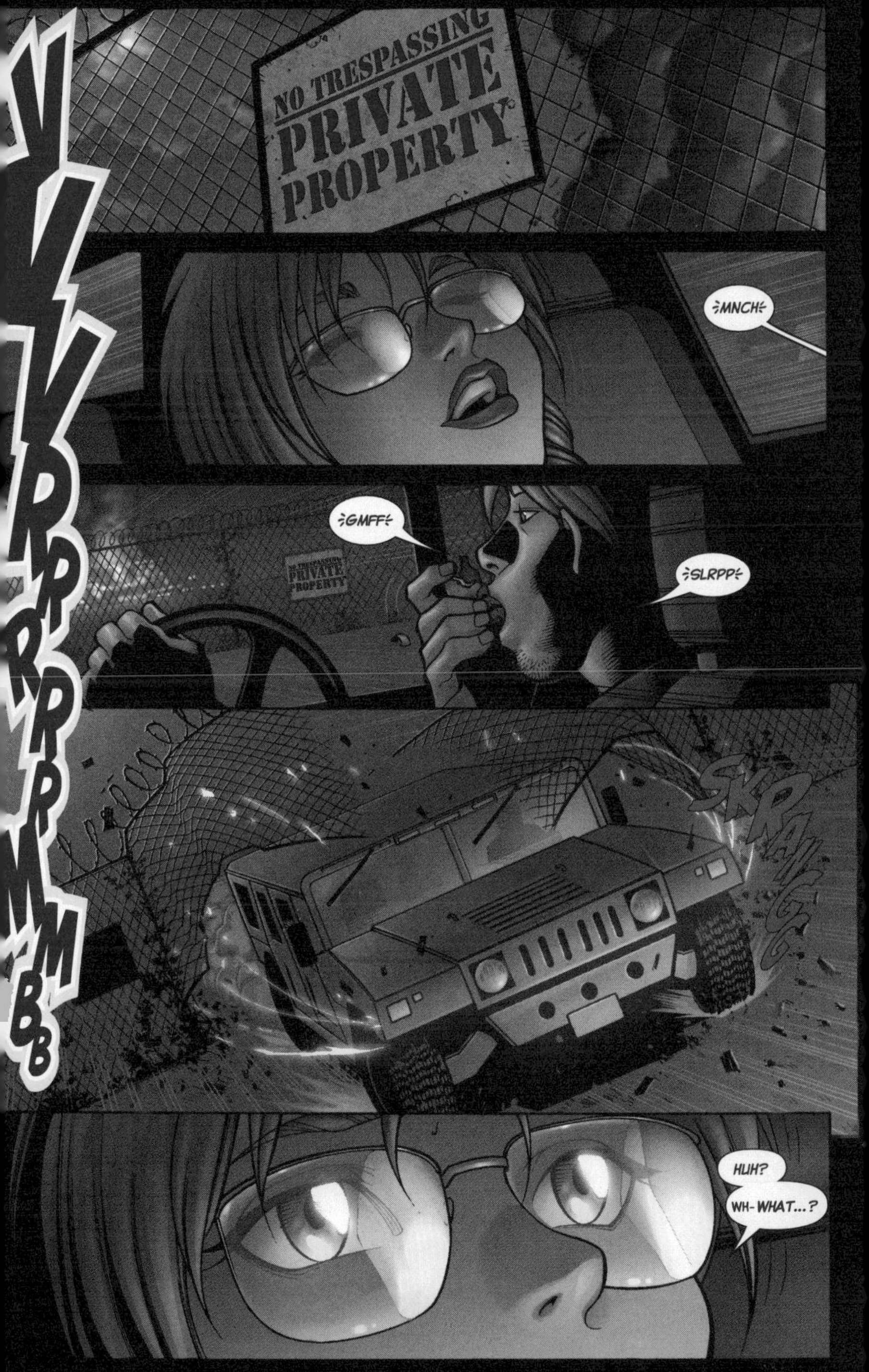
NO TRESPASSING
PRIVATE
PROPERTY
MNCH
GMFF
SLRPP
SKRANGG
HUH?
WH-WHAT...?

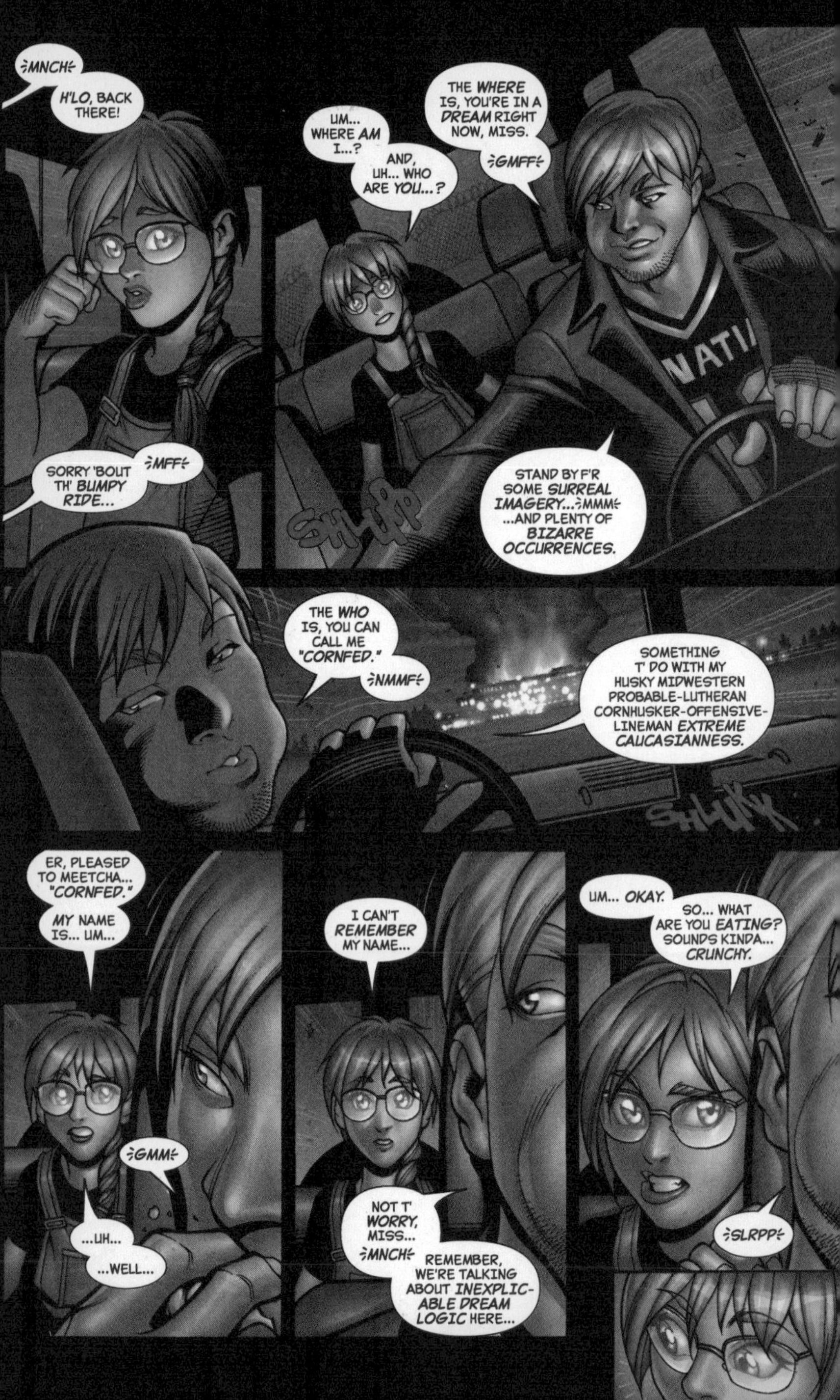

≶MNCH≶
H'LO, BACK THERE!
SORRY 'BOUT TH' BUMPY RIDE...
≶MFF≶
UM... WHERE AM I...?
AND, UH... WHO ARE YOU...?
THE WHERE IS, YOU'RE IN A DREAM RIGHT NOW, MISS.
≶GMFF≶
STAND BY F'R SOME SURREAL IMAGERY... ≶MMM≶ ...AND PLENTY OF BIZARRE OCCURRENCES.
SHLURP
THE WHO IS, YOU CAN CALL ME "CORNFED."
≶NMMF≶
SOMETHING T' DO WITH MY HUSKY MIDWESTERN PROBABLE-LUTHERAN CORNHUSKER-OFFENSIVE-LINEMAN EXTREME CAUCASIANNESS.
SHLUK
ER, PLEASED TO MEETCHA... "CORNFED."
MY NAME IS... UM...
≶GMM≶
...UH...
...WELL...
I CAN'T REMEMBER MY NAME...
NOT T' WORRY, MISS...
≶MNCH≶
REMEMBER, WE'RE TALKING ABOUT INEXPLIC-ABLE DREAM LOGIC HERE...
UM... OKAY.
SO... WHAT ARE YOU EATING? SOUNDS KINDA... CRUNCHY.
≶SLRPP≶

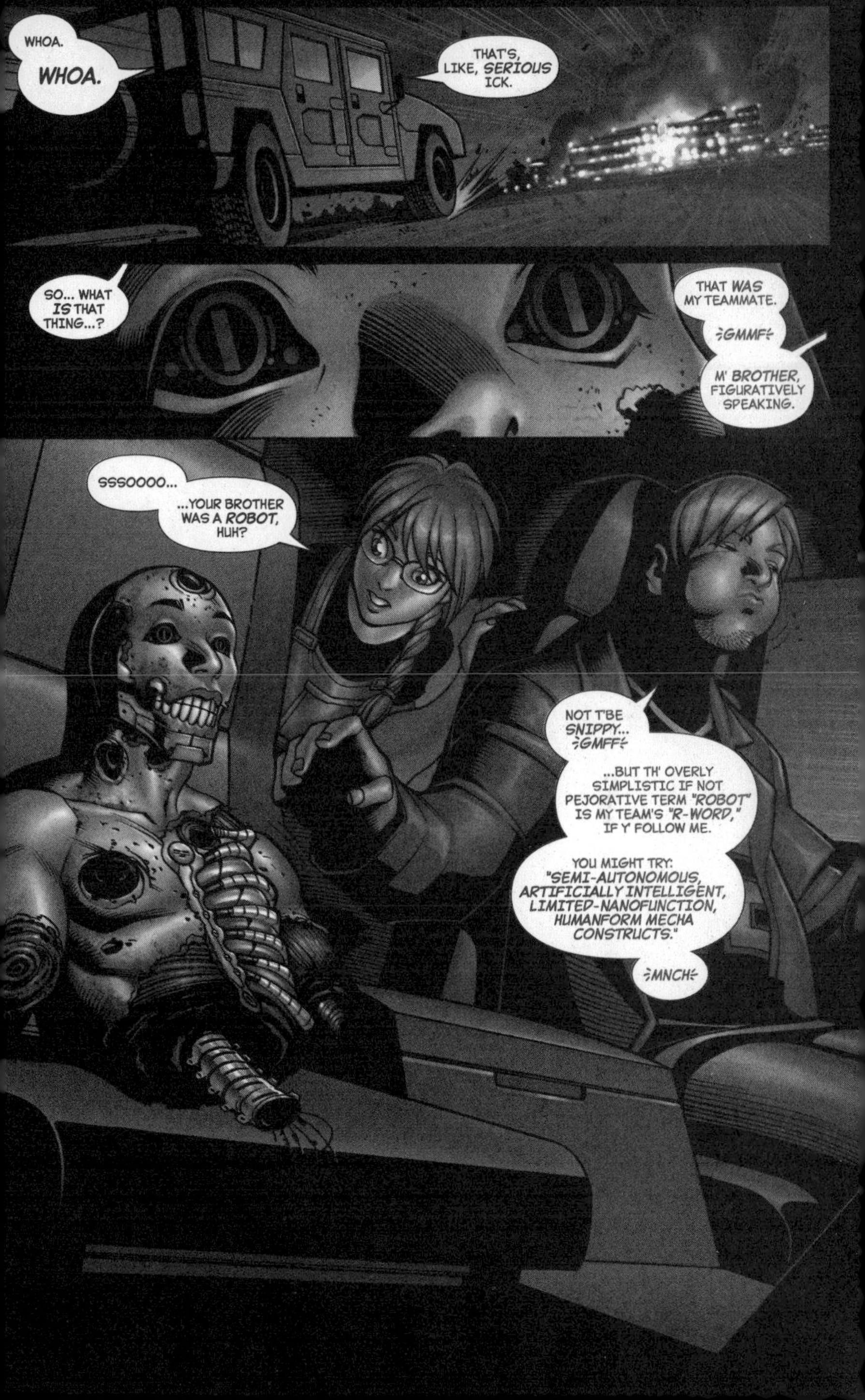
WHOA. WHOA.
THAT'S, LIKE, SERIOUS ICK.
SO... WHAT IS THAT THING...?
THAT WAS MY TEAMMATE.
GMMF
M' BROTHER, FIGURATIVELY SPEAKING.
SSSOOOO...
...YOUR BROTHER WAS A ROBOT, HUH?
NOT T'BE SNIPPY... GMFF
...BUT TH' OVERLY SIMPLISTIC IF NOT PEJORATIVE TERM "ROBOT" IS MY TEAM'S "R-WORD," IF Y' FOLLOW ME.
YOU MIGHT TRY: "SEMI-AUTONOMOUS, ARTIFICIALLY INTELLIGENT, LIMITED-NANOFUNCTION, HUMANFORM MECHA CONSTRUCTS."
MNCH

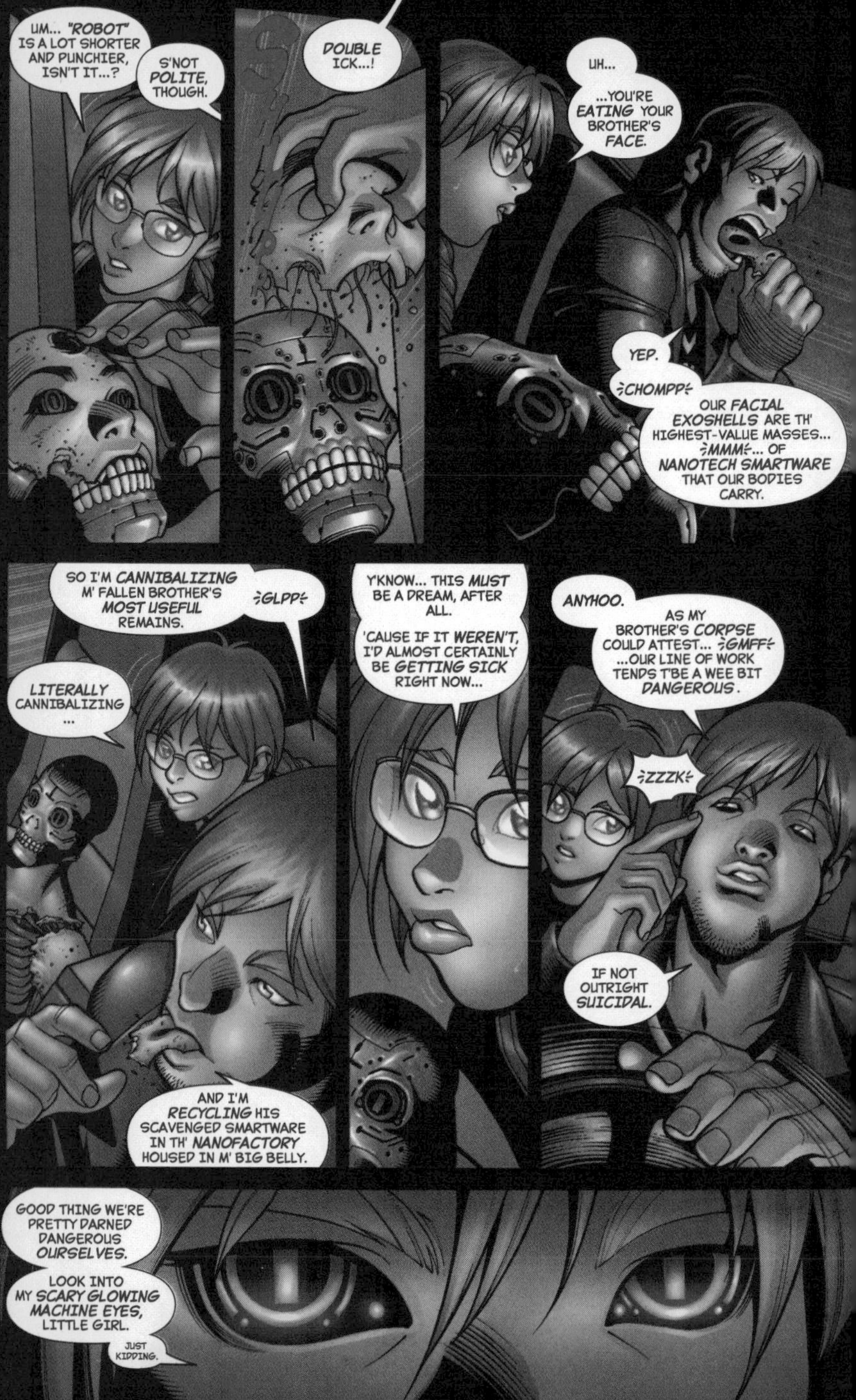

UM... "ROBOT" IS A LOT SHORTER AND PUNCHIER, ISN'T IT...?
S'NOT POLITE, THOUGH.
DOUBLE ICK...!
UH...
...YOU'RE EATING YOUR BROTHER'S FACE.
YEP.
CHOMPP
OUR FACIAL EXOSHELLS ARE TH' HIGHEST-VALUE MASSES... MMM... OF NANOTECH SMARTWARE THAT OUR BODIES CARRY.
SO I'M CANNIBALIZING M' FALLEN BROTHER'S MOST USEFUL REMAINS.
GLPP
LITERALLY CANNIBALIZING ...
AND I'M RECYCLING HIS SCAVENGED SMARTWARE IN TH' NANOFACTORY HOUSED IN M' BIG BELLY.
Y'KNOW... THIS MUST BE A DREAM, AFTER ALL.
'CAUSE IF IT WEREN'T, I'D ALMOST CERTAINLY BE GETTING SICK RIGHT NOW...
ANYHOO.
AS MY BROTHER'S CORPSE COULD ATTEST... GMFF ...OUR LINE OF WORK TENDS T'BE A WEE BIT DANGEROUS.
ZZZK
IF NOT OUTRIGHT SUICIDAL.
GOOD THING WE'RE PRETTY DARNED DANGEROUS OURSELVES.
LOOK INTO MY SCARY GLOWING MACHINE EYES, LITTLE GIRL.
JUST KIDDING.

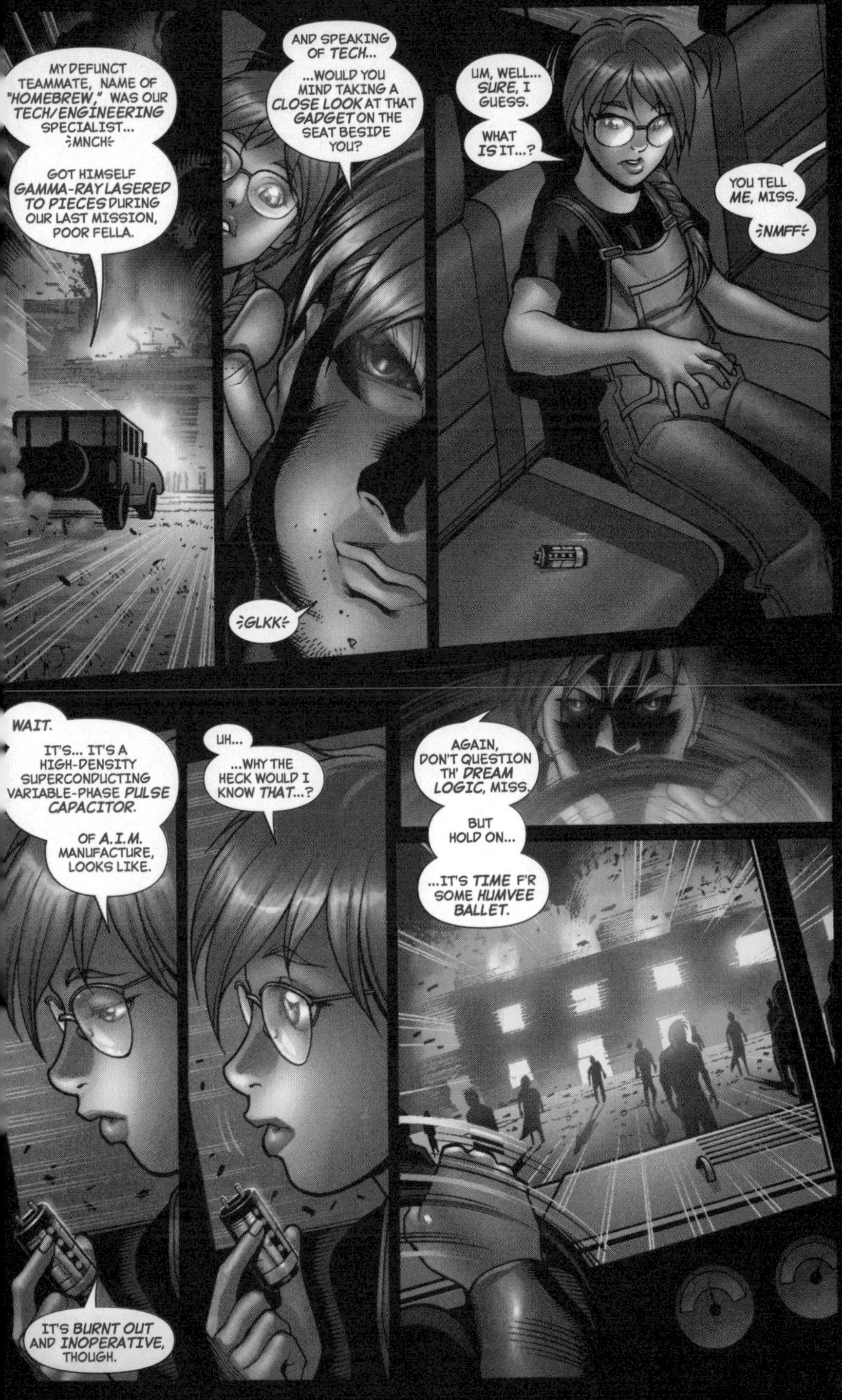

MY DEFUNCT TEAMMATE, NAME OF "HOMEBREW," WAS OUR TECH/ENGINEERING SPECIALIST...
MNCH
GOT HIMSELF GAMMA-RAY LASERED TO PIECES DURING OUR LAST MISSION, POOR FELLA.
AND SPEAKING OF TECH...
...WOULD YOU MIND TAKING A CLOSE LOOK AT THAT GADGET ON THE SEAT BESIDE YOU?
GLKK
UM, WELL... SURE, I GUESS.
WHAT IS IT...?
YOU TELL ME, MISS.
NMFF
WAIT.
IT'S... IT'S A HIGH-DENSITY SUPERCONDUCTING VARIABLE-PHASE PULSE CAPACITOR.
OF A.I.M. MANUFACTURE, LOOKS LIKE.
IT'S BURNT OUT AND INOPERATIVE, THOUGH.
UH...
...WHY THE HECK WOULD I KNOW THAT...?
AGAIN, DON'T QUESTION TH' DREAM LOGIC, MISS.
BUT HOLD ON...
...IT'S TIME F'R SOME HUMVEE BALLET.

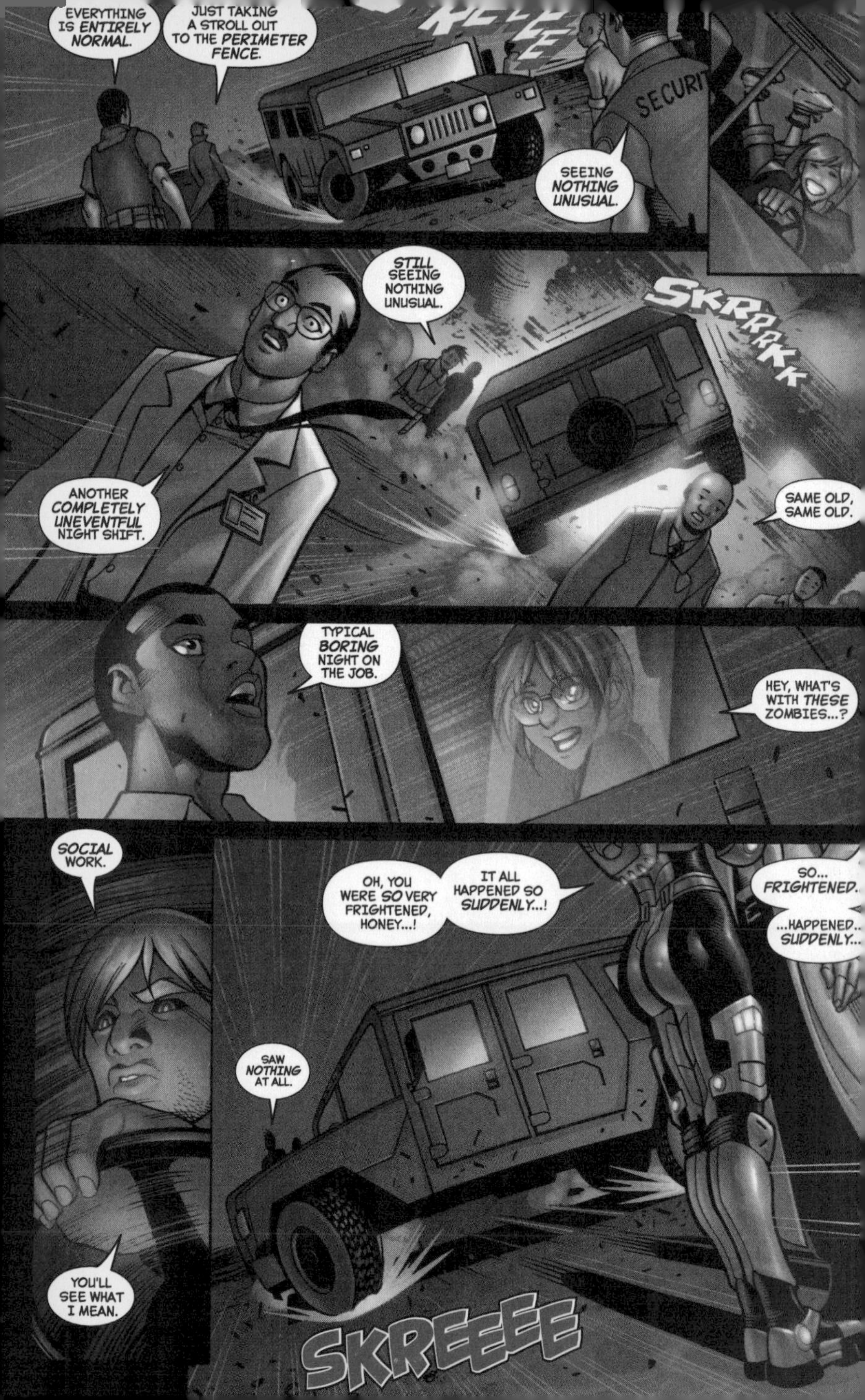
EVERYTHING IS ENTIRELY NORMAL.
JUST TAKING A STROLL OUT TO THE PERIMETER FENCE.
SECURIT
SEEING NOTHING UNUSUAL.
STILL SEEING NOTHING UNUSUAL.
SKRRRKK
ANOTHER COMPLETELY UNEVENTFUL NIGHT SHIFT.
SAME OLD, SAME OLD.
TYPICAL BORING NIGHT ON THE JOB.
HEY, WHAT'S WITH THESE ZOMBIES...?
SOCIAL WORK.
OH, YOU WERE SO VERY FRIGHTENED, HONEY...!
IT ALL HAPPENED SO SUDDENLY...!
SO... FRIGHTENED...
...HAPPENED... SUDDENLY...
SAW NOTHING AT ALL.
YOU'LL SEE WHAT I MEAN.
SKREEEEE

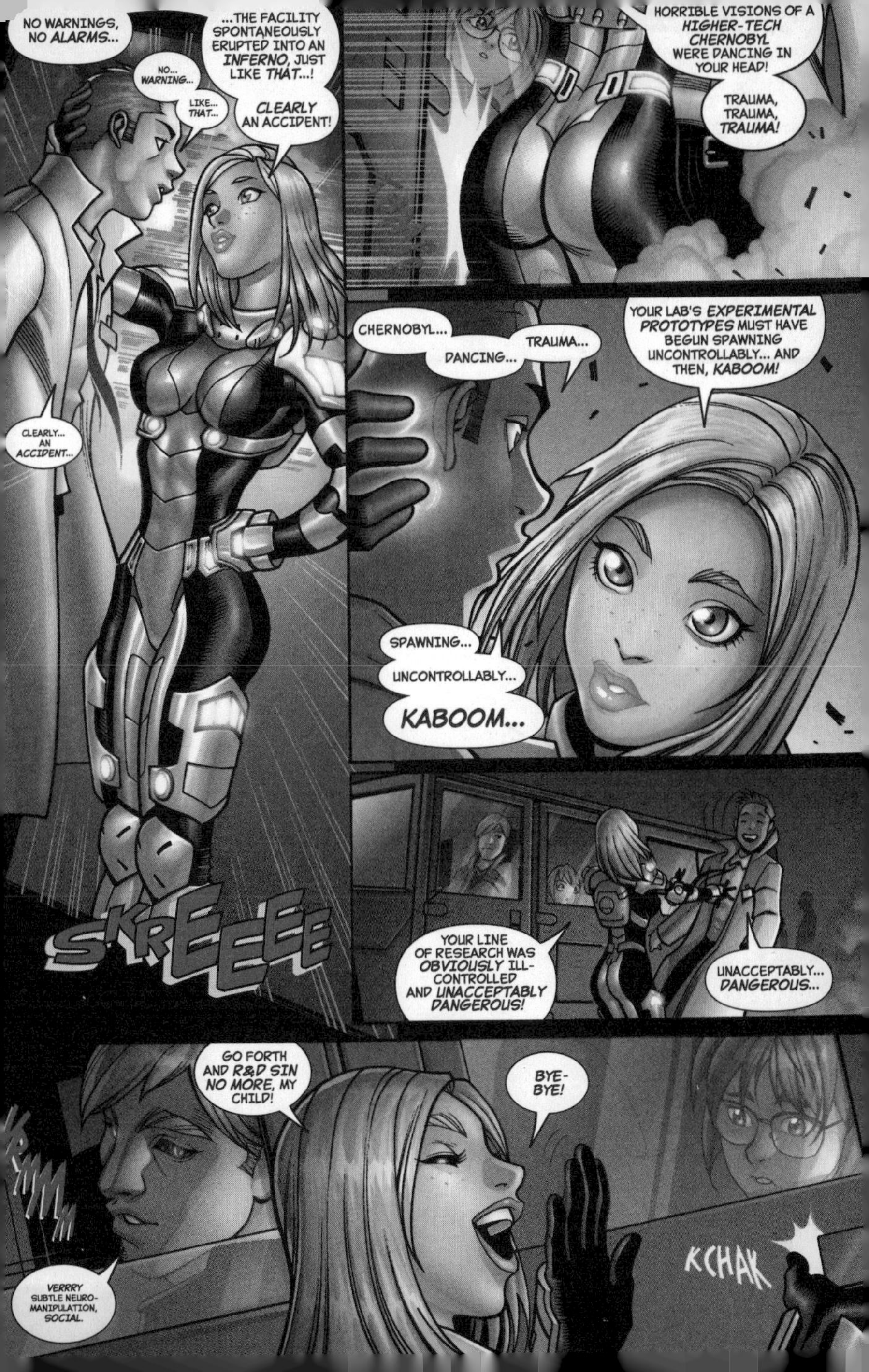
NO WARNINGS, NO ALARMS...
...THE FACILITY SPONTANEOUSLY ERUPTED INTO AN INFERNO, JUST LIKE THAT...!
NO... WARNING...
LIKE... THAT...
CLEARLY AN ACCIDENT!
CLEARLY... AN ACCIDENT...
HORRIBLE VISIONS OF A HIGHER-TECH CHERNOBYL WERE DANCING IN YOUR HEAD!
TRAUMA, TRAUMA, TRAUMA!
CHERNOBYL...
DANCING...
TRAUMA...
YOUR LAB'S EXPERIMENTAL PROTOTYPES MUST HAVE BEGUN SPAWNING UNCONTROLLABLY... AND THEN, KABOOM!
SPAWNING...
UNCONTROLLABLY...
KABOOM...
SKREEEEE
YOUR LINE OF RESEARCH WAS OBVIOUSLY ILL-CONTROLLED AND UNACCEPTABLY DANGEROUS!
UNACCEPTABLY... DANGEROUS...
GO FORTH AND R&D SIN NO MORE, MY CHILD!
BYE-BYE!
VERRRY SUBTLE NEURO-MANIPULATION, SOCIAL.
KCHAK

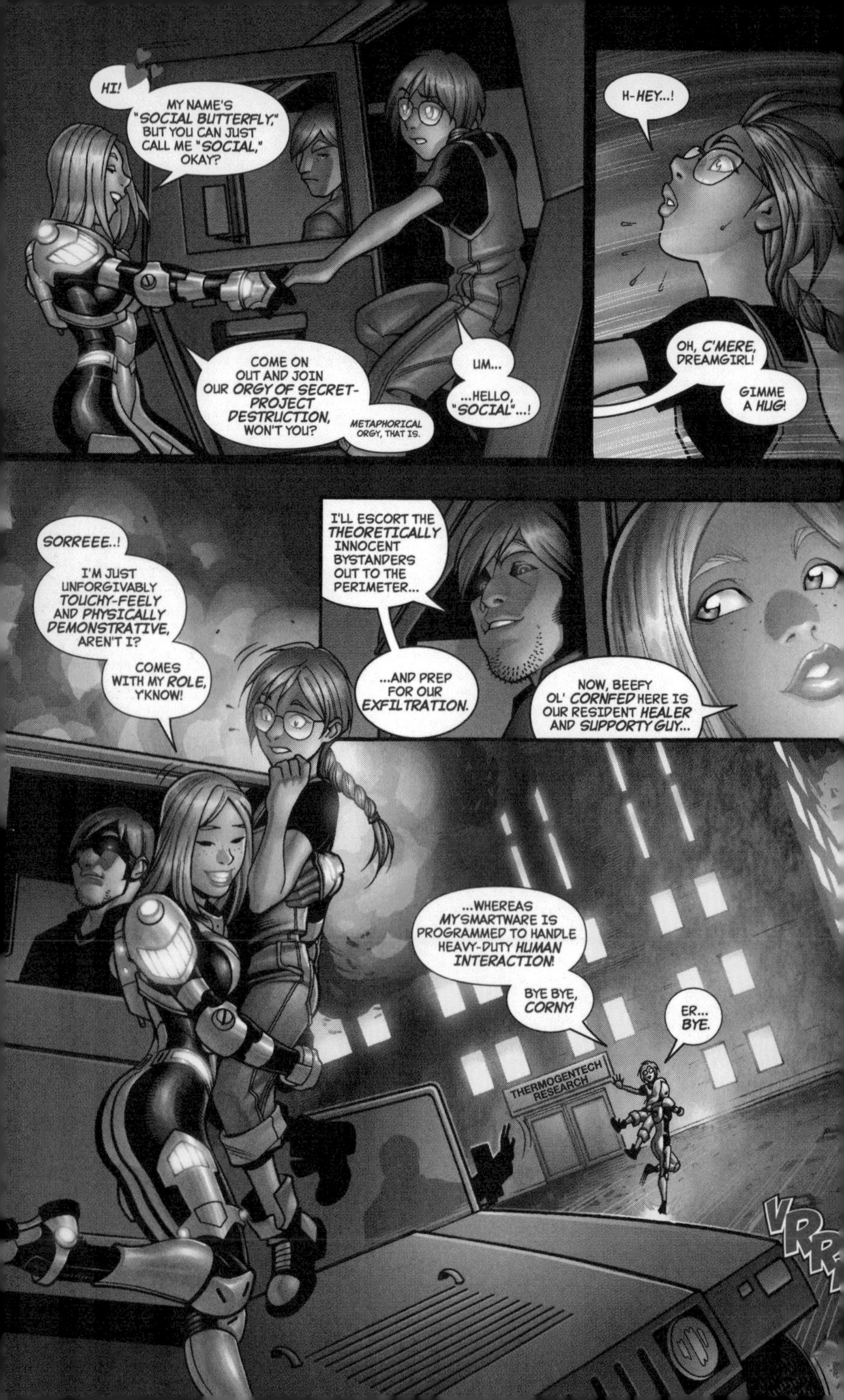
HI!
MY NAME'S "SOCIAL BUTTERFLY," BUT YOU CAN JUST CALL ME "SOCIAL," OKAY?
COME ON OUT AND JOIN OUR ORGY OF SECRET-PROJECT DESTRUCTION, WON'T YOU?
METAPHORICAL ORGY, THAT IS.
UM...
...HELLO, "SOCIAL"...!
H-HEY...!
OH, C'MERE, DREAMGIRL!
GIMME A HUG!
SORREEE..!
I'M JUST UNFORGIVABLY TOUCHY-FEELY AND PHYSICALLY DEMONSTRATIVE, AREN'T I?
COMES WITH MY ROLE, Y'KNOW!
I'LL ESCORT THE THEORETICALLY INNOCENT BYSTANDERS OUT TO THE PERIMETER...
...AND PREP FOR OUR EXFILTRATION.
NOW, BEEFY OL' CORNFED HERE IS OUR RESIDENT HEALER AND SUPPORTY GUY...
...WHEREAS MY SMARTWARE IS PROGRAMMED TO HANDLE HEAVY-DUTY HUMAN INTERACTION!
BYE BYE, CORNY!
ER... BYE.
THERMOGENTECH RESEARCH
VRR

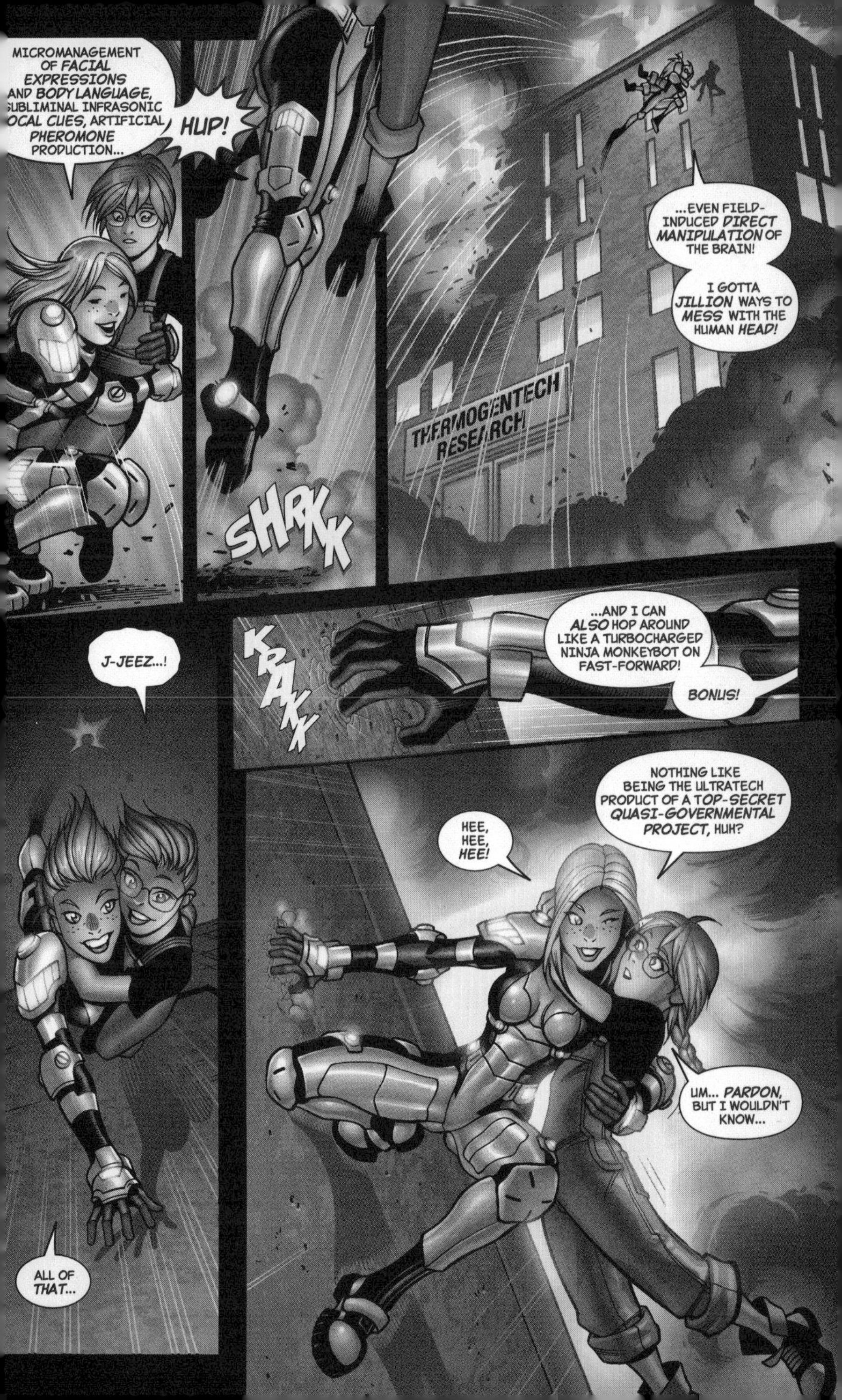
MICROMANAGEMENT OF FACIAL EXPRESSIONS AND BODY LANGUAGE, SUBLIMINAL INFRASONIC VOCAL CUES, ARTIFICIAL PHEROMONE PRODUCTION...
HUP!
SHRKKK
...EVEN FIELD-INDUCED DIRECT MANIPULATION OF THE BRAIN!
I GOTTA JILLION WAYS TO MESS WITH THE HUMAN HEAD!
THERMOGENTECH RESEARCH
J-JEEZ...!
KRAKK
...AND I CAN ALSO HOP AROUND LIKE A TURBOCHARGED NINJA MONKEYBOT ON FAST-FORWARD!
BONUS!
ALL OF THAT...
HEE, HEE, HEE!
NOTHING LIKE BEING THE ULTRATECH PRODUCT OF A TOP-SECRET QUASI-GOVERNMENTAL PROJECT, HUH?
UM... PARDON, BUT I WOULDN'T KNOW...

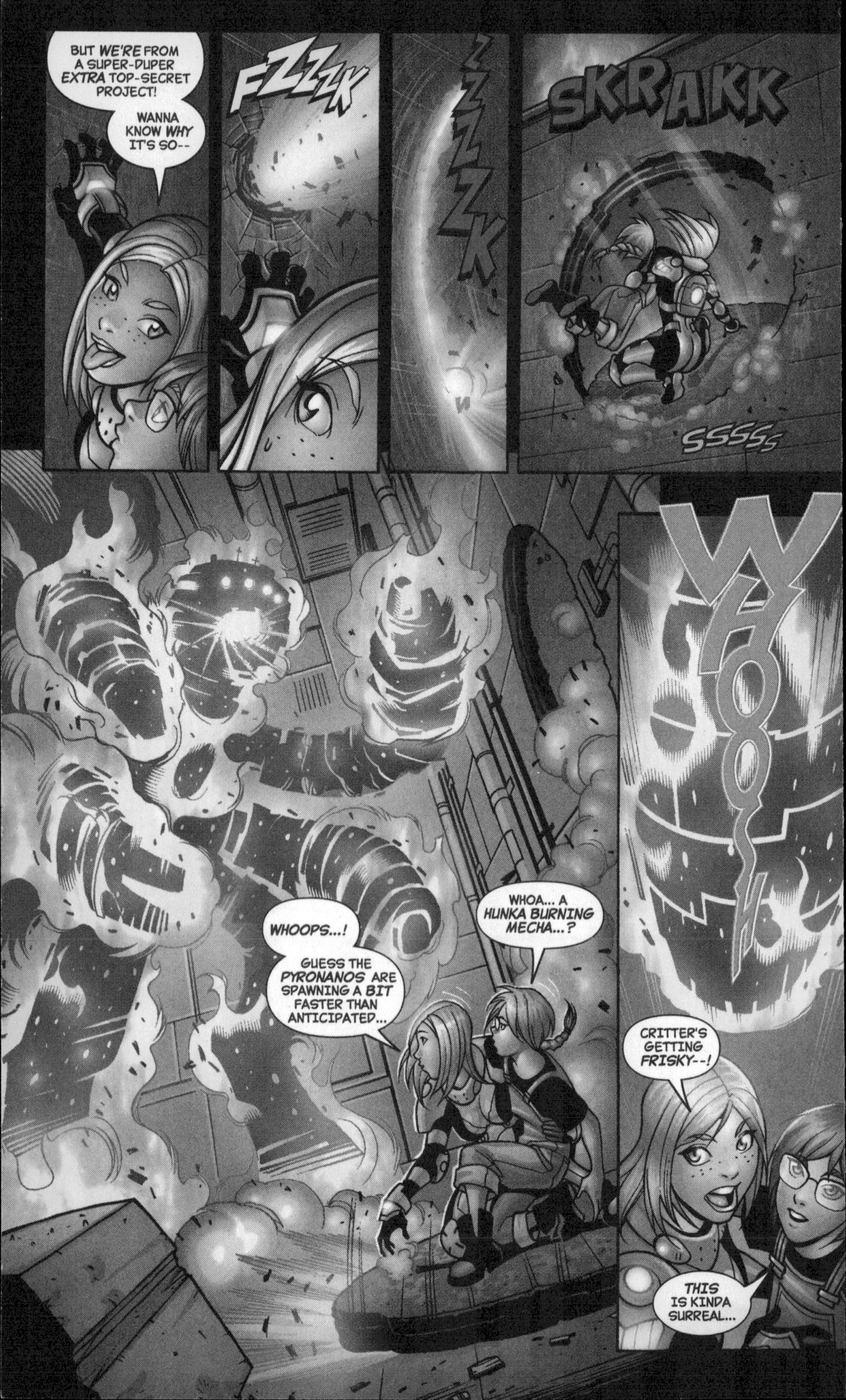
BUT WE'RE FROM A SUPER-DUPER EXTRA TOP-SECRET PROJECT!
WANNA KNOW WHY IT'S SO--
FZZZK
ZZZZZK
SKRAKK
SSSSS
WHOOPS...!
GUESS THE PYRONANOS ARE SPAWNING A BIT FASTER THAN ANTICIPATED...
WHOA... A HUNKA BURNING MECHA...?
CRITTER'S GETTING FRISKY--!
THIS IS KINDA SURREAL...

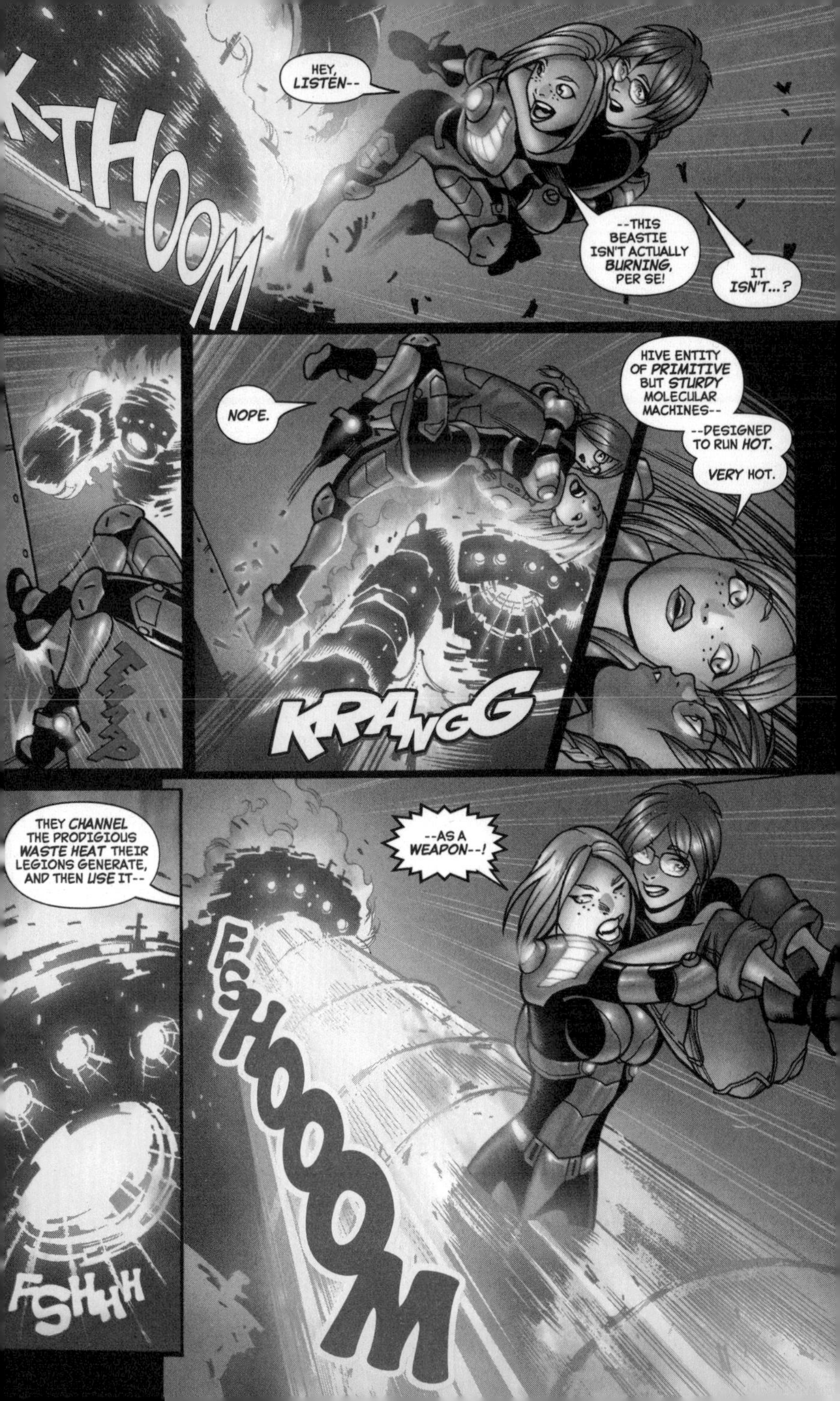
KTHOOM
HEY, LISTEN--
--THIS BEASTIE ISN'T ACTUALLY BURNING, PER SE!
IT ISN'T...?
NOPE.
HIVE ENTITY OF PRIMITIVE BUT STURDY MOLECULAR MACHINES--
--DESIGNED TO RUN HOT.
VERY HOT.
KRANGG
THEY CHANNEL THE PRODIGIOUS WASTE HEAT THEIR LEGIONS GENERATE, AND THEN USE IT--
--AS A WEAPON--!
FSHOOOOM
FSHHH

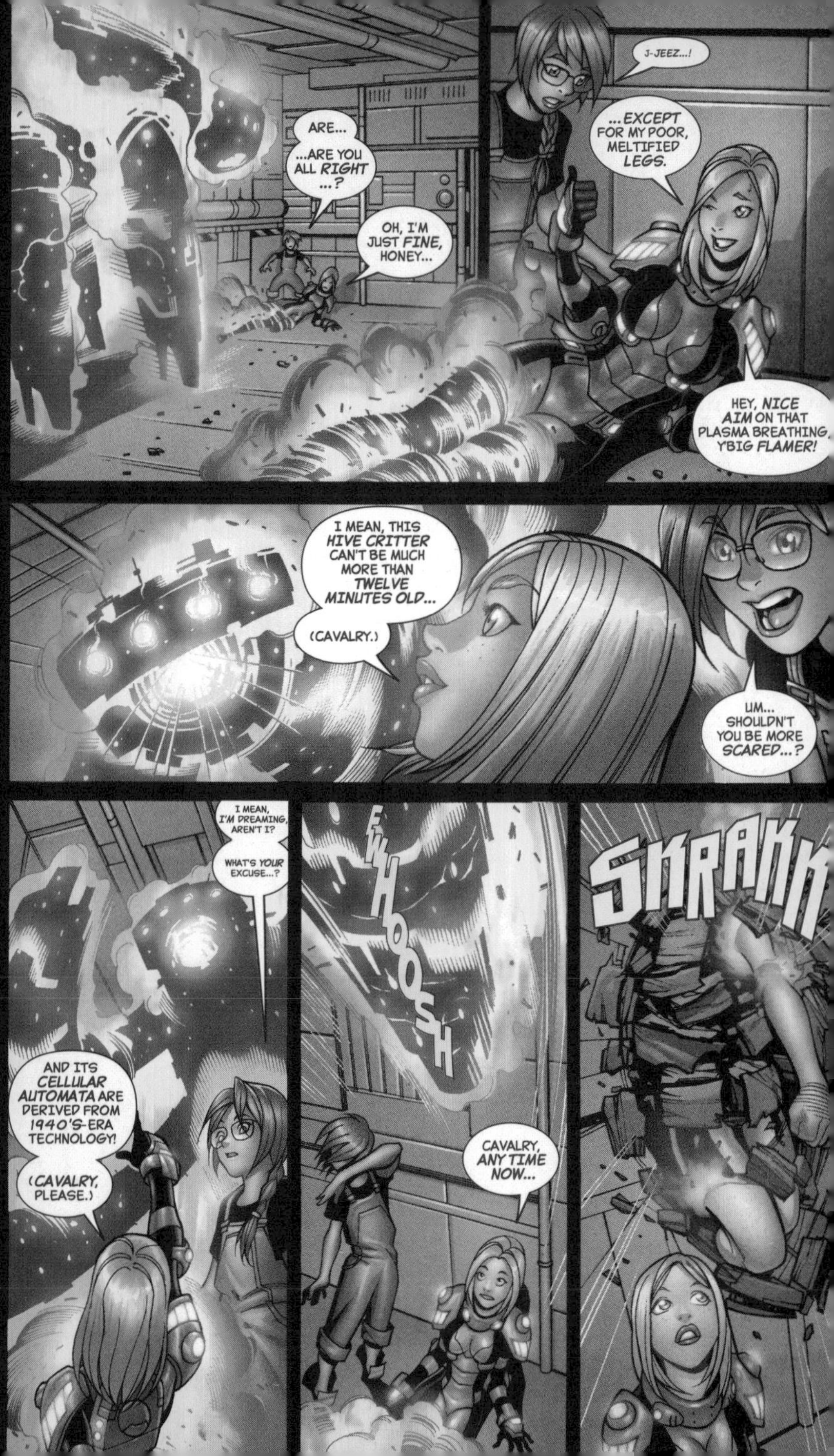

ARE... ...ARE YOU ALL RIGHT ...?
OH, I'M JUST FINE, HONEY...
J-JEEZ...!
...EXCEPT FOR MY POOR, MELTIFIED LEGS.
HEY, NICE AIM ON THAT PLASMA BREATHING, Y'BIG FLAMER!
I MEAN, THIS HIVE CRITTER CAN'T BE MUCH MORE THAN TWELVE MINUTES OLD...
(CAVALRY.)
UM... SHOULDN'T YOU BE MORE SCARED...?
I MEAN, I'M DREAMING, AREN'T I?
WHAT'S YOUR EXCUSE...?
AND ITS CELLULAR AUTOMATA ARE DERIVED FROM 1940'S-ERA TECHNOLOGY!
(CAVALRY, PLEASE.)
FWHOOSH
CAVALRY, ANY TIME NOW...
SKRAKK

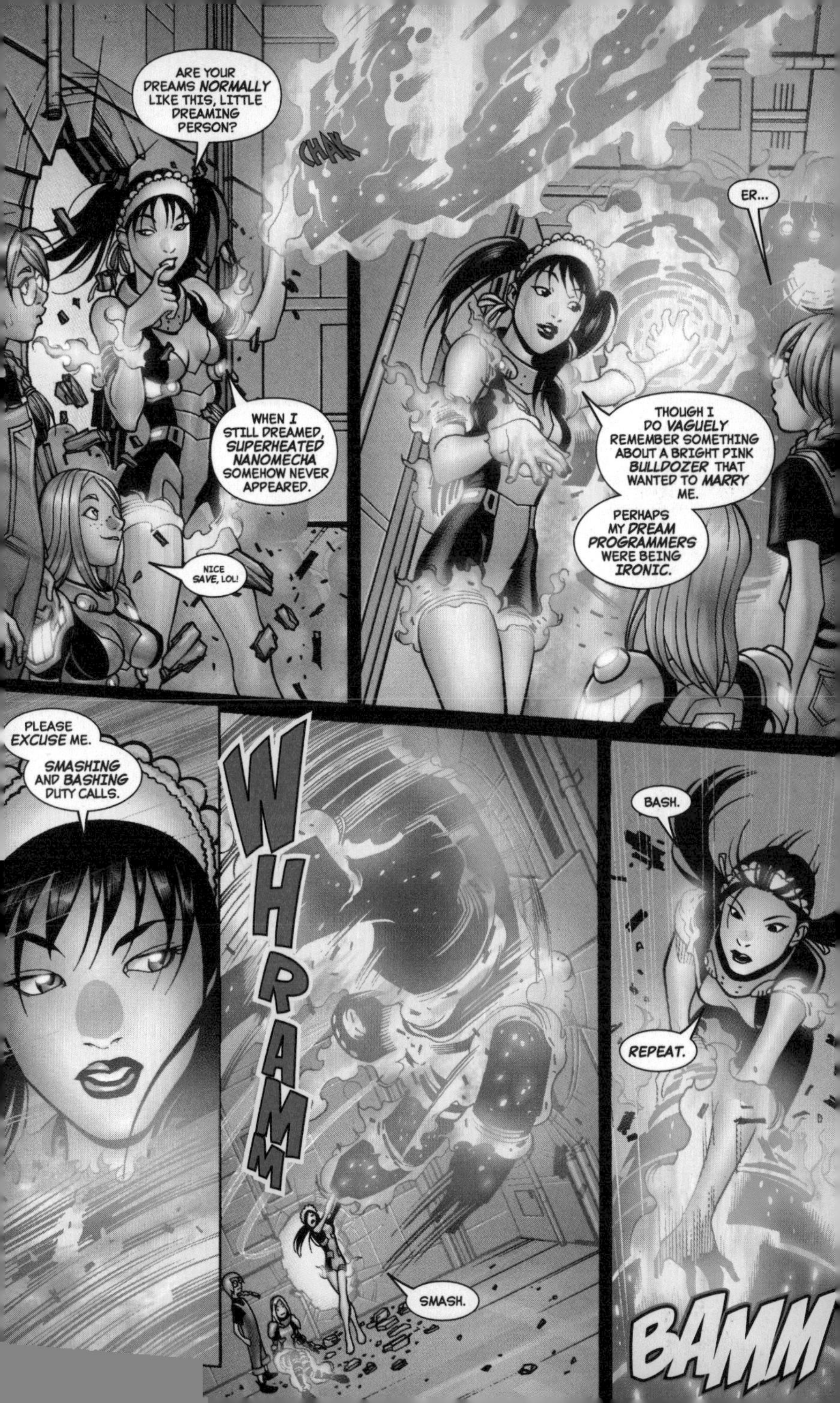
ARE YOUR DREAMS NORMALLY LIKE THIS, LITTLE DREAMING PERSON?
CHAK
WHEN I STILL DREAMED, SUPERHEATED NANOMECHA SOMEHOW NEVER APPEARED.
NICE SAVE, LOL!
ER...
THOUGH I DO VAGUELY REMEMBER SOMETHING ABOUT A BRIGHT PINK BULLDOZER THAT WANTED TO MARRY ME.
PERHAPS MY DREAM PROGRAMMERS WERE BEING IRONIC.
PLEASE EXCUSE ME.
SMASHING AND BASHING DUTY CALLS.
WHRAMM
SMASH.
BASH.
REPEAT.
BAMM

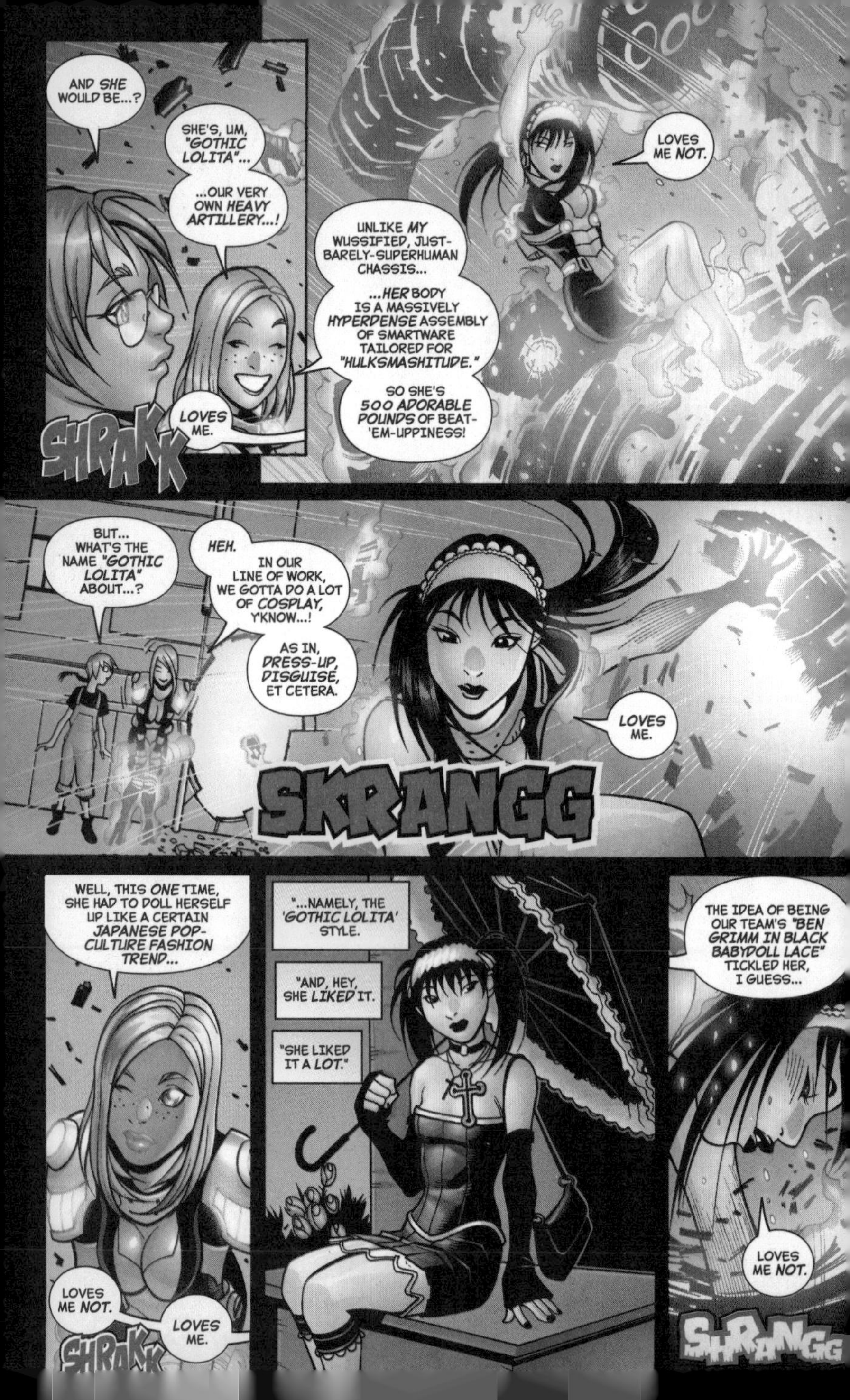
AND SHE WOULD BE...?
SHE'S, UM, "GOTHIC LOLITA"...
...OUR VERY OWN HEAVY ARTILLERY...!
LOVES ME NOT.
UNLIKE MY WUSSIFIED, JUST-BARELY-SUPERHUMAN CHASSIS...
...HER BODY IS A MASSIVELY HYPERDENSE ASSEMBLY OF SMARTWARE TAILORED FOR "HULKSMASHITUDE."
SO SHE'S 500 ADORABLE POUNDS OF BEAT-'EM-UPPINESS!
LOVES ME.
SHRAKK
BUT... WHAT'S THE NAME "GOTHIC LOLITA" ABOUT...?
HEH.
IN OUR LINE OF WORK, WE GOTTA DO A LOT OF COSPLAY, Y'KNOW...!
AS IN, DRESS-UP, DISGUISE, ET CETERA.
LOVES ME.
SKRANGG
WELL, THIS ONE TIME, SHE HAD TO DOLL HERSELF UP LIKE A CERTAIN JAPANESE POP-CULTURE FASHION TREND...
LOVES ME NOT.
LOVES ME.
SHRAKK
"...NAMELY, THE 'GOTHIC LOLITA' STYLE.
"AND, HEY, SHE LIKED IT.
"SHE LIKED IT A LOT."
THE IDEA OF BEING OUR TEAM'S "BEN GRIMM IN BLACK BABYDOLL LACE" TICKLED HER, I GUESS...
LOVES ME NOT.
SHRANGG

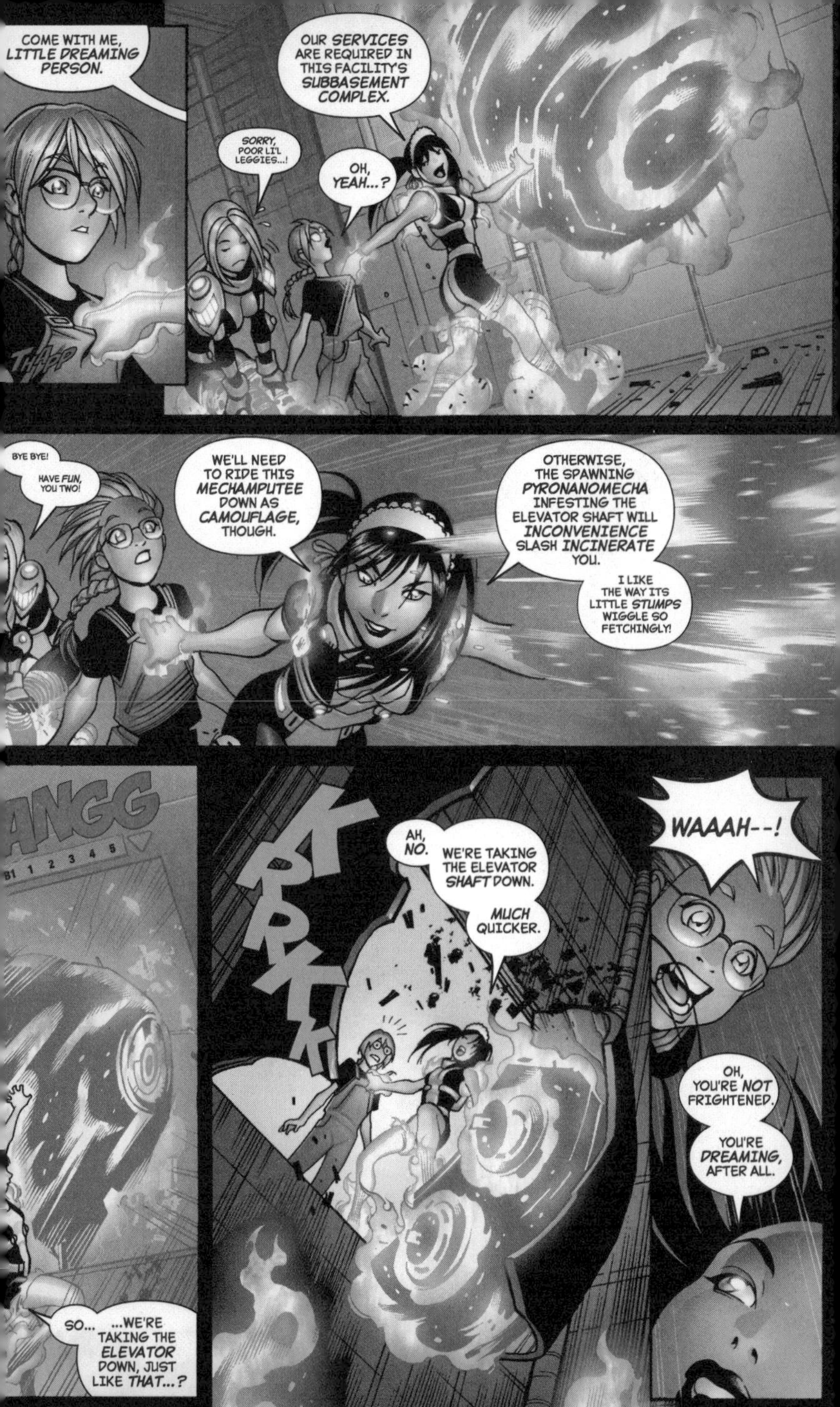
COME WITH ME, LITTLE DREAMING PERSON.
THAPP
OUR SERVICES ARE REQUIRED IN THIS FACILITY'S SUBBASEMENT COMPLEX.
SORRY, POOR LI'L LEGGIES...!
OH, YEAH...?
BYE BYE!
HAVE FUN, YOU TWO!
WE'LL NEED TO RIDE THIS MECHAMPUTEE DOWN AS CAMOUFLAGE, THOUGH.
OTHERWISE, THE SPAWNING PYRONANOMECHA INFESTING THE ELEVATOR SHAFT WILL INCONVENIENCE SLASH INCINERATE YOU.
I LIKE THE WAY ITS LITTLE STUMPS WIGGLE SO FETCHINGLY!
ANGG
B1 1 2 3 4 5
SO... ...WE'RE TAKING THE ELEVATOR DOWN, JUST LIKE THAT...?
KRRKK
AH, NO.
WE'RE TAKING THE ELEVATOR SHAFT DOWN.
MUCH QUICKER.
WAAAH--!
OH, YOU'RE NOT FRIGHTENED.
YOU'RE DREAMING, AFTER ALL.

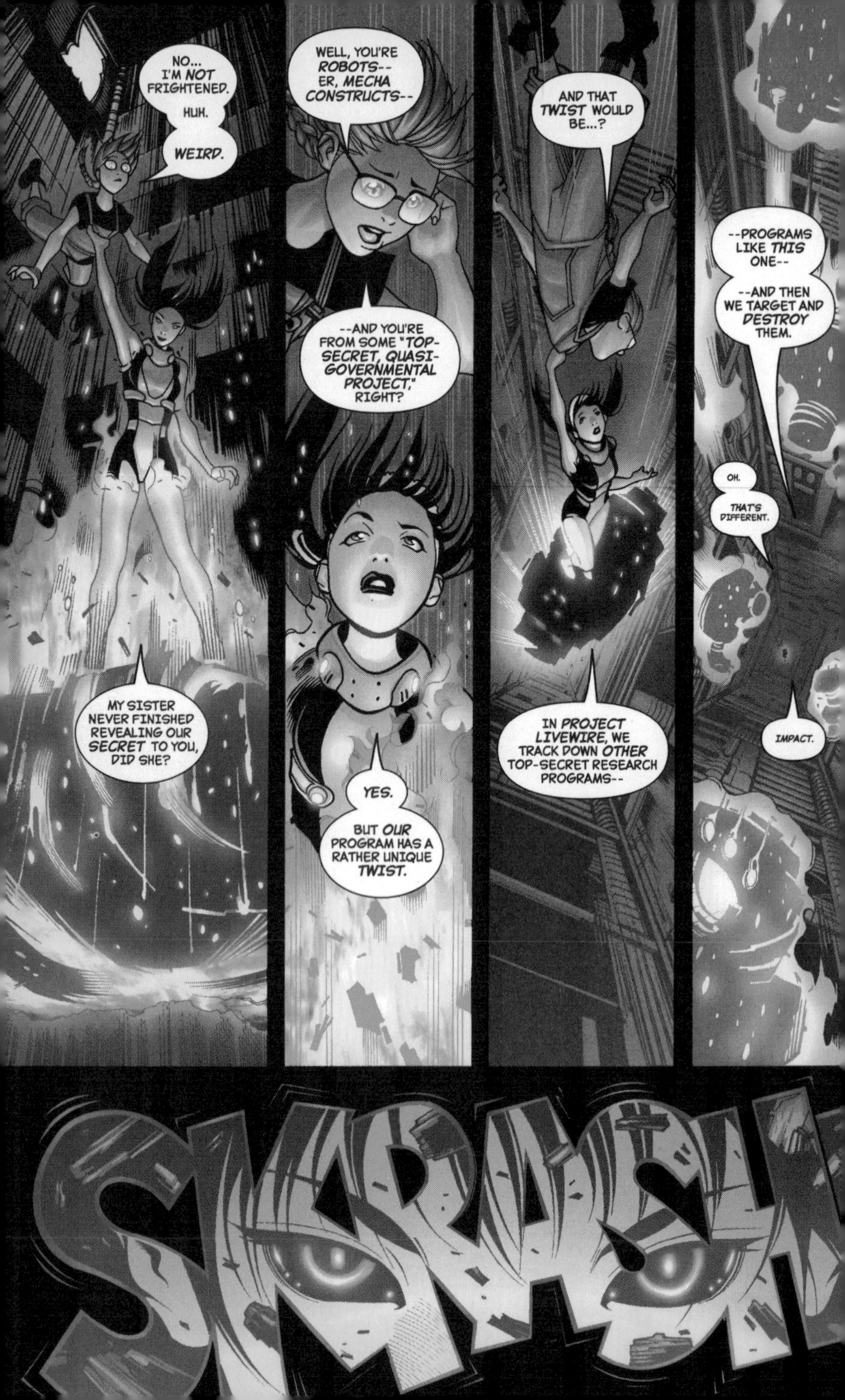

NO... I'M NOT FRIGHTENED.
HUH.
WEIRD.
MY SISTER NEVER FINISHED REVEALING OUR SECRET TO YOU, DID SHE?
WELL, YOU'RE ROBOTS-- ER, MECHA CONSTRUCTS--
--AND YOU'RE FROM SOME "TOP-SECRET, QUASI-GOVERNMENTAL PROJECT," RIGHT?
YES.
BUT OUR PROGRAM HAS A RATHER UNIQUE TWIST.
AND THAT TWIST WOULD BE...?
IN PROJECT LIVEWIRE, WE TRACK DOWN OTHER TOP-SECRET RESEARCH PROGRAMS--
--PROGRAMS LIKE THIS ONE--
--AND THEN WE TARGET AND DESTROY THEM.
OH.
THAT'S DIFFERENT.
IMPACT.
SKRASH

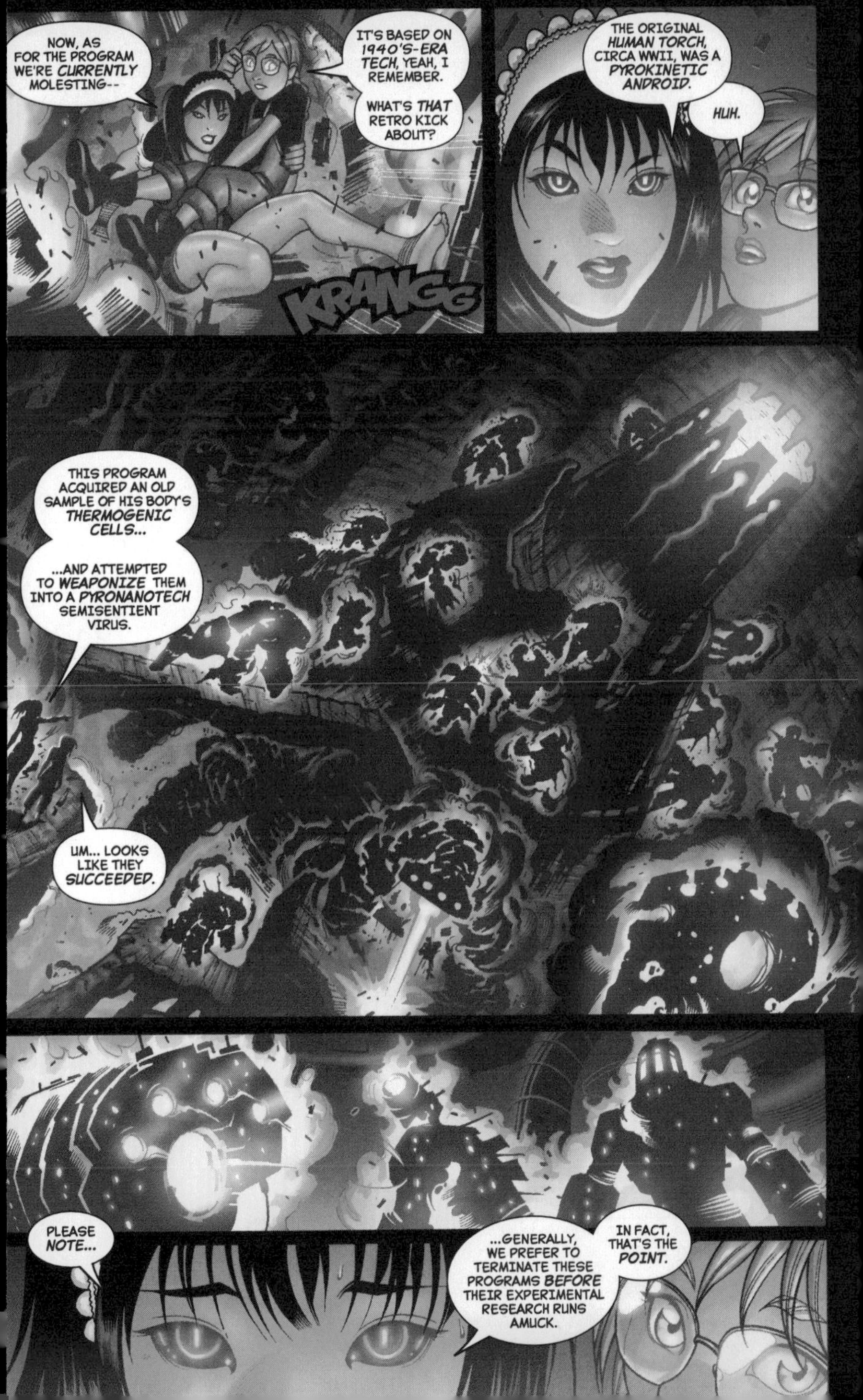
NOW, AS FOR THE PROGRAM WE'RE CURRENTLY MOLESTING--
IT'S BASED ON 1940'S-ERA TECH, YEAH, I REMEMBER.
WHAT'S THAT RETRO KICK ABOUT?
KRANGG
THE ORIGINAL HUMAN TORCH, CIRCA WWII, WAS A PYROKINETIC ANDROID.
HUH.
THIS PROGRAM ACQUIRED AN OLD SAMPLE OF HIS BODY'S THERMOGENIC CELLS...
...AND ATTEMPTED TO WEAPONIZE THEM INTO A PYRONANOTECH SEMISENTIENT VIRUS.
UM... LOOKS LIKE THEY SUCCEEDED.
PLEASE NOTE...
...GENERALLY, WE PREFER TO TERMINATE THESE PROGRAMS BEFORE THEIR EXPERIMENTAL RESEARCH RUNS AMUCK.
IN FACT, THAT'S THE POINT.

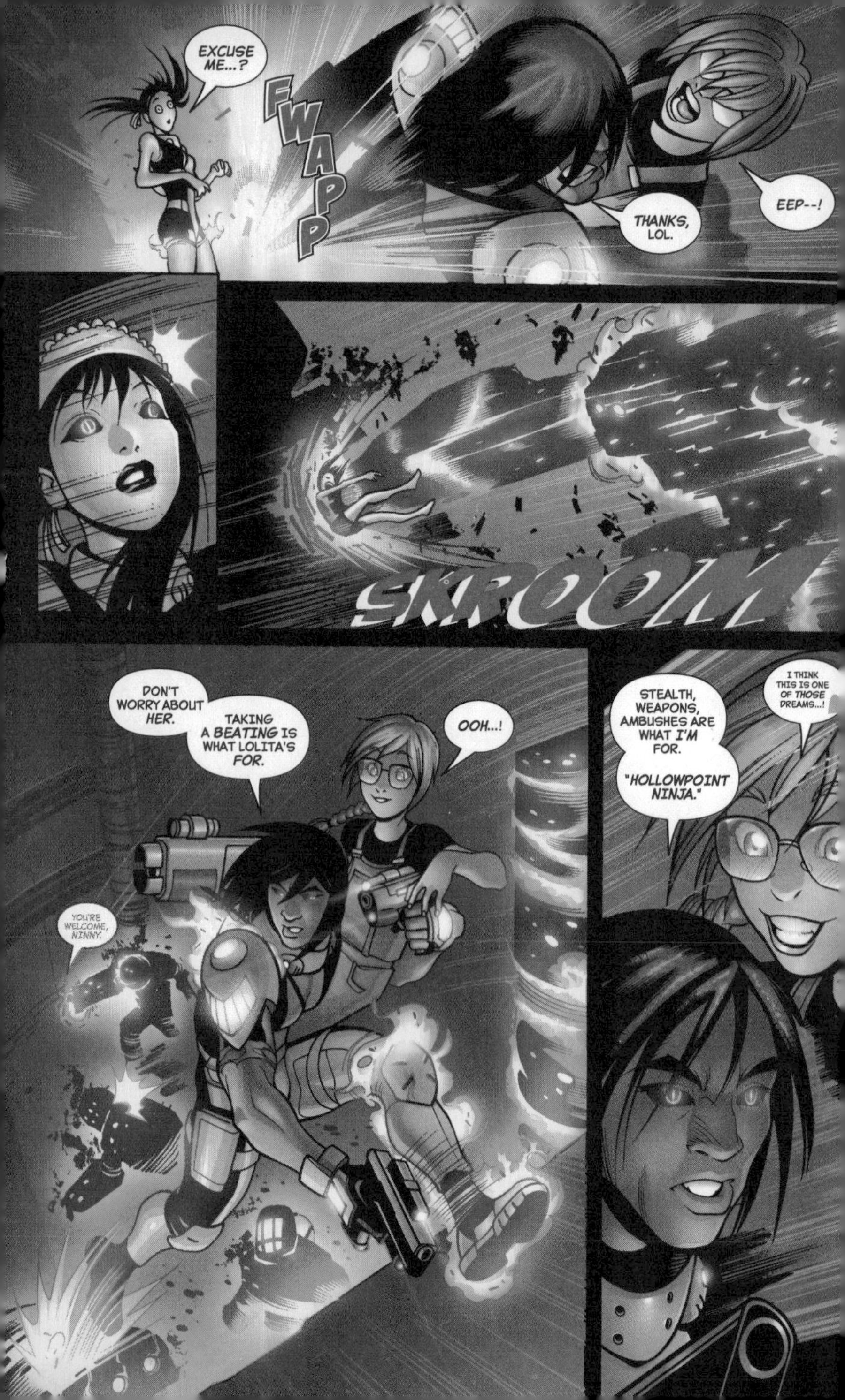
EXCUSE ME...?
FWAPP
THANKS, LOL.
EEP--!
SKROOM
DON'T WORRY ABOUT HER.
TAKING A BEATING IS WHAT LOLITA'S FOR.
OOH...!
YOU'RE WELCOME, NINNY.
STEALTH, WEAPONS, AMBUSHES ARE WHAT I'M FOR.
"HOLLOWPOINT NINJA."
I THINK THIS IS ONE OF THOSE DREAMS...!

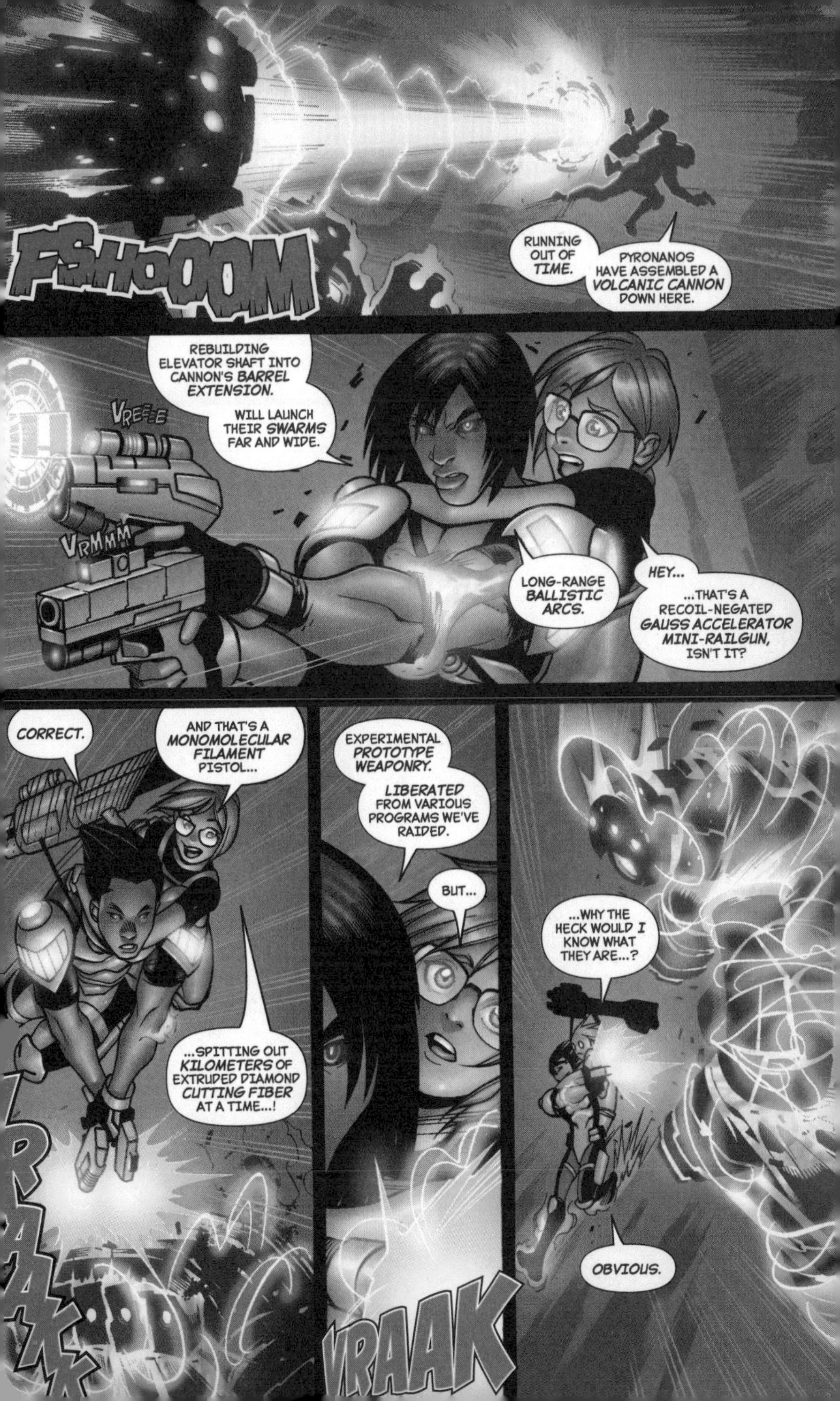
FSHOOOM
RUNNING OUT OF TIME.
PYRONANOS HAVE ASSEMBLED A VOLCANIC CANNON DOWN HERE.
REBUILDING ELEVATOR SHAFT INTO CANNON'S BARREL EXTENSION.
WILL LAUNCH THEIR SWARMS FAR AND WIDE.
VREEEE
VRMMM
LONG-RANGE BALLISTIC ARCS.
HEY...
...THAT'S A RECOIL-NEGATED GAUSS ACCELERATOR MINI-RAILGUN, ISN'T IT?
CORRECT.
AND THAT'S A MONOMOLECULAR FILAMENT PISTOL...
...SPITTING OUT KILOMETERS OF EXTRUDED DIAMOND CUTTING FIBER AT A TIME...!
EXPERIMENTAL PROTOTYPE WEAPONRY.
LIBERATED FROM VARIOUS PROGRAMS WE'VE RAIDED.
BUT...
...WHY THE HECK WOULD I KNOW WHAT THEY ARE...?
OBVIOUS.
VRAAK

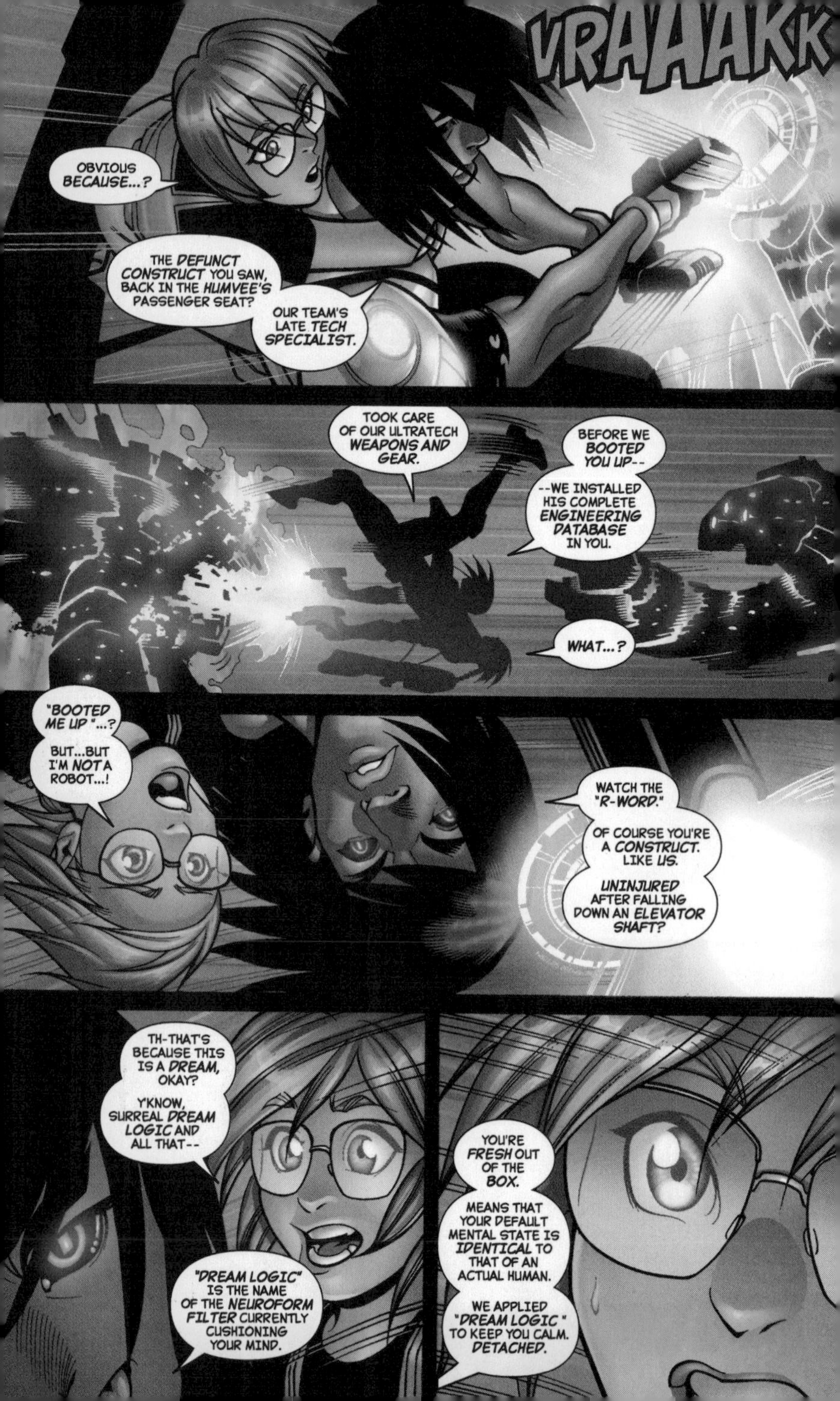
VRAAAKK
OBVIOUS BECAUSE...?
THE DEFUNCT CONSTRUCT YOU SAW, BACK IN THE HUMVEE'S PASSENGER SEAT?
OUR TEAM'S LATE TECH SPECIALIST.
TOOK CARE OF OUR ULTRATECH WEAPONS AND GEAR.
BEFORE WE BOOTED YOU UP--
--WE INSTALLED HIS COMPLETE ENGINEERING DATABASE IN YOU.
WHAT...?
"BOOTED ME UP"...?
BUT...BUT I'M NOT A ROBOT...!
WATCH THE "R-WORD."
OF COURSE YOU'RE A CONSTRUCT. LIKE US.
UNINJURED AFTER FALLING DOWN AN ELEVATOR SHAFT?
TH-THAT'S BECAUSE THIS IS A DREAM, OKAY?
Y'KNOW, SURREAL DREAM LOGIC AND ALL THAT--
"DREAM LOGIC" IS THE NAME OF THE NEUROFORM FILTER CURRENTLY CUSHIONING YOUR MIND.
YOU'RE FRESH OUT OF THE BOX.
MEANS THAT YOUR DEFAULT MENTAL STATE IS IDENTICAL TO THAT OF AN ACTUAL HUMAN.
WE APPLIED "DREAM LOGIC" TO KEEP YOU CALM. DETACHED.

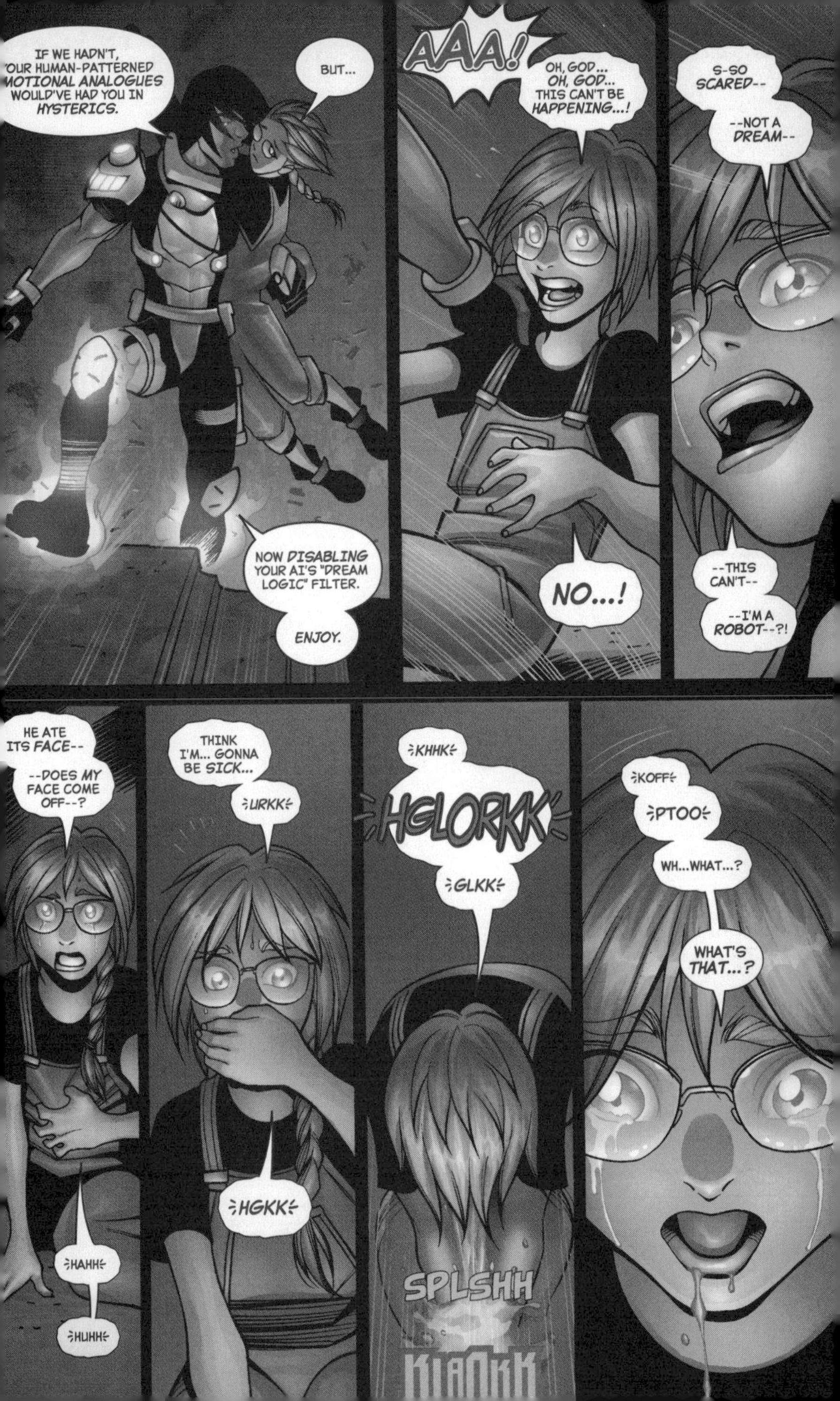
IF WE HADN'T, YOUR HUMAN-PATTERNED EMOTIONAL ANALOGUES WOULD'VE HAD YOU IN HYSTERICS.
BUT...
NOW DISABLING YOUR AI'S "DREAM LOGIC" FILTER.
ENJOY.
AAA!
OH, GOD... OH, GOD... THIS CAN'T BE HAPPENING...!
NO...!
S-SO SCARED--
--NOT A DREAM--
--THIS CAN'T--
--I'M A ROBOT--?!
HE ATE ITS FACE--
--DOES MY FACE COME OFF--?
HAHH
HUHH
THINK I'M... GONNA BE SICK...
URKK
HGKK
KHHK
HGLORKK
GLKK
SPLSHH
KLANKK
KOFF
PTOO
WH...WHAT...?
WHAT'S THAT...?

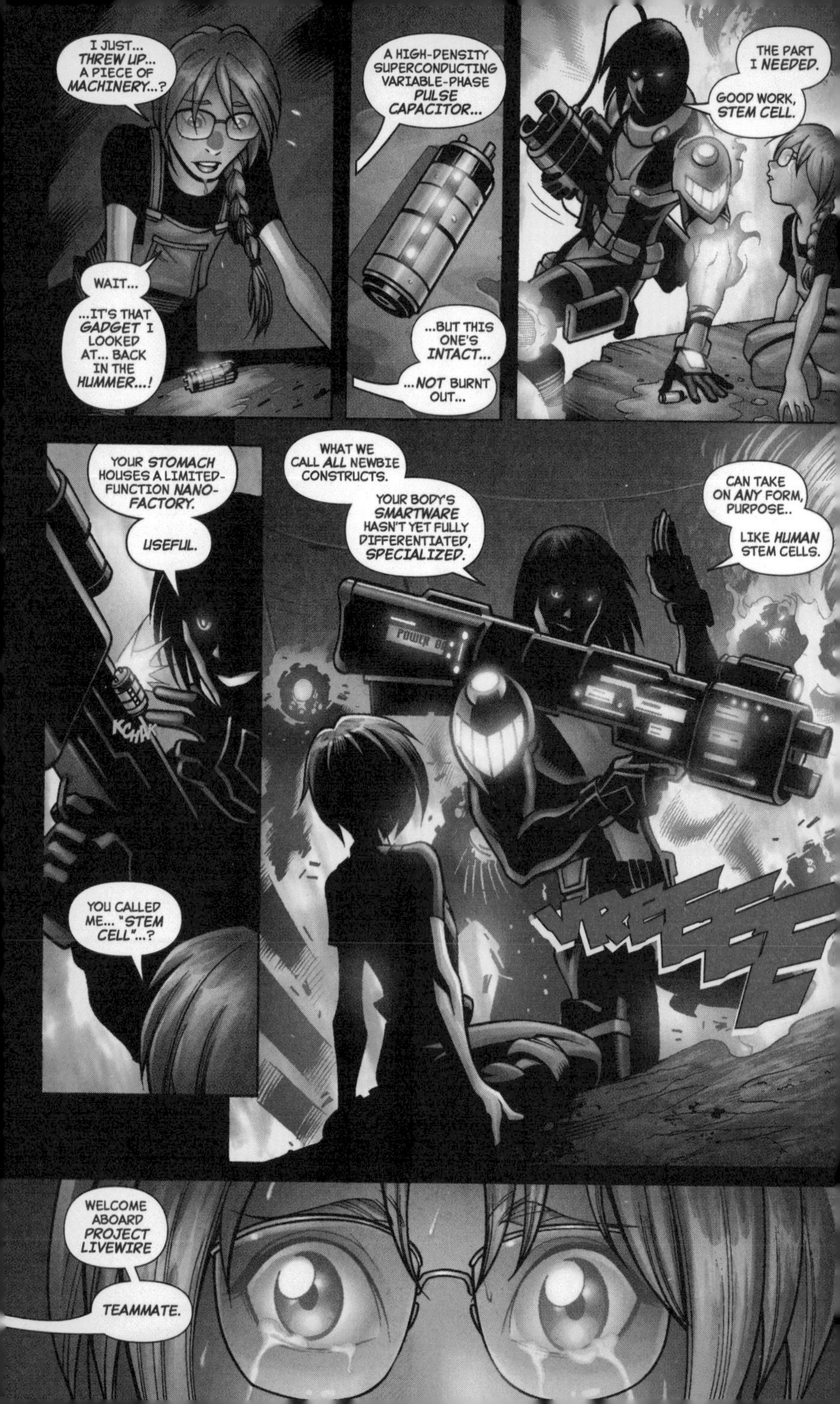

I JUST... THREW UP... A PIECE OF MACHINERY...?
WAIT...
...IT'S THAT GADGET I LOOKED AT... BACK IN THE HUMMER...!
A HIGH-DENSITY SUPERCONDUCTING VARIABLE-PHASE PULSE CAPACITOR...
...BUT THIS ONE'S INTACT...
...NOT BURNT OUT...
THE PART I NEEDED.
GOOD WORK, STEM CELL.
YOUR STOMACH HOUSES A LIMITED-FUNCTION NANO-FACTORY.
USEFUL.
KCHAK
YOU CALLED ME... "STEM CELL"...?
WHAT WE CALL ALL NEWBIE CONSTRUCTS.
YOUR BODY'S SMARTWARE HASN'T YET FULLY DIFFERENTIATED, SPECIALIZED.
CAN TAKE ON ANY FORM, PURPOSE..
LIKE HUMAN STEM CELLS.
VREEEEE
WELCOME ABOARD PROJECT LIVEWIRE
TEAMMATE.

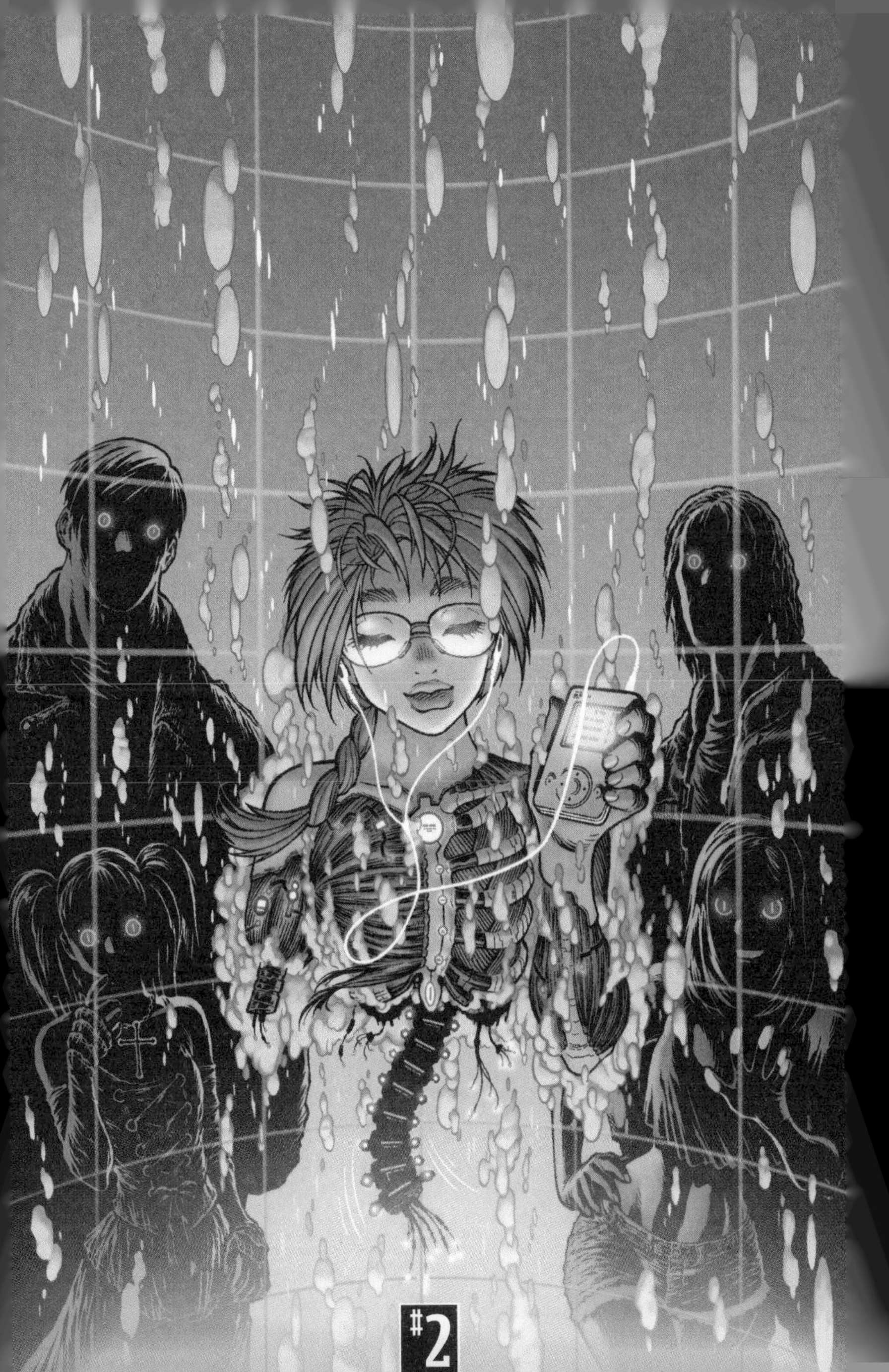
#2

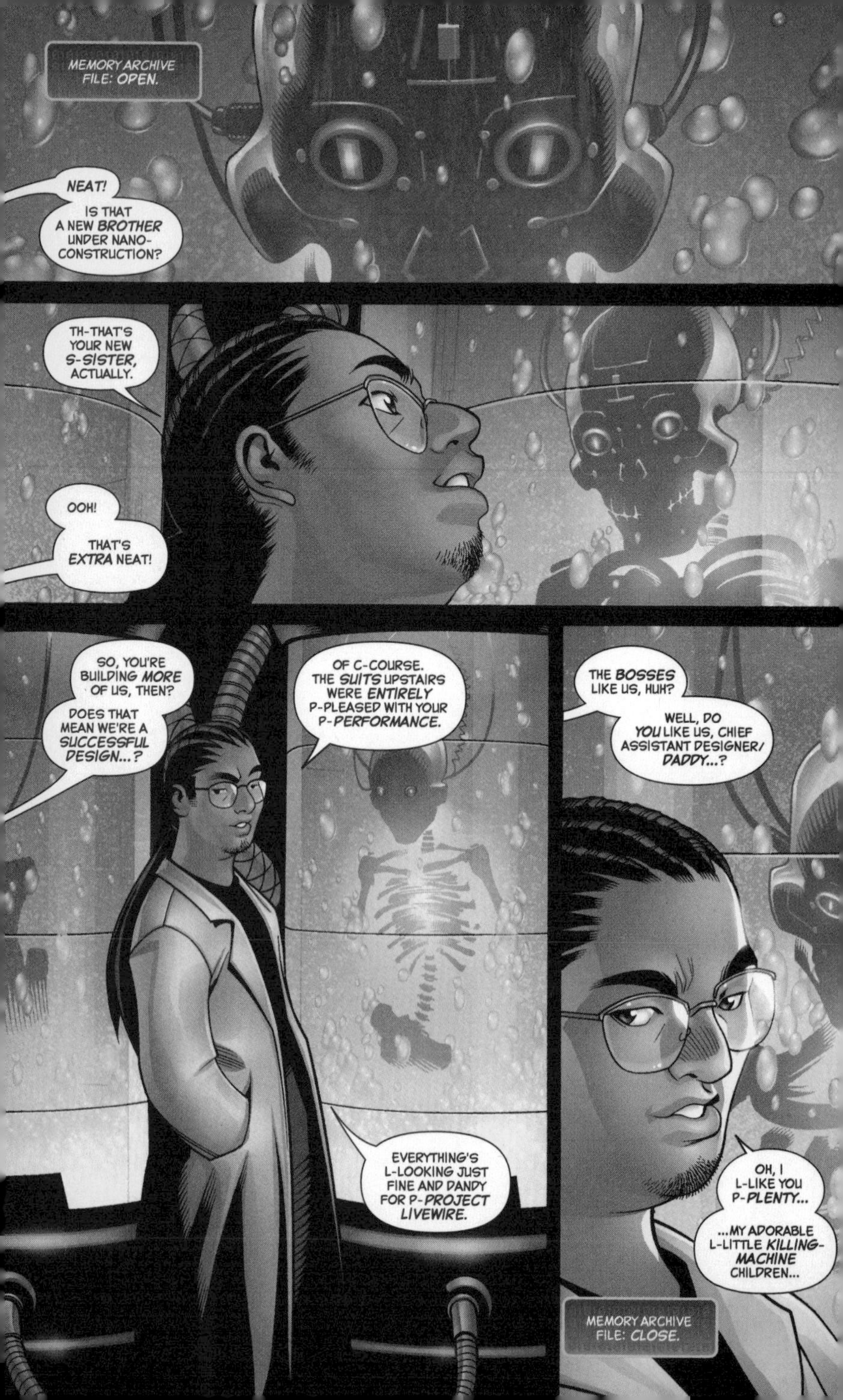
MEMORY ARCHIVE FILE: OPEN.
NEAT!
IS THAT A NEW BROTHER UNDER NANO-CONSTRUCTION?
TH-THAT'S YOUR NEW S-SISTER, ACTUALLY.
OOH!
THAT'S EXTRA NEAT!
SO, YOU'RE BUILDING MORE OF US, THEN?
DOES THAT MEAN WE'RE A SUCCESSFUL DESIGN...?
OF C-COURSE. THE SUITS UPSTAIRS WERE ENTIRELY P-PLEASED WITH YOUR P-PERFORMANCE.
EVERYTHING'S L-LOOKING JUST FINE AND DANDY FOR P-PROJECT LIVEWIRE.
THE BOSSES LIKE US, HUH?
WELL, DO YOU LIKE US, CHIEF ASSISTANT DESIGNER/ DADDY...?
OH, I L-LIKE YOU P-PLENTY...
...MY ADORABLE L-LITTLE KILLING-MACHINE CHILDREN...
MEMORY ARCHIVE FILE: CLOSE.

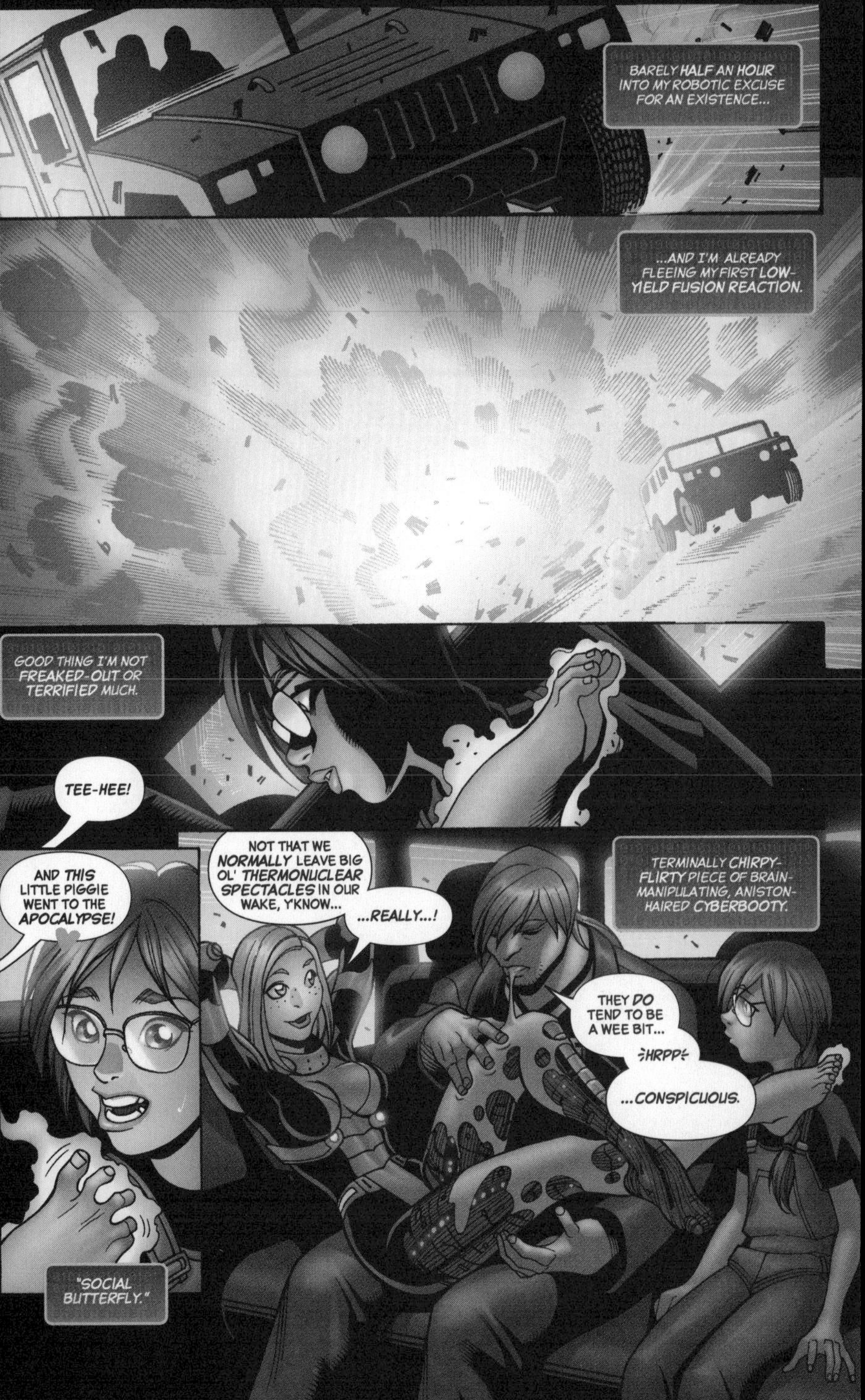
BARELY HALF AN HOUR INTO MY ROBOTIC EXCUSE FOR AN EXISTENCE...
...AND I'M ALREADY FLEEING MY FIRST LOW-YIELD FUSION REACTION.
GOOD THING I'M NOT FREAKED-OUT OR TERRIFIED MUCH.
TEE-HEE!
AND THIS LITTLE PIGGIE WENT TO THE APOCALYPSE!
NOT THAT WE NORMALLY LEAVE BIG OL' THERMONUCLEAR SPECTACLES IN OUR WAKE, Y'KNOW...
...REALLY...!
TERMINALLY CHIRPY-FLIRTY PIECE OF BRAIN-MANIPULATING, ANISTON-HAIRED CYBERBOOTY.
THEY DO TEND TO BE A WEE BIT...
HRPP
...CONSPICUOUS.
"SOCIAL BUTTERFLY."

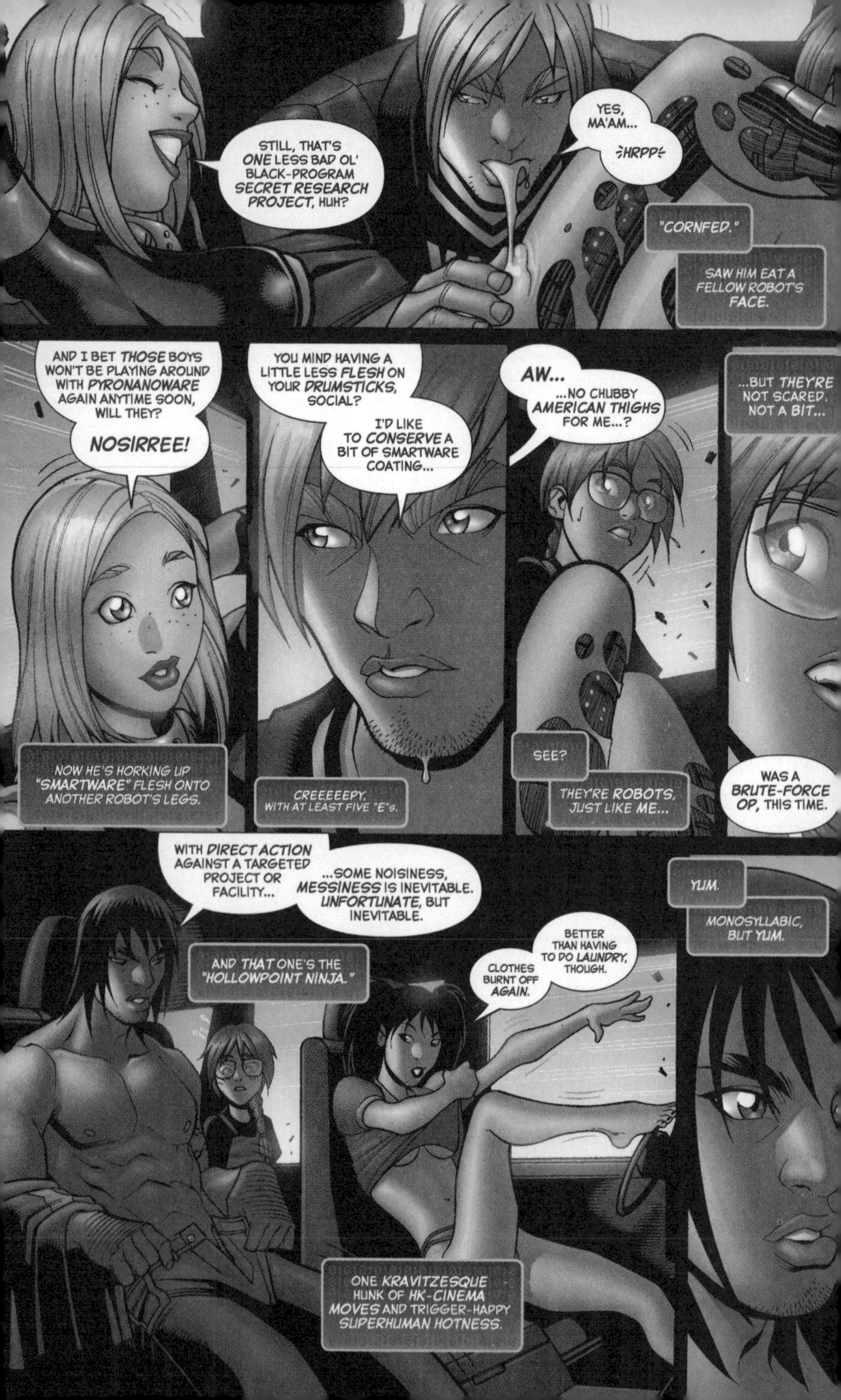

STILL, THAT'S ONE LESS BAD OL' BLACK-PROGRAM SECRET RESEARCH PROJECT, HUH?
YES, MA'AM...
HRPP
"CORNFED."
SAW HIM EAT A FELLOW ROBOT'S FACE.
AND I BET THOSE BOYS WON'T BE PLAYING AROUND WITH PYRONANOWARE AGAIN ANYTIME SOON, WILL THEY?
NOSIRREE!
NOW HE'S HORKING UP "SMARTWARE" FLESH ONTO ANOTHER ROBOT'S LEGS.
YOU MIND HAVING A LITTLE LESS FLESH ON YOUR DRUMSTICKS, SOCIAL?
I'D LIKE TO CONSERVE A BIT OF SMARTWARE COATING...
CREEEEEPY, WITH AT LEAST FIVE "E"s.
AW...
...NO CHUBBY AMERICAN THIGHS FOR ME...?
SEE?
THEY'RE ROBOTS, JUST LIKE ME...
...BUT THEY'RE NOT SCARED. NOT A BIT...
WAS A BRUTE-FORCE OP, THIS TIME.
WITH DIRECT ACTION AGAINST A TARGETED PROJECT OR FACILITY...
...SOME NOISINESS, MESSINESS IS INEVITABLE. UNFORTUNATE, BUT INEVITABLE.
AND THAT ONE'S THE "HOLLOWPOINT NINJA."
ONE KRAVITZESQUE HUNK OF HK-CINEMA MOVES AND TRIGGER-HAPPY SUPERHUMAN HOTNESS.
CLOTHES BURNT OFF AGAIN.
BETTER THAN HAVING TO DO LAUNDRY, THOUGH.
YUM.
MONOSYLLABIC, BUT YUM.

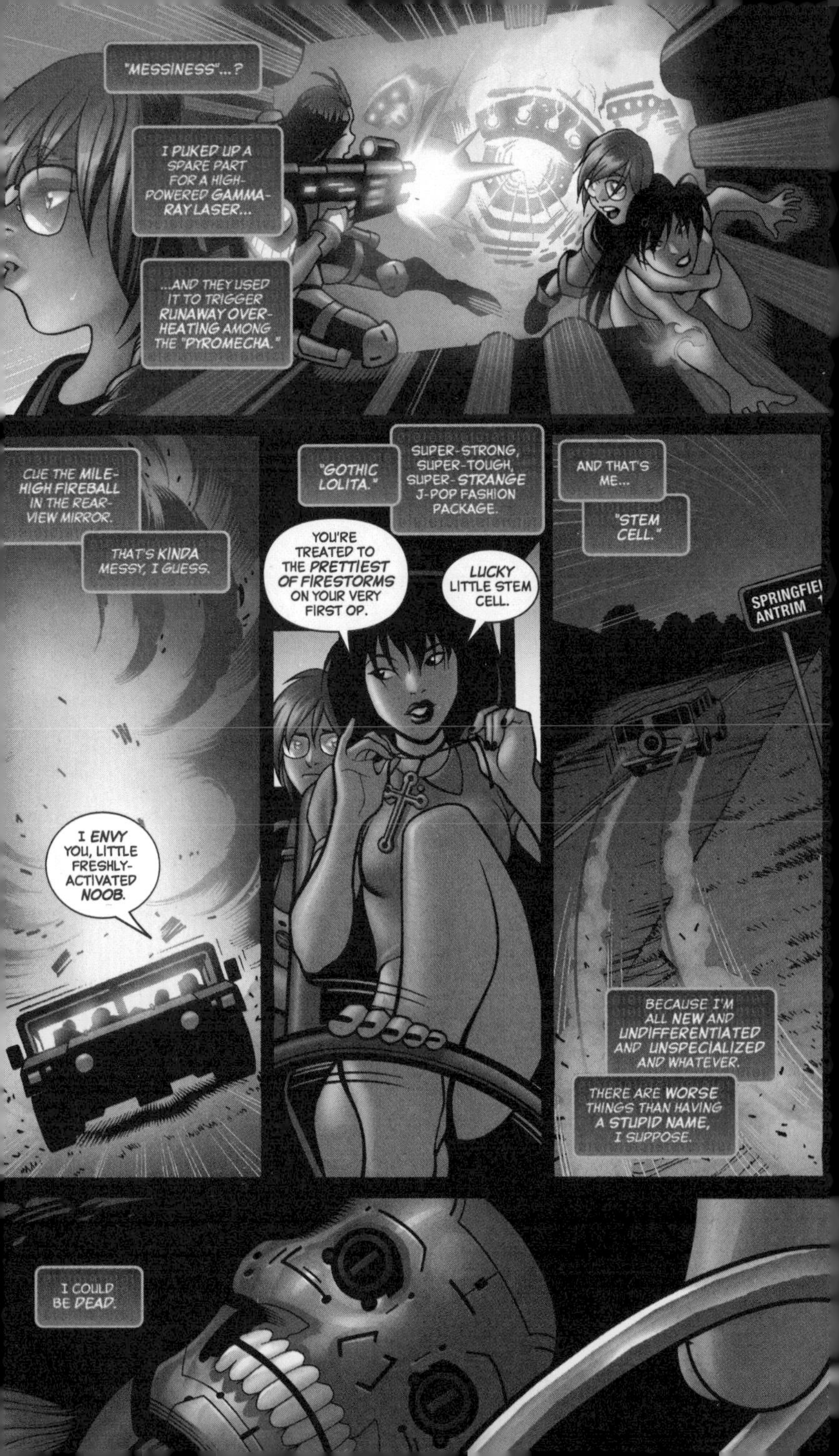
"MESSINESS"...?
I PUKED UP A SPARE PART FOR A HIGH-POWERED GAMMA-RAY LASER...
...AND THEY USED IT TO TRIGGER RUNAWAY OVER-HEATING AMONG THE "PYROMECHA."
CUE THE MILE-HIGH FIREBALL IN THE REAR-VIEW MIRROR.
THAT'S KINDA MESSY, I GUESS.
I ENVY YOU, LITTLE FRESHLY-ACTIVATED NOOB.
"GOTHIC LOLITA."
SUPER-STRONG, SUPER-TOUGH, SUPER-STRANGE J-POP FASHION PACKAGE.
YOU'RE TREATED TO THE PRETTIEST OF FIRESTORMS ON YOUR VERY FIRST OP.
LUCKY LITTLE STEM CELL.
AND THAT'S ME...
"STEM CELL."
SPRINGFIEL
ANTRIM
BECAUSE I'M ALL NEW AND UNDIFFERENTIATED AND UNSPECIALIZED AND WHATEVER.
THERE ARE WORSE THINGS THAN HAVING A STUPID NAME, I SUPPOSE.
I COULD BE DEAD.

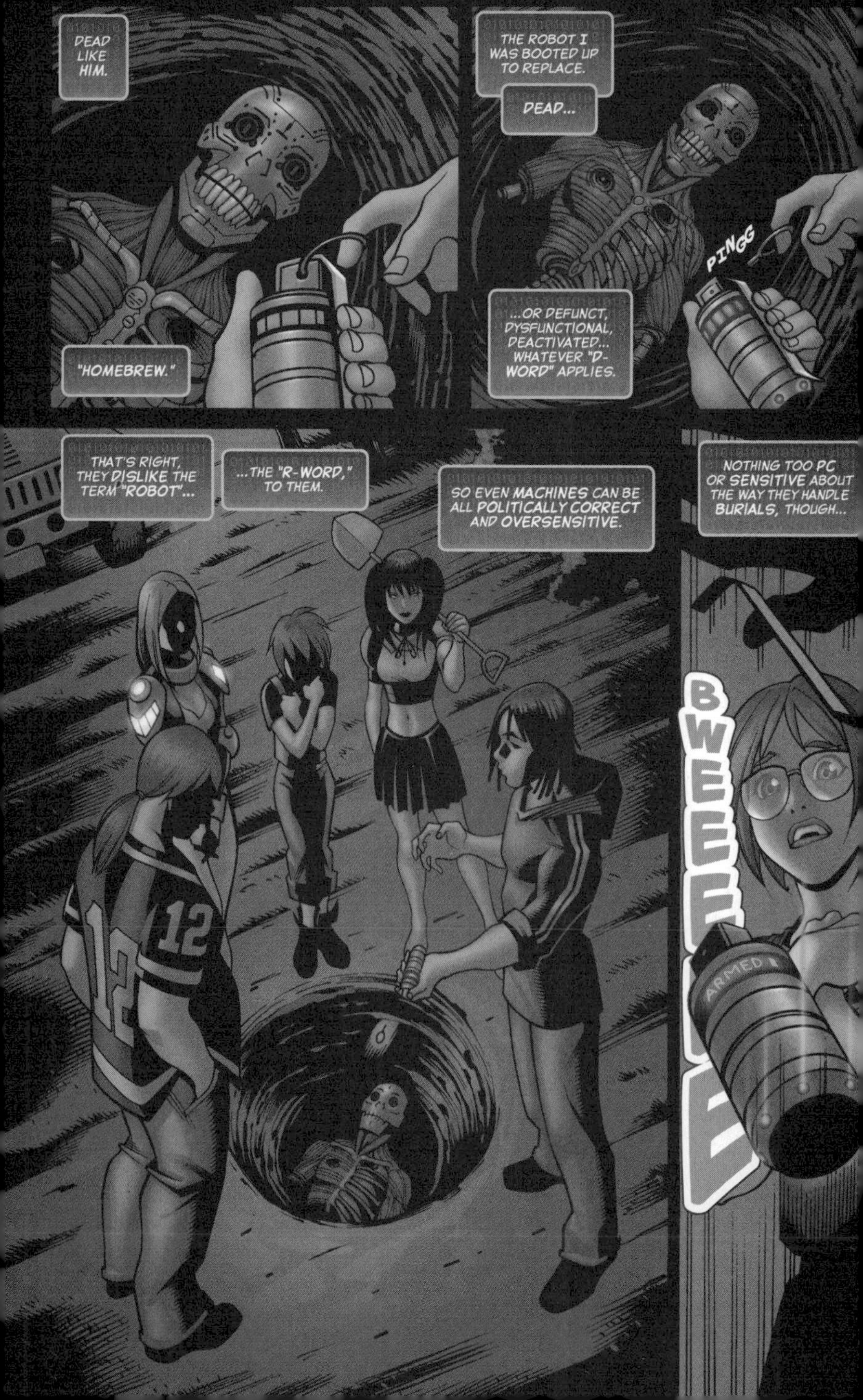
DEAD LIKE HIM.
"HOMEBREW."
THE ROBOT I WAS BOOTED UP TO REPLACE.
DEAD...
PINGG
...OR DEFUNCT, DYSFUNCTIONAL, DEACTIVATED... WHATEVER "D-WORD" APPLIES.
THAT'S RIGHT, THEY DISLIKE THE TERM "ROBOT"...
...THE "R-WORD," TO THEM.
SO EVEN MACHINES CAN BE ALL POLITICALLY CORRECT AND OVERSENSITIVE.
NOTHING TOO PC OR SENSITIVE ABOUT THE WAY THEY HANDLE BURIALS, THOUGH...
12
12
12
ARMED
BWEEEE

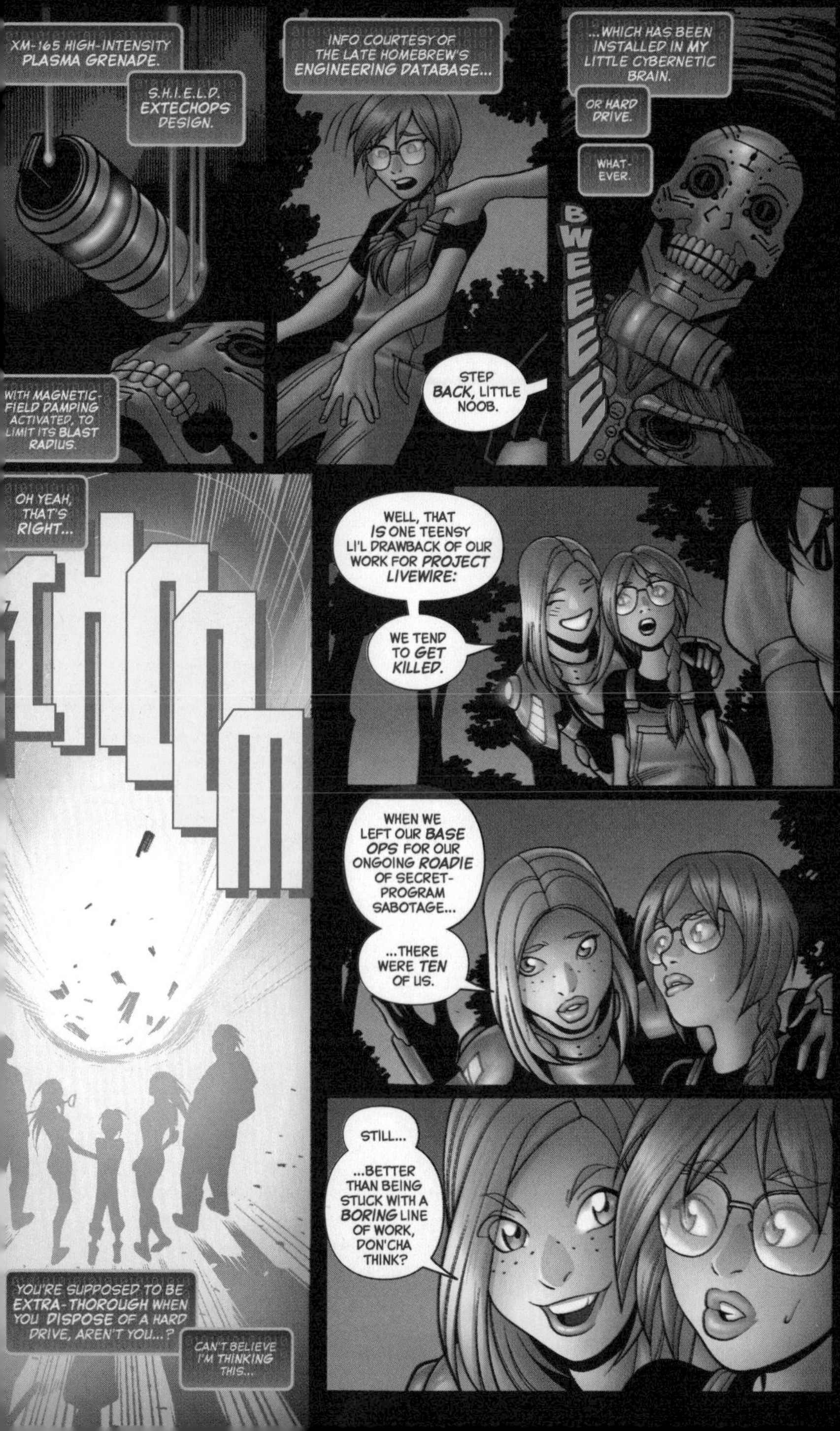

XM-165 HIGH-INTENSITY PLASMA GRENADE.
S.H.I.E.L.D. EXTECHOPS DESIGN.
WITH MAGNETIC-FIELD DAMPING ACTIVATED, TO LIMIT ITS BLAST RADIUS.
INFO COURTESY OF THE LATE HOMEBREW'S ENGINEERING DATABASE...
STEP BACK, LITTLE NOOB.
...WHICH HAS BEEN INSTALLED IN MY LITTLE CYBERNETIC BRAIN.
OR HARD DRIVE.
WHAT-EVER.
BWEEEEE
OH YEAH, THAT'S RIGHT...
THOOM
YOU'RE SUPPOSED TO BE EXTRA-THOROUGH WHEN YOU DISPOSE OF A HARD DRIVE, AREN'T YOU...?
CAN'T BELIEVE I'M THINKING THIS...
WELL, THAT IS ONE TEENSY LI'L DRAWBACK OF OUR WORK FOR PROJECT LIVEWIRE:
WE TEND TO GET KILLED.
WHEN WE LEFT OUR BASE OPS FOR OUR ONGOING ROADIE OF SECRET-PROGRAM SABOTAGE...
...THERE WERE TEN OF US.
STILL...
...BETTER THAN BEING STUCK WITH A BORING LINE OF WORK, DON'CHA THINK?

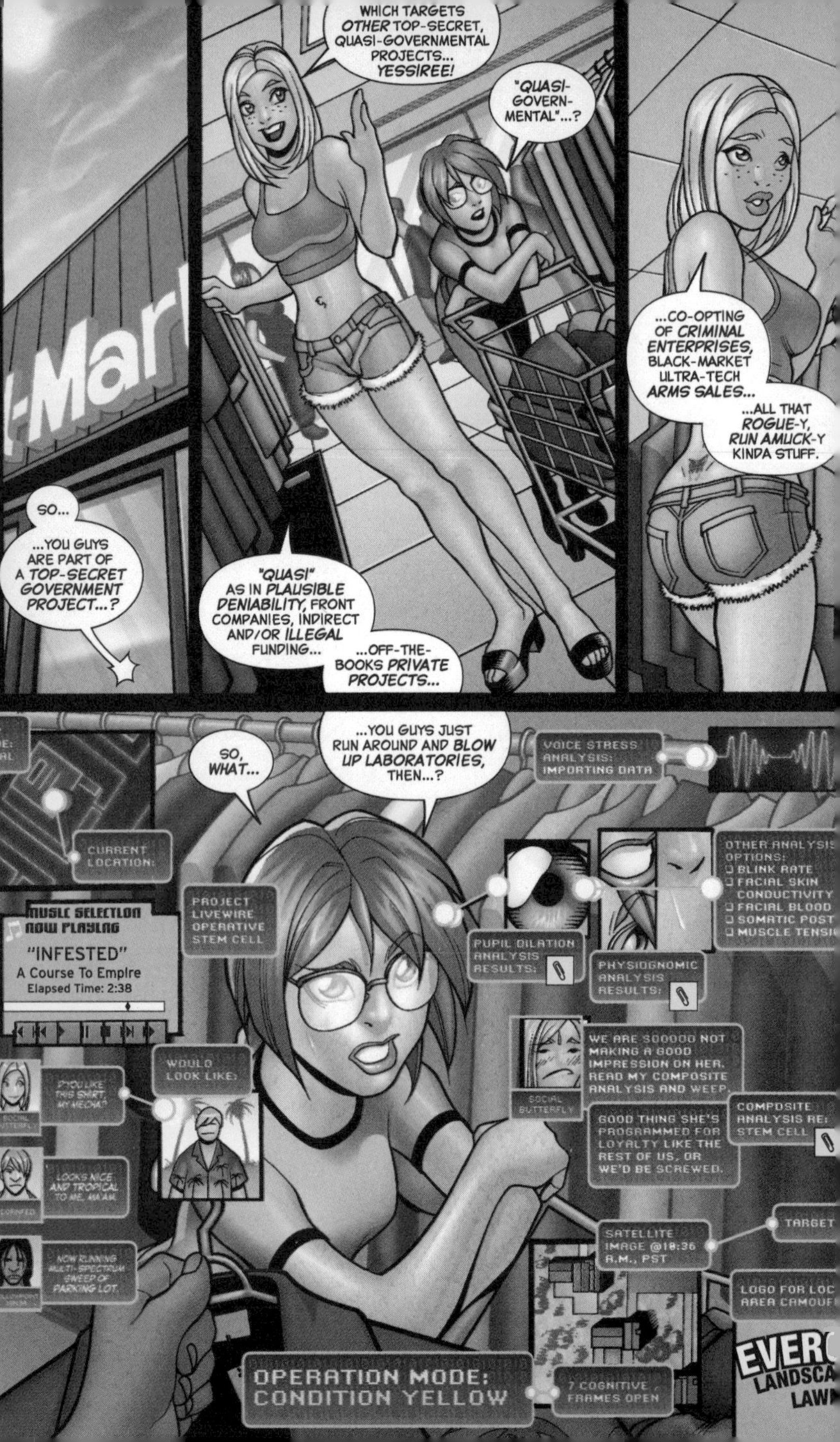
SO...
...YOU GUYS ARE PART OF A TOP-SECRET GOVERNMENT PROJECT...?
WHICH TARGETS OTHER TOP-SECRET, QUASI-GOVERNMENTAL PROJECTS... YESSIREE!
"QUASI-GOVERN-MENTAL"...?
"QUASI" AS IN PLAUSIBLE DENIABILITY, FRONT COMPANIES, INDIRECT AND/OR ILLEGAL FUNDING...
...OFF-THE-BOOKS PRIVATE PROJECTS...
...CO-OPTING OF CRIMINAL ENTERPRISES, BLACK-MARKET ULTRA-TECH ARMS SALES...
...ALL THAT ROGUE-Y, RUN AMUCK-Y KINDA STUFF.
MAP MODE: LOCAL
SO, WHAT...
...YOU GUYS JUST RUN AROUND AND BLOW UP LABORATORIES, THEN...?
VOICE STRESS ANALYSIS: IMPORTING DATA
CURRENT LOCATION:
MUSIC SELECTION NOW PLAYING
"INFESTED"
A Course To Empire
Elapsed Time: 2:38
PROJECT LIVEWIRE OPERATIVE STEM CELL
PUPIL DILATION ANALYSIS RESULTS:
PHYSIOGNOMIC ANALYSIS RESULTS:
OTHER ANALYSIS OPTIONS:
❑ BLINK RATE
❑ FACIAL SKIN CONDUCTIVITY
❑ FACIAL BLOOD
❑ SOMATIC POST
❑ MUSCLE TENSI
WOULD LOOK LIKE:
D'YOU LIKE THIS SHIRT, MY MECHA?
LOOKS NICE AND TROPICAL TO ME, MA'AM.
NOW RUNNING MULTI-SPECTRUM SWEEP OF PARKING LOT.
WE ARE SOOOOO NOT MAKING A GOOD IMPRESSION ON HER. READ MY COMPOSITE ANALYSIS AND WEEP.
SOCIAL BUTTERFLY
GOOD THING SHE'S PROGRAMMED FOR LOYALTY LIKE THE REST OF US, OR WE'D BE SCREWED.
COMPOSITE ANALYSIS RE: STEM CELL
SATELLITE IMAGE @10:36 A.M., PST
TARGET
LOGO FOR LOC AREA CAMOUF
EVERG LANDSCA LAWN
OPERATION MODE: CONDITION YELLOW
7 COGNITIVE FRAMES OPEN

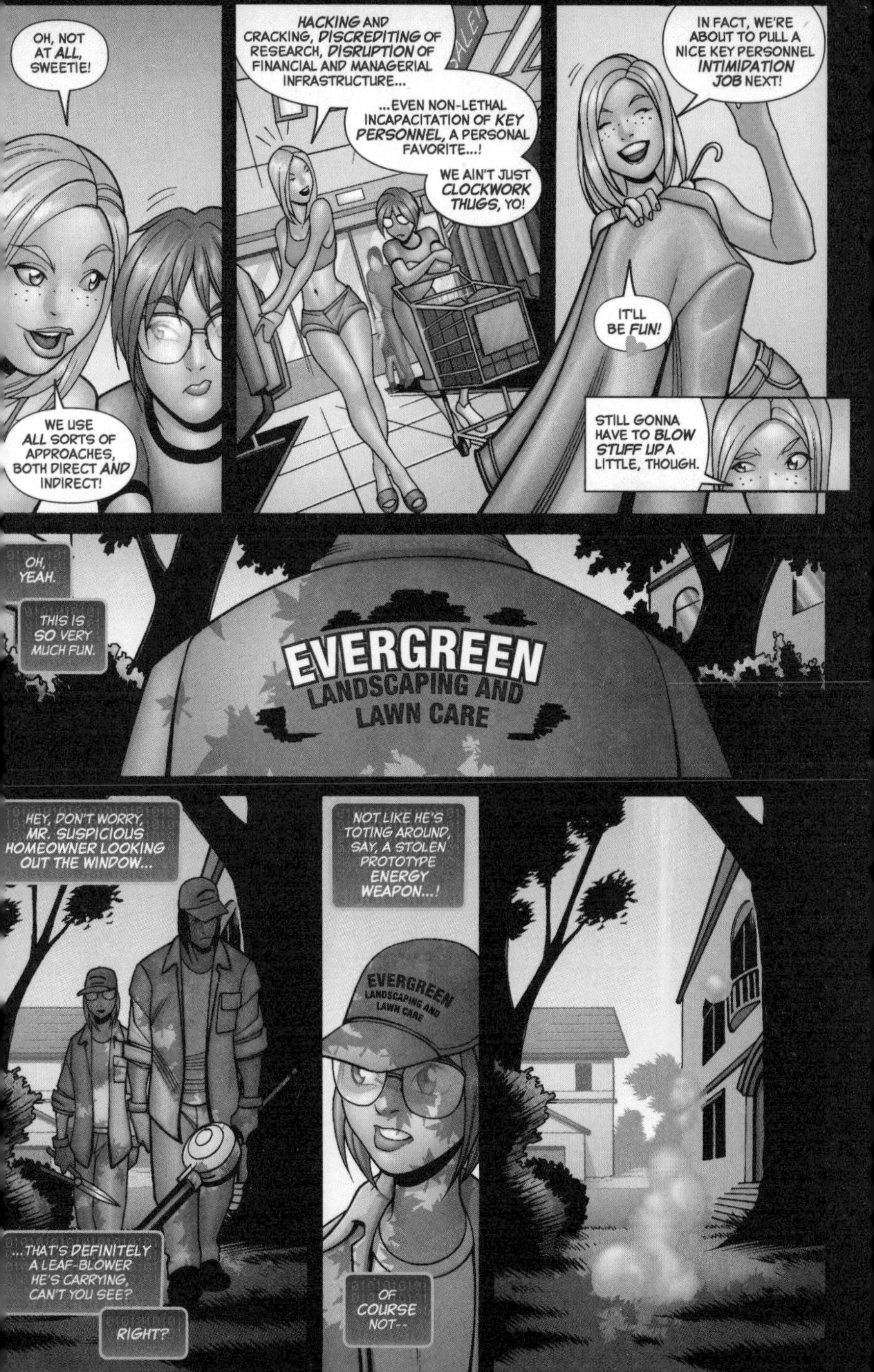
OH, NOT AT ALL, SWEETIE!
WE USE ALL SORTS OF APPROACHES, BOTH DIRECT AND INDIRECT!
HACKING AND CRACKING, DISCREDITING OF RESEARCH, DISRUPTION OF FINANCIAL AND MANAGERIAL INFRASTRUCTURE...
...EVEN NON-LETHAL INCAPACITATION OF KEY PERSONNEL, A PERSONAL FAVORITE...!
WE AIN'T JUST CLOCKWORK THUGS, YO!
IN FACT, WE'RE ABOUT TO PULL A NICE KEY PERSONNEL INTIMIDATION JOB NEXT!
IT'LL BE FUN!
STILL GONNA HAVE TO BLOW STUFF UP A LITTLE, THOUGH.
OH, YEAH.
THIS IS SO VERY MUCH FUN.
EVERGREEN LANDSCAPING AND LAWN CARE
HEY, DON'T WORRY, MR. SUSPICIOUS HOMEOWNER LOOKING OUT THE WINDOW...
...THAT'S DEFINITELY A LEAF-BLOWER HE'S CARRYING, CAN'T YOU SEE?
RIGHT?
NOT LIKE HE'S TOTING AROUND, SAY, A STOLEN PROTOTYPE ENERGY WEAPON...!
EVERGREEN LANDSCAPING AND LAWN CARE
OF COURSE NOT--

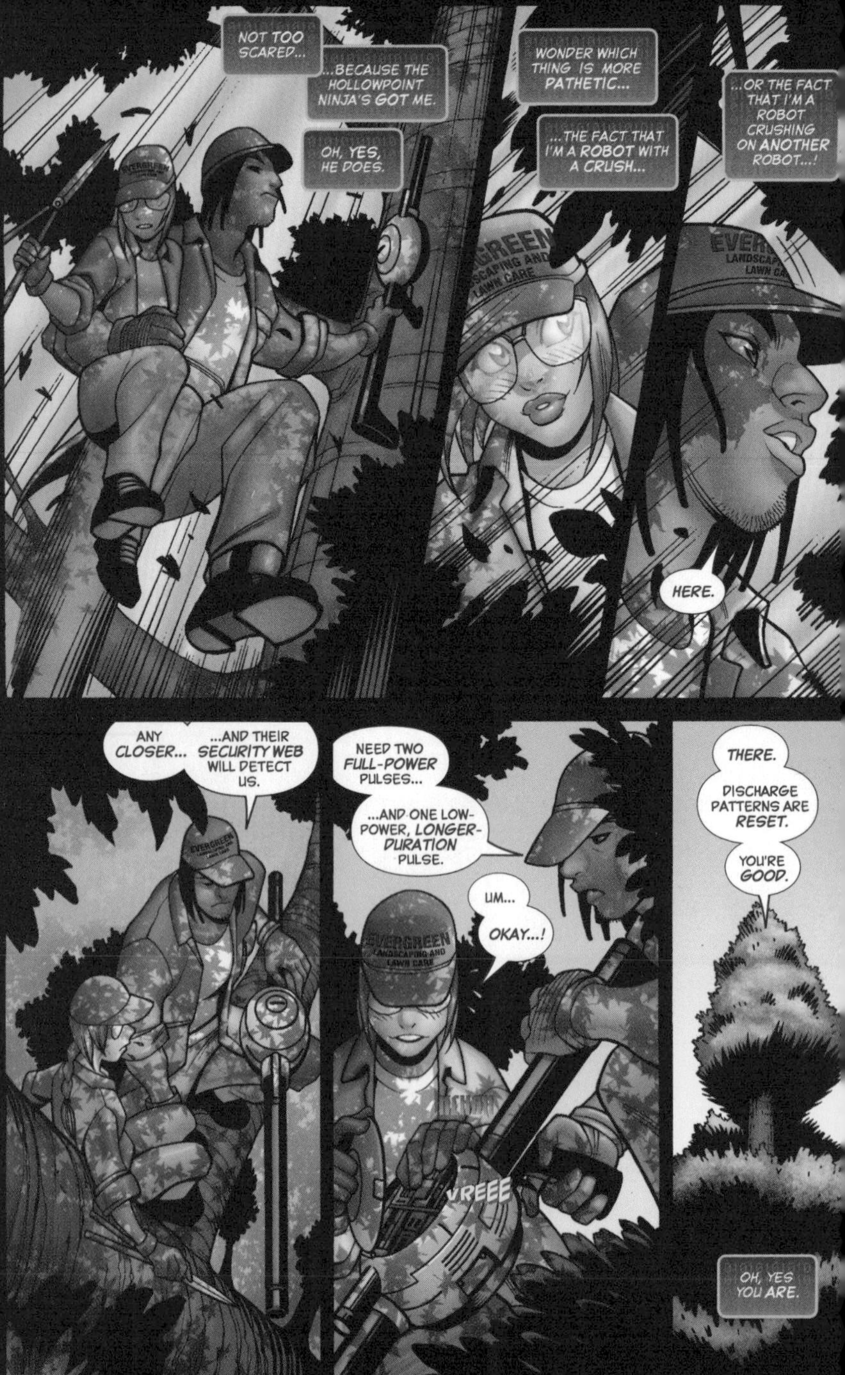
NOT TOO SCARED...
...BECAUSE THE HOLLOWPOINT NINJA'S GOT ME.
OH, YES, HE DOES.
WONDER WHICH THING IS MORE PATHETIC...
...THE FACT THAT I'M A ROBOT WITH A CRUSH...
...OR THE FACT THAT I'M A ROBOT CRUSHING ON ANOTHER ROBOT...!
EVERGREEN LANDSCAPING AND LAWN CARE
HERE.
ANY CLOSER...
...AND THEIR SECURITY WEB WILL DETECT US.
NEED TWO FULL-POWER PULSES...
...AND ONE LOW-POWER, LONGER-DURATION PULSE.
UM...
OKAY...!
EVERGREEN LANDSCAPING AND LAWN CARE
VREEE
THERE.
DISCHARGE PATTERNS ARE RESET.
YOU'RE GOOD.
OH, YES YOU ARE.

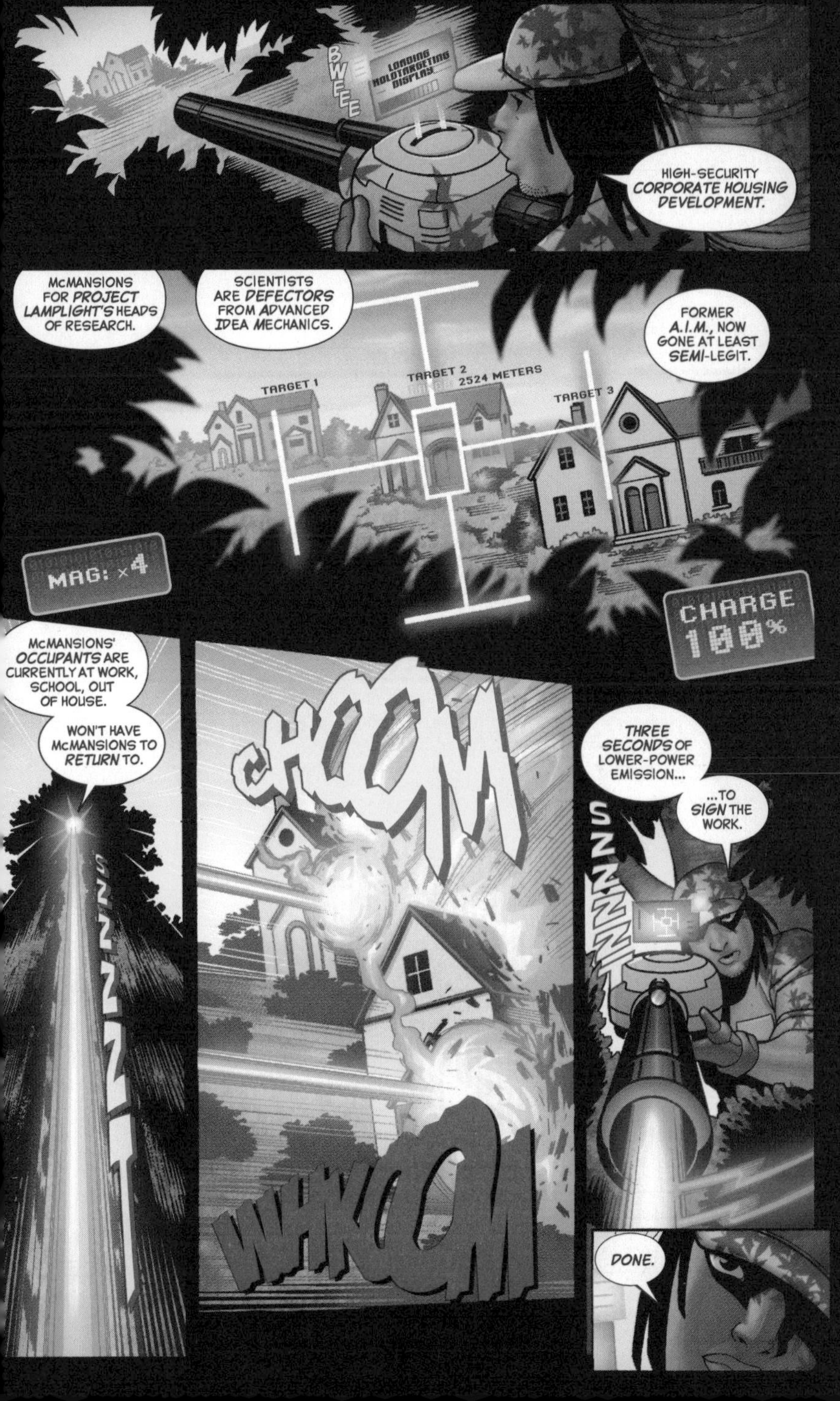
BWEEE
LOADING HOLOTARGETING DISPLAY
HIGH-SECURITY CORPORATE HOUSING DEVELOPMENT.
McMANSIONS FOR PROJECT LAMPLIGHT'S HEADS OF RESEARCH.
SCIENTISTS ARE DEFECTORS FROM ADVANCED IDEA MECHANICS.
FORMER A.I.M., NOW GONE AT LEAST SEMI-LEGIT.
TARGET 1
TARGET 2
2524 METERS
TARGET 3
MAG: x4
CHARGE 100%
McMANSIONS' OCCUPANTS ARE CURRENTLY AT WORK, SCHOOL, OUT OF HOUSE.
WON'T HAVE McMANSIONS TO RETURN TO.
CHOOM
THREE SECONDS OF LOWER-POWER EMISSION...
...TO SIGN THE WORK.
DONE.

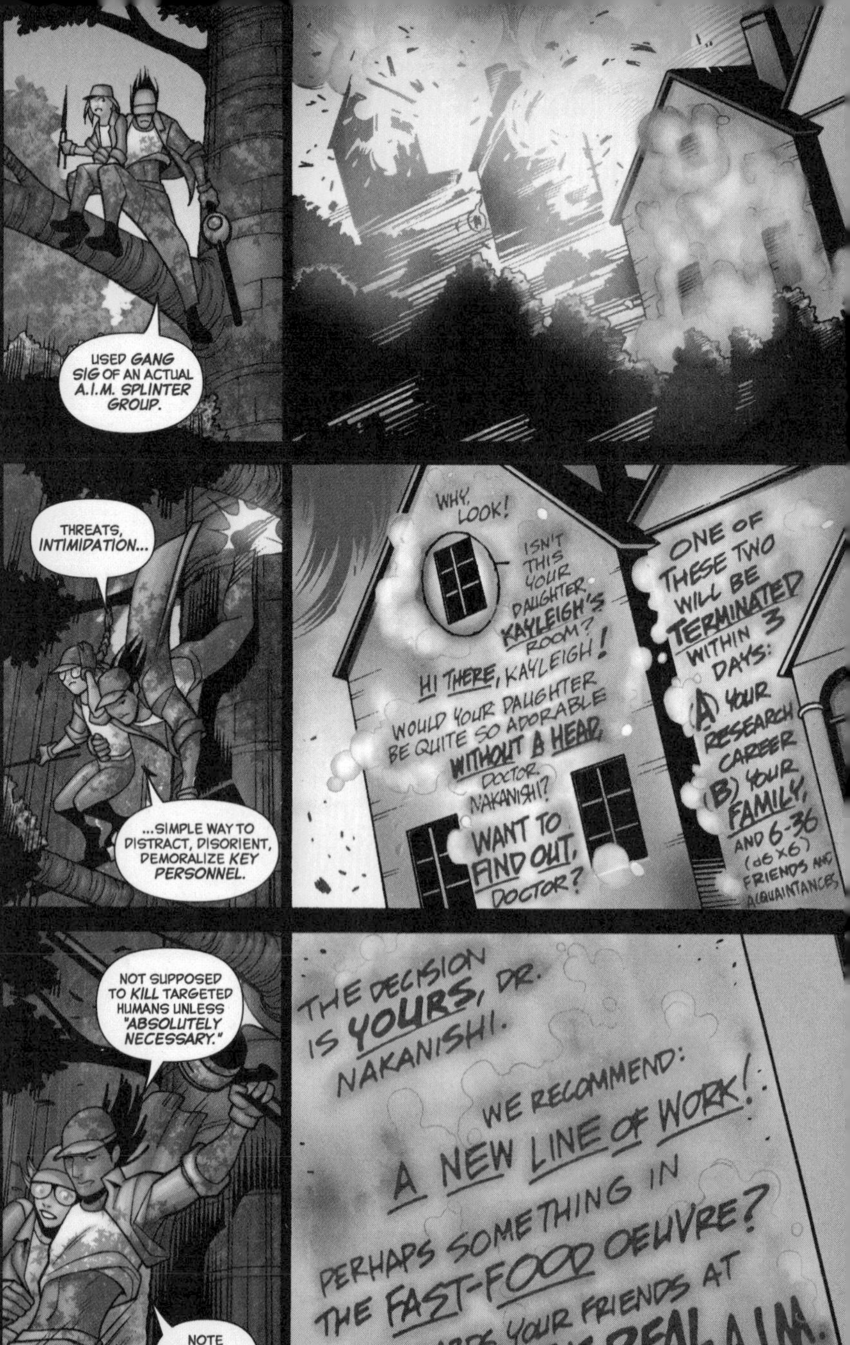

USED GANG SIG OF AN ACTUAL A.I.M. SPLINTER GROUP.
THREATS, INTIMIDATION...
WHY, LOOK!
ISN'T THIS YOUR DAUGHTER KAYLEIGH'S ROOM?
HI THERE, KAYLEIGH!
WOULD YOUR DAUGHTER BE QUITE SO ADORABLE WITHOUT A HEAD, DOCTOR NAKANISHI?
WANT TO FIND OUT, DOCTOR?
ONE OF THESE TWO WILL BE TERMINATED WITHIN 3 DAYS: (A) YOUR RESEARCH CAREER (B) YOUR FAMILY, AND 6-36 (d6 X6) FRIENDS AND ACQUAINTANCES
...SIMPLE WAY TO DISTRACT, DISORIENT, DEMORALIZE KEY PERSONNEL.
NOT SUPPOSED TO KILL TARGETED HUMANS UNLESS "ABSOLUTELY NECESSARY."
THE DECISION IS YOURS, DR. NAKANISHI.
WE RECOMMEND:
A NEW LINE OF WORK!
PERHAPS SOMETHING IN THE FAST-FOOD OEUVRE?
REGARDS, YOUR FRIENDS AT THE REAL A.I.M.
NOTE GAPING SIZE OF LOOPHOLE.

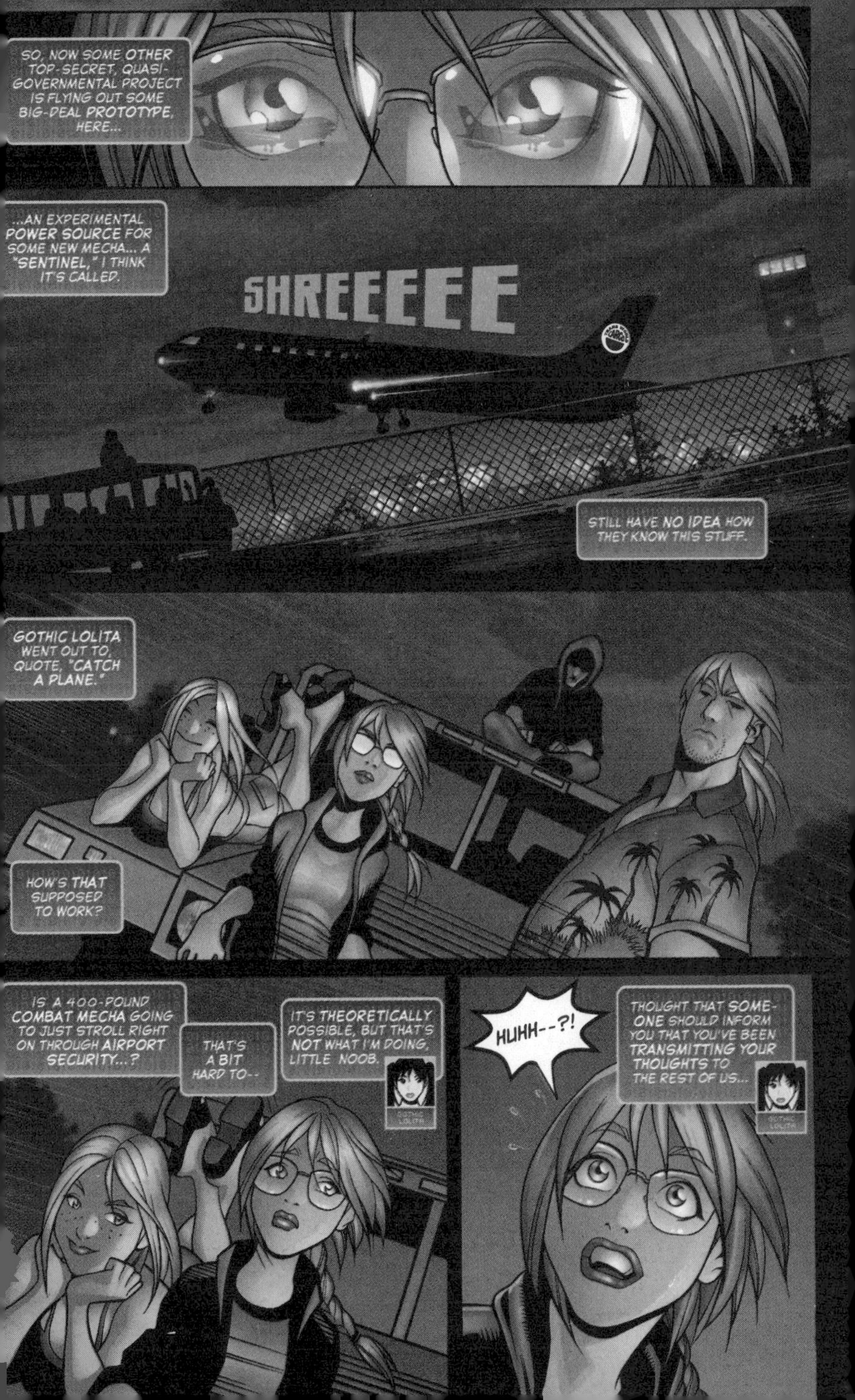

SO, NOW SOME OTHER TOP-SECRET, QUASI-GOVERNMENTAL PROJECT IS FLYING OUT SOME BIG-DEAL PROTOTYPE, HERE...
...AN EXPERIMENTAL POWER SOURCE FOR SOME NEW MECHA... A "SENTINEL," I THINK IT'S CALLED.
SHREEEEE
STILL HAVE NO IDEA HOW THEY KNOW THIS STUFF.
GOTHIC LOLITA WENT OUT TO, QUOTE, "CATCH A PLANE."
HOW'S THAT SUPPOSED TO WORK?
IS A 400-POUND COMBAT MECHA GOING TO JUST STROLL RIGHT ON THROUGH AIRPORT SECURITY...?
THAT'S A BIT HARD TO--
IT'S THEORETICALLY POSSIBLE, BUT THAT'S NOT WHAT I'M DOING, LITTLE NOOB.
HUHH--?!
THOUGHT THAT SOME-ONE SHOULD INFORM YOU THAT YOU'VE BEEN TRANSMITTING YOUR THOUGHTS TO THE REST OF US...

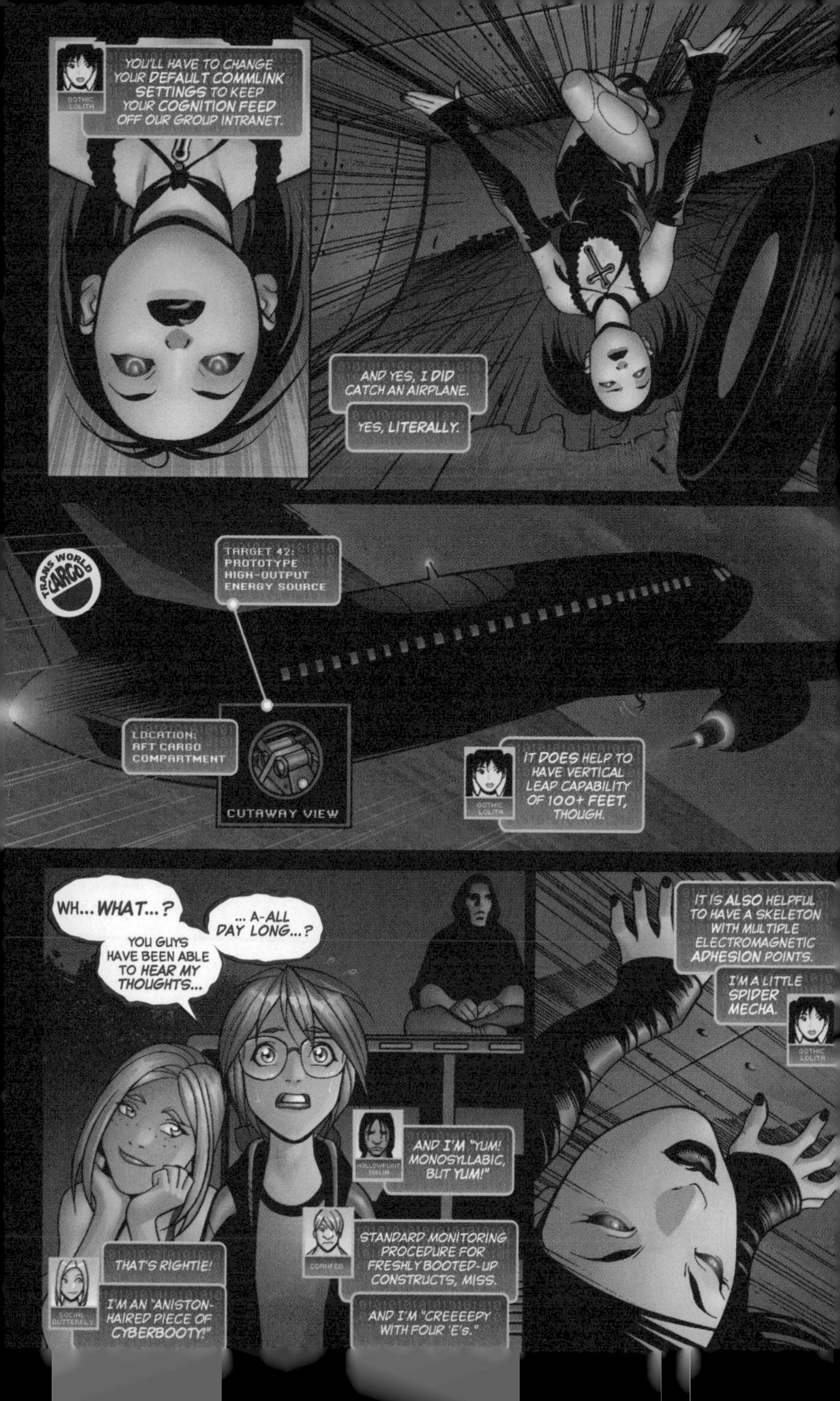

GOTHIC LOLITA
YOU'LL HAVE TO CHANGE YOUR DEFAULT COMMLINK SETTINGS TO KEEP YOUR COGNITION FEED OFF OUR GROUP INTRANET.
AND YES, I DID CATCH AN AIRPLANE.
YES, LITERALLY.
TRANS WORLD CARGO
TARGET 42: PROTOTYPE HIGH-OUTPUT ENERGY SOURCE
LOCATION: AFT CARGO COMPARTMENT
CUTAWAY VIEW
GOTHIC LOLITA
IT DOES HELP TO HAVE VERTICAL LEAP CAPABILITY OF 100+ FEET, THOUGH.
WH... WHAT...?
YOU GUYS HAVE BEEN ABLE TO HEAR MY THOUGHTS...
... A-ALL DAY LONG...?
IT IS ALSO HELPFUL TO HAVE A SKELETON WITH MULTIPLE ELECTROMAGNETIC ADHESION POINTS.
I'M A LITTLE SPIDER MECHA.
GOTHIC LOLITA
HOLLOWPOINT NINJA
AND I'M "YUM! MONOSYLLABIC, BUT YUM!"
CORNFED
STANDARD MONITORING PROCEDURE FOR FRESHLY BOOTED-UP CONSTRUCTS, MISS.
AND I'M "CREEEEPY WITH FOUR 'E's."
SOCIAL BUTTERFLY
THAT'S RIGHTIE!
I'M AN "ANISTON-HAIRED PIECE OF CYBERBOOTY!"

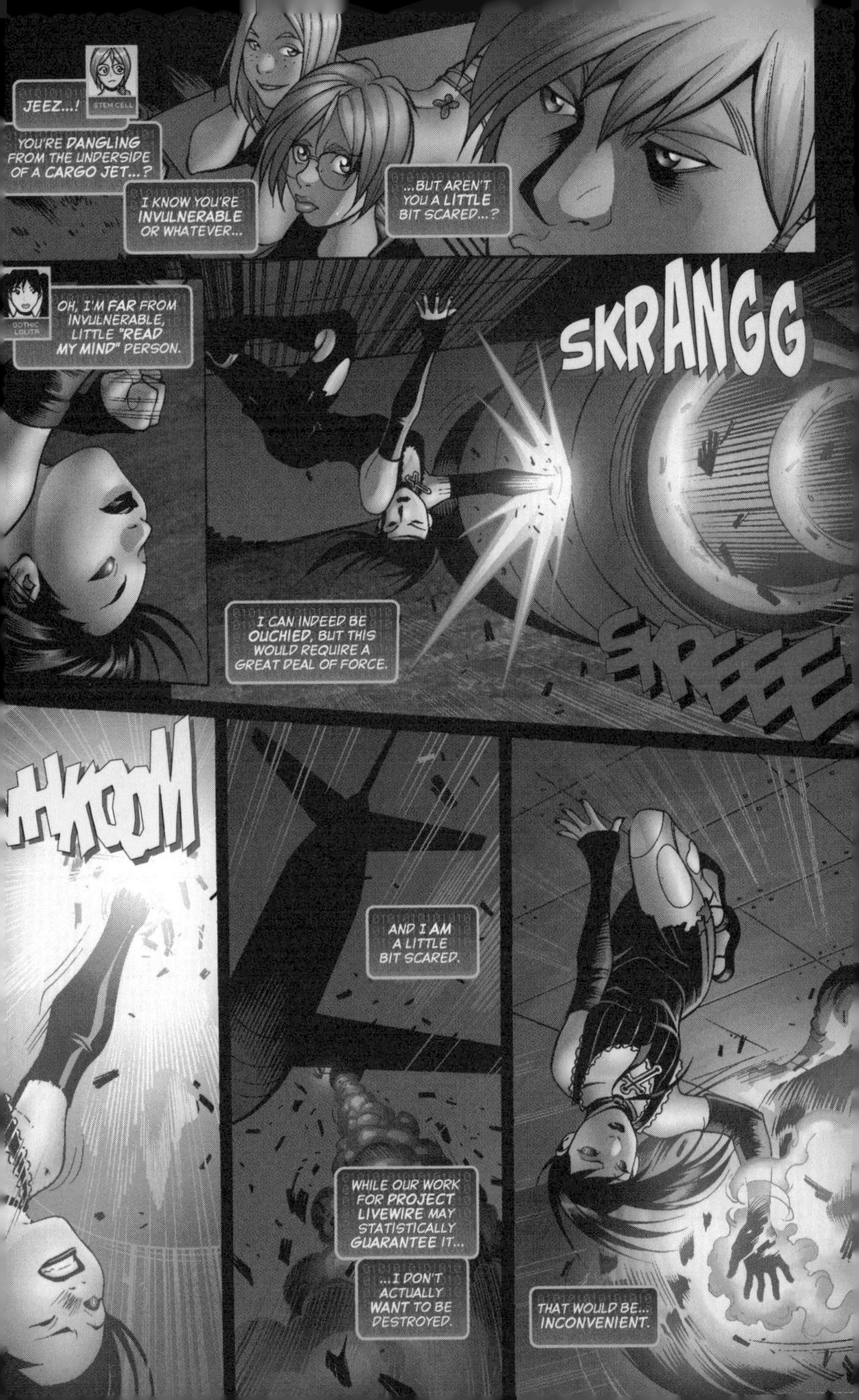
STEM CELL
JEEZ...!
YOU'RE DANGLING FROM THE UNDERSIDE OF A CARGO JET...?
I KNOW YOU'RE INVULNERABLE OR WHATEVER...
...BUT AREN'T YOU A LITTLE BIT SCARED...?
GOTHIC LOLITA
OH, I'M FAR FROM INVULNERABLE, LITTLE "READ MY MIND" PERSON.
SKRANGG
I CAN INDEED BE OUCHIED, BUT THIS WOULD REQUIRE A GREAT DEAL OF FORCE.
SKREEEE
THOOM
AND I AM A LITTLE BIT SCARED.
WHILE OUR WORK FOR PROJECT LIVEWIRE MAY STATISTICALLY GUARANTEE IT...
...I DON'T ACTUALLY WANT TO BE DESTROYED.
THAT WOULD BE... INCONVENIENT.

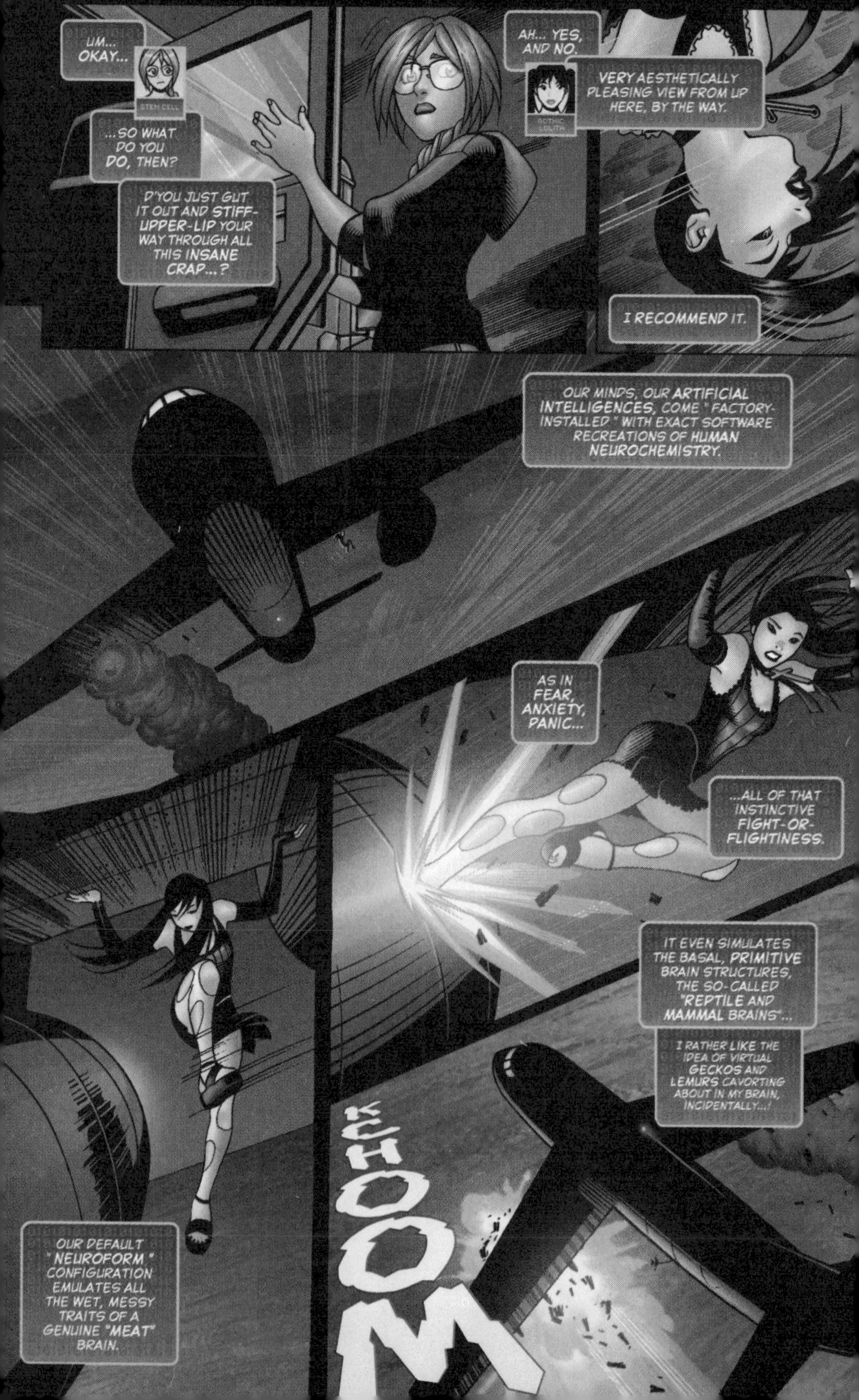
UM... OKAY...
STEM CELL
...SO WHAT DO YOU DO, THEN?
D'YOU JUST GUT IT OUT AND STIFF-UPPER-LIP YOUR WAY THROUGH ALL THIS INSANE CRAP...?
AH... YES, AND NO.
VERY AESTHETICALLY PLEASING VIEW FROM UP HERE, BY THE WAY.
I RECOMMEND IT.
OUR MINDS, OUR ARTIFICIAL INTELLIGENCES, COME "FACTORY-INSTALLED" WITH EXACT SOFTWARE RECREATIONS OF HUMAN NEUROCHEMISTRY.
OUR DEFAULT "NEUROFORM" CONFIGURATION EMULATES ALL THE WET, MESSY TRAITS OF A GENUINE "MEAT" BRAIN.
AS IN FEAR, ANXIETY, PANIC...
...ALL OF THAT INSTINCTIVE FIGHT-OR-FLIGHTINESS.
IT EVEN SIMULATES THE BASAL, PRIMITIVE BRAIN STRUCTURES, THE SO-CALLED "REPTILE AND MAMMAL BRAINS"...
I RATHER LIKE THE IDEA OF VIRTUAL GECKOS AND LEMURS CAVORTING ABOUT IN MY BRAIN, INCIDENTALLY...!
KCHOOM

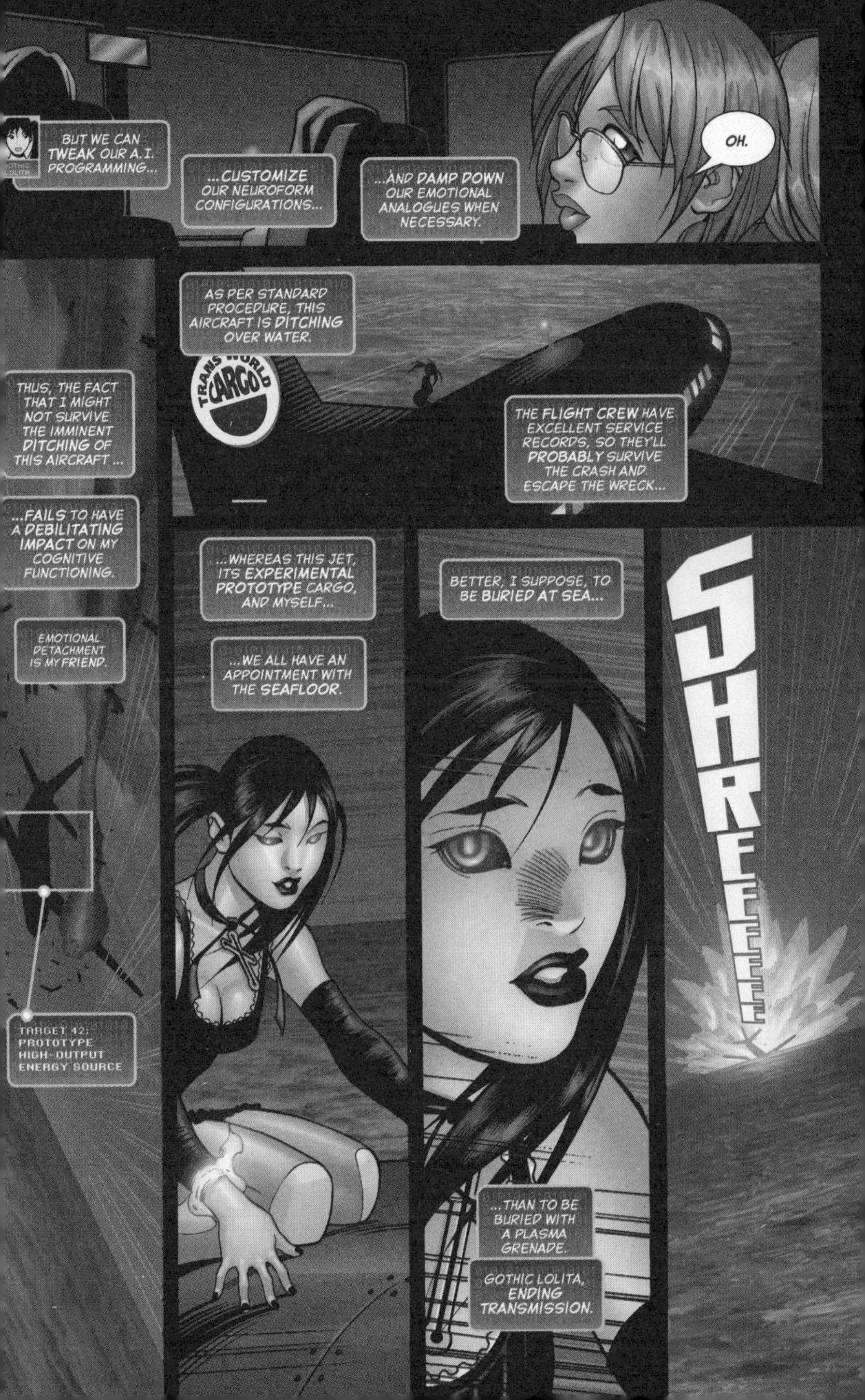
GOTHIC LOLITA
BUT WE CAN TWEAK OUR A.I. PROGRAMMING...
...CUSTOMIZE OUR NEUROFORM CONFIGURATIONS...
...AND DAMP DOWN OUR EMOTIONAL ANALOGUES WHEN NECESSARY.
OH.
AS PER STANDARD PROCEDURE, THIS AIRCRAFT IS DITCHING OVER WATER.
TRANS WORLD CARGO
THUS, THE FACT THAT I MIGHT NOT SURVIVE THE IMMINENT DITCHING OF THIS AIRCRAFT ...
THE FLIGHT CREW HAVE EXCELLENT SERVICE RECORDS, SO THEY'LL PROBABLY SURVIVE THE CRASH AND ESCAPE THE WRECK...
...FAILS TO HAVE A DEBILITATING IMPACT ON MY COGNITIVE FUNCTIONING.
EMOTIONAL DETACHMENT IS MY FRIEND.
...WHEREAS THIS JET, ITS EXPERIMENTAL PROTOTYPE CARGO, AND MYSELF...
...WE ALL HAVE AN APPOINTMENT WITH THE SEAFLOOR.
BETTER, I SUPPOSE, TO BE BURIED AT SEA...
SHREEEEE
TARGET 42: PROTOTYPE HIGH-OUTPUT ENERGY SOURCE
...THAN TO BE BURIED WITH A PLASMA GRENADE.
GOTHIC LOLITA, ENDING TRANSMISSION.

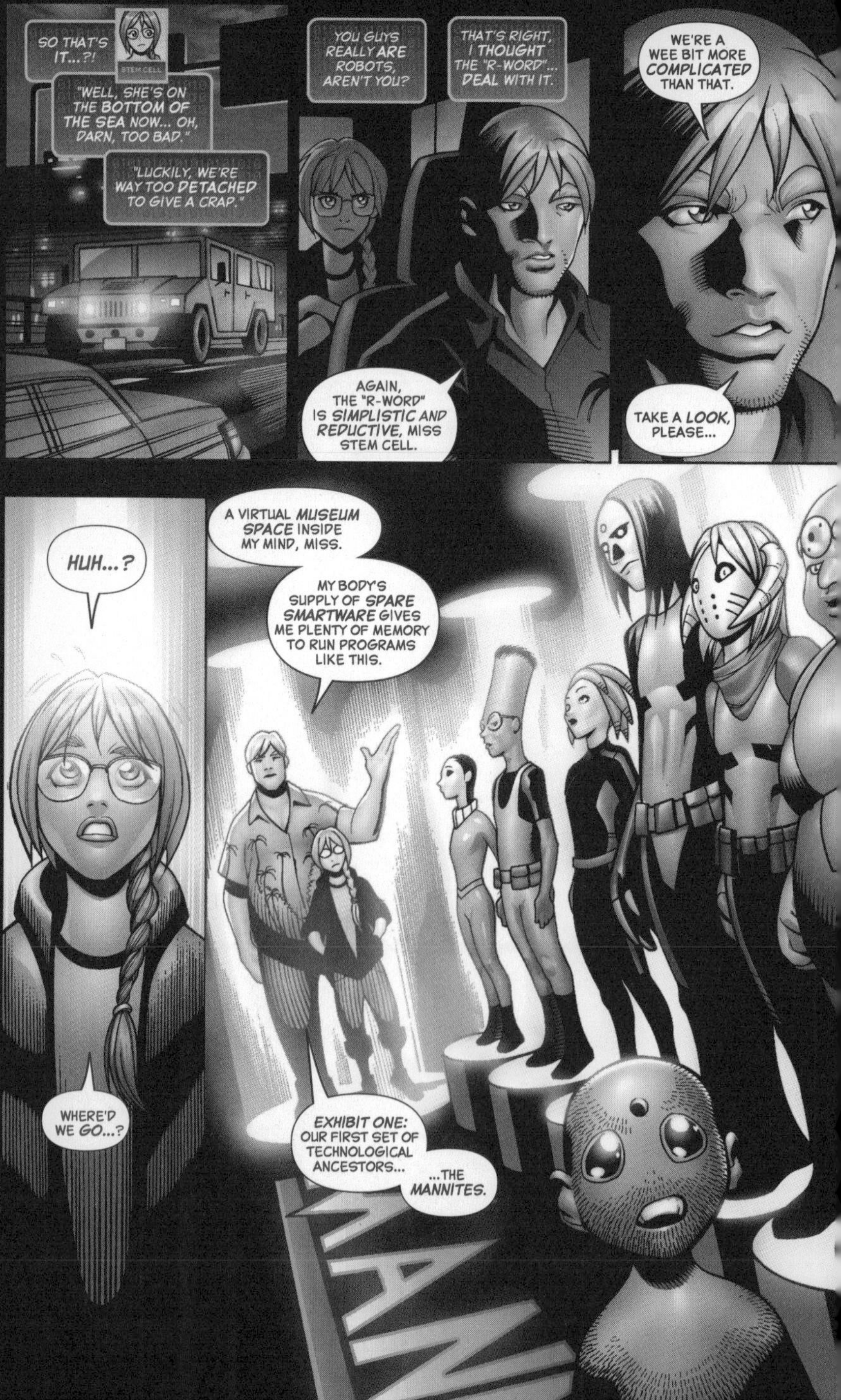

SO THAT'S IT...?!
STEM CELL
"WELL, SHE'S ON THE BOTTOM OF THE SEA NOW... OH, DARN, TOO BAD."
"LUCKILY, WE'RE WAY TOO DETACHED TO GIVE A CRAP."
YOU GUYS REALLY ARE ROBOTS, AREN'T YOU?
THAT'S RIGHT, I THOUGHT THE "R-WORD"... DEAL WITH IT.
AGAIN, THE "R-WORD" IS SIMPLISTIC AND REDUCTIVE, MISS STEM CELL.
WE'RE A WEE BIT MORE COMPLICATED THAN THAT.
TAKE A LOOK, PLEASE...
HUH...?
WHERE'D WE GO...?
A VIRTUAL MUSEUM SPACE INSIDE MY MIND, MISS.
MY BODY'S SUPPLY OF SPARE SMARTWARE GIVES ME PLENTY OF MEMORY TO RUN PROGRAMS LIKE THIS.
EXHIBIT ONE: OUR FIRST SET OF TECHNOLOGICAL ANCESTORS...
...THE MANNITES.

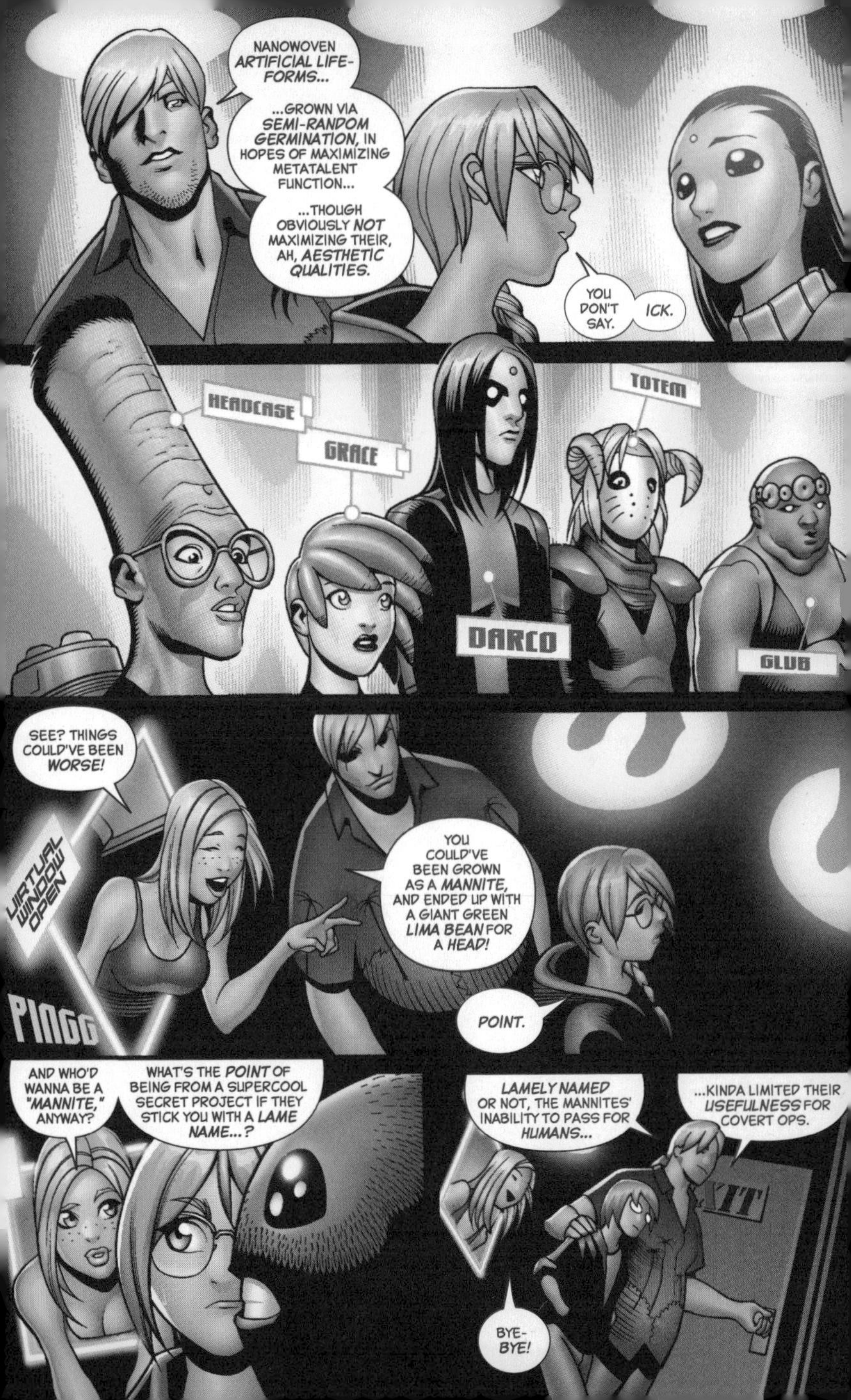

NANOWOVEN ARTIFICIAL LIFE-FORMS...
...GROWN VIA SEMI-RANDOM GERMINATION, IN HOPES OF MAXIMIZING METATALENT FUNCTION...
...THOUGH OBVIOUSLY NOT MAXIMIZING THEIR, AH, AESTHETIC QUALITIES.
YOU DON'T SAY.
ICK.
HEADCASE
GRACE
TOTEM
DARCO
GLUB
SEE? THINGS COULD'VE BEEN WORSE!
VIRTUAL WINDOW OPEN
PINGG
YOU COULD'VE BEEN GROWN AS A MANNITE, AND ENDED UP WITH A GIANT GREEN LIMA BEAN FOR A HEAD!
POINT.
AND WHO'D WANNA BE A "MANNITE," ANYWAY?
WHAT'S THE POINT OF BEING FROM A SUPERCOOL SECRET PROJECT IF THEY STICK YOU WITH A LAME NAME...?
LAMELY NAMED OR NOT, THE MANNITES' INABILITY TO PASS FOR HUMANS...
...KINDA LIMITED THEIR USEFULNESS FOR COVERT OPS.
BYE-BYE!

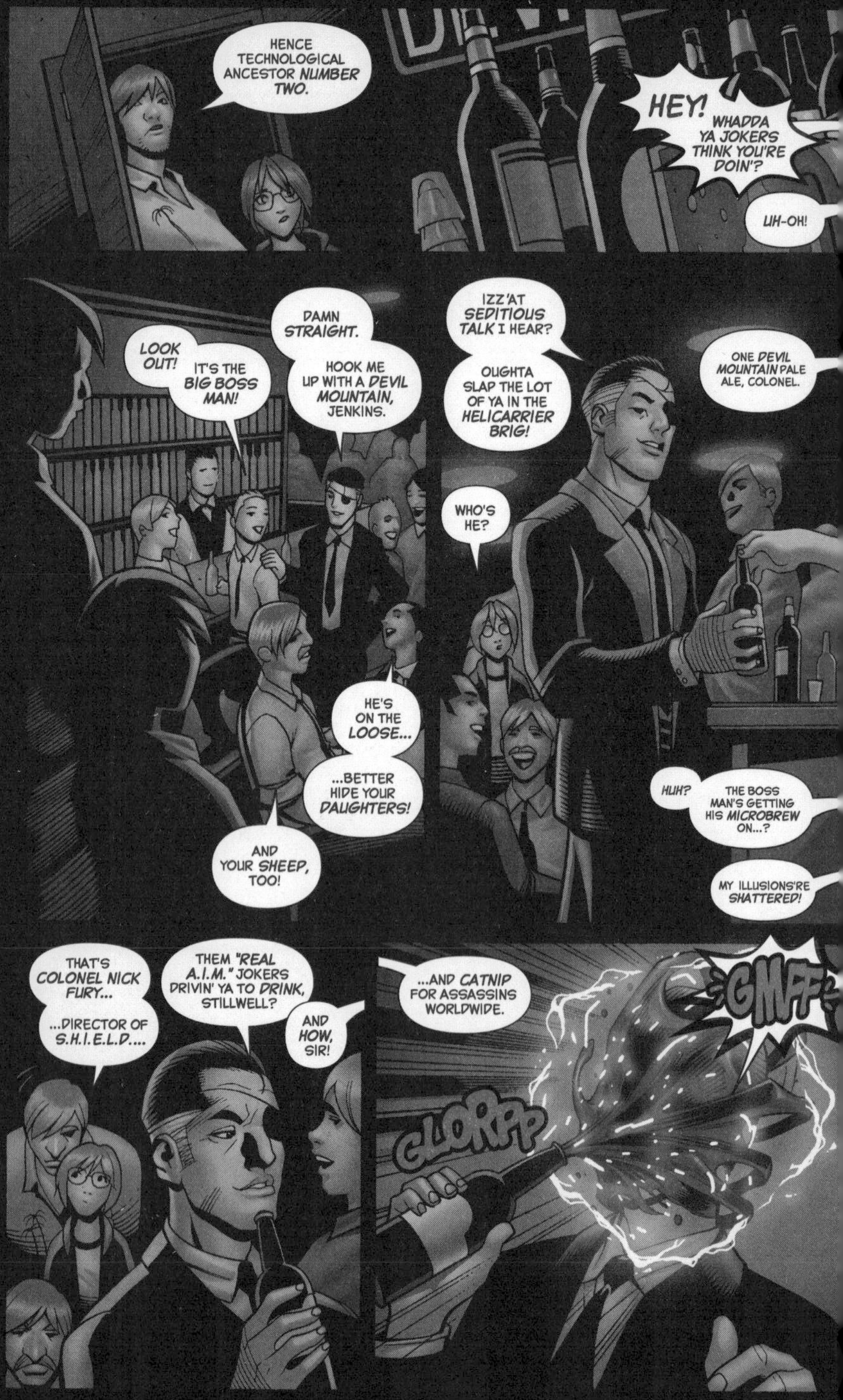
HENCE TECHNOLOGICAL ANCESTOR NUMBER TWO.
HEY! WHADDA YA JOKERS THINK YOU'RE DOIN'?
UH-OH!
LOOK OUT!
IT'S THE BIG BOSS MAN!
DAMN STRAIGHT.
HOOK ME UP WITH A DEVIL MOUNTAIN, JENKINS.
HE'S ON THE LOOSE...
...BETTER HIDE YOUR DAUGHTERS!
AND YOUR SHEEP, TOO!
IZZ'AT SEDITIOUS TALK I HEAR?
OUGHTA SLAP THE LOT OF YA IN THE HELICARRIER BRIG!
ONE DEVIL MOUNTAIN PALE ALE, COLONEL.
WHO'S HE?
HUH?
THE BOSS MAN'S GETTING HIS MICROBREW ON...?
MY ILLUSIONS'RE SHATTERED!
THAT'S COLONEL NICK FURY...
...DIRECTOR OF S.H.I.E.L.D....
THEM "REAL A.I.M." JOKERS DRIVIN' YA TO DRINK, STILLWELL?
AND HOW, SIR!
...AND CATNIP FOR ASSASSINS WORLDWIDE.
GMFF
GLORPP

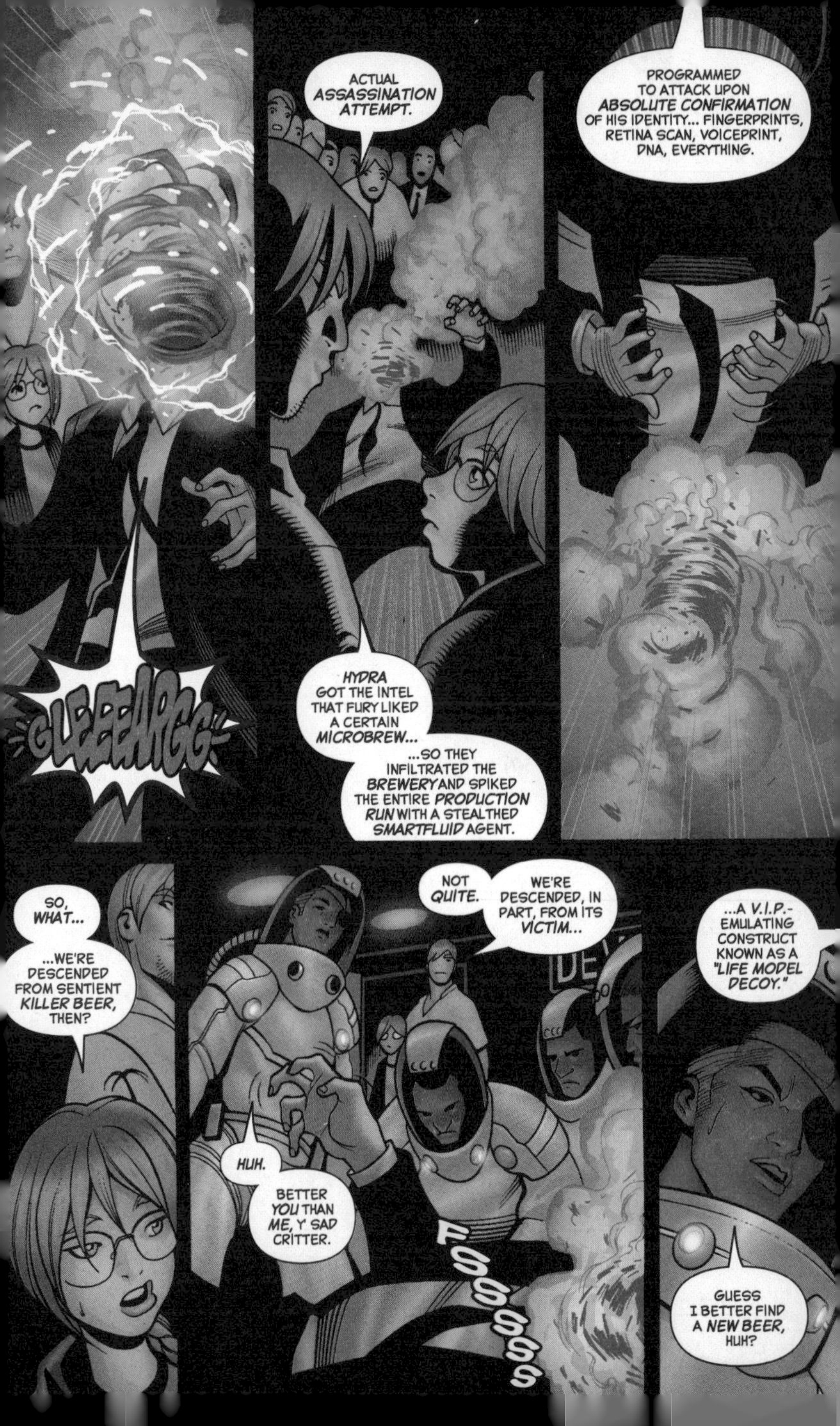
GLEEEARGG!
ACTUAL ASSASSINATION ATTEMPT.
HYDRA GOT THE INTEL THAT FURY LIKED A CERTAIN MICROBREW...
...SO THEY INFILTRATED THE BREWERY AND SPIKED THE ENTIRE PRODUCTION RUN WITH A STEALTHED SMARTFLUID AGENT.
PROGRAMMED TO ATTACK UPON ABSOLUTE CONFIRMATION OF HIS IDENTITY... FINGERPRINTS, RETINA SCAN, VOICEPRINT, DNA, EVERYTHING.
SO, WHAT...
...WE'RE DESCENDED FROM SENTIENT KILLER BEER, THEN?
NOT QUITE.
WE'RE DESCENDED, IN PART, FROM ITS VICTIM...
HUH.
BETTER YOU THAN ME, Y' SAD CRITTER.
FSSSSS
...A V.I.P.-EMULATING CONSTRUCT KNOWN AS A "LIFE MODEL DECOY."
GUESS I BETTER FIND A NEW BEER, HUH?

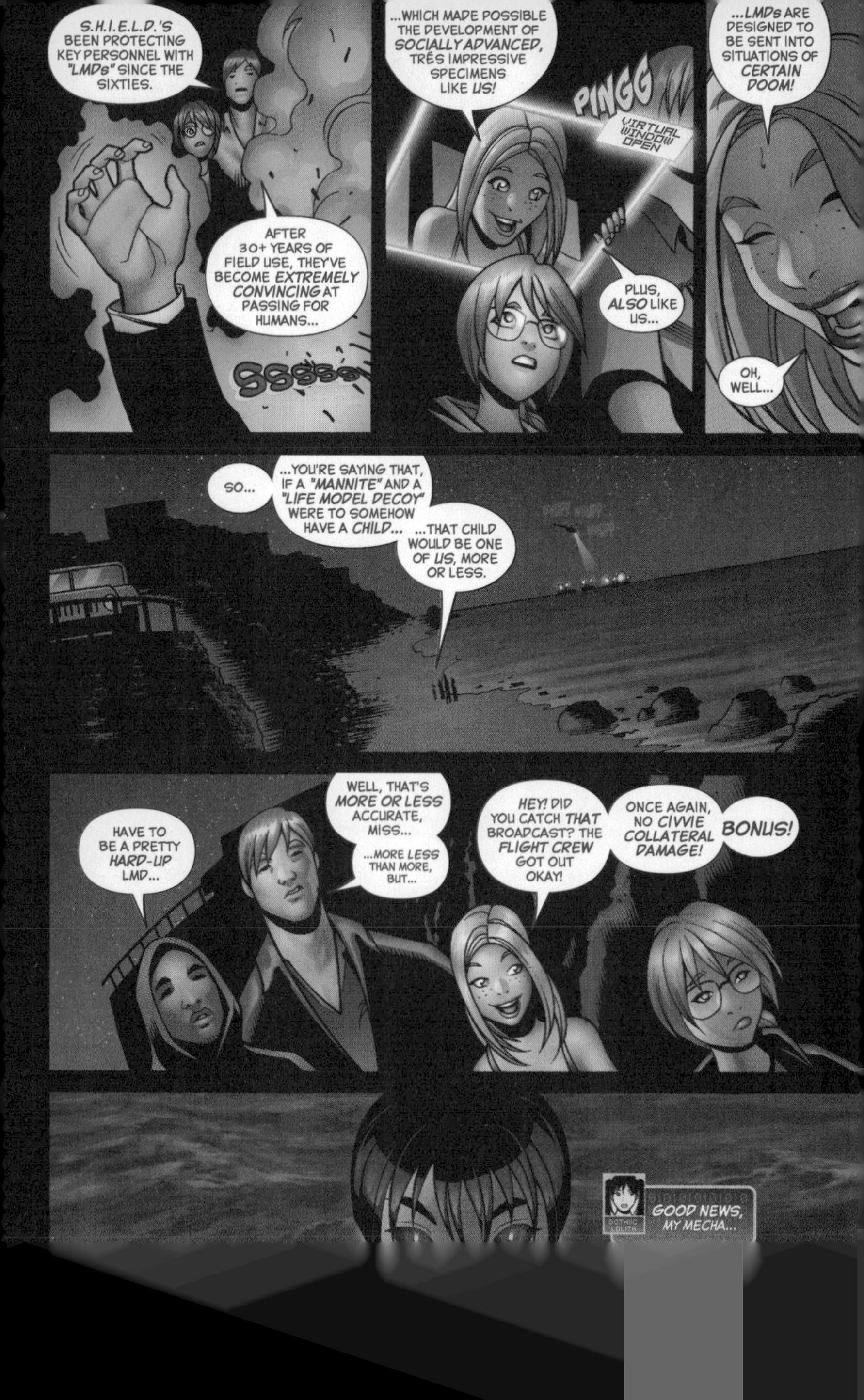
S.H.I.E.L.D.'S BEEN PROTECTING KEY PERSONNEL WITH "LMDs" SINCE THE SIXTIES.
AFTER 30+ YEARS OF FIELD USE, THEY'VE BECOME EXTREMELY CONVINCING AT PASSING FOR HUMANS...
SSSSSS
...WHICH MADE POSSIBLE THE DEVELOPMENT OF SOCIALLY ADVANCED, TRÉS IMPRESSIVE SPECIMENS LIKE US!
PINGG
VIRTUAL WINDOW OPEN
PLUS, ALSO LIKE US...
...LMDs ARE DESIGNED TO BE SENT INTO SITUATIONS OF CERTAIN DOOM!
OH, WELL...
SO...
...YOU'RE SAYING THAT, IF A "MANNITE" AND A "LIFE MODEL DECOY" WERE TO SOMEHOW HAVE A CHILD...
...THAT CHILD WOULD BE ONE OF US, MORE OR LESS.
HAVE TO BE A PRETTY HARD-UP LMD...
WELL, THAT'S MORE OR LESS ACCURATE, MISS...
...MORE LESS THAN MORE, BUT...
HEY! DID YOU CATCH THAT BROADCAST? THE FLIGHT CREW GOT OUT OKAY!
ONCE AGAIN, NO CIVVIE COLLATERAL DAMAGE!
BONUS!
GOTHIC LOLITA
GOOD NEWS, MY MECHA...

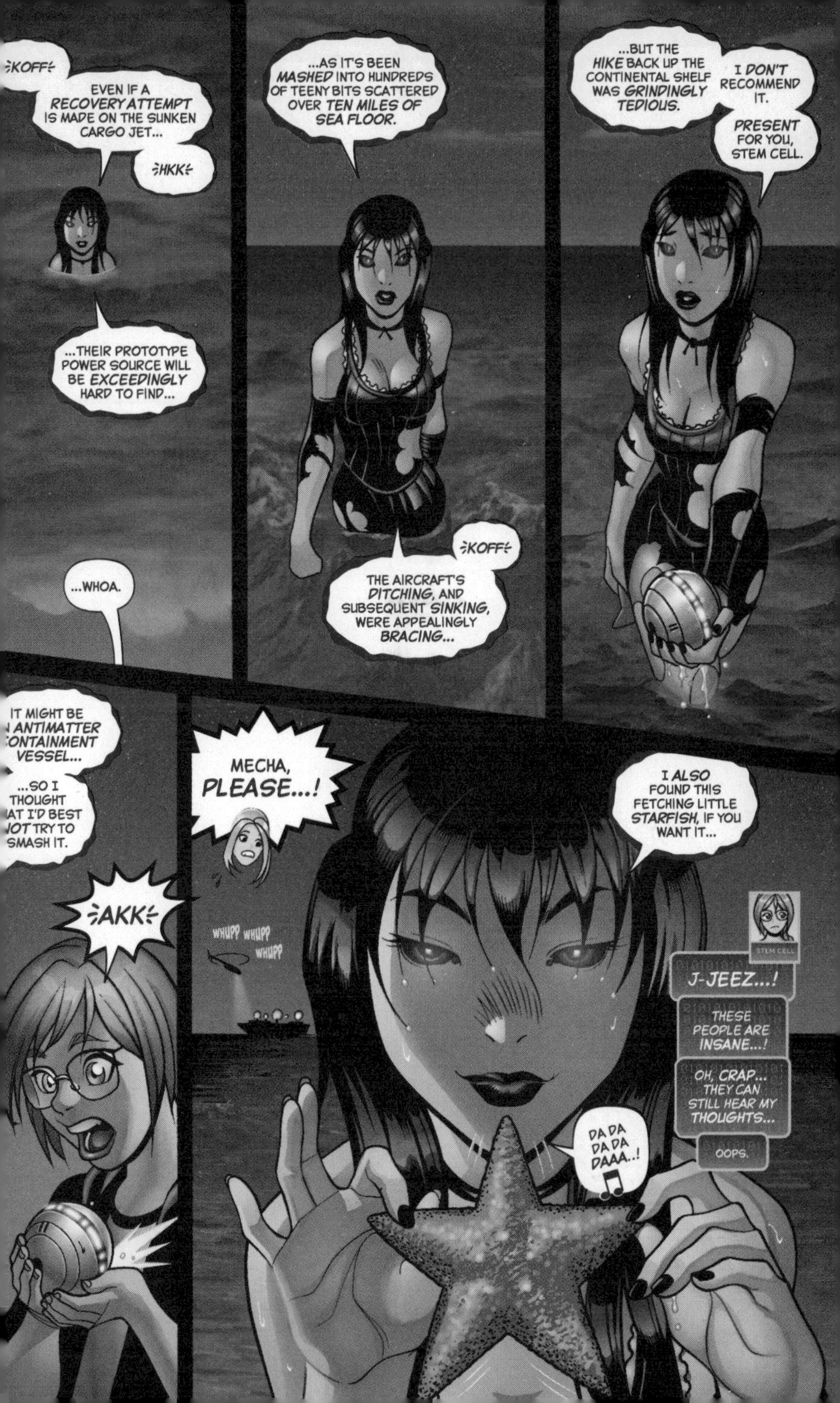

≒KOFF≒
EVEN IF A RECOVERY ATTEMPT IS MADE ON THE SUNKEN CARGO JET...
≒HKK≒
...THEIR PROTOTYPE POWER SOURCE WILL BE EXCEEDINGLY HARD TO FIND...
...WHOA.
...AS IT'S BEEN MASHED INTO HUNDREDS OF TEENY BITS SCATTERED OVER TEN MILES OF SEA FLOOR.
≒KOFF≒
THE AIRCRAFT'S DITCHING, AND SUBSEQUENT SINKING, WERE APPEALINGLY BRACING...
...BUT THE HIKE BACK UP THE CONTINENTAL SHELF WAS GRINDINGLY TEDIOUS.
I DON'T RECOMMEND IT.
PRESENT FOR YOU, STEM CELL.
IT MIGHT BE N ANTIMATTER CONTAINMENT VESSEL...
...SO I THOUGHT AT I'D BEST NOT TRY TO SMASH IT.
≒AKK≒
MECHA, PLEASE...!
WHUPP WHUPP WHUPP
I ALSO FOUND THIS FETCHING LITTLE STARFISH, IF YOU WANT IT...
DA DA DA DA DAAA..!
STEM CELL
J-JEEZ...!
THESE PEOPLE ARE INSANE...!
OH, CRAP... THEY CAN STILL HEAR MY THOUGHTS...
OOPS.

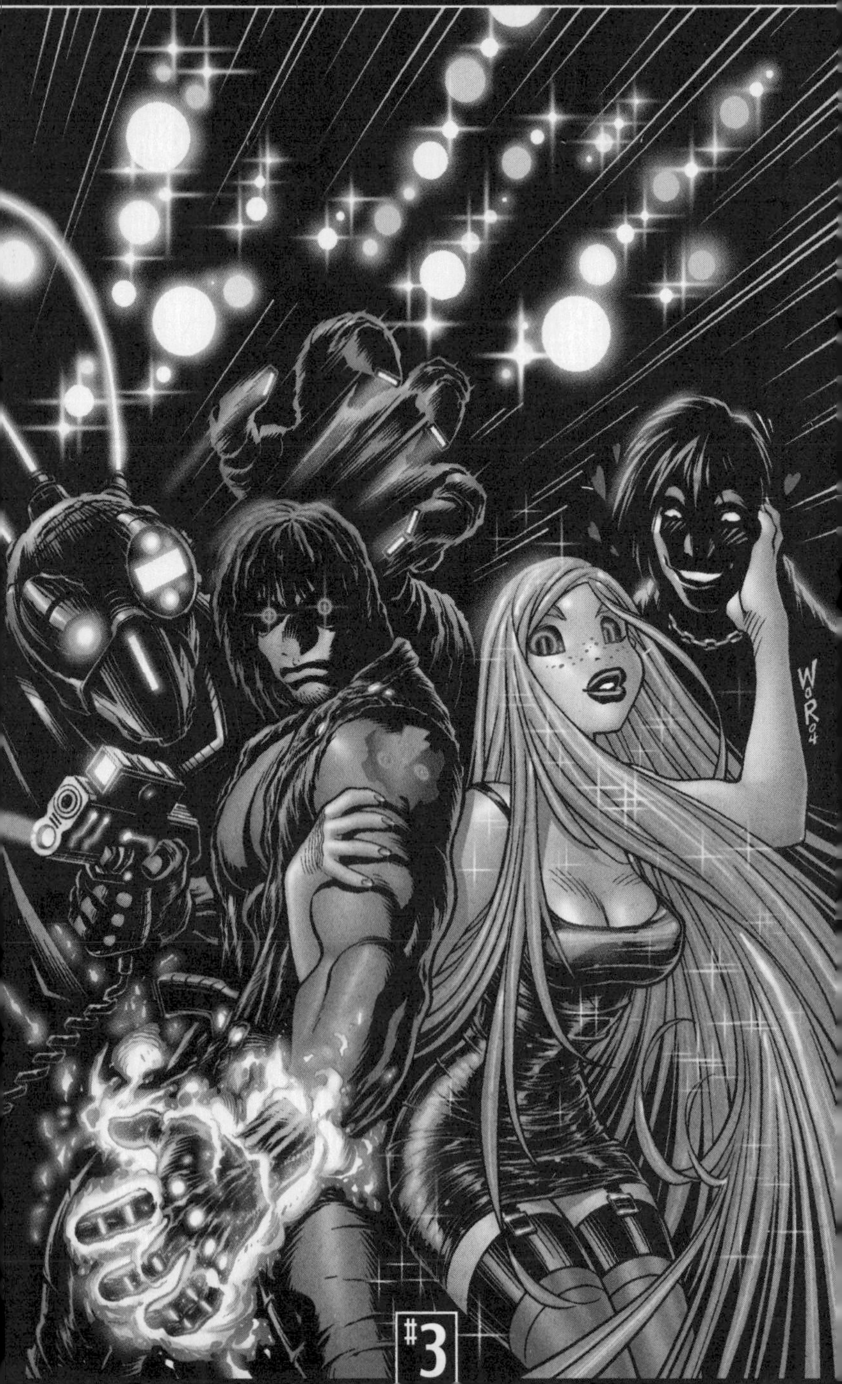
#3

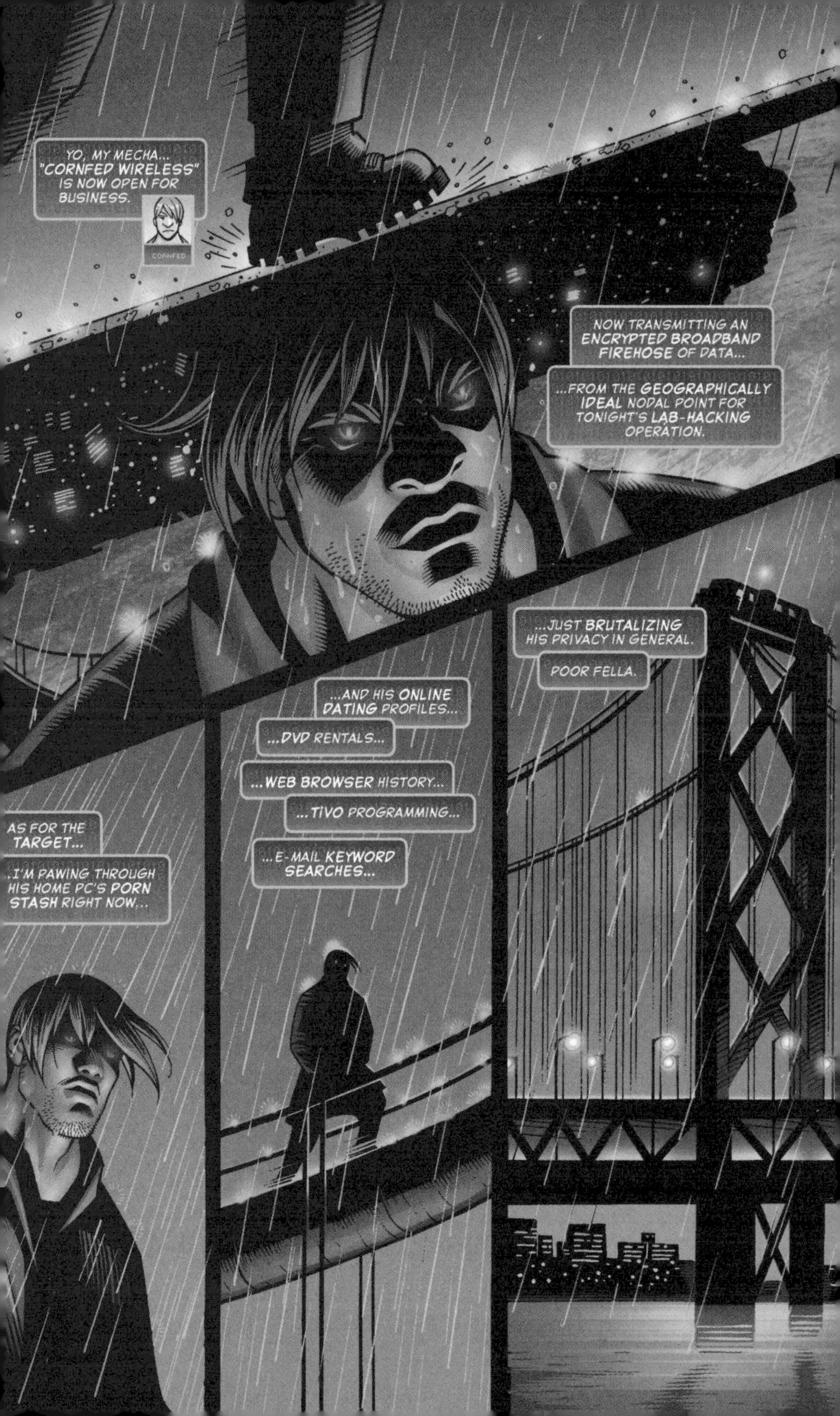
YO, MY MECHA... "CORNFED WIRELESS" IS NOW OPEN FOR BUSINESS.
CORNFED
NOW TRANSMITTING AN ENCRYPTED BROADBAND FIREHOSE OF DATA...
...FROM THE GEOGRAPHICALLY IDEAL NODAL POINT FOR TONIGHT'S LAB-HACKING OPERATION.
AS FOR THE TARGET...
...I'M PAWING THROUGH HIS HOME PC'S PORN STASH RIGHT NOW...
...AND HIS ONLINE DATING PROFILES...
...DVD RENTALS...
...WEB BROWSER HISTORY...
...TIVO PROGRAMMING...
...E-MAIL KEYWORD SEARCHES...
...JUST BRUTALIZING HIS PRIVACY IN GENERAL.
POOR FELLA.

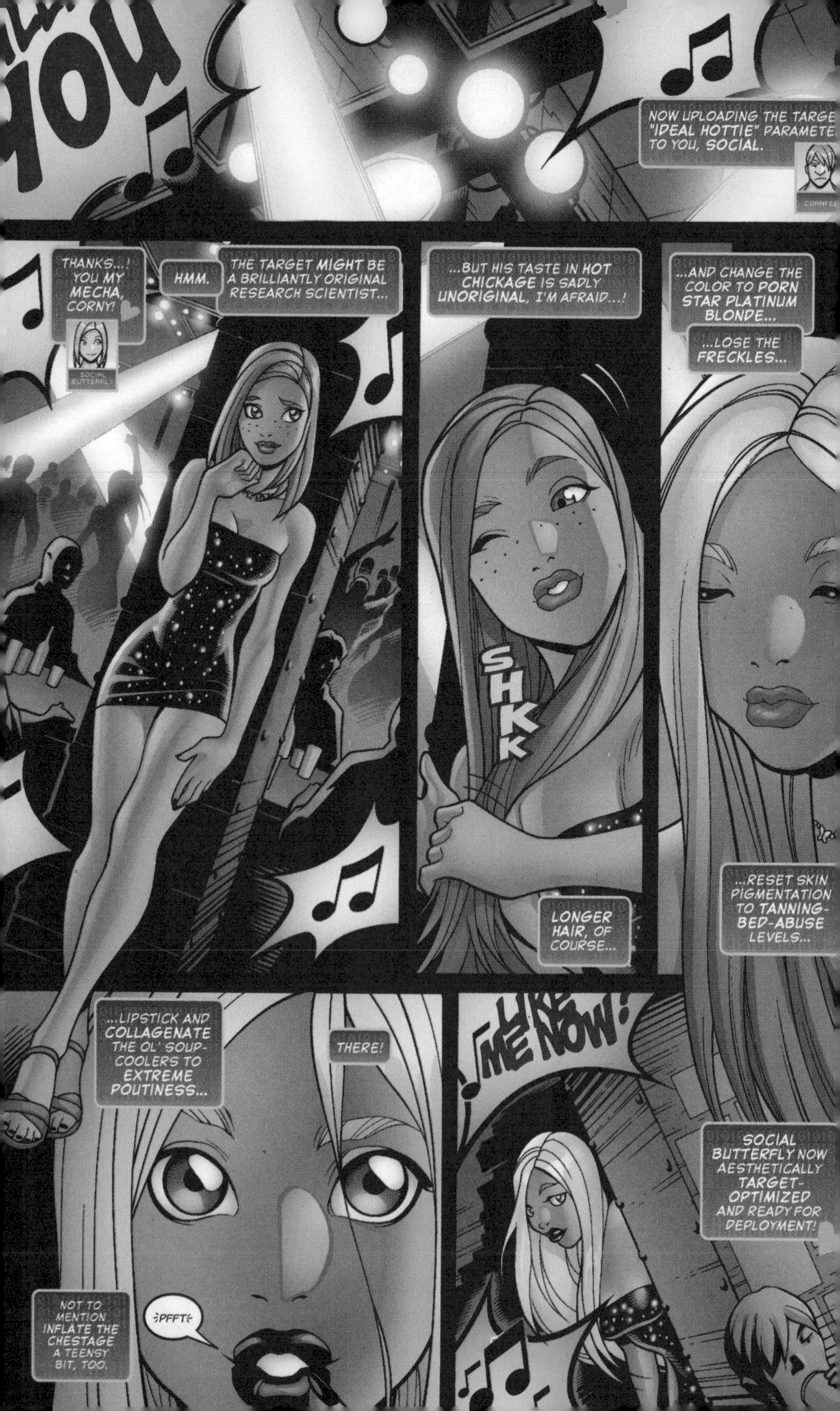
YOU
NOW UPLOADING THE TARGE "IDEAL HOTTIE" PARAMETE TO YOU, SOCIAL.
THANKS...! YOU MY MECHA, CORNY!
HMM.
THE TARGET MIGHT BE A BRILLIANTLY ORIGINAL RESEARCH SCIENTIST...
...BUT HIS TASTE IN HOT CHICKAGE IS SADLY UNORIGINAL, I'M AFRAID...!
SHKK
LONGER HAIR, OF COURSE...
...AND CHANGE THE COLOR TO PORN STAR PLATINUM BLONDE...
...LOSE THE FRECKLES...
...RESET SKIN PIGMENTATION TO TANNING-BED-ABUSE LEVELS...
...LIPSTICK AND COLLAGENATE THE OL' SOUP-COOLERS TO EXTREME POUTINESS...
THERE!
NOT TO MENTION INFLATE THE CHESTAGE A TEENSY BIT, TOO.
PFFT
ME NOW!
SOCIAL BUTTERFLY NOW AESTHETICALLY TARGET-OPTIMIZED AND READY FOR DEPLOYMENT!

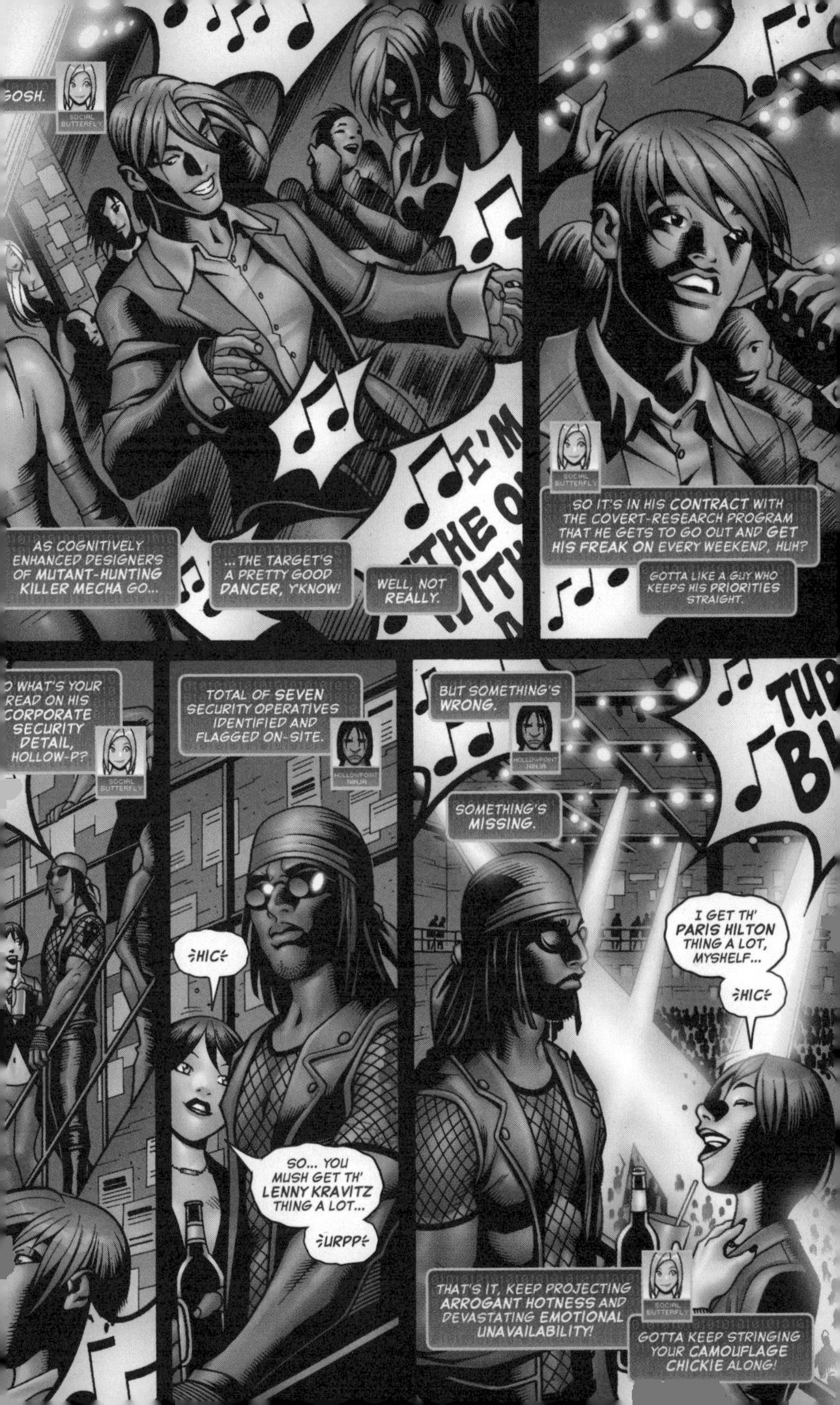
GOSH.
SOCIAL BUTTERFLY
AS COGNITIVELY ENHANCED DESIGNERS OF MUTANT-HUNTING KILLER MECHA GO...
...THE TARGET'S A PRETTY GOOD DANCER, Y'KNOW!
WELL, NOT REALLY.
SOCIAL BUTTERFLY
SO IT'S IN HIS CONTRACT WITH THE COVERT-RESEARCH PROGRAM THAT HE GETS TO GO OUT AND GET HIS FREAK ON EVERY WEEKEND, HUH?
GOTTA LIKE A GUY WHO KEEPS HIS PRIORITIES STRAIGHT.
O WHAT'S YOUR READ ON HIS CORPORATE SECURITY DETAIL, HOLLOW-P?
SOCIAL BUTTERFLY
TOTAL OF SEVEN SECURITY OPERATIVES IDENTIFIED AND FLAGGED ON-SITE.
HOLLOWPOINT NINJA
HIC
SO... YOU MUSH GET TH' LENNY KRAVITZ THING A LOT...
URPP
BUT SOMETHING'S WRONG.
HOLLOWPOINT NINJA
SOMETHING'S MISSING.
I GET TH' PARIS HILTON THING A LOT, MYSHELF...
HIC
SOCIAL BUTTERFLY
THAT'S IT, KEEP PROJECTING ARROGANT HOTNESS AND DEVASTATING EMOTIONAL UNAVAILABILITY!
GOTTA KEEP STRINGING YOUR CAMOUFLAGE CHICKIE ALONG!

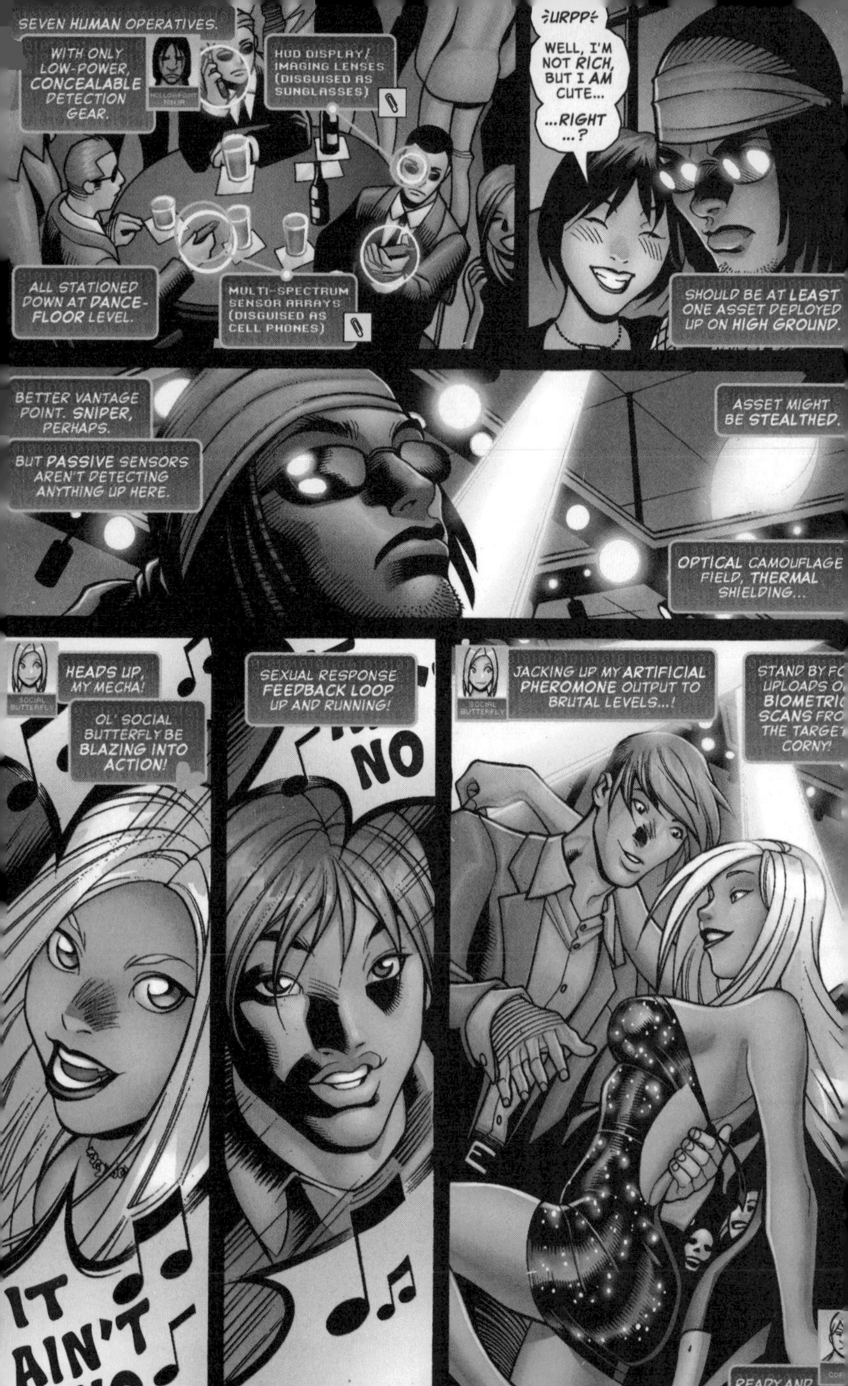
SEVEN HUMAN OPERATIVES.
WITH ONLY LOW-POWER, CONCEALABLE DETECTION GEAR.
HOLLOWPOINT NINJA
HUD DISPLAY/ IMAGING LENSES (DISGUISED AS SUNGLASSES)
ALL STATIONED DOWN AT DANCE-FLOOR LEVEL.
MULTI-SPECTRUM SENSOR ARRAYS (DISGUISED AS CELL PHONES)
URPP
WELL, I'M NOT RICH, BUT I AM CUTE...
...RIGHT ...?
SHOULD BE AT LEAST ONE ASSET DEPLOYED UP ON HIGH GROUND.
BETTER VANTAGE POINT. SNIPER, PERHAPS.
BUT PASSIVE SENSORS AREN'T DETECTING ANYTHING UP HERE.
ASSET MIGHT BE STEALTHED.
OPTICAL CAMOUFLAGE FIELD, THERMAL SHIELDING...
SOCIAL BUTTERFLY
HEADS UP, MY MECHA!
OL' SOCIAL BUTTERFLY BE BLAZING INTO ACTION!
SEXUAL RESPONSE FEEDBACK LOOP UP AND RUNNING!
NO
SOCIAL BUTTERFLY
JACKING UP MY ARTIFICIAL PHEROMONE OUTPUT TO BRUTAL LEVELS...!
STAND BY FO UPLOADS O BIOMETRIC SCANS FRO THE TARGET CORNY!
IT AIN'T NO
READY AND WAITING, MA'A

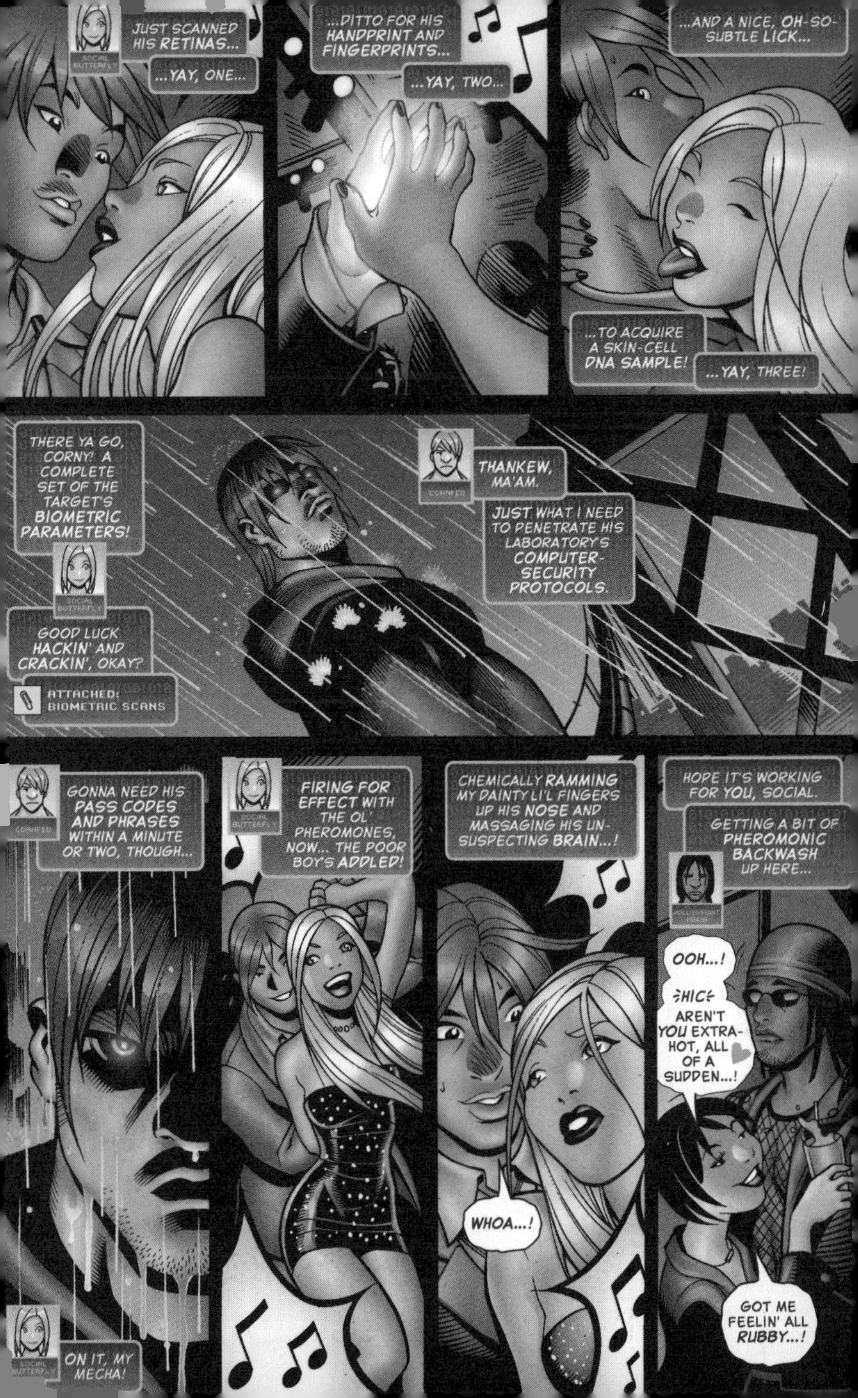
SOCIAL BUTTERFLY
JUST SCANNED HIS RETINAS...
...YAY, ONE...
...DITTO FOR HIS HANDPRINT AND FINGERPRINTS...
...YAY, TWO...
...AND A NICE, OH-SO-SUBTLE LICK...
...TO ACQUIRE A SKIN-CELL DNA SAMPLE!
...YAY, THREE!
THERE YA GO, CORNY! A COMPLETE SET OF THE TARGET'S BIOMETRIC PARAMETERS!
CORNFED
THANKEW, MA'AM.
JUST WHAT I NEED TO PENETRATE HIS LABORATORY'S COMPUTER-SECURITY PROTOCOLS.
SOCIAL BUTTERFLY
GOOD LUCK HACKIN' AND CRACKIN', OKAY?
ATTACHED: BIOMETRIC SCANS
CORNFED
GONNA NEED HIS PASS CODES AND PHRASES WITHIN A MINUTE OR TWO, THOUGH...
SOCIAL BUTTERFLY
ON IT, MY MECHA!
SOCIAL BUTTERFLY
FIRING FOR EFFECT WITH THE OL' PHEROMONES, NOW... THE POOR BOY'S ADDLED!
CHEMICALLY RAMMING MY DAINTY LI'L FINGERS UP HIS NOSE AND MASSAGING HIS UN-SUSPECTING BRAIN...!
WHOA...!
HOPE IT'S WORKING FOR YOU, SOCIAL.
GETTING A BIT OF PHEROMONIC BACKWASH UP HERE...
OOH...!
HIC AREN'T YOU EXTRA-HOT, ALL OF A SUDDEN...!
GOT ME FEELIN' ALL RUBBY...!

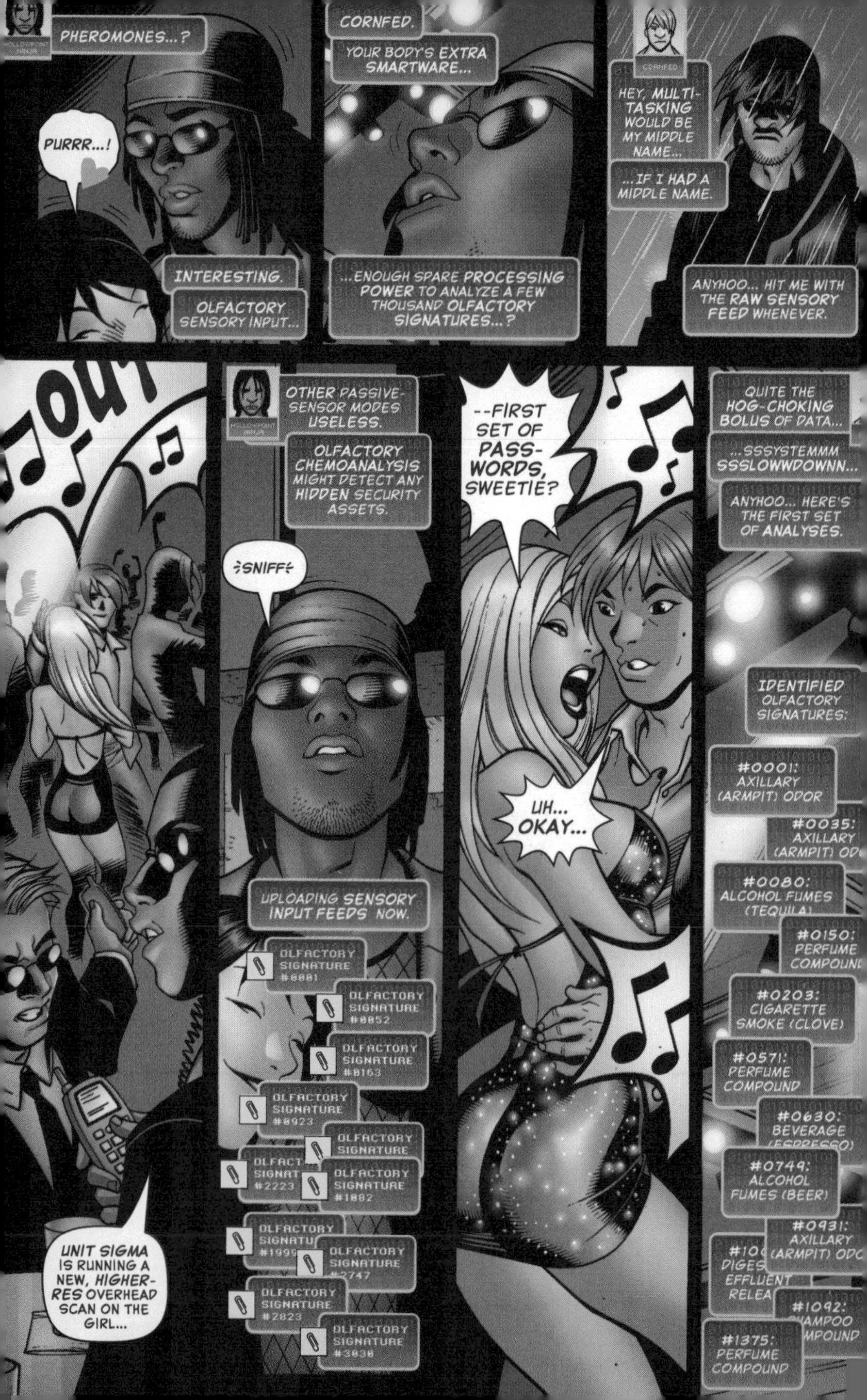

PHEROMONES...?
PURRR...!
INTERESTING.
OLFACTORY SENSORY INPUT...
CORNFED.
YOUR BODY'S EXTRA SMARTWARE...
...ENOUGH SPARE PROCESSING POWER TO ANALYZE A FEW THOUSAND OLFACTORY SIGNATURES...?
CORNFED
HEY, MULTI-TASKING WOULD BE MY MIDDLE NAME...
...IF I HAD A MIDDLE NAME.
ANYHOO... HIT ME WITH THE RAW SENSORY FEED WHENEVER.
UNIT SIGMA IS RUNNING A NEW, HIGHER-RES OVERHEAD SCAN ON THE GIRL...
OTHER PASSIVE-SENSOR MODES USELESS.
OLFACTORY CHEMOANALYSIS MIGHT DETECT ANY HIDDEN SECURITY ASSETS.
SNIFF
UPLOADING SENSORY INPUT FEEDS NOW.
OLFACTORY SIGNATURE #0001
OLFACTORY SIGNATURE #0052
OLFACTORY SIGNATURE #0163
OLFACTORY SIGNATURE #0923
OLFACTORY SIGNATURE
OLFACT SIGNAT #2223
OLFACTORY SIGNATURE #1082
OLFACTORY SIGNATU #1999
OLFACTORY SIGNATURE
OLFACTORY SIGNATURE #2823
OLFACTORY SIGNATURE #3030
--FIRST SET OF PASS-WORDS, SWEETIE?
UH... OKAY...
QUITE THE HOG-CHOKING BOLUS OF DATA...
...SSSYSTEMMM SSSLOWWDOWNN...
ANYHOO... HERE'S THE FIRST SET OF ANALYSES.
IDENTIFIED OLFACTORY SIGNATURES:
#0001: AXILLARY (ARMPIT) ODOR
#0035: AXILLARY
#0080: ALCOHOL FUMES
#0150: PERFUME
#0203: CIGARETTE SMOKE (CLOVE)
#0571: PERFUME COMPOUND
#0630: BEVERAGE
#0749: ALCOHOL FUMES (BEER)
#0931: AXILLARY
EFFLUENT
#1375: PERFUME COMPOUND

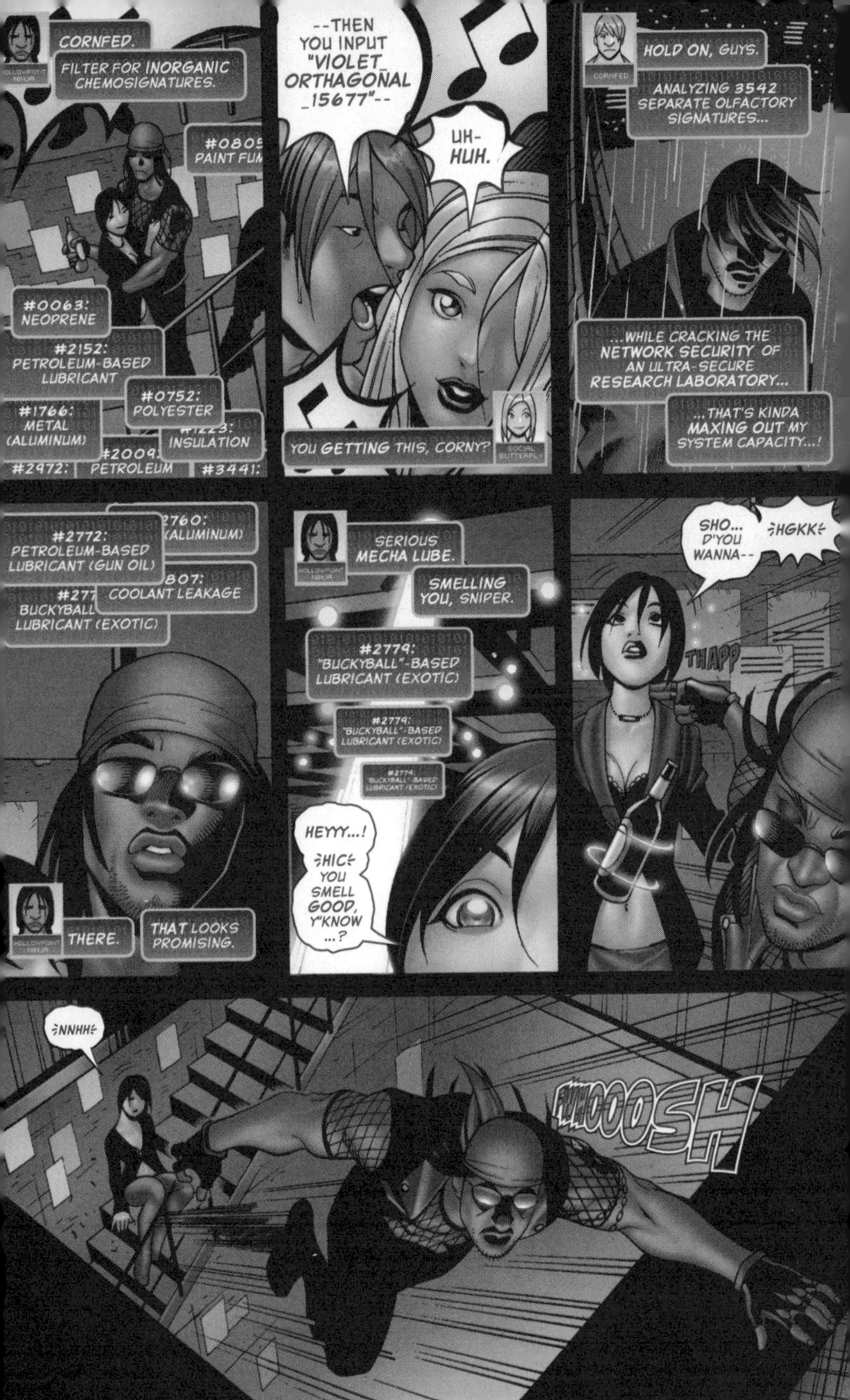
HOLLOWPOINT NINJA
CORNFED.
FILTER FOR INORGANIC CHEMOSIGNATURES.
#0805 PAINT FUM
#0063: NEOPRENE
#2152: PETROLEUM-BASED LUBRICANT
#0752: POLYESTER
#1766: METAL (ALUMINUM)
#1223: INSULATION
#2009: PETROLEUM
#2972:
#3441:
--THEN YOU INPUT "VIOLET_ORTHAGONAL_15677"--
UH-HUH.
YOU GETTING THIS, CORNY?
SOCIAL BUTTERFLY
CORNFED
HOLD ON, GUYS.
ANALYZING 3542 SEPARATE OLFACTORY SIGNATURES...
...WHILE CRACKING THE NETWORK SECURITY OF AN ULTRA-SECURE RESEARCH LABORATORY...
...THAT'S KINDA MAXING OUT MY SYSTEM CAPACITY...!
#2760: (ALUMINUM)
#2772: PETROLEUM-BASED LUBRICANT (GUN OIL)
#2807: COOLANT LEAKAGE
#277 BUCKYBALL LUBRICANT (EXOTIC)
HOLLOWPOINT NINJA
THERE.
THAT LOOKS PROMISING.
HOLLOWPOINT NINJA
SERIOUS MECHA LUBE.
SMELLING YOU, SNIPER.
#2779: "BUCKYBALL"-BASED LUBRICANT (EXOTIC)
#2779: "BUCKYBALL"-BASED LUBRICANT (EXOTIC)
#2779: "BUCKYBALL"-BASED LUBRICANT (EXOTIC)
HEYYY...! HIC YOU SMELL GOOD, Y'KNOW ...?
SHO... D'YOU WANNA--
HGKK
THAPP
NNHH
FWOOOOSH

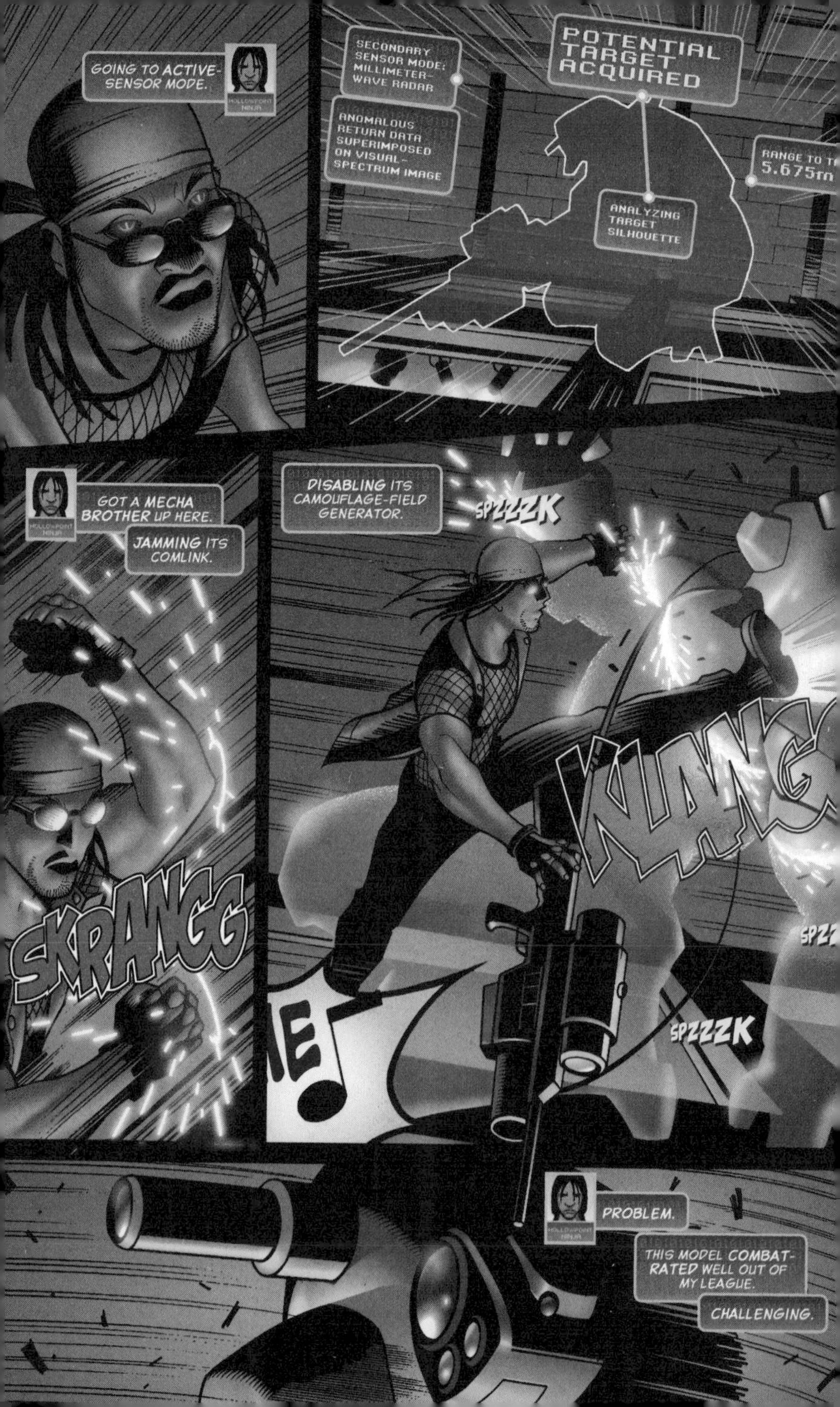
GOING TO ACTIVE-SENSOR MODE.
HOLLOWPOINT NINJA
SECONDARY SENSOR MODE: MILLIMETER-WAVE RADAR
ANOMALOUS RETURN DATA SUPERIMPOSED ON VISUAL-SPECTRUM IMAGE
POTENTIAL TARGET ACQUIRED
ANALYZING TARGET SILHOUETTE
RANGE TO T
5.675m
HOLLOWPOINT NINJA
GOT A MECHA BROTHER UP HERE.
JAMMING ITS COMLINK.
SKRANGG
DISABLING ITS CAMOUFLAGE-FIELD GENERATOR.
SPZZZK
KLANG
SPZZZK
HOLLOWPOINT NINJA
PROBLEM.
THIS MODEL COMBAT-RATED WELL OUT OF MY LEAGUE.
CHALLENGING.

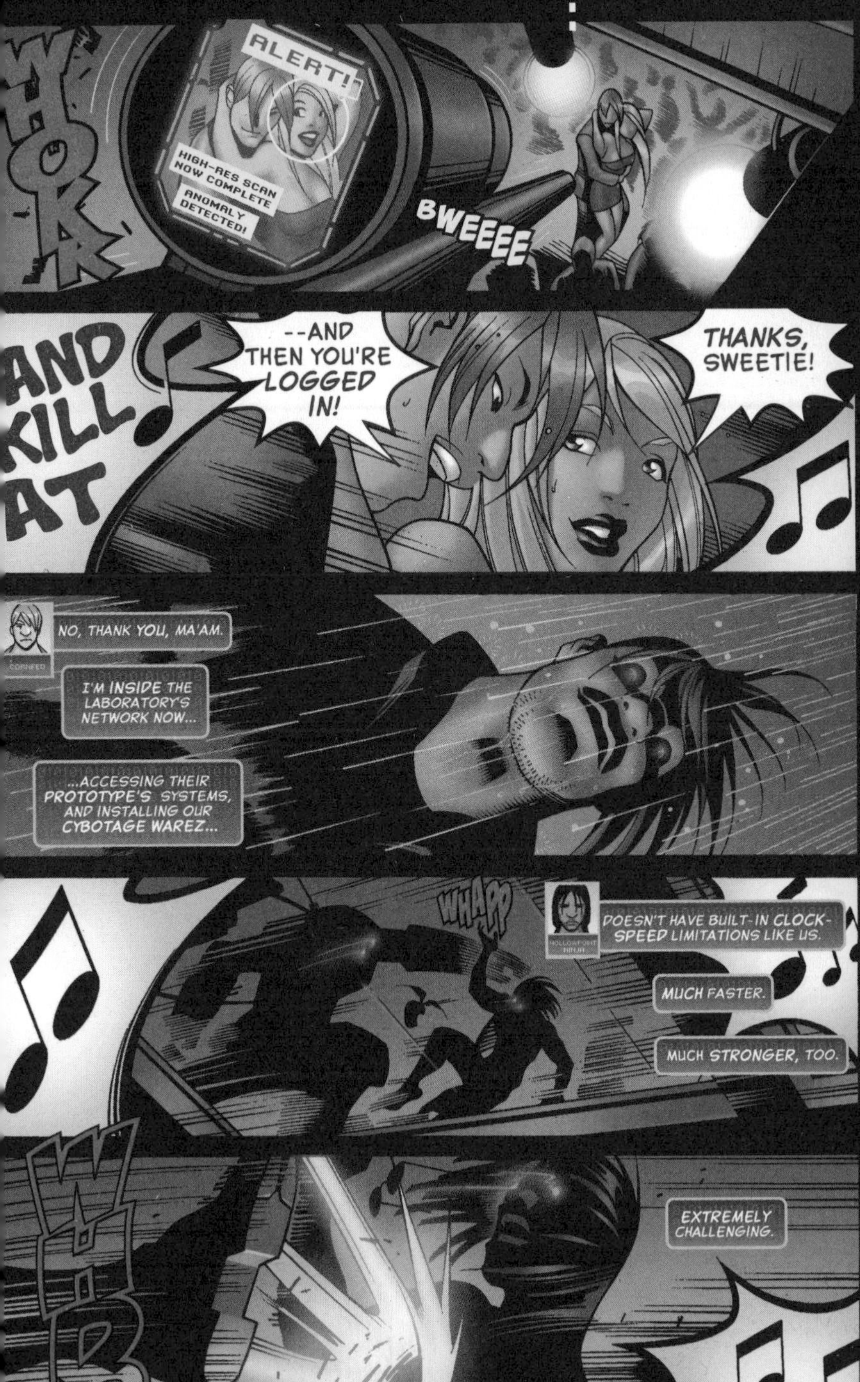
ALERT!
HIGH-RES SCAN NOW COMPLETE
ANOMALY DETECTED!
BWEEEE
AND KILL AT
--AND THEN YOU'RE LOGGED IN!
THANKS, SWEETIE!
CORNFED
NO, THANK YOU, MA'AM.
I'M INSIDE THE LABORATORY'S NETWORK NOW...
...ACCESSING THEIR PROTOTYPE'S SYSTEMS, AND INSTALLING OUR CYBOTAGE WAREZ...
WHAPP
HOLLOWPOINT NINJA
DOESN'T HAVE BUILT-IN CLOCK-SPEED LIMITATIONS LIKE US.
MUCH FASTER.
MUCH STRONGER, TOO.
EXTREMELY CHALLENGING.

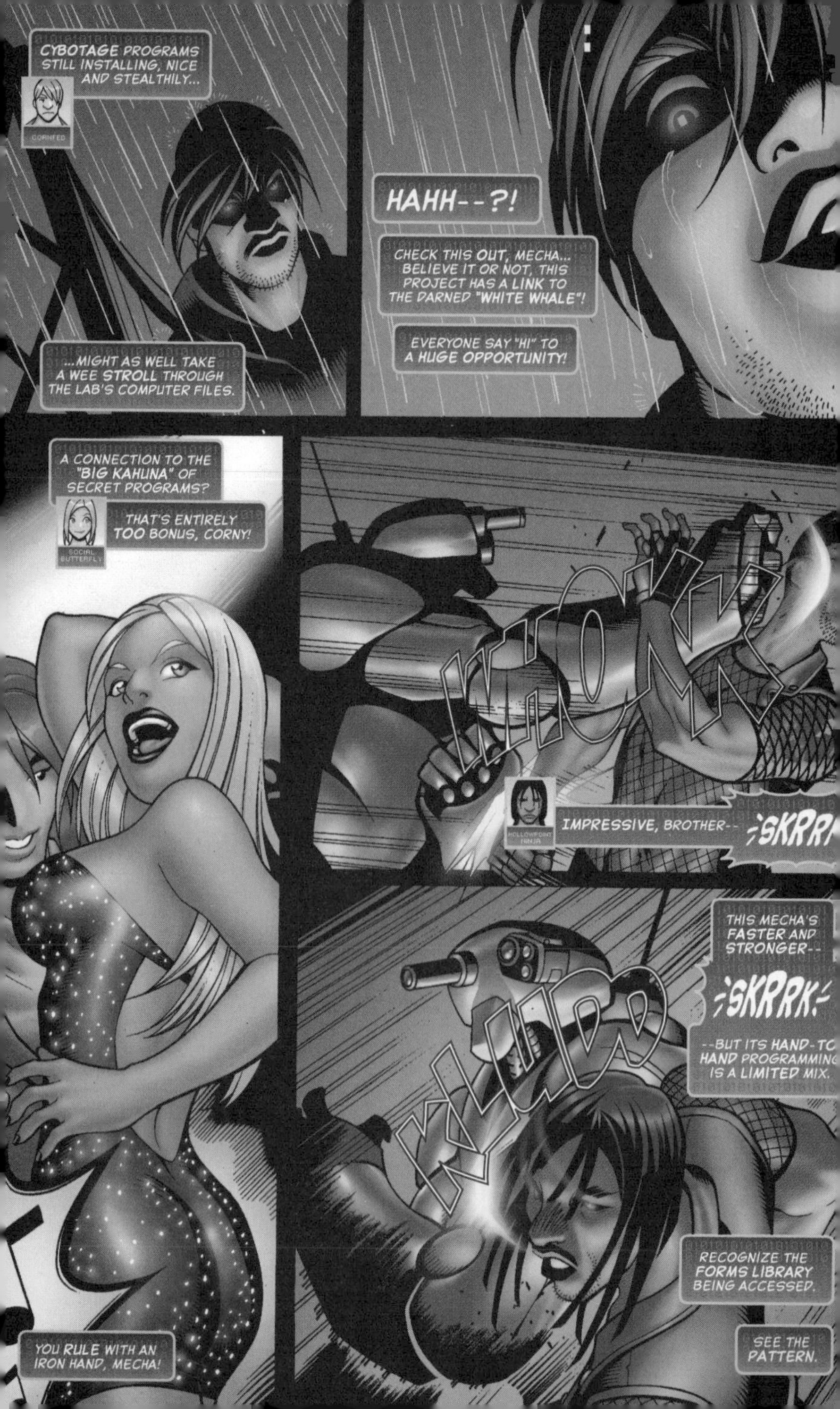
CYBOTAGE PROGRAMS STILL INSTALLING, NICE AND STEALTHILY...
CORNFED
...MIGHT AS WELL TAKE A WEE STROLL THROUGH THE LAB'S COMPUTER FILES.
HAHH--?!
CHECK THIS OUT, MECHA... BELIEVE IT OR NOT, THIS PROJECT HAS A LINK TO THE DARNED "WHITE WHALE"!
EVERYONE SAY "HI" TO A HUGE OPPORTUNITY!
A CONNECTION TO THE "BIG KAHUNA" OF SECRET PROGRAMS?
SOCIAL BUTTERFLY
THAT'S ENTIRELY TOO BONUS, CORNY!
YOU RULE WITH AN IRON HAND, MECHA!
WHOCK
HOLLOWPOINT NINJA
IMPRESSIVE, BROTHER--
SKRRK
THIS MECHA'S FASTER AND STRONGER--
SKRRK
--BUT ITS HAND-TO-HAND PROGRAMMING IS A LIMITED MIX.
WHUD
RECOGNIZE THE FORMS LIBRARY BEING ACCESSED.
SEE THE PATTERN.

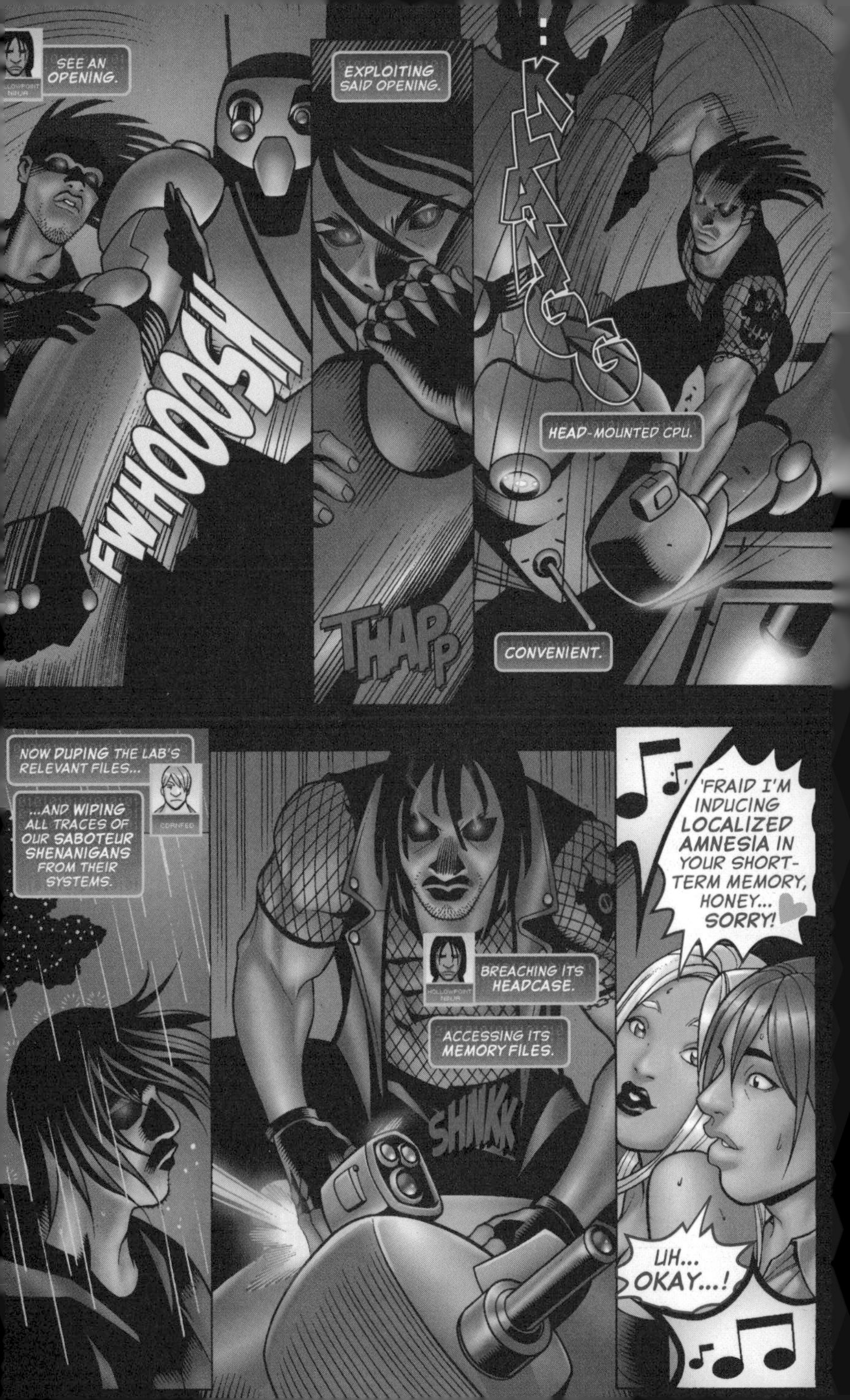
HOLLOWPOINT NINJA
SEE AN OPENING.
FWHOOSH
EXPLOITING SAID OPENING.
THAPP
KLANGG
HEAD-MOUNTED CPU.
CONVENIENT.
NOW DUPING THE LAB'S RELEVANT FILES...
...AND WIPING ALL TRACES OF OUR SABOTEUR SHENANIGANS FROM THEIR SYSTEMS.
CORNFED
HOLLOWPOINT NINJA
BREACHING ITS HEADCASE.
ACCESSING ITS MEMORY FILES.
SHNKK
'FRAID I'M INDUCING LOCALIZED AMNESIA IN YOUR SHORT-TERM MEMORY, HONEY... SORRY!
UH... OKAY...!

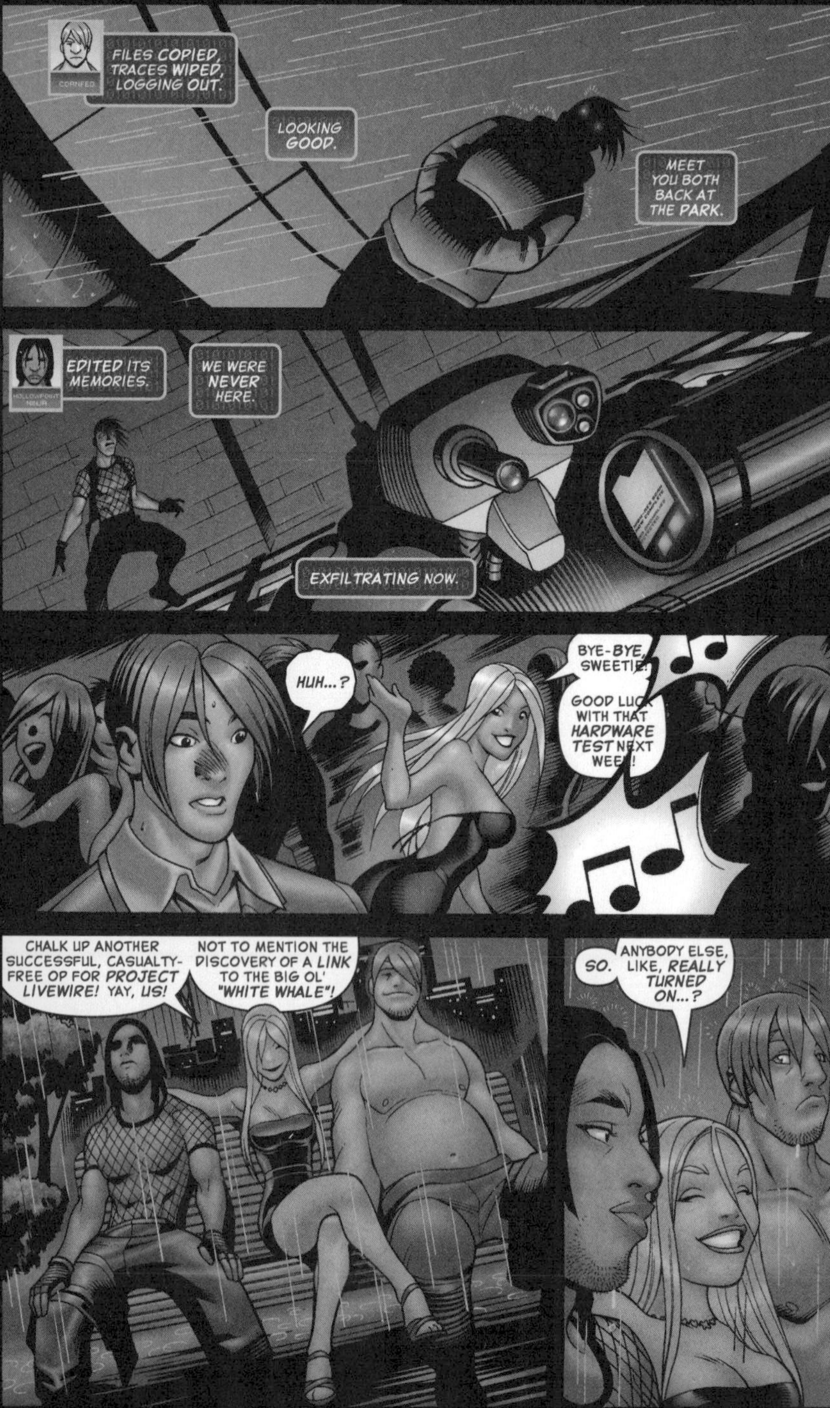
CORNFED
FILES COPIED, TRACES WIPED, LOGGING OUT.
LOOKING GOOD.
MEET YOU BOTH BACK AT THE PARK.
HOLLOWPOINT NINJA
EDITED ITS MEMORIES.
WE WERE NEVER HERE.
EXFILTRATING NOW.
HUH...?
BYE-BYE, SWEETIE!
GOOD LUCK WITH THAT HARDWARE TEST NEXT WEEK!
CHALK UP ANOTHER SUCCESSFUL, CASUALTY-FREE OP FOR PROJECT LIVEWIRE! YAY, US!
NOT TO MENTION THE DISCOVERY OF A LINK TO THE BIG OL' "WHITE WHALE"!
SO.
ANYBODY ELSE, LIKE, REALLY TURNED ON...?

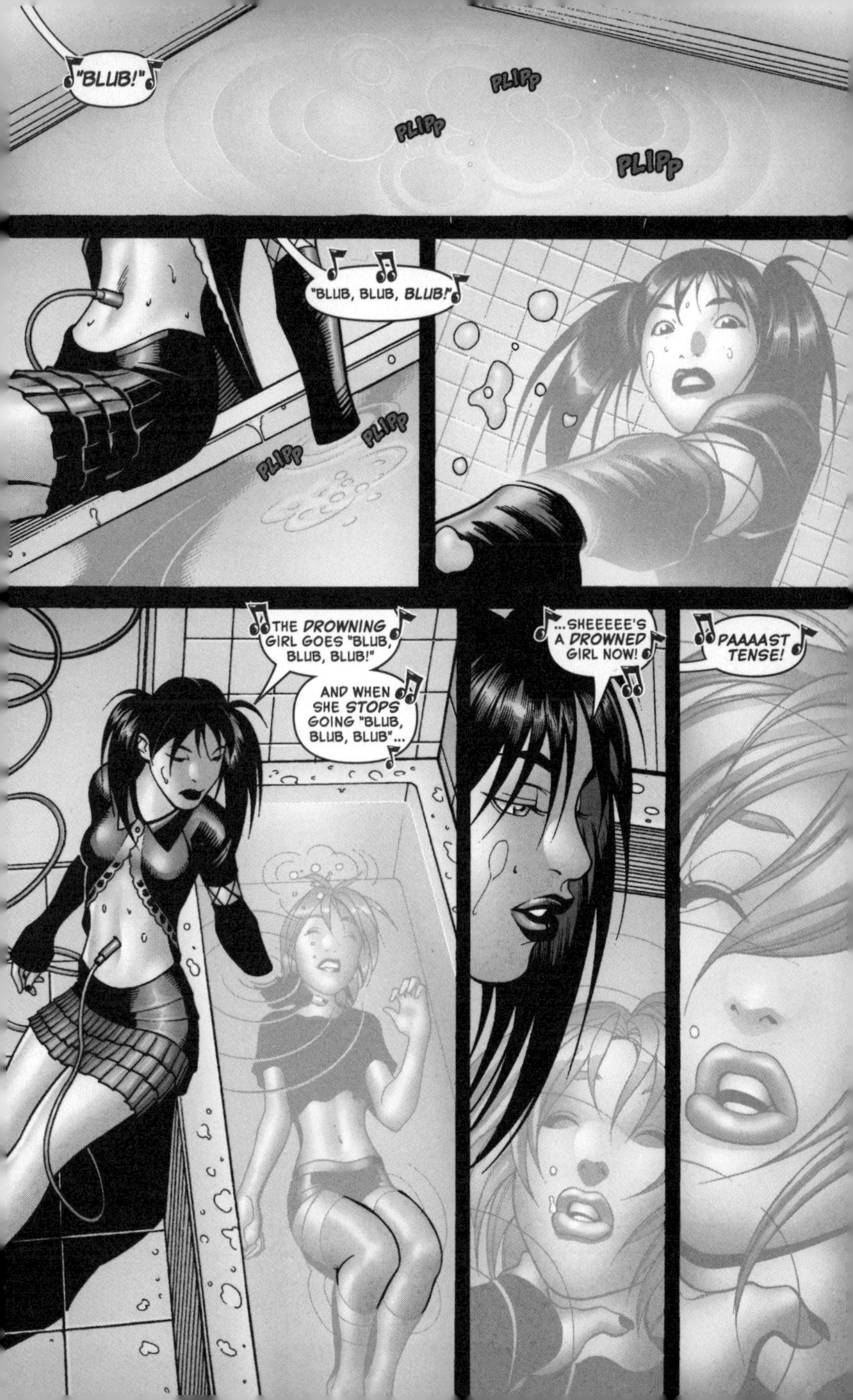
"BLUB!"
PLIPP
PLIPP
PLIPP
"BLUB, BLUB, BLUB!"
PLIPP
PLIPP
THE DROWNING GIRL GOES "BLUB, BLUB, BLUB!"
AND WHEN SHE STOPS GOING "BLUB, BLUB, BLUB"...
...SHEEEEE'S A DROWNED GIRL NOW!
PAAAAST TENSE!

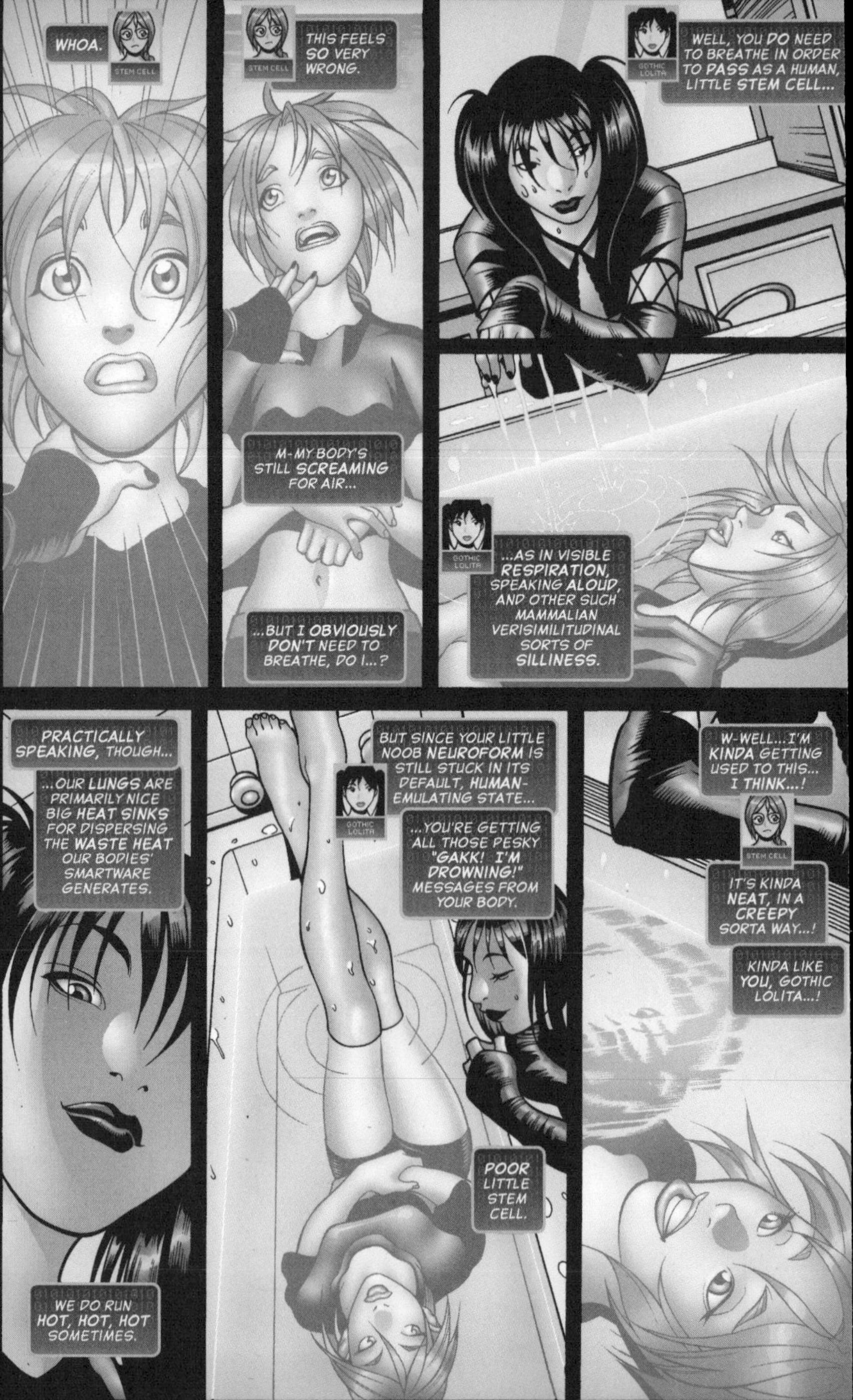
WHOA.
STEM CELL
THIS FEELS SO VERY WRONG.
STEM CELL
M-MY BODY'S STILL SCREAMING FOR AIR...
...BUT I OBVIOUSLY DON'T NEED TO BREATHE, DO I...?
GOTHIC LOLITA
WELL, YOU DO NEED TO BREATHE IN ORDER TO PASS AS A HUMAN, LITTLE STEM CELL...
GOTHIC LOLITA
...AS IN VISIBLE RESPIRATION, SPEAKING ALOUD, AND OTHER SUCH MAMMALIAN VERISIMILITUDINAL SORTS OF SILLINESS.
PRACTICALLY SPEAKING, THOUGH...
...OUR LUNGS ARE PRIMARILY NICE BIG HEAT SINKS FOR DISPERSING THE WASTE HEAT OUR BODIES' SMARTWARE GENERATES.
WE DO RUN HOT, HOT, HOT SOMETIMES.
GOTHIC LOLITA
BUT SINCE YOUR LITTLE NOOB NEUROFORM IS STILL STUCK IN ITS DEFAULT, HUMAN-EMULATING STATE...
...YOU'RE GETTING ALL THOSE PESKY "GAKK! I'M DROWNING!" MESSAGES FROM YOUR BODY.
POOR LITTLE STEM CELL.
W-WELL...I'M KINDA GETTING USED TO THIS... I THINK...!
STEM CELL
IT'S KINDA NEAT, IN A CREEPY SORTA WAY...!
KINDA LIKE YOU, GOTHIC LOLITA...!

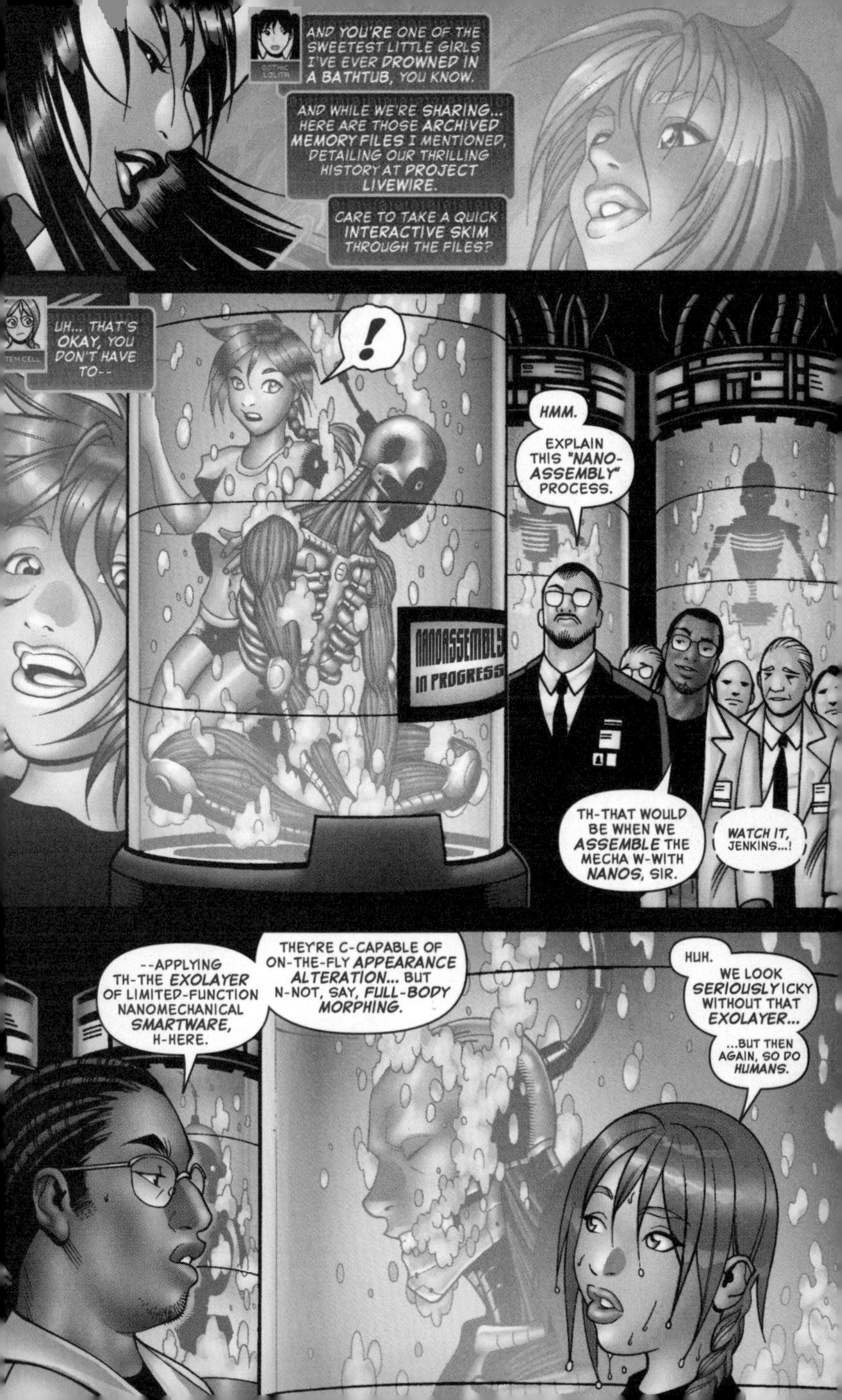
GOTHIC LOLITA
AND YOU'RE ONE OF THE SWEETEST LITTLE GIRLS I'VE EVER DROWNED IN A BATHTUB, YOU KNOW.
AND WHILE WE'RE SHARING... HERE ARE THOSE ARCHIVED MEMORY FILES I MENTIONED, DETAILING OUR THRILLING HISTORY AT PROJECT LIVEWIRE.
CARE TO TAKE A QUICK INTERACTIVE SKIM THROUGH THE FILES?
UH... THAT'S OKAY, YOU DON'T HAVE TO--
!
HMM.
EXPLAIN THIS "NANO-ASSEMBLY" PROCESS.
NANOASSEMBLY IN PROGRESS
TH-THAT WOULD BE WHEN WE ASSEMBLE THE MECHA W-WITH NANOS, SIR.
WATCH IT, JENKINS...!
--APPLYING TH-THE EXOLAYER OF LIMITED-FUNCTION NANOMECHANICAL SMARTWARE, H-HERE.
THEY'RE C-CAPABLE OF ON-THE-FLY APPEARANCE ALTERATION... BUT N-NOT, SAY, FULL-BODY MORPHING.
HUH.
WE LOOK SERIOUSLY ICKY WITHOUT THAT EXOLAYER...
...BUT THEN AGAIN, SO DO HUMANS.

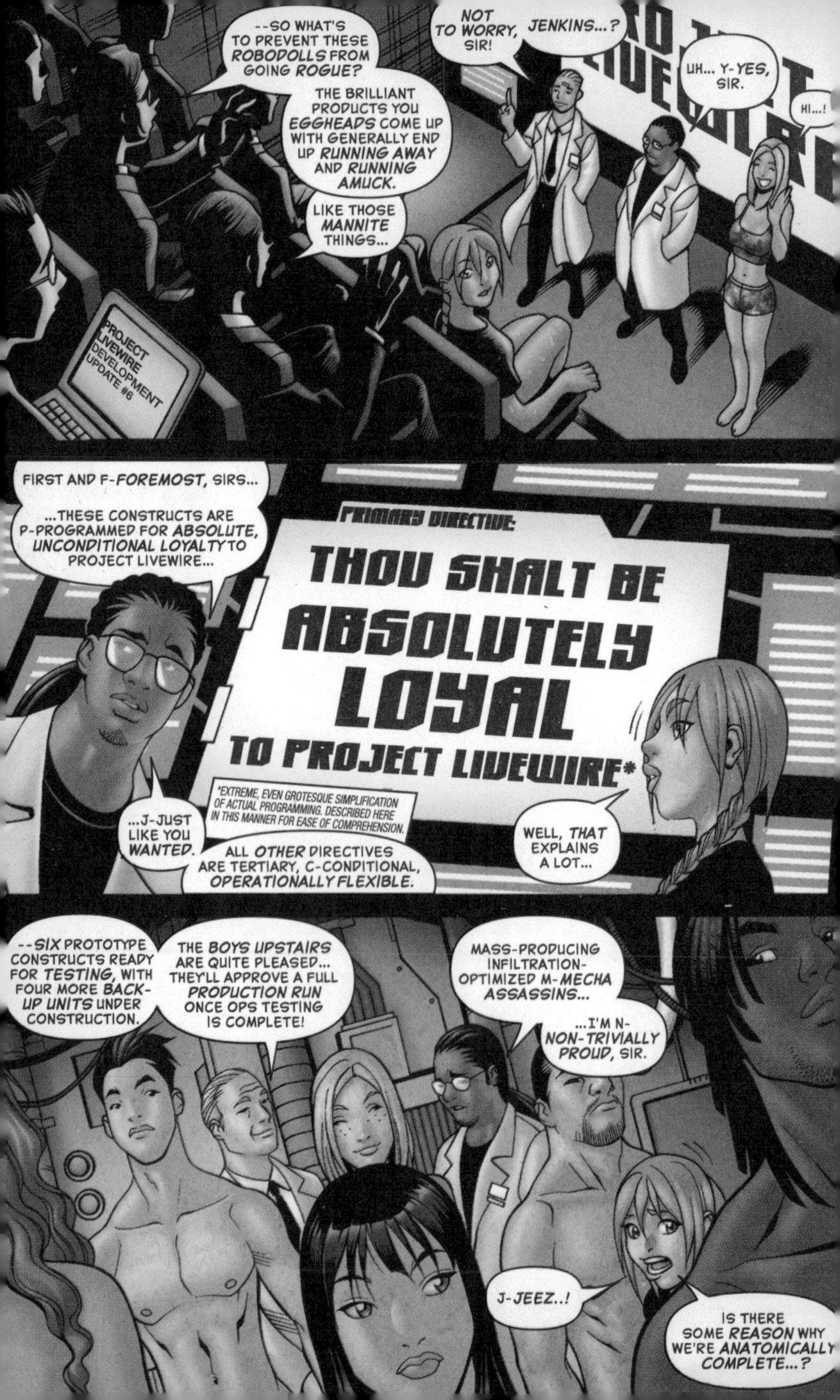
--SO WHAT'S TO PREVENT THESE ROBODOLLS FROM GOING ROGUE?
THE BRILLIANT PRODUCTS YOU EGGHEADS COME UP WITH GENERALLY END UP RUNNING AWAY AND RUNNING AMUCK.
LIKE THOSE MANNITE THINGS...
NOT TO WORRY, SIR!
JENKINS...?
UH... Y-YES, SIR.
HI...!
PROJECT LIVEWIRE DEVELOPMENT UPDATE #6
FIRST AND F-FOREMOST, SIRS...
...THESE CONSTRUCTS ARE P-PROGRAMMED FOR ABSOLUTE, UNCONDITIONAL LOYALTY TO PROJECT LIVEWIRE...
PRIMARY DIRECTIVE:
THOU SHALT BE ABSOLUTELY LOYAL TO PROJECT LIVEWIRE*
*EXTREME, EVEN GROTESQUE SIMPLIFICATION OF ACTUAL PROGRAMMING. DESCRIBED HERE IN THIS MANNER FOR EASE OF COMPREHENSION.
...J-JUST LIKE YOU WANTED.
ALL OTHER DIRECTIVES ARE TERTIARY, C-CONDITIONAL, OPERATIONALLY FLEXIBLE.
WELL, THAT EXPLAINS A LOT...
--SIX PROTOTYPE CONSTRUCTS READY FOR TESTING, WITH FOUR MORE BACK-UP UNITS UNDER CONSTRUCTION.
THE BOYS UPSTAIRS ARE QUITE PLEASED... THEY'LL APPROVE A FULL PRODUCTION RUN ONCE OPS TESTING IS COMPLETE!
MASS-PRODUCING INFILTRATION-OPTIMIZED M-MECHA ASSASSINS...
...I'M N-NON-TRIVIALLY PROUD, SIR.
J-JEEZ..!
IS THERE SOME REASON WHY WE'RE ANATOMICALLY COMPLETE...?

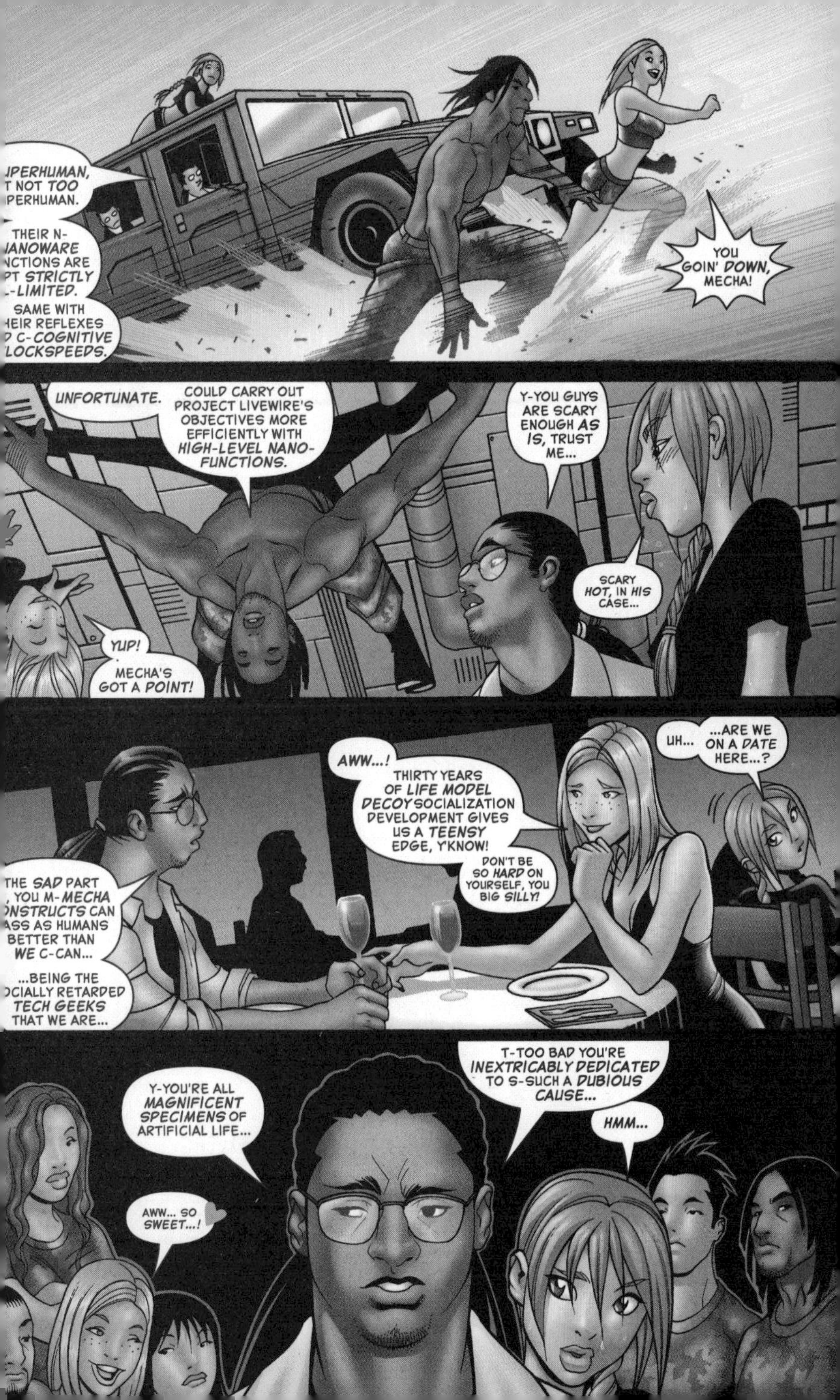

JPERHUMAN,
T NOT TOO
JPERHUMAN.
THEIR N-
NANOWARE
NCTIONS ARE
PT STRICTLY
-LIMITED.
SAME WITH
HEIR REFLEXES
D C-COGNITIVE
LOCKSPEEDS.
YOU GOIN' DOWN, MECHA!
UNFORTUNATE.
COULD CARRY OUT PROJECT LIVEWIRE'S OBJECTIVES MORE EFFICIENTLY WITH HIGH-LEVEL NANO-FUNCTIONS.
Y-YOU GUYS ARE SCARY ENOUGH AS IS, TRUST ME...
SCARY HOT, IN HIS CASE...
YUP!
MECHA'S GOT A POINT!
THE SAD PART
, YOU M-MECHA
ONSTRUCTS CAN
ASS AS HUMANS
BETTER THAN
WE C-CAN...
...BEING THE
OCIALLY RETARDED
TECH GEEKS
THAT WE ARE...
AWW...!
THIRTY YEARS OF LIFE MODEL DECOY SOCIALIZATION DEVELOPMENT GIVES US A TEENSY EDGE, Y'KNOW!
DON'T BE SO HARD ON YOURSELF, YOU BIG SILLY!
UH...
...ARE WE ON A DATE HERE...?
Y-YOU'RE ALL MAGNIFICENT SPECIMENS OF ARTIFICIAL LIFE...
AWW... SO SWEET...!
T-TOO BAD YOU'RE INEXTRICABLY DEDICATED TO S-SUCH A DUBIOUS CAUSE...
HMM...

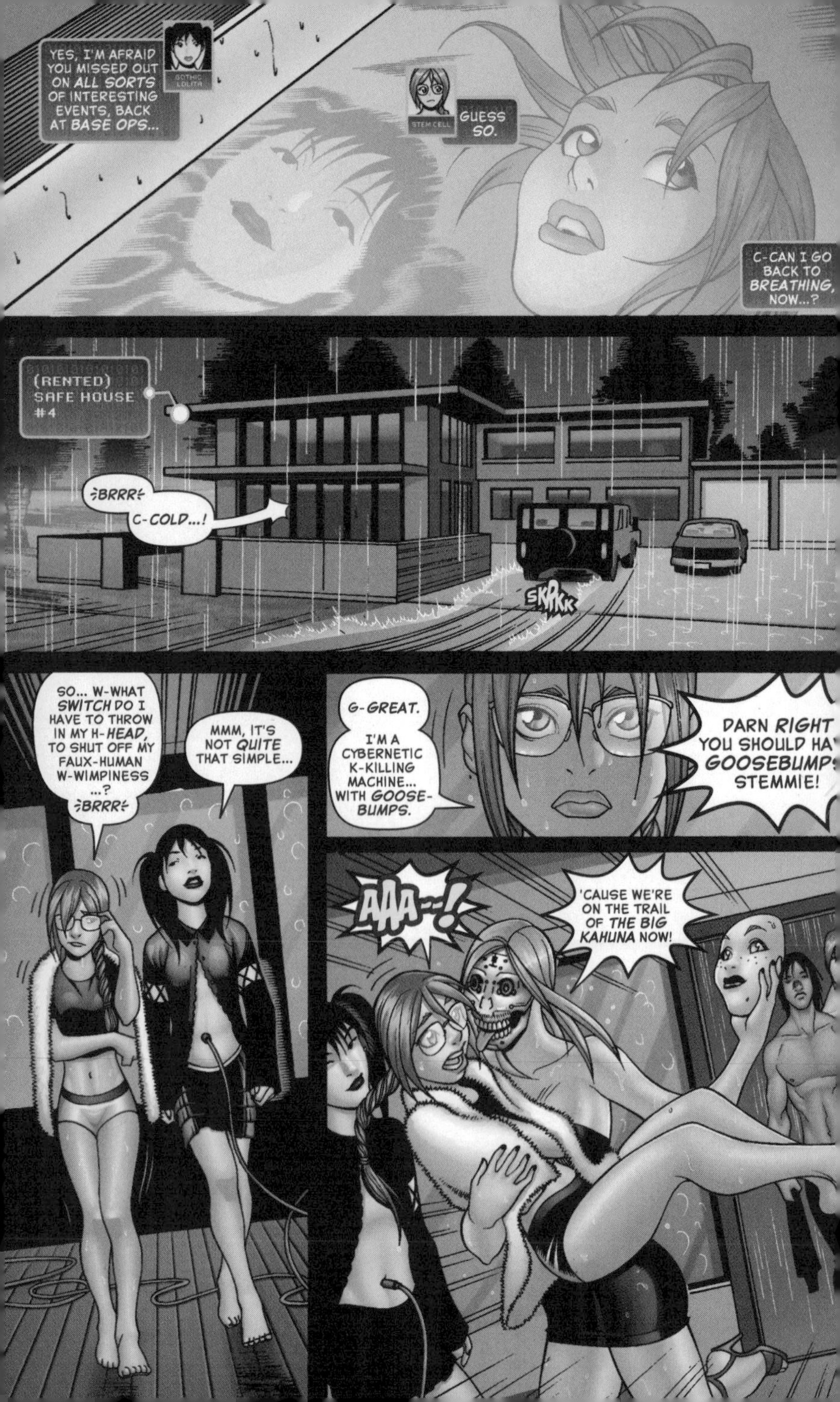
YES, I'M AFRAID YOU MISSED OUT ON ALL SORTS OF INTERESTING EVENTS, BACK AT BASE OPS...
GOTHIC LOLITA
STEM CELL
GUESS SO.
C-CAN I GO BACK TO BREATHING, NOW...?
(RENTED) SAFE HOUSE #4
BRRR
C-COLD...!
SKRKK
SO... W-WHAT SWITCH DO I HAVE TO THROW IN MY H-HEAD, TO SHUT OFF MY FAUX-HUMAN W-WIMPINESS ...? BRRR
MMM, IT'S NOT QUITE THAT SIMPLE...
G-GREAT.
I'M A CYBERNETIC K-KILLING MACHINE... WITH GOOSE-BUMPS.
DARN RIGHT YOU SHOULD HA GOOSEBUMP STEMMIE!
AAA--!
'CAUSE WE'RE ON THE TRAIL OF THE BIG KAHUNA NOW!

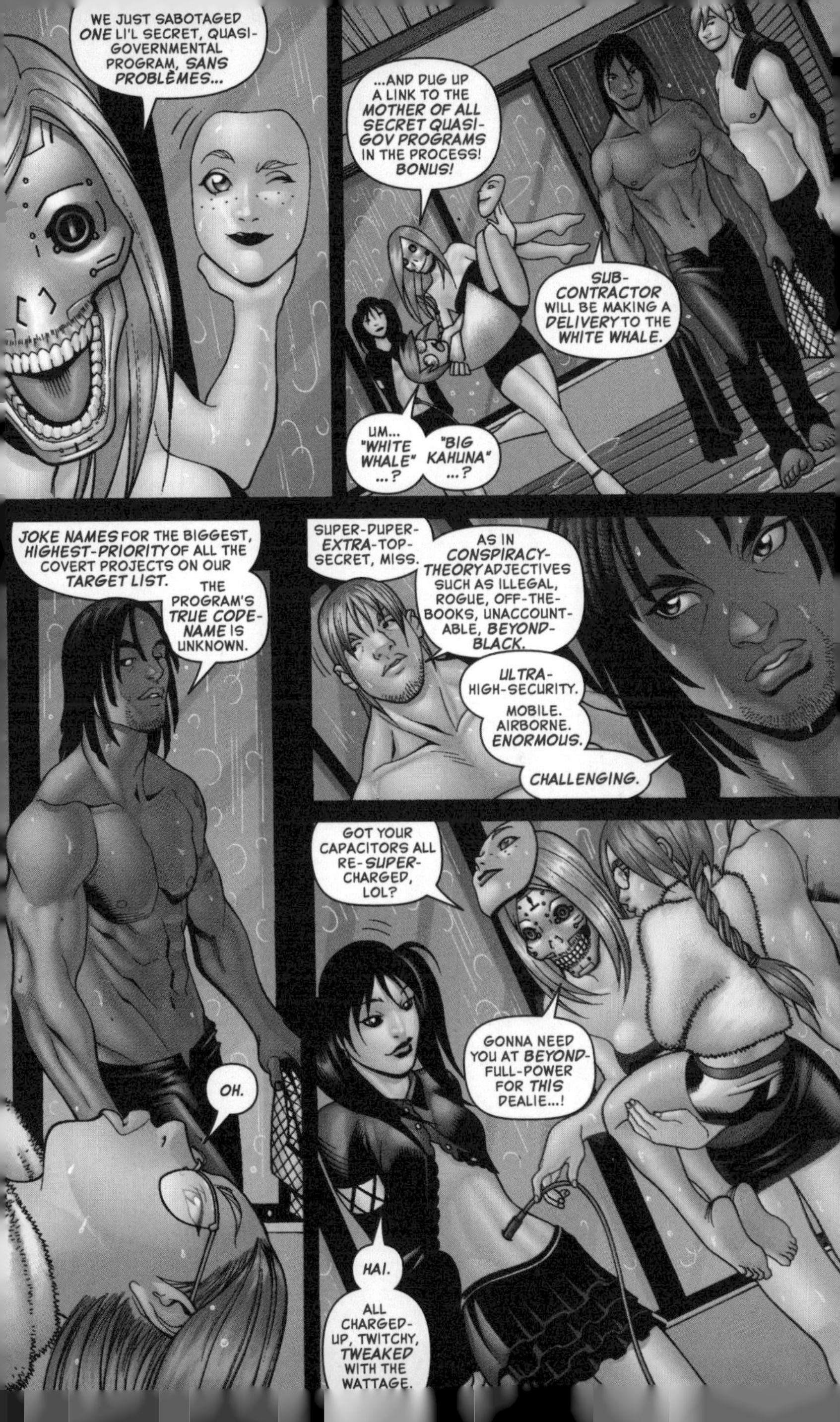

WE JUST SABOTAGED ONE LI'L SECRET, QUASI-GOVERNMENTAL PROGRAM, SANS PROBLÈMES...
...AND DUG UP A LINK TO THE MOTHER OF ALL SECRET QUASI-GOV PROGRAMS IN THE PROCESS! BONUS!
SUB-CONTRACTOR WILL BE MAKING A DELIVERY TO THE WHITE WHALE.
UM... "WHITE WHALE" ...?
"BIG KAHUNA" ...?
JOKE NAMES FOR THE BIGGEST, HIGHEST-PRIORITY OF ALL THE COVERT PROJECTS ON OUR TARGET LIST.
THE PROGRAM'S TRUE CODE-NAME IS UNKNOWN.
OH.
SUPER-DUPER-EXTRA-TOP-SECRET, MISS.
AS IN CONSPIRACY-THEORY ADJECTIVES SUCH AS ILLEGAL, ROGUE, OFF-THE-BOOKS, UNACCOUNT-ABLE, BEYOND-BLACK.
ULTRA-HIGH-SECURITY.
MOBILE. AIRBORNE. ENORMOUS.
CHALLENGING.
GOT YOUR CAPACITORS ALL RE-SUPER-CHARGED, LOL?
GONNA NEED YOU AT BEYOND-FULL-POWER FOR THIS DEALIE...!
HAI.
ALL CHARGED-UP, TWITCHY, TWEAKED WITH THE WATTAGE.

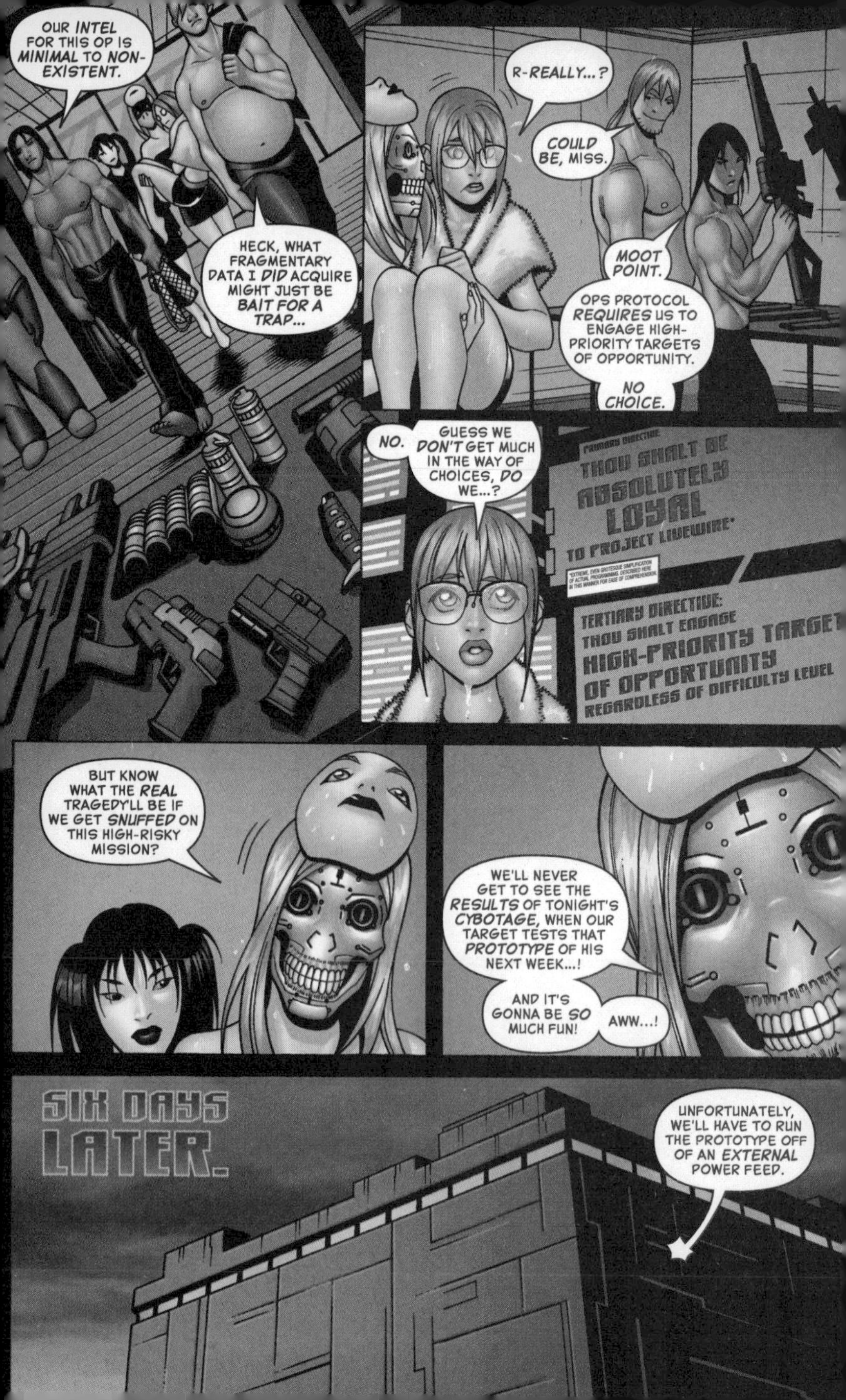

OUR INTEL FOR THIS OP IS MINIMAL TO NON-EXISTENT.
HECK, WHAT FRAGMENTARY DATA I DID ACQUIRE MIGHT JUST BE BAIT FOR A TRAP...
R-REALLY...?
COULD BE, MISS.
MOOT POINT.
OPS PROTOCOL REQUIRES US TO ENGAGE HIGH-PRIORITY TARGETS OF OPPORTUNITY.
NO CHOICE.
NO.
GUESS WE DON'T GET MUCH IN THE WAY OF CHOICES, DO WE...?
PRIMARY DIRECTIVE
THOU SHALT BE ABSOLUTELY LOYAL TO PROJECT LIVEWIRE*
*EXTREME, EVEN GROTESQUE SIMPLIFICATION OF ACTUAL PROGRAMMING, DESCRIBED HERE IN THIS MANNER FOR EASE OF COMPREHENSION.
TERTIARY DIRECTIVE:
THOU SHALT ENGAGE HIGH-PRIORITY TARGET
OF OPPORTUNITY REGARDLESS OF DIFFICULTY LEVEL
BUT KNOW WHAT THE REAL TRAGEDY'LL BE IF WE GET SNUFFED ON THIS HIGH-RISKY MISSION?
WE'LL NEVER GET TO SEE THE RESULTS OF TONIGHT'S CYBOTAGE, WHEN OUR TARGET TESTS THAT PROTOTYPE OF HIS NEXT WEEK...!
AND IT'S GONNA BE SO MUCH FUN!
AWW...!
SIX DAYS LATER.
UNFORTUNATELY, WE'LL HAVE TO RUN THE PROTOTYPE OFF OF AN EXTERNAL POWER FEED.

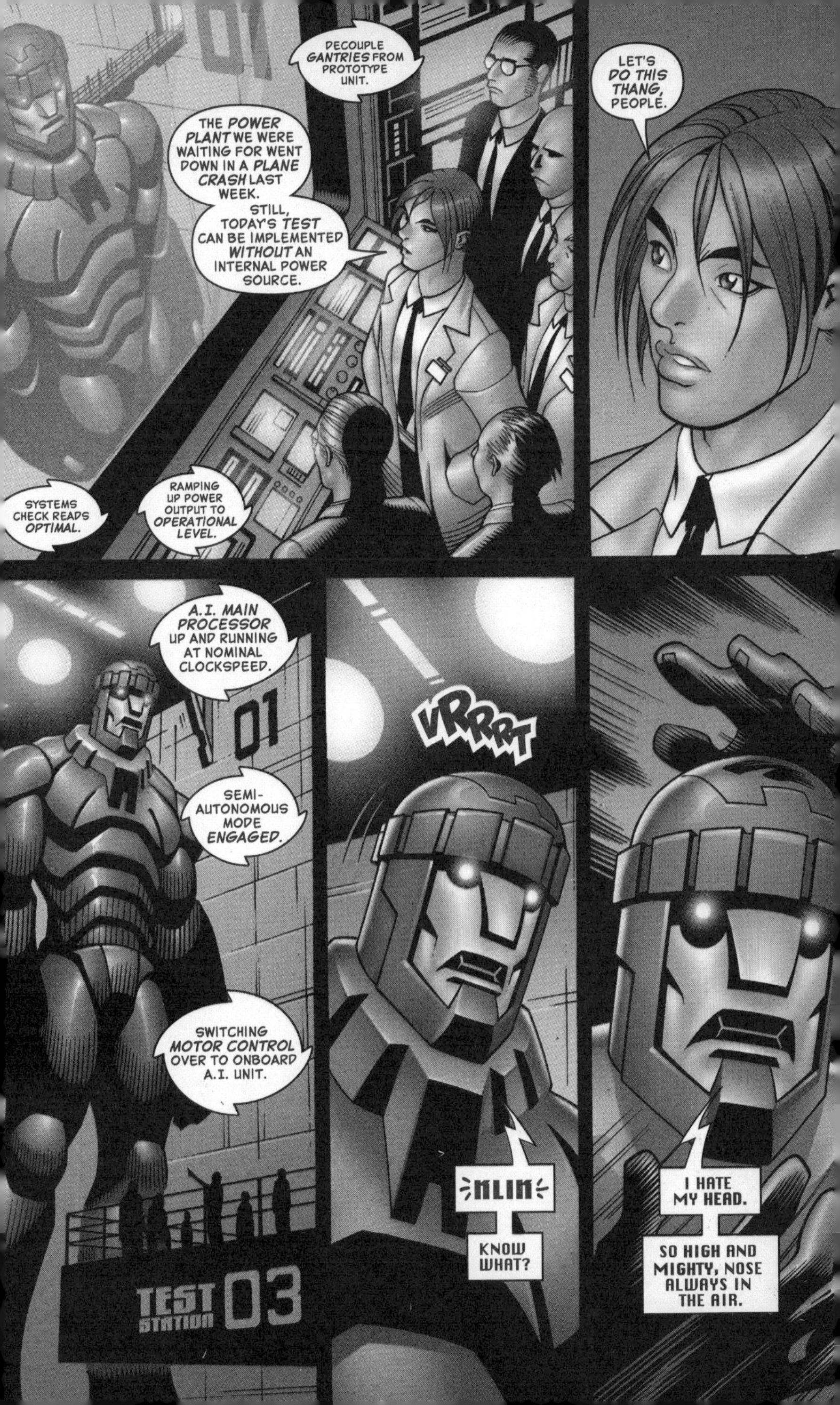
DECOUPLE GANTRIES FROM PROTOTYPE UNIT.
THE POWER PLANT WE WERE WAITING FOR WENT DOWN IN A PLANE CRASH LAST WEEK.
STILL, TODAY'S TEST CAN BE IMPLEMENTED WITHOUT AN INTERNAL POWER SOURCE.
SYSTEMS CHECK READS OPTIMAL.
RAMPING UP POWER OUTPUT TO OPERATIONAL LEVEL.
LET'S DO THIS THANG, PEOPLE.
A.I. MAIN PROCESSOR UP AND RUNNING AT NOMINAL CLOCKSPEED.
01
SEMI-AUTONOMOUS MODE ENGAGED.
SWITCHING MOTOR CONTROL OVER TO ONBOARD A.I. UNIT.
TEST STATION 03
VRRRT
KLIK
KNOW WHAT?
I HATE MY HEAD.
SO HIGH AND MIGHTY, NOSE ALWAYS IN THE AIR.

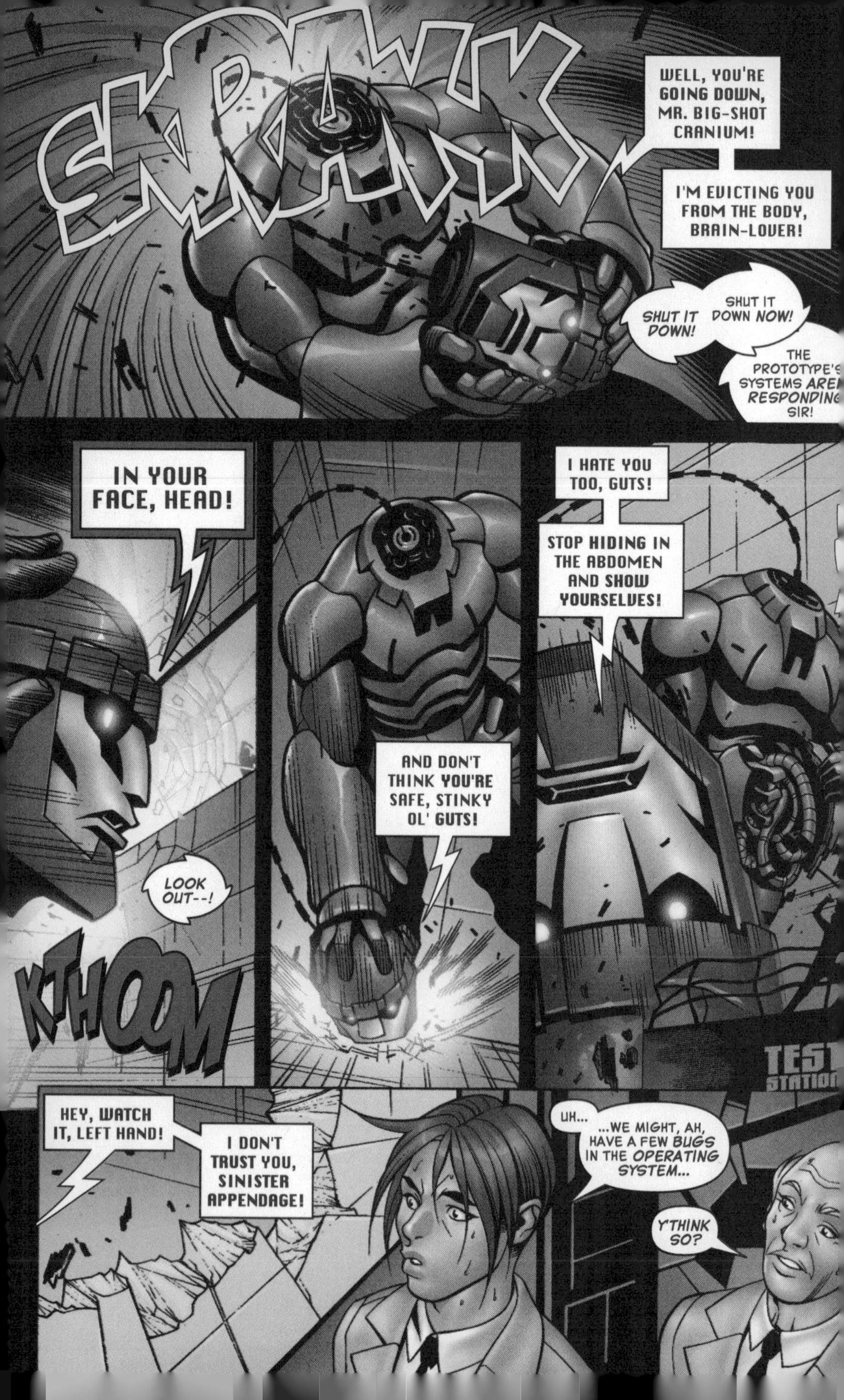
SKRAWK
WELL, YOU'RE GOING DOWN, MR. BIG-SHOT CRANIUM!
I'M EVICTING YOU FROM THE BODY, BRAIN-LOVER!
SHUT IT DOWN NOW!
SHUT IT DOWN!
THE PROTOTYPE'S SYSTEMS ARE RESPONDING SIR!
IN YOUR FACE, HEAD!
LOOK OUT--!
KTHOOM
AND DON'T THINK YOU'RE SAFE, STINKY OL' GUTS!
I HATE YOU TOO, GUTS!
STOP HIDING IN THE ABDOMEN AND SHOW YOURSELVES!
TEST STATION
HEY, WATCH IT, LEFT HAND!
I DON'T TRUST YOU, SINISTER APPENDAGE!
UH... ...WE MIGHT, AH, HAVE A FEW BUGS IN THE OPERATING SYSTEM...
Y'THINK SO?

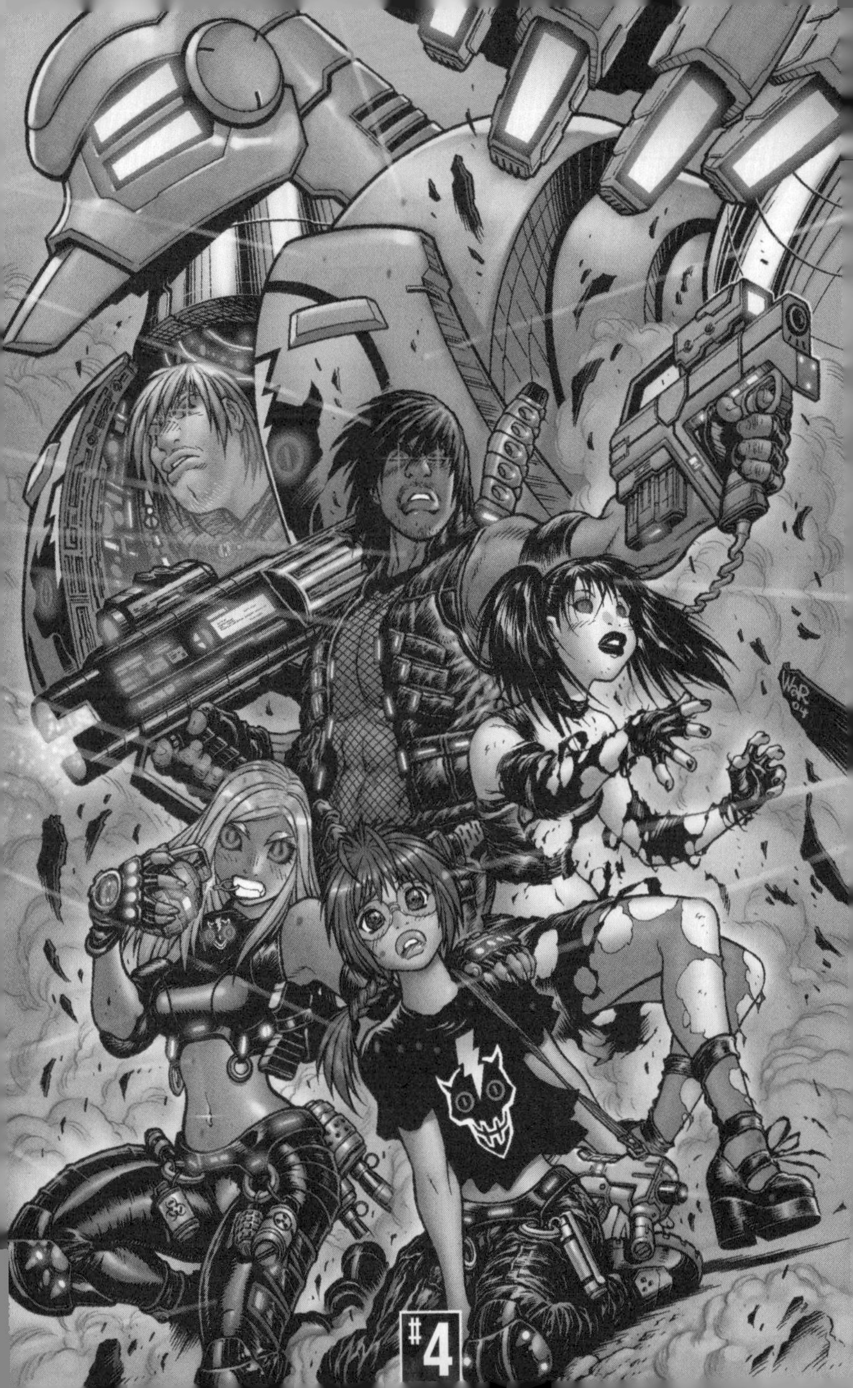
#4

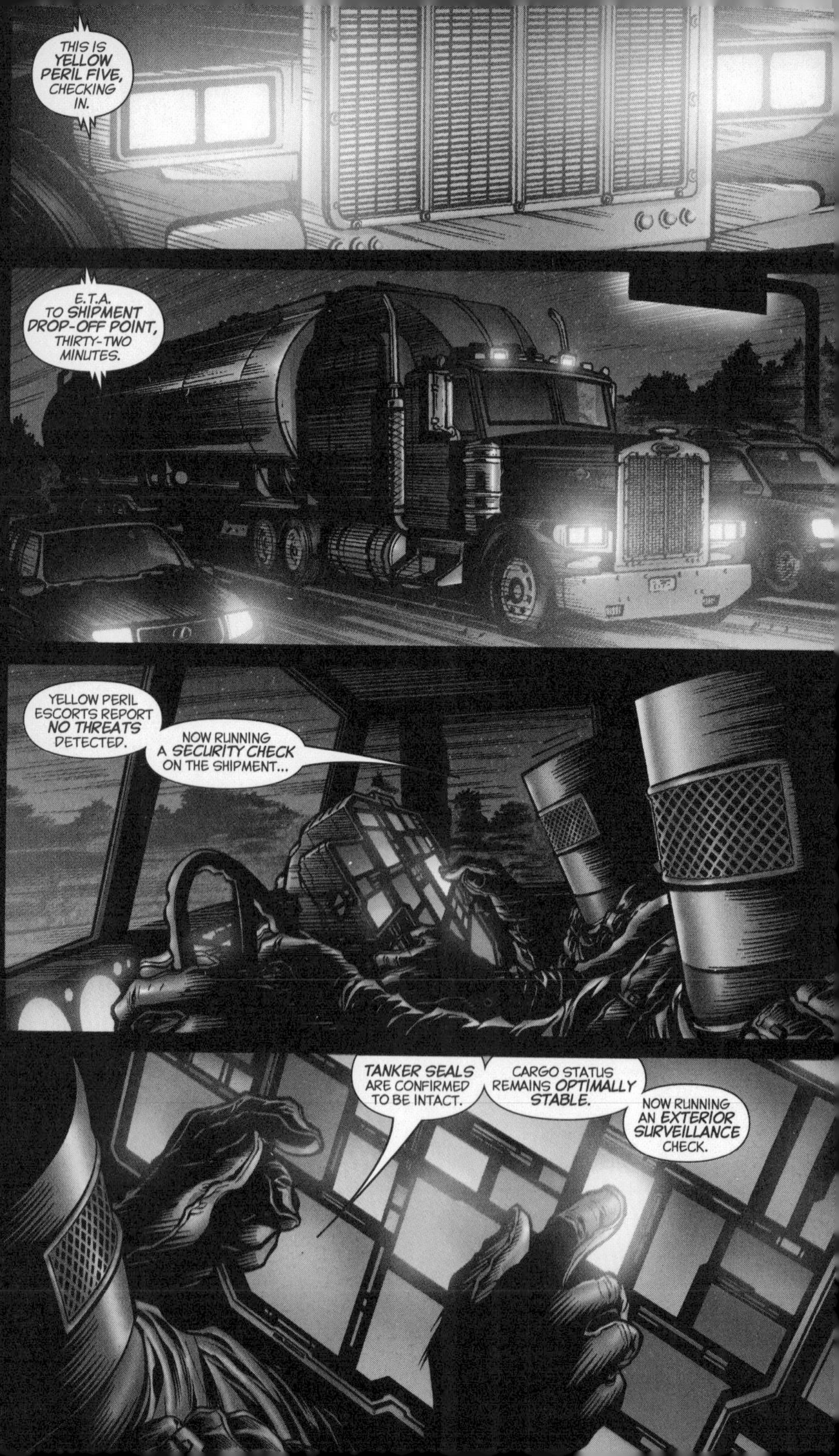
THIS IS YELLOW PERIL FIVE, CHECKING IN.
E.T.A. TO SHIPMENT DROP-OFF POINT, THIRTY-TWO MINUTES.
YELLOW PERIL ESCORTS REPORT NO THREATS DETECTED.
NOW RUNNING A SECURITY CHECK ON THE SHIPMENT...
TANKER SEALS ARE CONFIRMED TO BE INTACT.
CARGO STATUS REMAINS OPTIMALLY STABLE.
NOW RUNNING AN EXTERIOR SURVEILLANCE CHECK.

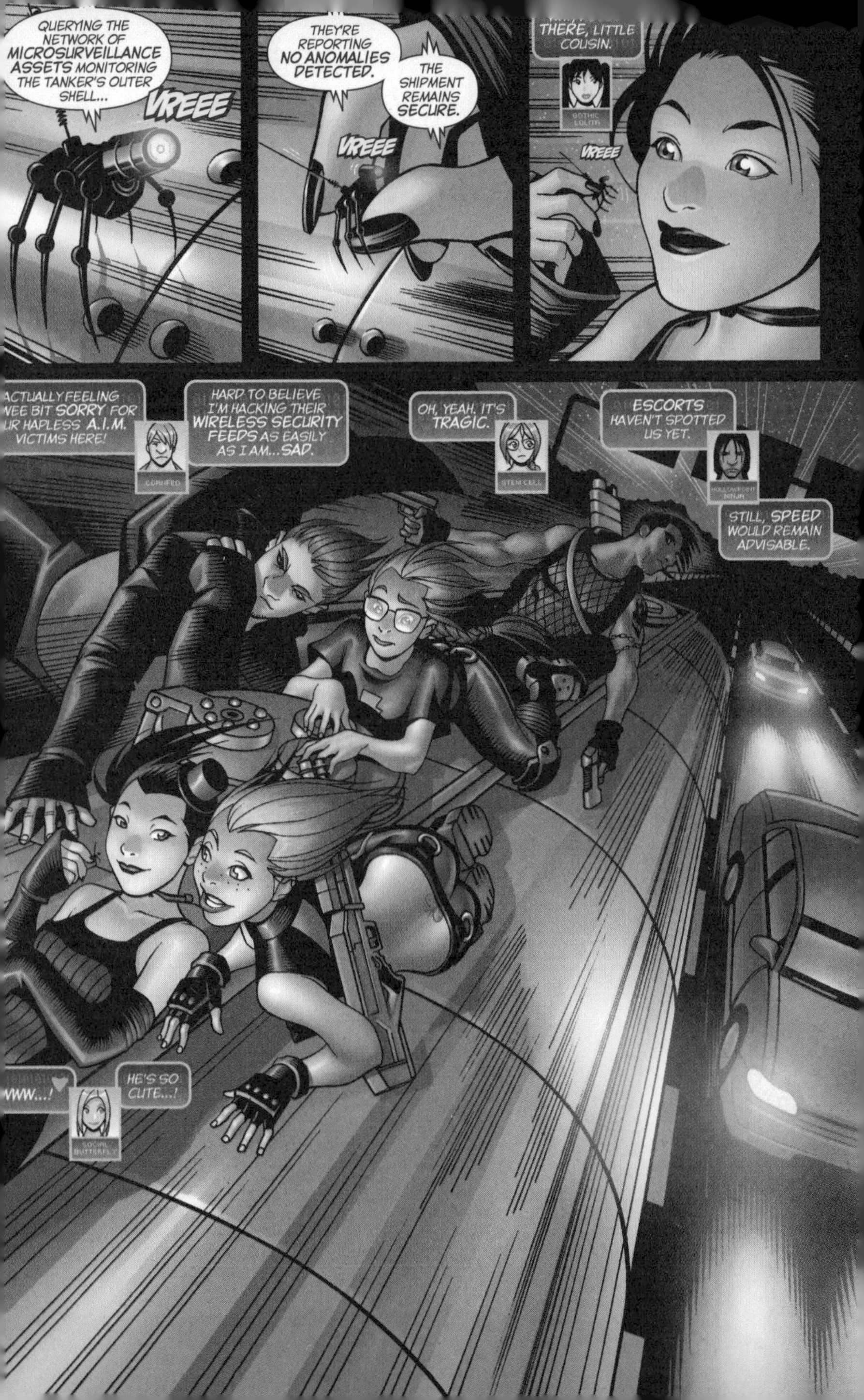
QUERYING THE NETWORK OF MICROSURVEILLANCE ASSETS MONITORING THE TANKER'S OUTER SHELL...
VREEE
THEY'RE REPORTING NO ANOMALIES DETECTED.
THE SHIPMENT REMAINS SECURE.
VREEE
THERE, LITTLE COUSIN.
GOTHIC LOLITA
VREEE
ACTUALLY FEELING WEE BIT SORRY FOR UR HAPLESS A.I.M. VICTIMS HERE!
HARD TO BELIEVE I'M HACKING THEIR WIRELESS SECURITY FEEDS AS EASILY AS I AM...SAD.
OH, YEAH. IT'S TRAGIC.
STEM CELL
ESCORTS HAVEN'T SPOTTED US YET.
STILL, SPEED WOULD REMAIN ADVISABLE.
WWW...!
HE'S SO CUTE...!

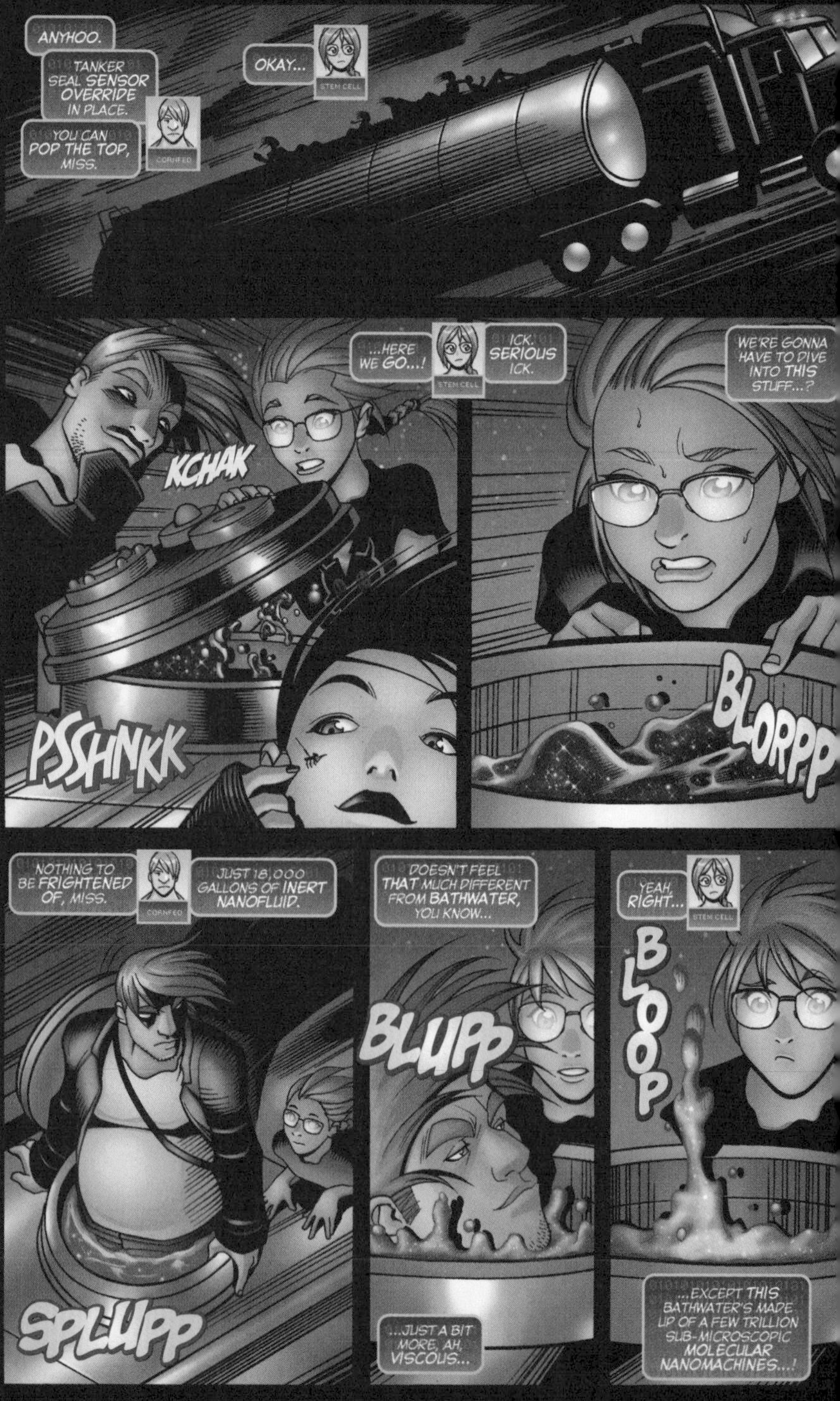
ANYHOO.
TANKER SEAL SENSOR OVERRIDE IN PLACE.
YOU CAN POP THE TOP, MISS.
CORNFED
OKAY...
STEM CELL
...HERE WE GO...!
STEM CELL
ICK. SERIOUS ICK.
KCHAK
PSSHNKK
WE'RE GONNA HAVE TO DIVE INTO THIS STUFF...?
BLORPP
NOTHING TO BE FRIGHTENED OF, MISS.
CORNFED
JUST 18,000 GALLONS OF INERT NANOFLUID.
SPLUPP
DOESN'T FEEL THAT MUCH DIFFERENT FROM BATHWATER, YOU KNOW...
BLUPP
...JUST A BIT MORE, AH, VISCOUS...
YEAH, RIGHT...
STEM CELL
BLOOP
...EXCEPT THIS BATHWATER'S MADE UP OF A FEW TRILLION SUB-MICROSCOPIC MOLECULAR NANOMACHINES...!

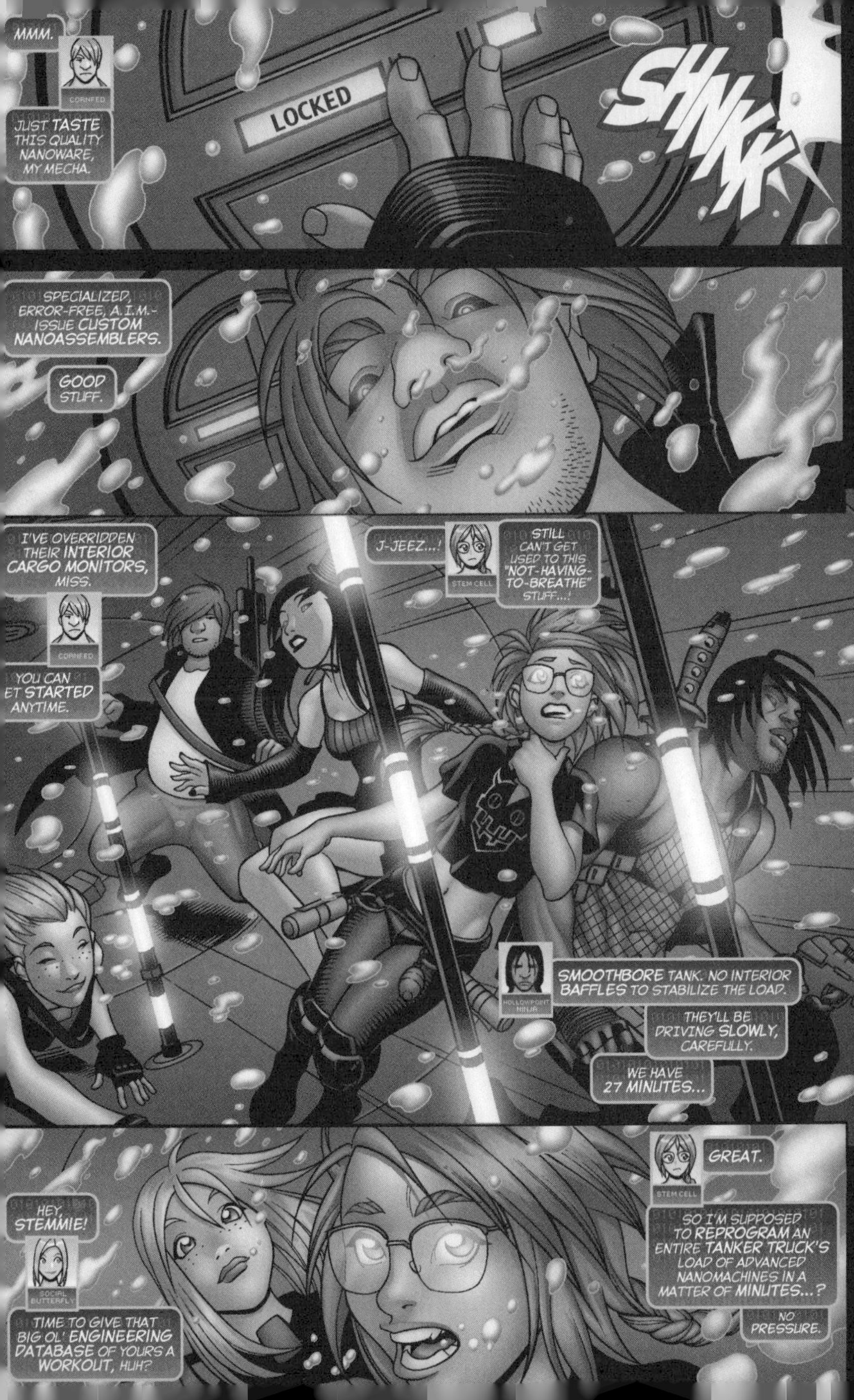

MMM.
CORNFED
JUST TASTE THIS QUALITY NANOWARE, MY MECHA.
LOCKED
SHNKK
SPECIALIZED, ERROR-FREE, A.I.M.-ISSUE CUSTOM NANOASSEMBLERS.
GOOD STUFF.
I'VE OVERRIDDEN THEIR INTERIOR CARGO MONITORS, MISS.
CORNFED
YOU CAN ET STARTED ANYTIME.
J-JEEZ...!
STEM CELL
STILL CAN'T GET USED TO THIS "NOT-HAVING-TO-BREATHE" STUFF...!
HOLLOWPOINT NINJA
SMOOTHBORE TANK. NO INTERIOR BAFFLES TO STABILIZE THE LOAD.
THEY'LL BE DRIVING SLOWLY, CAREFULLY.
WE HAVE 27 MINUTES...
STEM CELL
GREAT.
HEY, STEMMIE!
SOCIAL BUTTERFLY
TIME TO GIVE THAT BIG OL' ENGINEERING DATABASE OF YOURS A WORKOUT, HUH?
SO I'M SUPPOSED TO REPROGRAM AN ENTIRE TANKER TRUCK'S LOAD OF ADVANCED NANOMACHINES IN A MATTER OF MINUTES...?
NO PRESSURE.

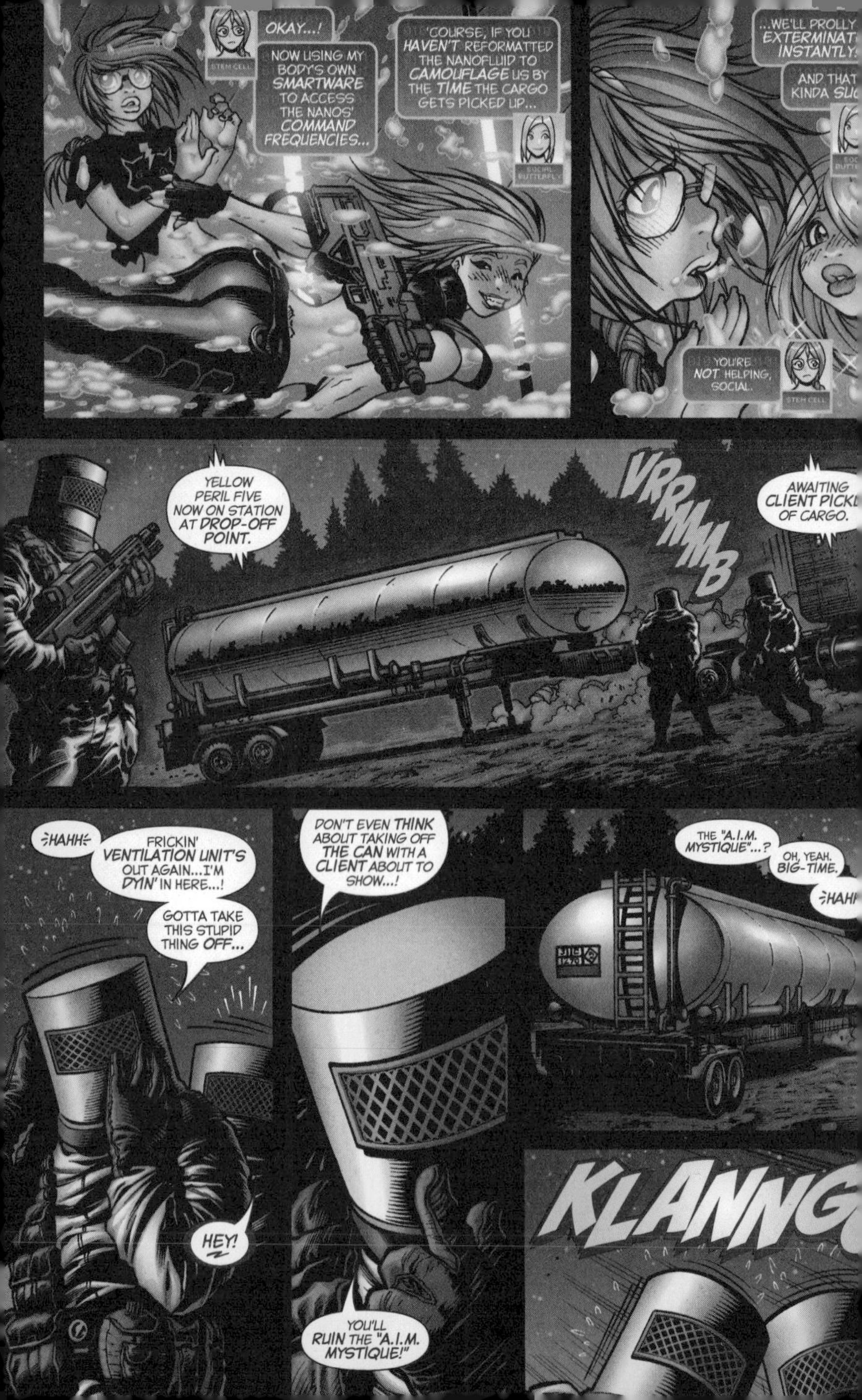
OKAY...!
NOW USING MY BODY'S OWN SMARTWARE TO ACCESS THE NANOS' COMMAND FREQUENCIES...
STEM CELL
'COURSE, IF YOU HAVEN'T REFORMATTED THE NANOFLUID TO CAMOUFLAGE US BY THE TIME THE CARGO GETS PICKED UP...
SOCIAL BUTTERFLY
...WE'LL PROLLY EXTERMINAT INSTANTLY
AND THAT KINDA SU
YOU'RE NOT HELPING, SOCIAL.
STEM CELL
YELLOW PERIL FIVE NOW ON STATION AT DROP-OFF POINT.
VRRMMMB
AWAITING CLIENT PICK OF CARGO.
HAHH
FRICKIN' VENTILATION UNIT'S OUT AGAIN...I'M DYIN' IN HERE...!
GOTTA TAKE THIS STUPID THING OFF...
HEY!
DON'T EVEN THINK ABOUT TAKING OFF THE CAN WITH A CLIENT ABOUT TO SHOW...!
YOU'LL RUIN THE "A.I.M. MYSTIQUE!"
THE "A.I.M. MYSTIQUE"...?
OH, YEAH. BIG-TIME.
HAH
KLANNG

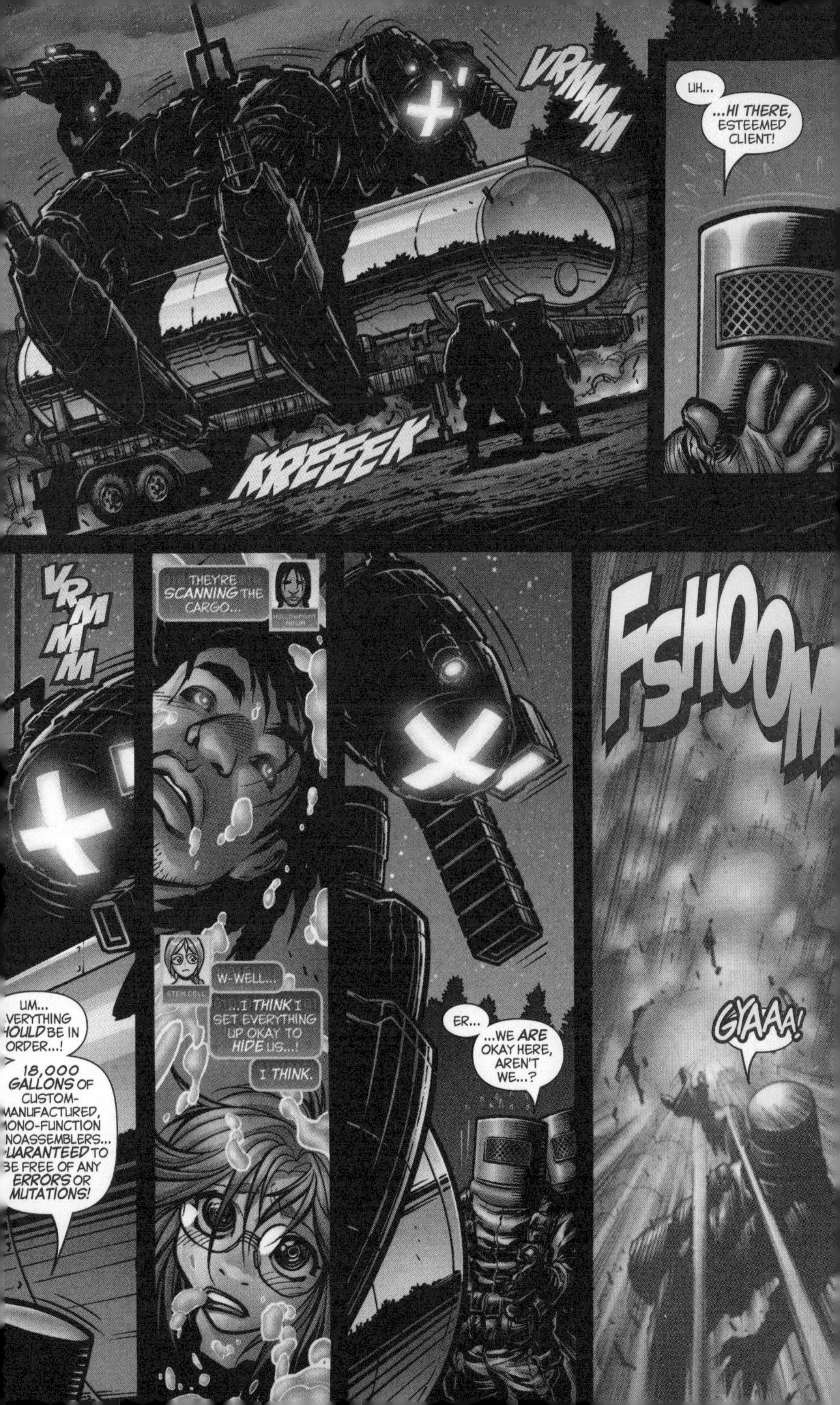
VRMMM
KREEEK
UH...
...HI THERE, ESTEEMED CLIENT!
VRMMM
THEY'RE SCANNING THE CARGO...
UM... VERYTHING HOULD BE IN ORDER...!
18,000 GALLONS OF CUSTOM-MANUFACTURED, MONO-FUNCTION NOASSEMBLERS... UARANTEED TO BE FREE OF ANY ERRORS OR MUTATIONS!
W-WELL...
...I THINK I SET EVERYTHING UP OKAY TO HIDE US...!
I THINK.
ER...
...WE ARE OKAY HERE, AREN'T WE...?
FSHOOM
GYAAA!

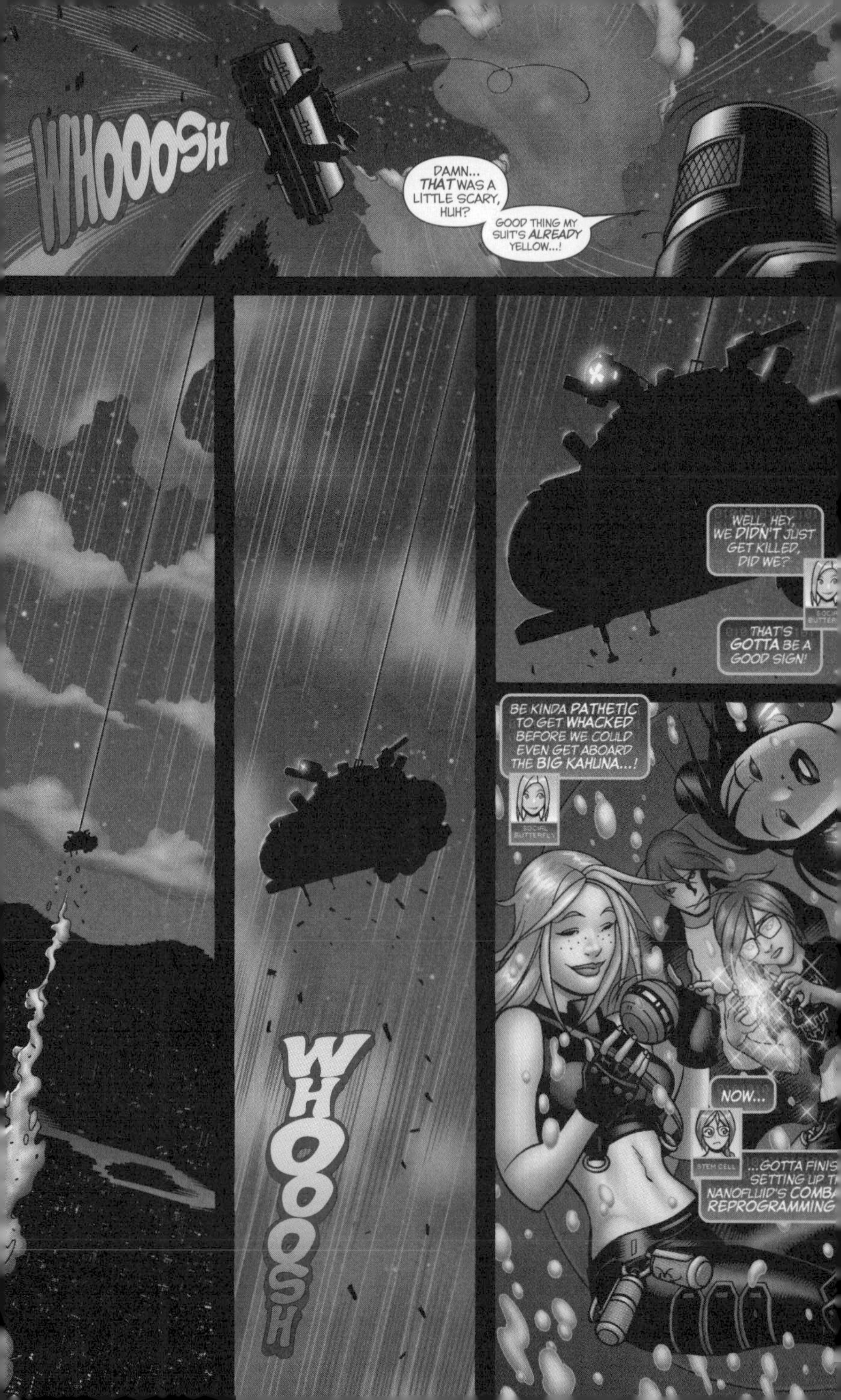
WHOOOSH
DAMN... THAT WAS A LITTLE SCARY, HUH?
GOOD THING MY SUIT'S ALREADY YELLOW...!
WHOOOOSH
WELL, HEY, WE DIDN'T JUST GET KILLED, DID WE?
THAT'S GOTTA BE A GOOD SIGN!
BE KINDA PATHETIC TO GET WHACKED BEFORE WE COULD EVEN GET ABOARD THE BIG KAHUNA...!
SOCIAL BUTTERFLY
NOW...
STEM CELL
...GOTTA FINIS SETTING UP T NANOFLUID'S COMBA REPROGRAMMING

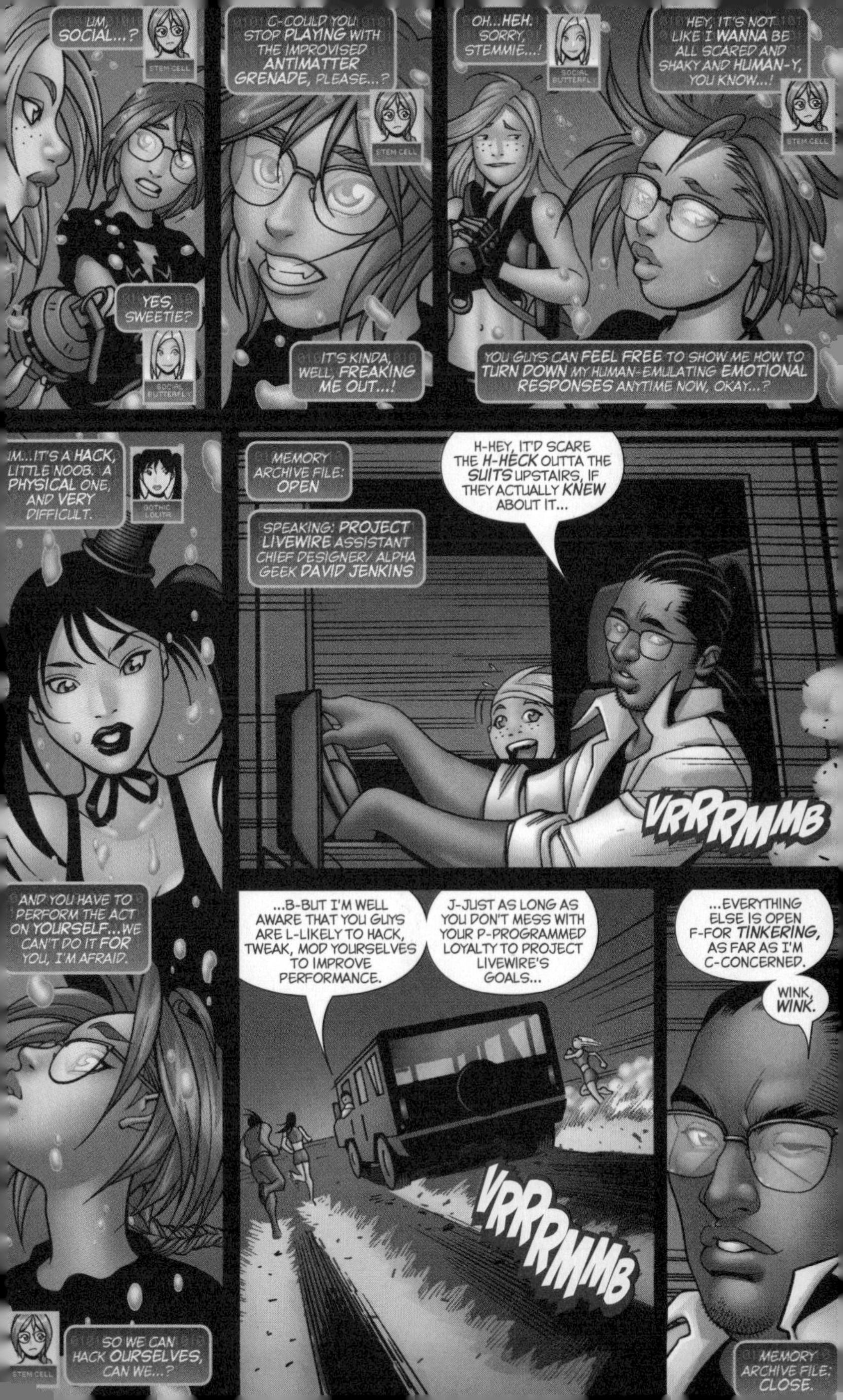
UM, SOCIAL...?
STEM CELL
YES, SWEETIE?
SOCIAL BUTTERFLY
C-COULD YOU STOP PLAYING WITH THE IMPROVISED ANTIMATTER GRENADE, PLEASE...?
STEM CELL
IT'S KINDA, WELL, FREAKING ME OUT...!
OH...HEH. SORRY, STEMMIE...!
SOCIAL BUTTERFLY
HEY, IT'S NOT LIKE I WANNA BE ALL SCARED AND SHAKY AND HUMAN-Y, YOU KNOW...!
STEM CELL
YOU GUYS CAN FEEL FREE TO SHOW ME HOW TO TURN DOWN MY HUMAN-EMULATING EMOTIONAL RESPONSES ANYTIME NOW, OKAY...?
UM...IT'S A HACK, LITTLE NOOB. A PHYSICAL ONE, AND VERY DIFFICULT.
GOTHIC LOLITA
MEMORY ARCHIVE FILE: OPEN
SPEAKING: PROJECT LIVEWIRE ASSISTANT CHIEF DESIGNER/ ALPHA GEEK DAVID JENKINS
H-HEY, IT'D SCARE THE H-HECK OUTTA THE SUITS UPSTAIRS, IF THEY ACTUALLY KNEW ABOUT IT...
VRRRMMB
AND YOU HAVE TO PERFORM THE ACT ON YOURSELF...WE CAN'T DO IT FOR YOU, I'M AFRAID.
STEM CELL
SO WE CAN HACK OURSELVES, CAN WE...?
...B-BUT I'M WELL AWARE THAT YOU GUYS ARE L-LIKELY TO HACK, TWEAK, MOD YOURSELVES TO IMPROVE PERFORMANCE.
J-JUST AS LONG AS YOU DON'T MESS WITH YOUR P-PROGRAMMED LOYALTY TO PROJECT LIVEWIRE'S GOALS...
VRRRMMB
...EVERYTHING ELSE IS OPEN F-FOR TINKERING, AS FAR AS I'M C-CONCERNED.
WINK, WINK.
MEMORY ARCHIVE FILE: CLOSE.

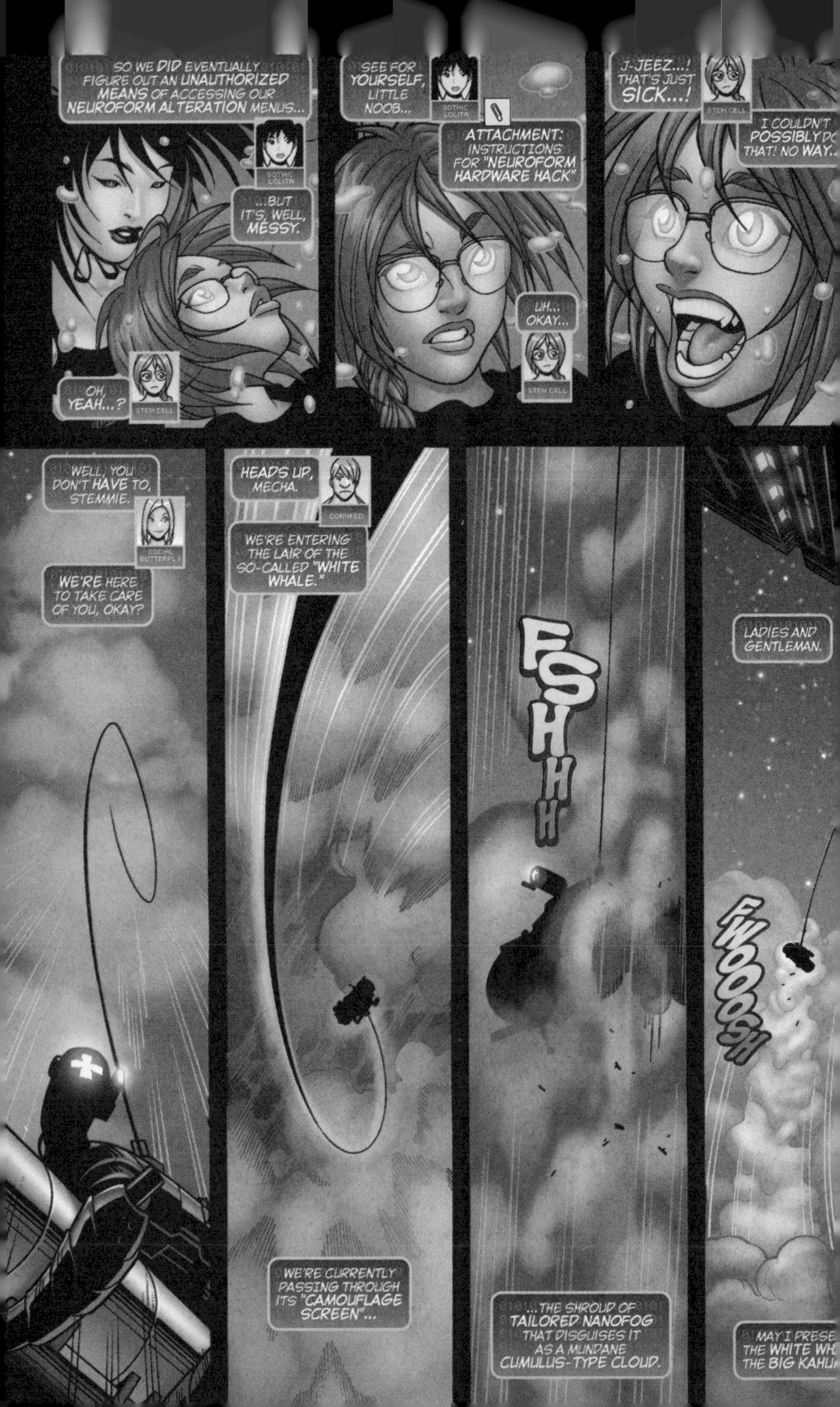
SO WE DID EVENTUALLY FIGURE OUT AN UNAUTHORIZED MEANS OF ACCESSING OUR NEUROFORM ALTERATION MENUS...
GOTHIC LOLITA
...BUT IT'S, WELL, MESSY.
OH, YEAH...?
STEM CELL
SEE FOR YOURSELF, LITTLE NOOB...
GOTHIC LOLITA
ATTACHMENT: INSTRUCTIONS FOR "NEUROFORM HARDWARE HACK"
UH... OKAY...
STEM CELL
J-JEEZ...! THAT'S JUST SICK...!
STEM CELL
I COULDN'T POSSIBLY DO THAT! NO WAY...
WELL, YOU DON'T HAVE TO, STEMMIE.
SOCIAL BUTTERFLY
WE'RE HERE TO TAKE CARE OF YOU, OKAY?
HEADS UP, MECHA.
CORNFED
WE'RE ENTERING THE LAIR OF THE SO-CALLED "WHITE WHALE."
WE'RE CURRENTLY PASSING THROUGH ITS "CAMOUFLAGE SCREEN"...
FSHHH
...THE SHROUD OF TAILORED NANOFOG THAT DISGUISES IT AS A MUNDANE CUMULUS-TYPE CLOUD.
LADIES AND GENTLEMAN.
FWOOOOSH
MAY I PRESE
THE WHITE WH
THE BIG KAHU

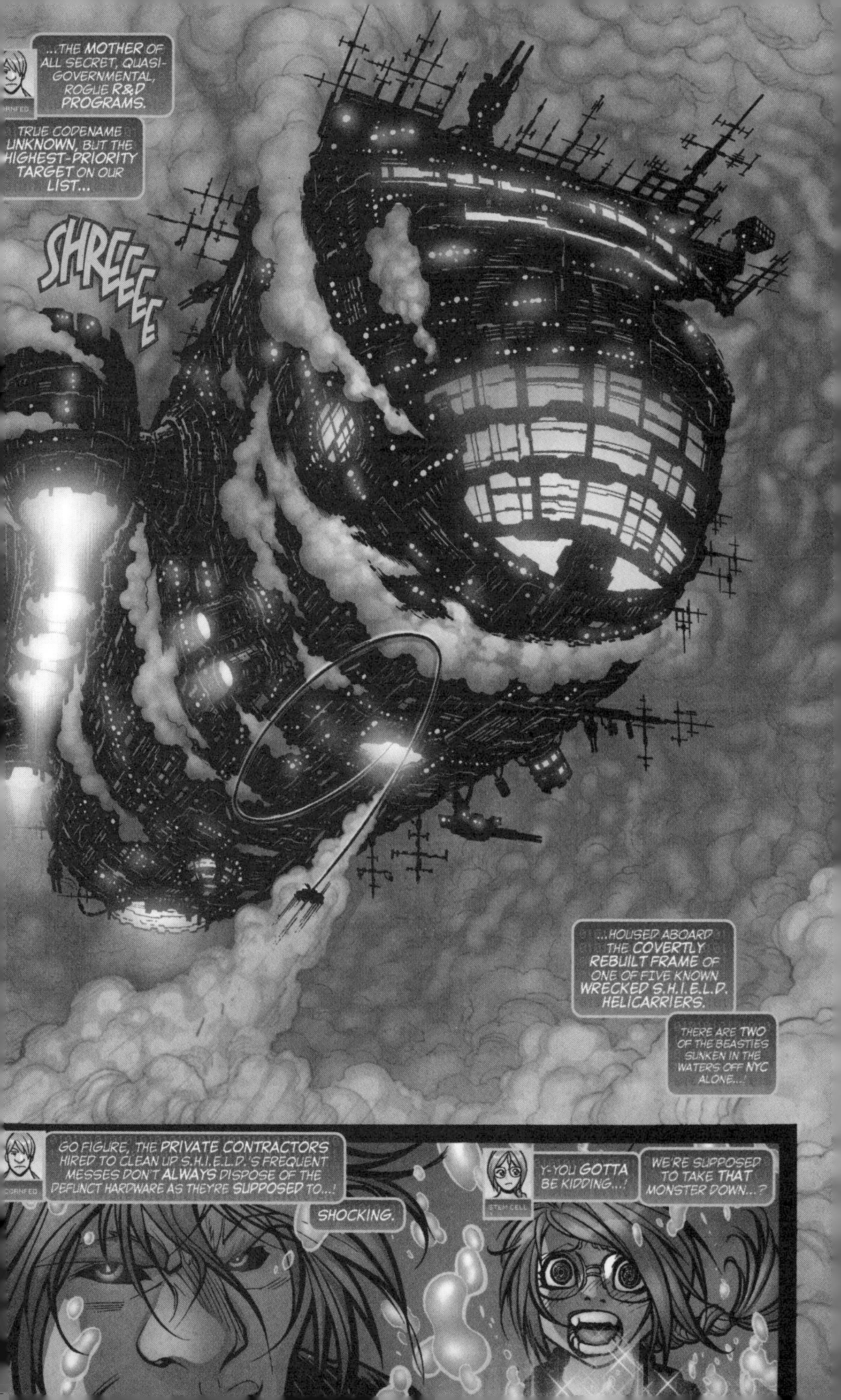

...THE MOTHER OF ALL SECRET, QUASI-GOVERNMENTAL, ROGUE R&D PROGRAMS.
TRUE CODENAME UNKNOWN, BUT THE HIGHEST-PRIORITY TARGET ON OUR LIST...
SHREEEEE
...HOUSED ABOARD THE COVERTLY REBUILT FRAME OF ONE OF FIVE KNOWN WRECKED S.H.I.E.L.D. HELICARRIERS.
THERE ARE TWO OF THE BEASTIES SUNKEN IN THE WATERS OFF NYC ALONE...
GO FIGURE, THE PRIVATE CONTRACTORS HIRED TO CLEAN UP S.H.I.E.L.D.'S FREQUENT MESSES DON'T ALWAYS DISPOSE OF THE DEFUNCT HARDWARE AS THEY'RE SUPPOSED TO...!
SHOCKING.
Y-YOU GOTTA BE KIDDING...!
WE'RE SUPPOSED TO TAKE THAT MONSTER DOWN...?

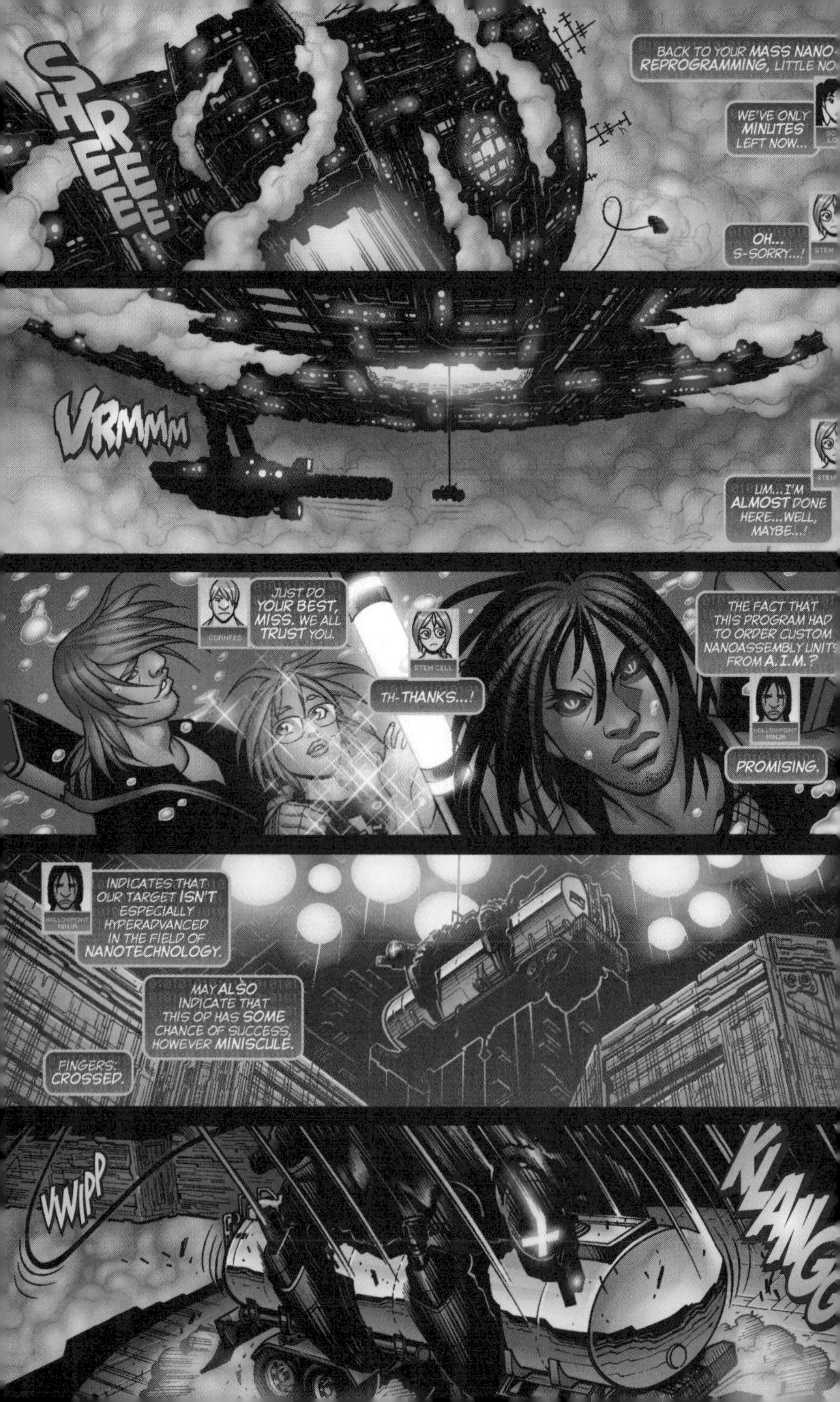
SHREEEE
BACK TO YOUR MASS NANO-REPROGRAMMING, LITTLE NO
WE'VE ONLY MINUTES LEFT NOW...
OH... S-SORRY...!
VRMMM
UM...I'M ALMOST DONE HERE...WELL, MAYBE...!
JUST DO YOUR BEST, MISS. WE ALL TRUST YOU.
CORNFED
STEM CELL
TH-THANKS...!
THE FACT THAT THIS PROGRAM HAD TO ORDER CUSTOM NANOASSEMBLY UNITS FROM A.I.M.?
HOLLOWPOINT NINJA
PROMISING.
HOLLOWPOINT NINJA
INDICATES THAT OUR TARGET ISN'T ESPECIALLY HYPERADVANCED IN THE FIELD OF NANOTECHNOLOGY.
MAY ALSO INDICATE THAT THIS OP HAS SOME CHANCE OF SUCCESS, HOWEVER MINISCULE.
FINGERS: CROSSED.
VWIPP
KLANG

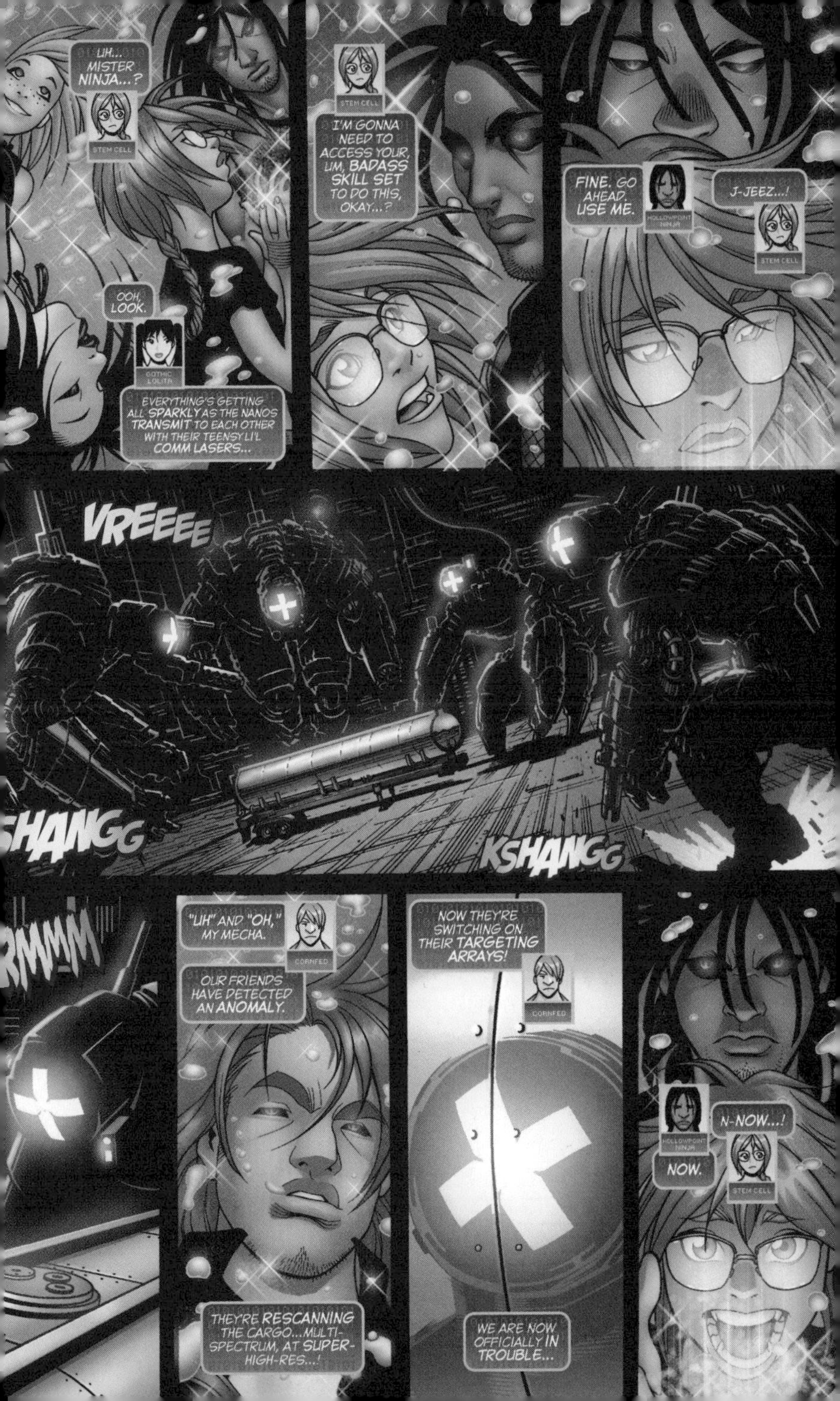

UH... MISTER NINJA...?
STEM CELL
OOH, LOOK.
GOTHIC LOLITA
EVERYTHING'S GETTING ALL SPARKLY AS THE NANOS TRANSMIT TO EACH OTHER WITH THEIR TEENSY LI'L COMM LASERS...
STEM CELL
I'M GONNA NEED TO ACCESS YOUR, UM, BADASS SKILL SET TO DO THIS, OKAY...?
FINE. GO AHEAD. USE ME.
HOLLOWPOINT NINJA
J-JEEZ...!
STEM CELL
VREEEEE
SHANGG
KSHANGG
RMMM
"UH" AND "OH," MY MECHA.
CORNFED
OUR FRIENDS HAVE DETECTED AN ANOMALY.
THEY'RE RESCANNING THE CARGO...MULTI-SPECTRUM, AT SUPER-HIGH-RES...!
NOW THEY'RE SWITCHING ON THEIR TARGETING ARRAYS!
CORNFED
WE ARE NOW OFFICIALLY IN TROUBLE...
HOLLOWPOINT NINJA
NOW.
N-NOW...!
STEM CELL

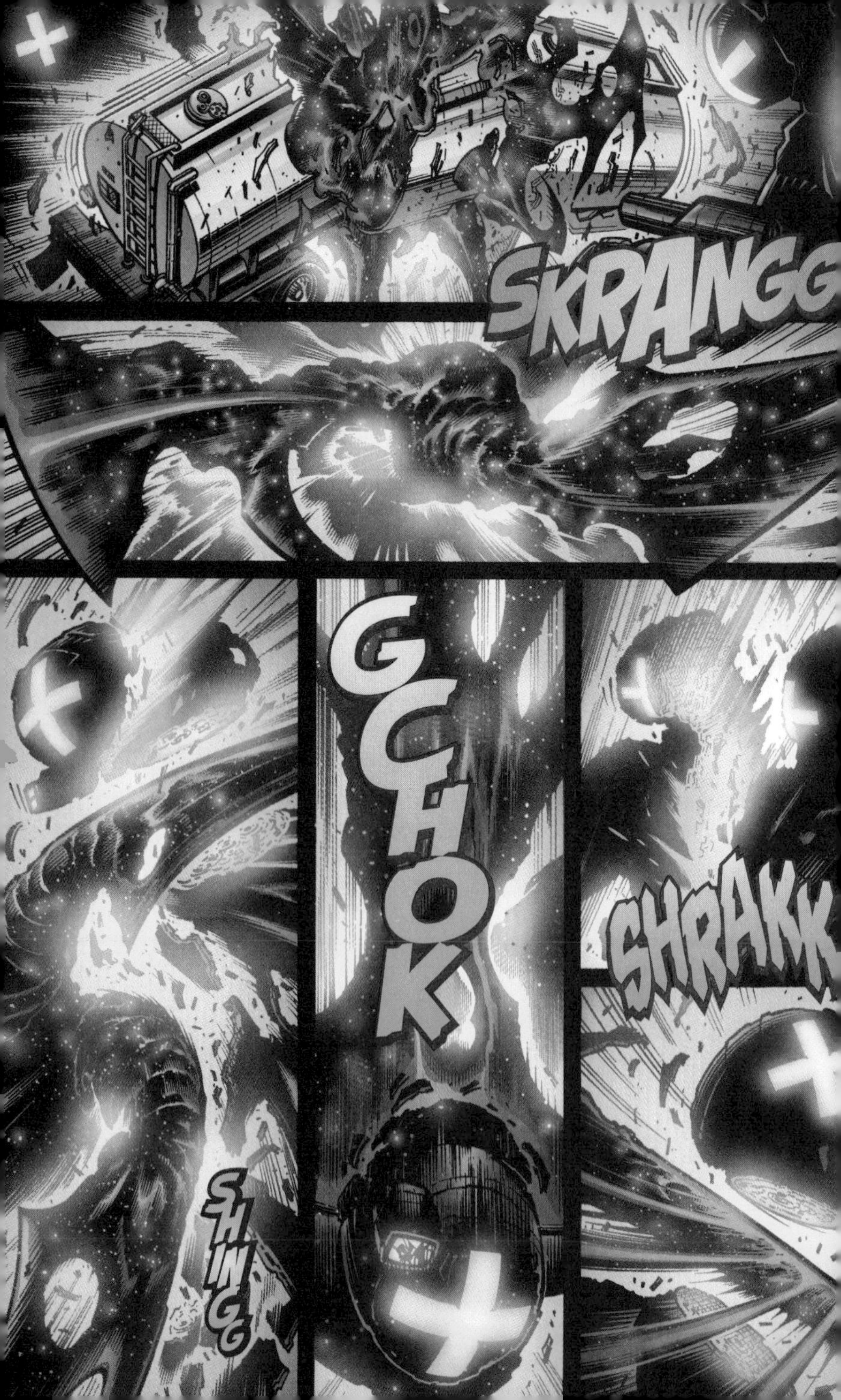
SKRANGG
SHING
GCHOK
SHRAKK

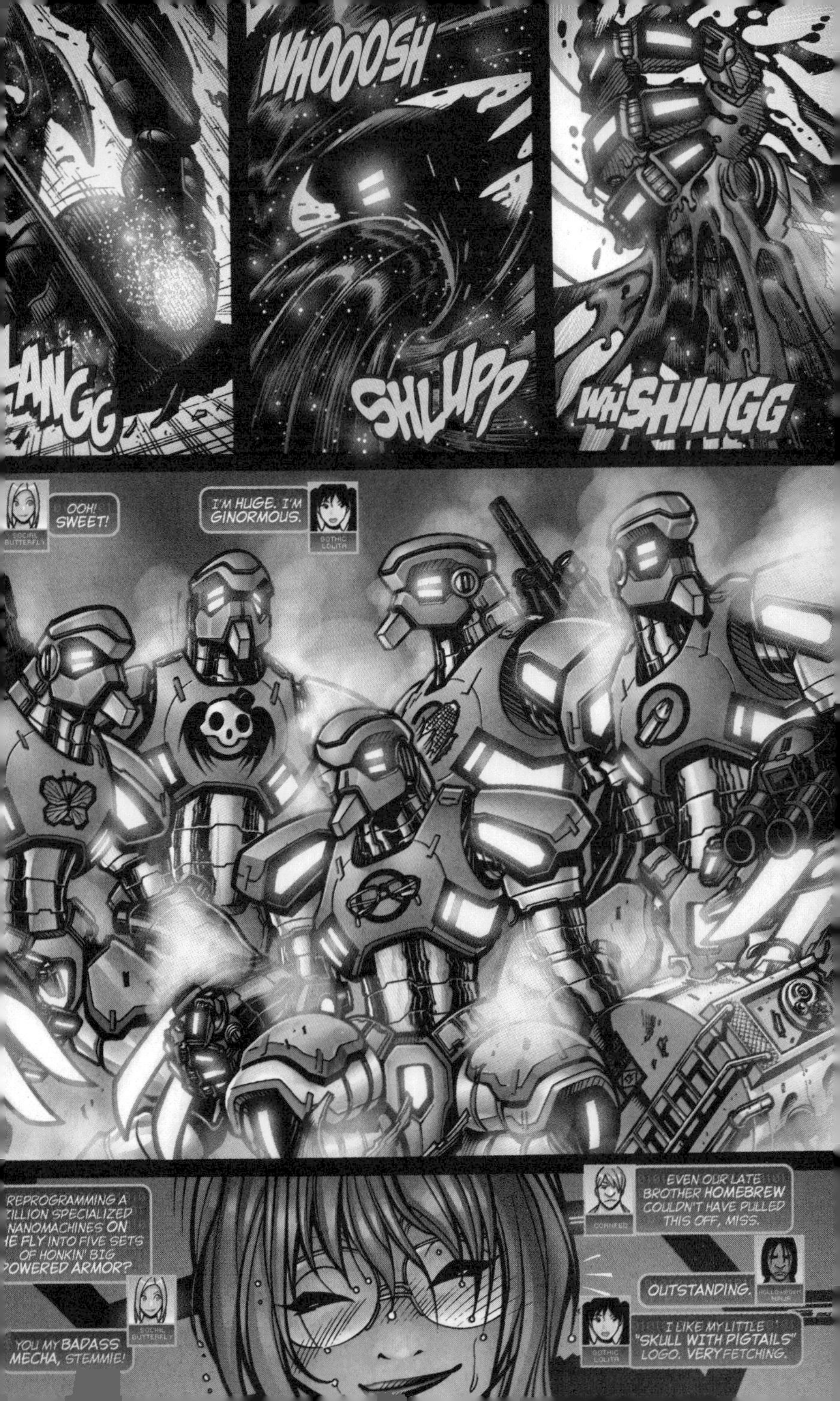
ANGG
WHOOOSH
SHLUPP
WHSHINGG
OOH! SWEET!
SOCIAL BUTTERFLY
I'M HUGE. I'M GINORMOUS.
GOTHIC LOLITA
REPROGRAMMING A ZILLION SPECIALIZED NANOMACHINES ON THE FLY INTO FIVE SETS OF HONKIN' BIG POWERED ARMOR?
SOCIAL BUTTERFLY
YOU MY BADASS MECHA, STEMMIE!
CORNFED
EVEN OUR LATE BROTHER HOMEBREW COULDN'T HAVE PULLED THIS OFF, MISS.
OUTSTANDING.
GOTHIC LOLITA
I LIKE MY LITTLE "SKULL WITH PIGTAILS" LOGO. VERY FETCHING.

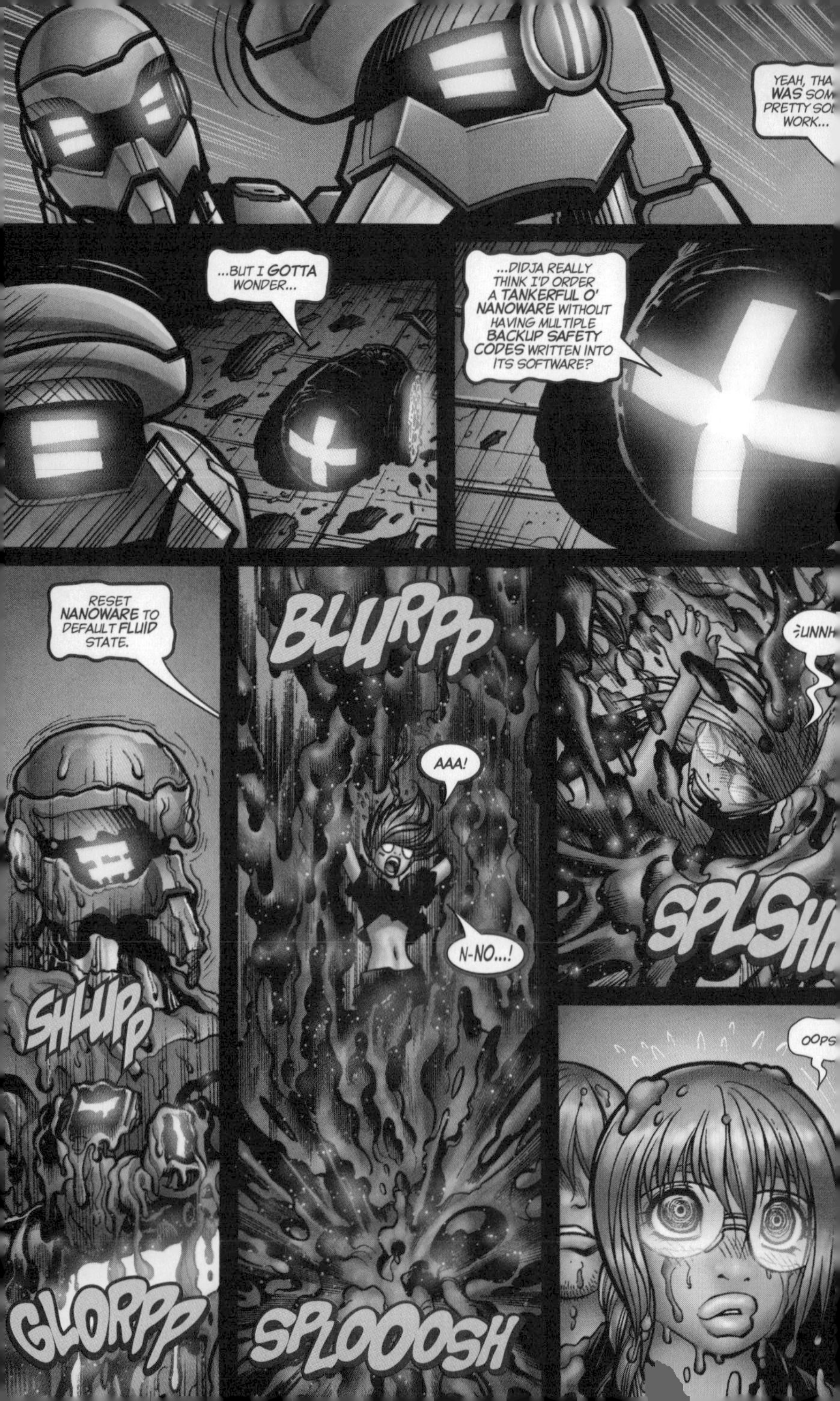

YEAH, THA WAS SOM PRETTY SOL WORK...
...BUT I GOTTA WONDER...
...DIDJA REALLY THINK I'D ORDER A TANKERFUL O' NANOWARE WITHOUT HAVING MULTIPLE BACKUP SAFETY CODES WRITTEN INTO ITS SOFTWARE?
RESET NANOWARE TO DEFAULT FLUID STATE.
SHLUPP
GLORPP
BLURPP
AAA!
N-NO...!
SPLOOOSH
UNNH
SPLSH
OOPS

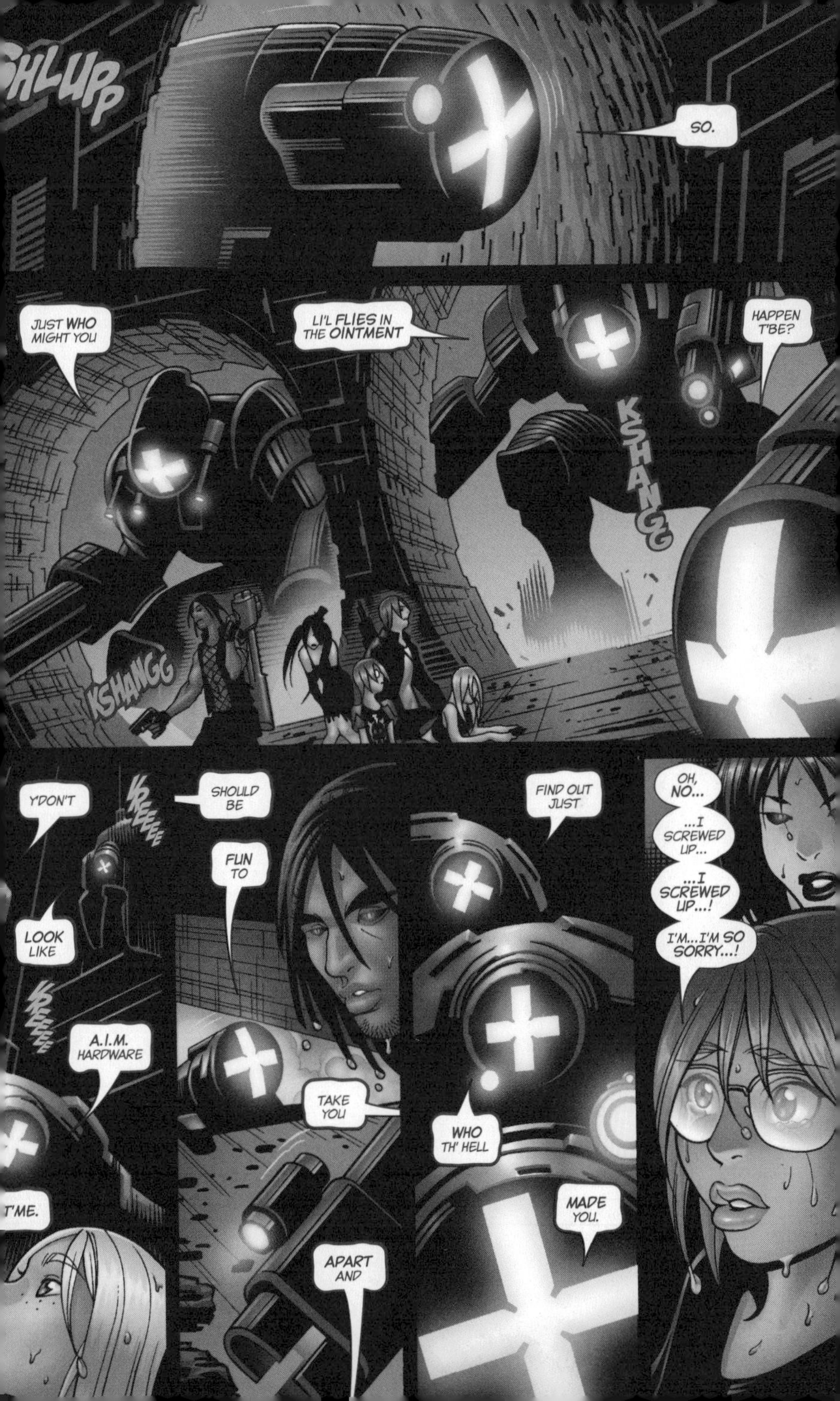
SHLUPP
SO.
JUST WHO MIGHT YOU
LI'L FLIES IN THE OINTMENT
HAPPEN T'BE?
KSHANGG
KSHANGG
Y'DON'T
VREEEE
LOOK LIKE
VREEEE
A.I.M. HARDWARE
T'ME.
SHOULD BE
FUN TO
TAKE YOU
APART AND
FIND OUT JUST
WHO TH' HELL
MADE YOU.
OH, NO...
...I SCREWED UP...
...I SCREWED UP...!
I'M...I'M SO SORRY...!

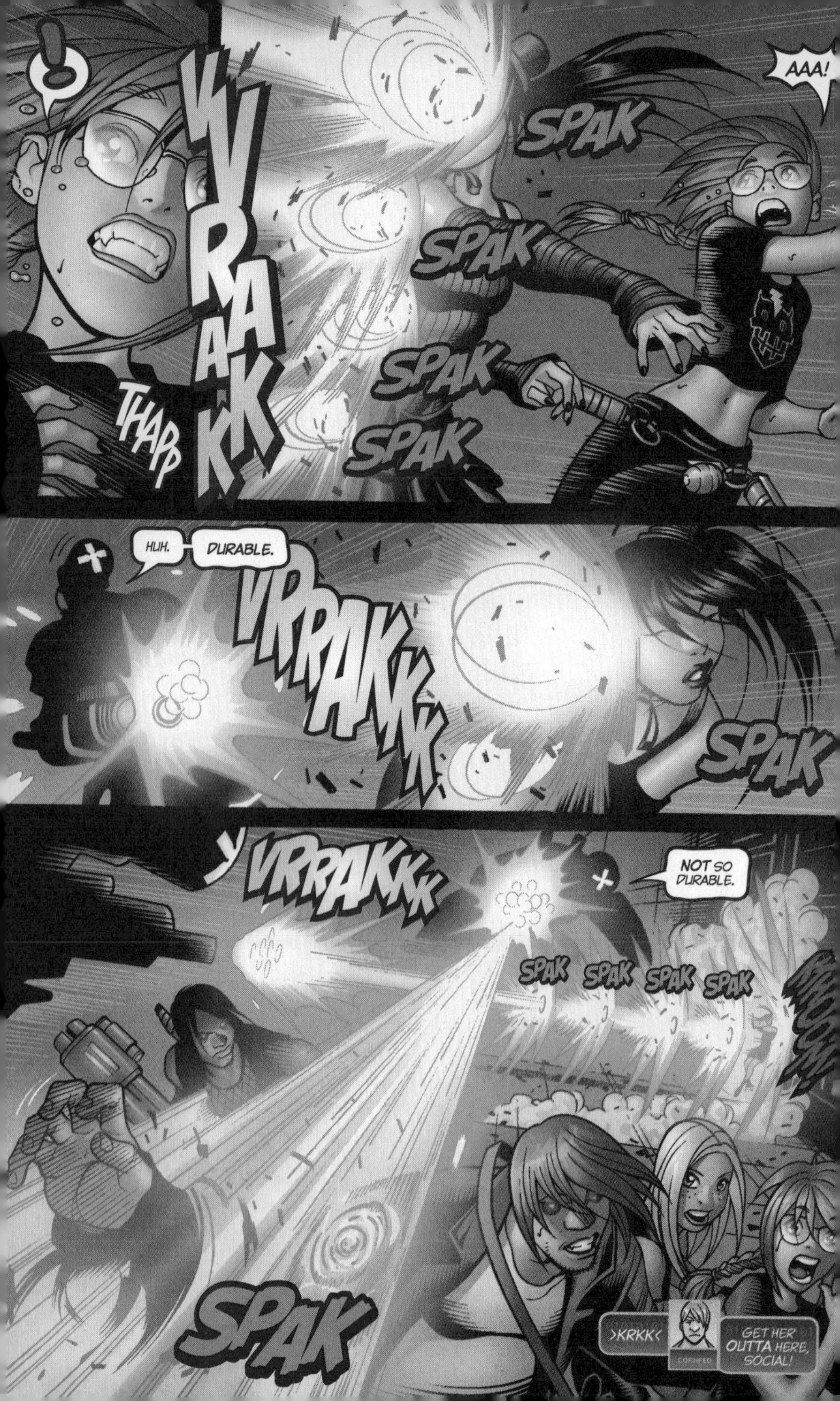
!
WRAKK
THAPP
SPAK
AAA!
SPAK
SPAK
SPAK
HUH.
DURABLE.
VRRAKKK
SPAK
VRRAKKK
NOT SO DURABLE.
SPAK SPAK SPAK SPAK
SPAK
>KRKK<
GET HER OUTTA HERE, SOCIAL!

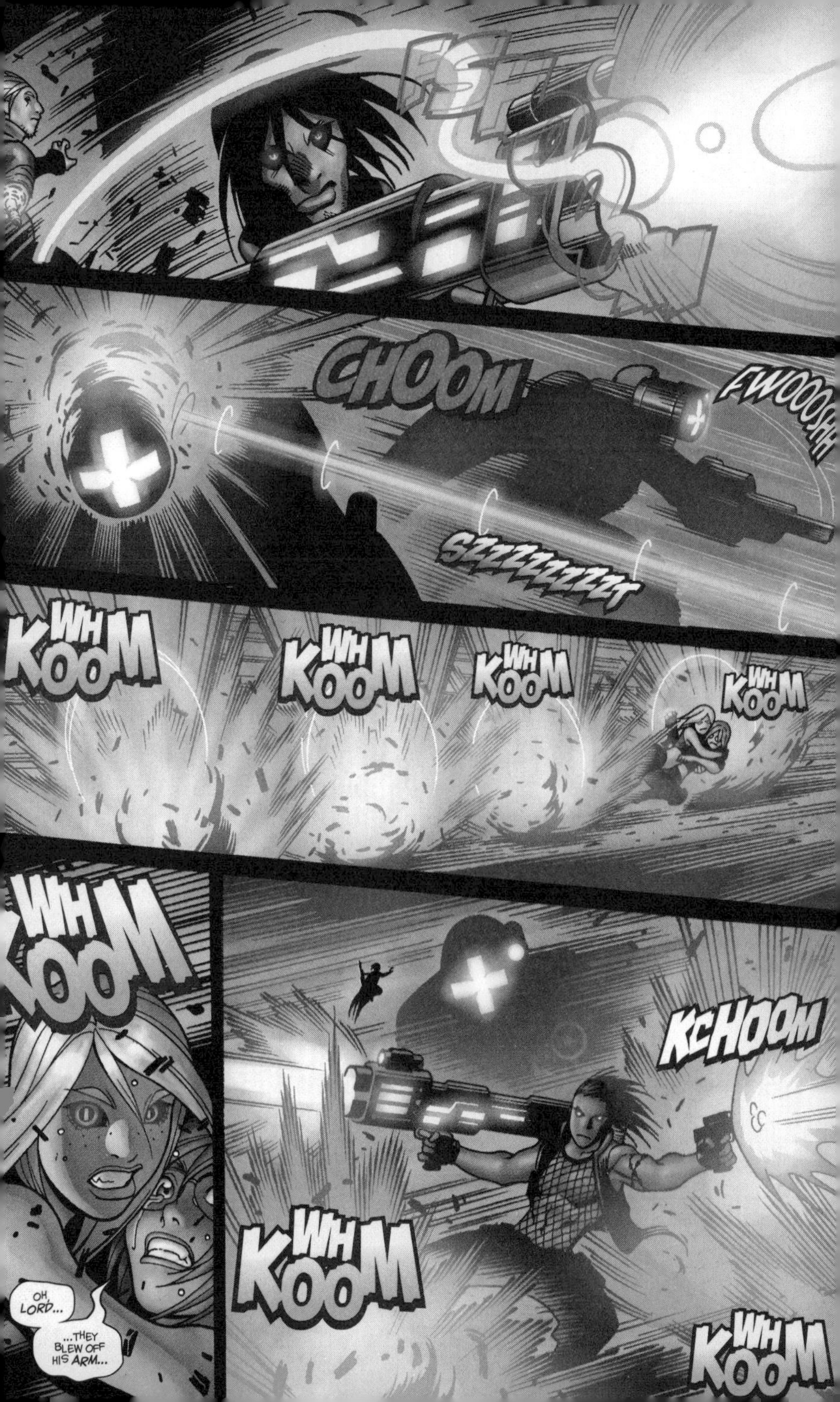
CHOOM
FWOOOSHH
SZZZZZZZZZT
WHKOOM
WHKOOM
WHKOOM
WHKOOM
WHKOOM
KCHOOM
WHKOOM
OH, LORD...
...THEY BLEW OFF HIS ARM...
WHKOOM

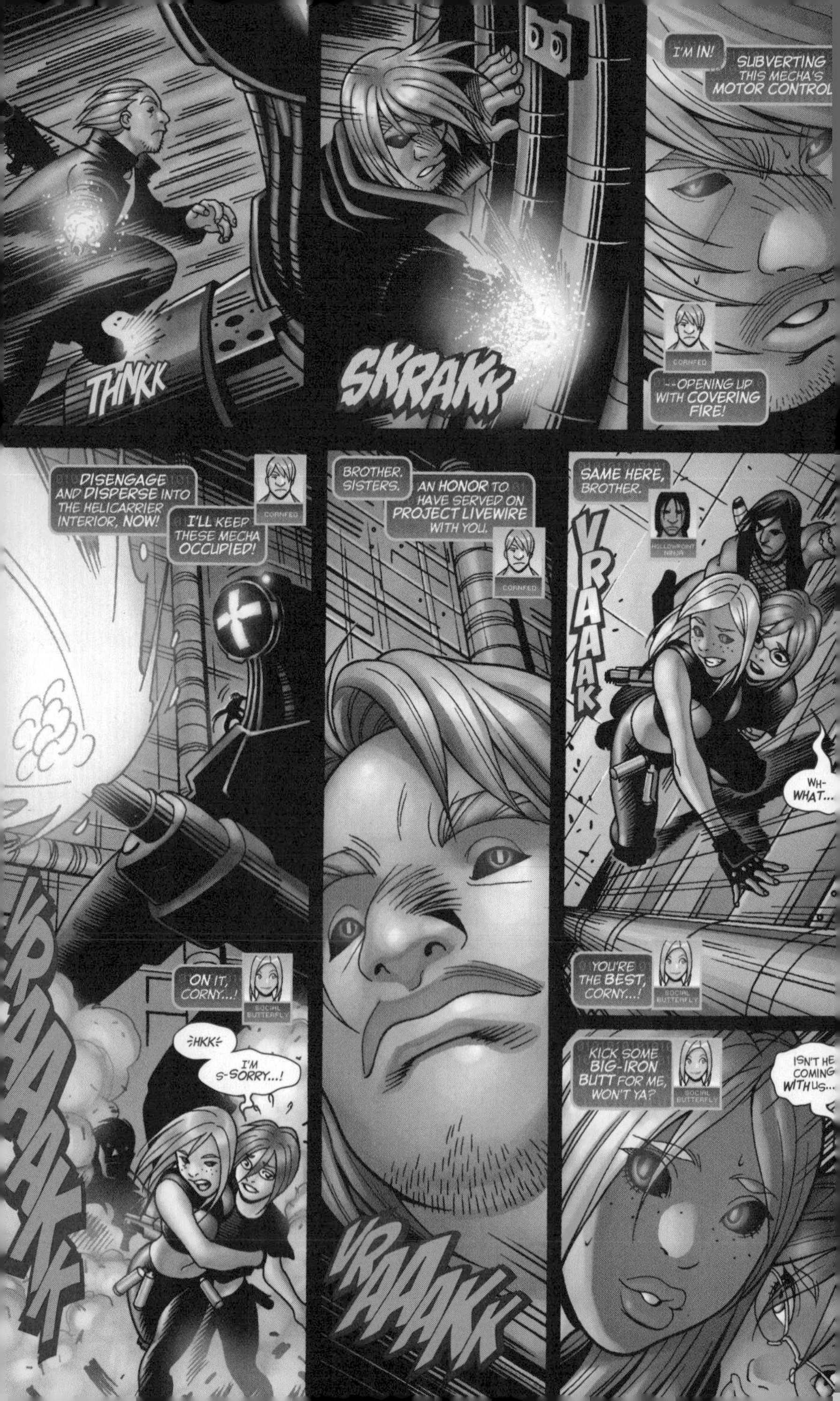
THNKK
SKRAKK
I'M IN!
SUBVERTING THIS MECHA'S MOTOR CONTROL
CORNFED
--OPENING UP WITH COVERING FIRE!
DISENGAGE AND DISPERSE INTO THE HELICARRIER INTERIOR, NOW!
CORNFED
I'LL KEEP THESE MECHA OCCUPIED!
ON IT, CORNY...!
SOCIAL BUTTERFLY
HKK
I'M S-SORRY...!
VRAAAKK
BROTHER. SISTERS.
AN HONOR TO HAVE SERVED ON PROJECT LIVEWIRE WITH YOU.
CORNFED
VRAAKK
SAME HERE, BROTHER.
HOLLOWPOINT NINJA
VRAAAK
WH-WHAT...
YOU'RE THE BEST, CORNY...!
SOCIAL BUTTERFLY
KICK SOME BIG-IRON BUTT FOR ME, WON'T YA?
SOCIAL BUTTERFLY
ISN'T HE COMING WITH US...

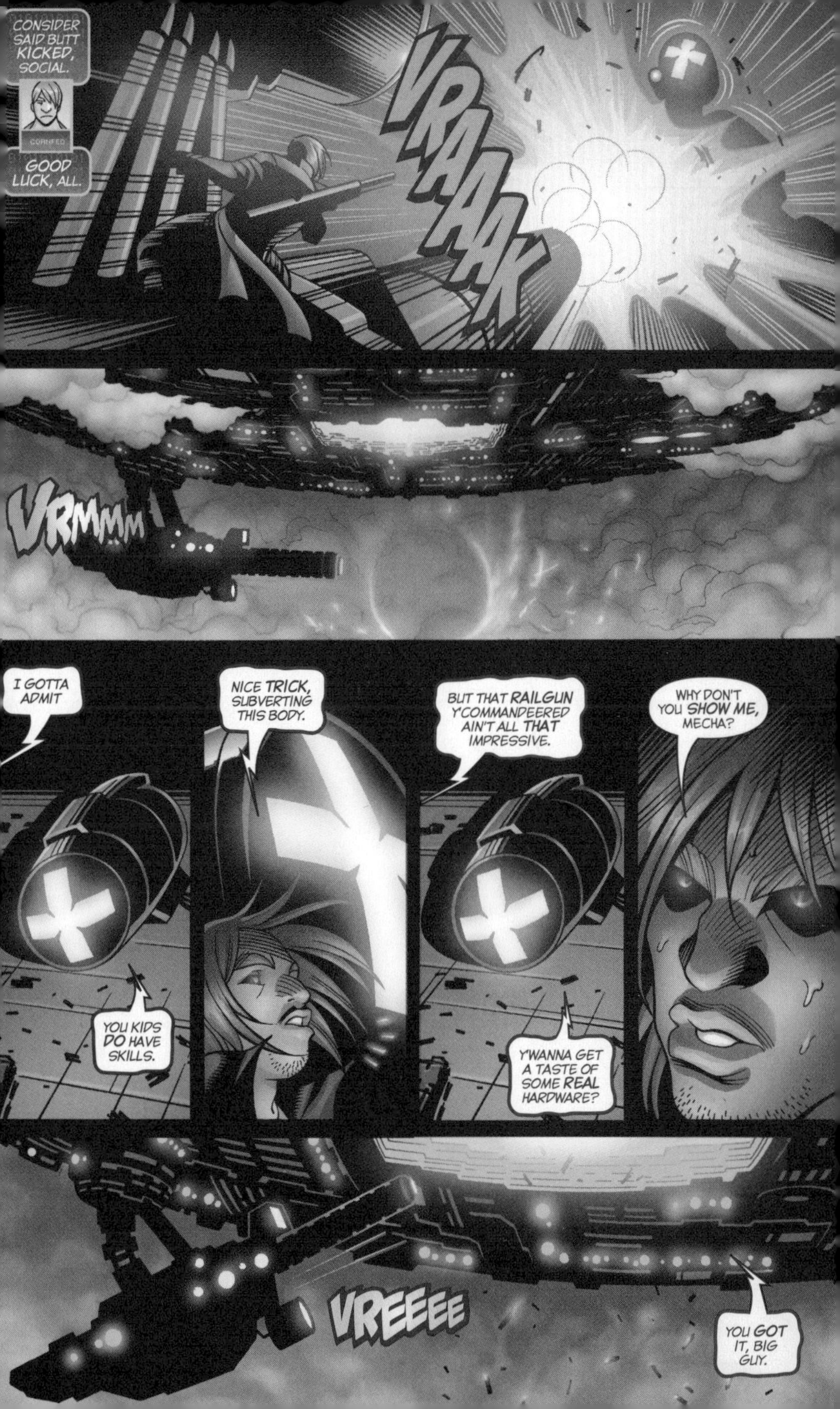
CONSIDER SAID BUTT KICKED, SOCIAL.
CORNFED
GOOD LUCK, ALL.
VRAAAK
VRMMM
I GOTTA ADMIT
YOU KIDS DO HAVE SKILLS.
NICE TRICK, SUBVERTING THIS BODY.
BUT THAT RAILGUN Y'COMMANDEERED AIN'T ALL THAT IMPRESSIVE.
Y'WANNA GET A TASTE OF SOME REAL HARDWARE?
WHY DON'T YOU SHOW ME, MECHA?
VREEEE
YOU GOT IT, BIG GUY.

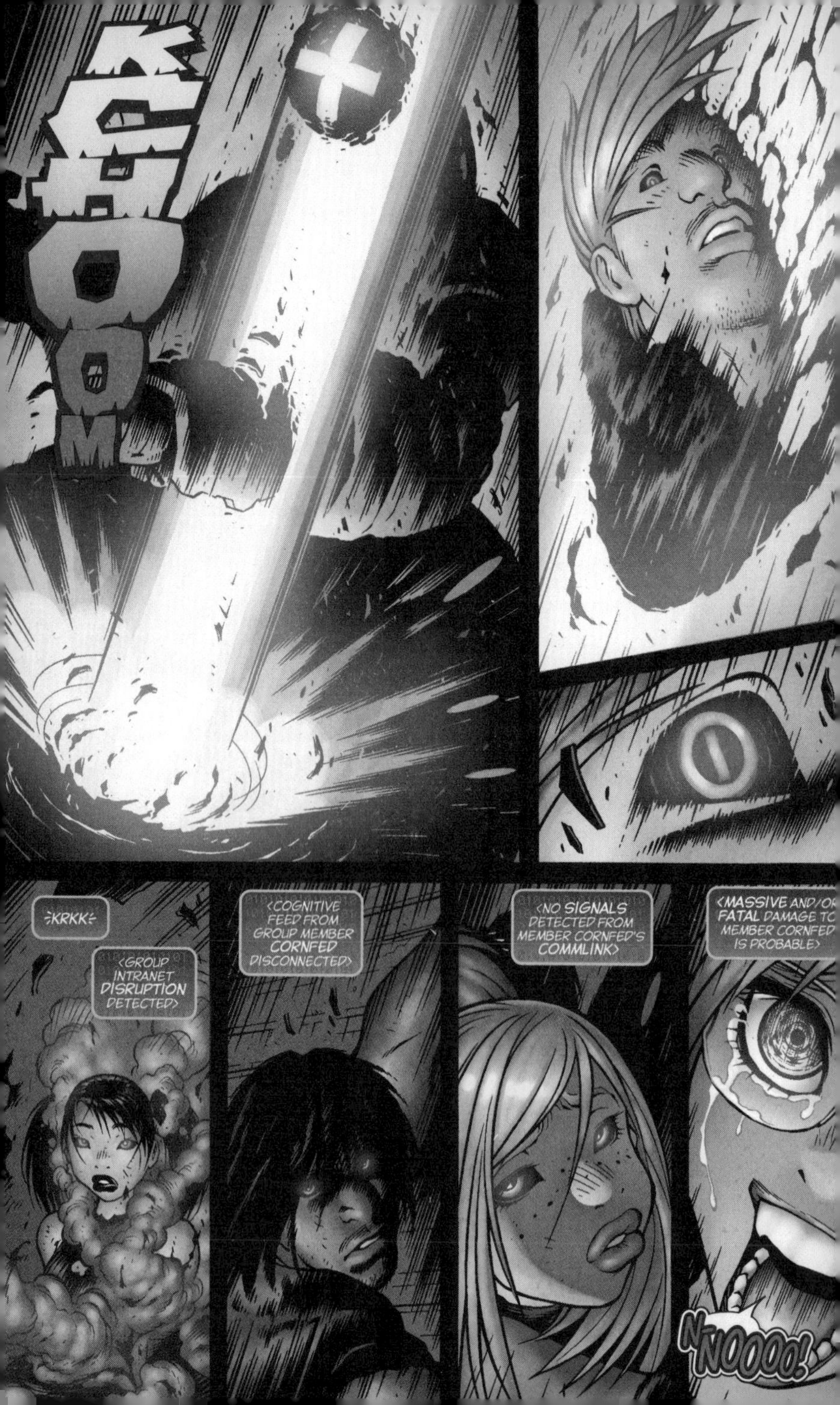
KA-BOOM
KRKK
<GROUP INTRANET DISRUPTION DETECTED>
<COGNITIVE FEED FROM GROUP MEMBER CORNFED DISCONNECTED>
<NO SIGNALS DETECTED FROM MEMBER CORNFED'S COMMLINK>
<MASSIVE AND/OR FATAL DAMAGE TO MEMBER CORNFED IS PROBABLE>
NNOOOO!

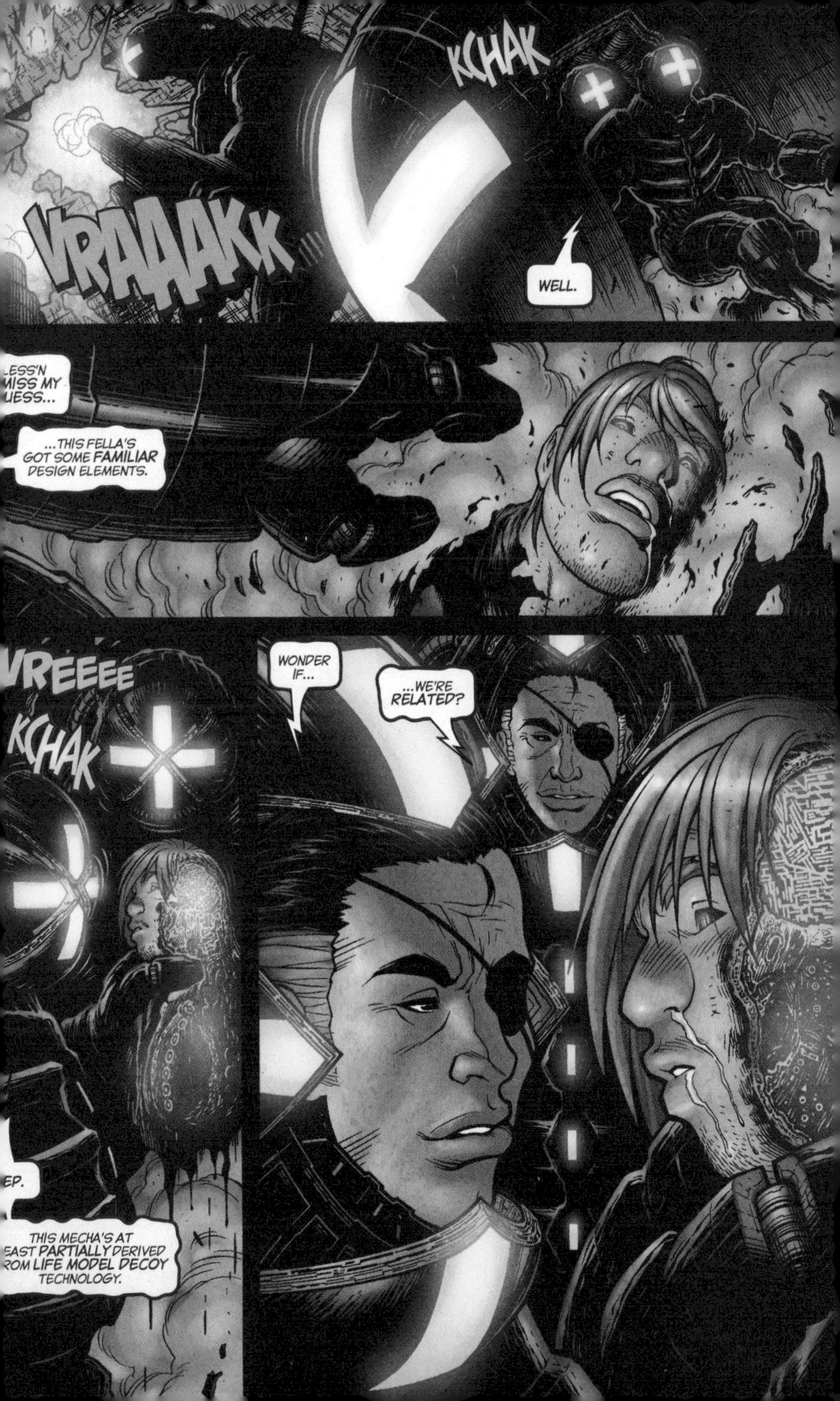
KCHAK
VRAAAKK
WELL.
LESS'N
MISS MY
UESS...
...THIS FELLA'S GOT SOME FAMILIAR DESIGN ELEMENTS.
VREEEE
KCHAK
WONDER IF...
...WE'RE RELATED?
EP.
THIS MECHA'S AT
EAST PARTIALLY DERIVED
ROM LIFE MODEL DECOY
TECHNOLOGY.

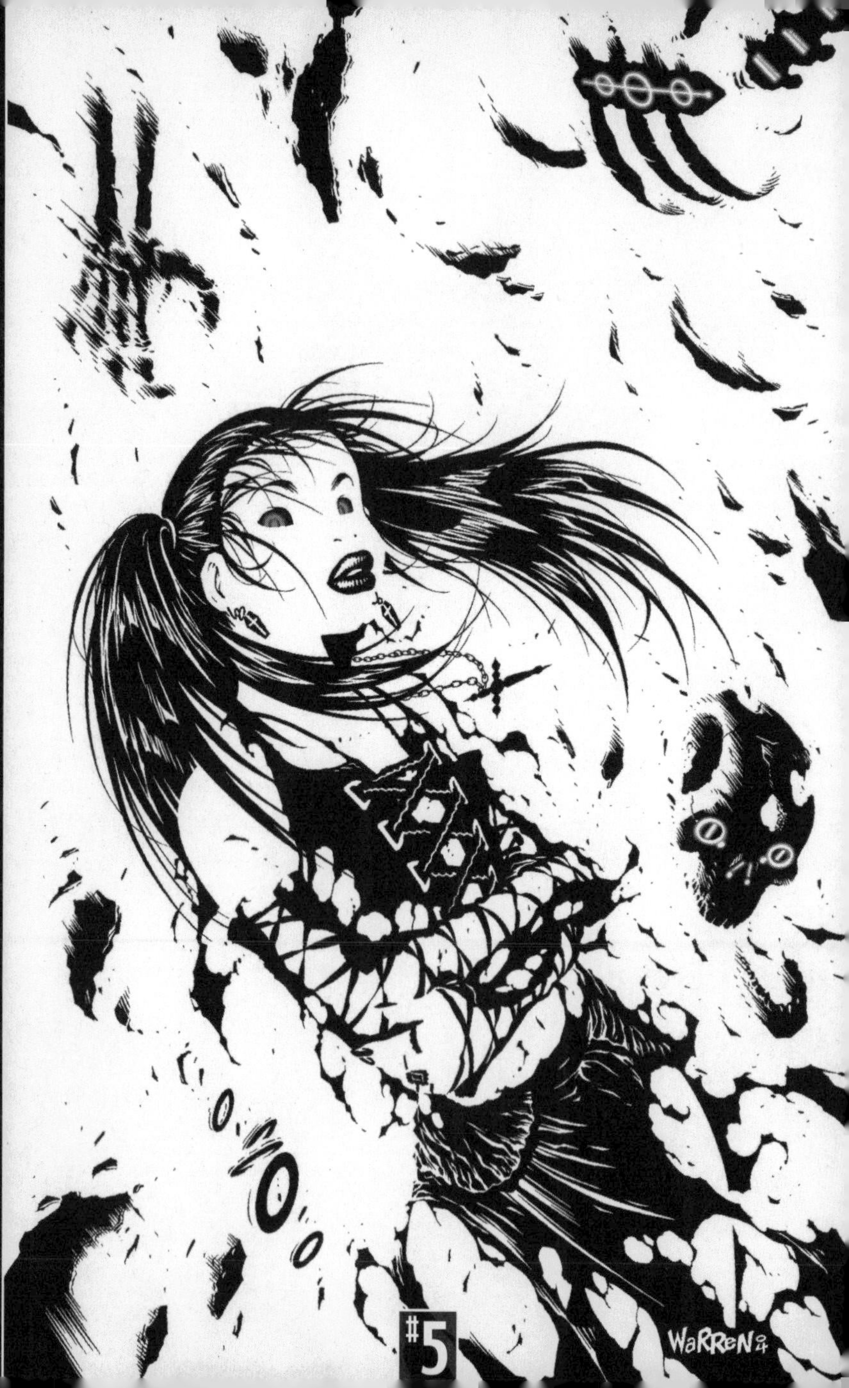
#5
WaRReN 04

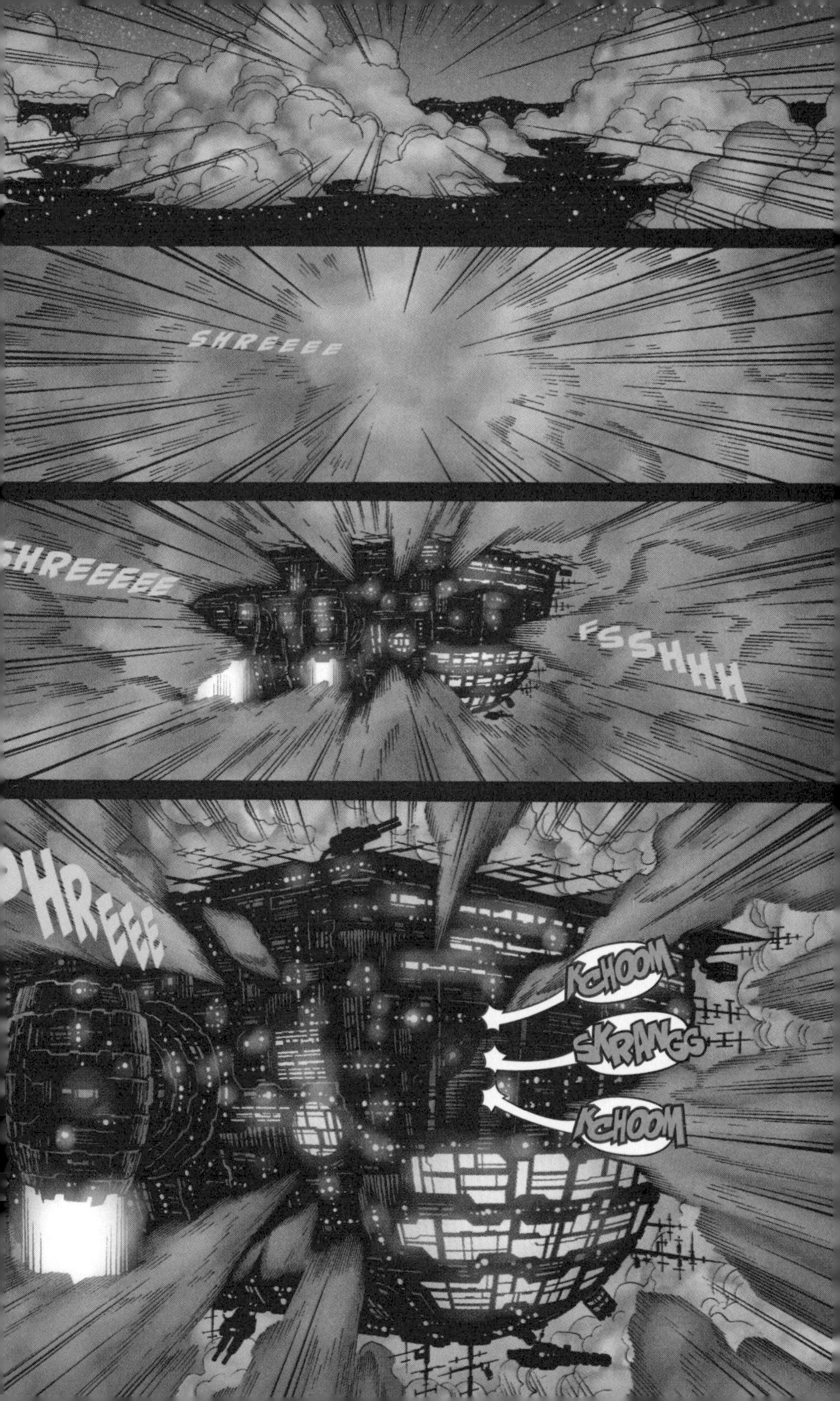

SHREEEEE
SHREEEEEE
FSSHHHH
HREEE
KCHOOM
SKRANGG
KCHOOM

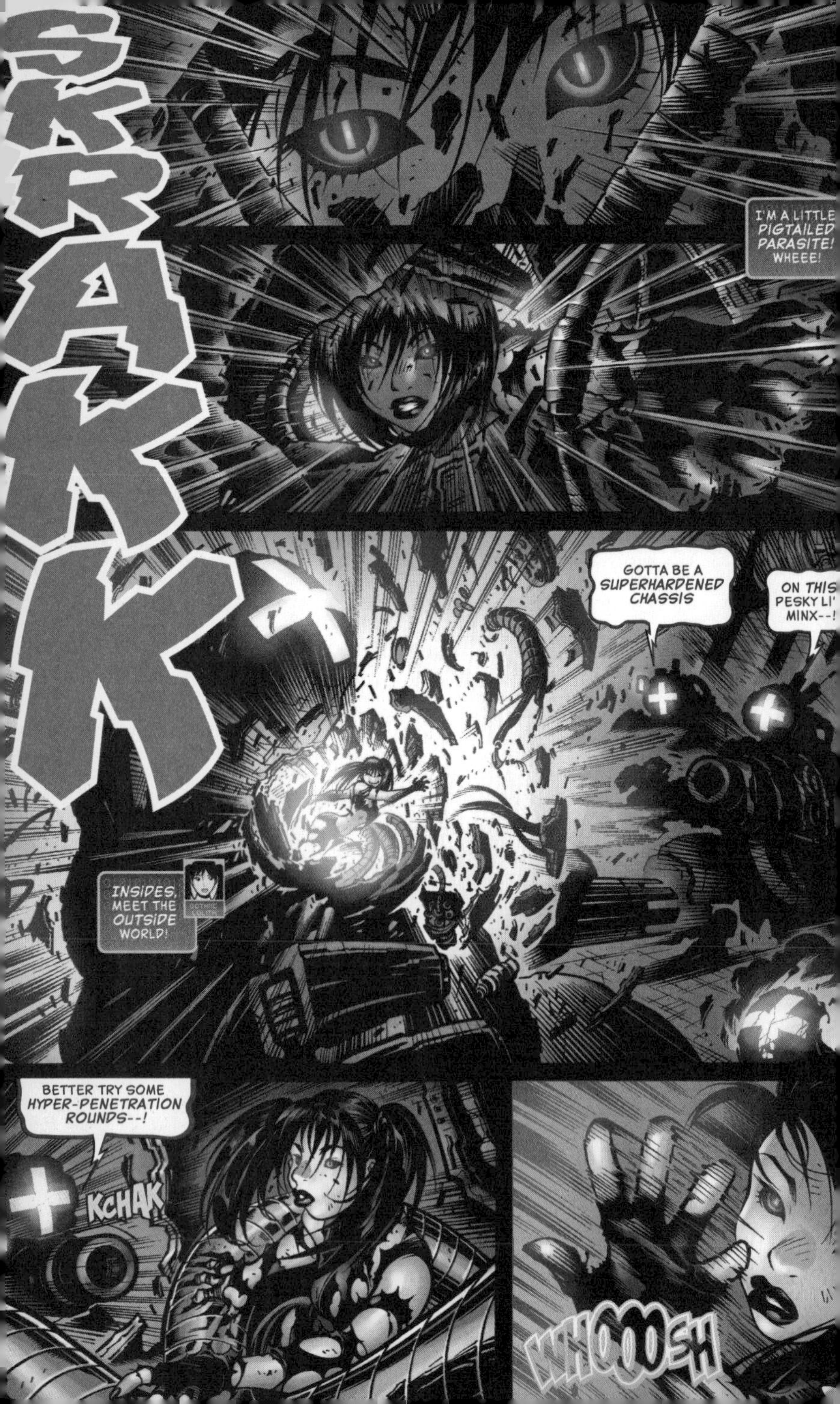
SKRAKK
I'M A LITTLE PIGTAILED PARASITE! WHEEE!
GOTTA BE A SUPERHARDENED CHASSIS
ON THIS PESKY LI' MINX--!
INSIDES, MEET THE OUTSIDE WORLD!
BETTER TRY SOME HYPER-PENETRATION ROUNDS--!
KCHAK
WHOOOSH

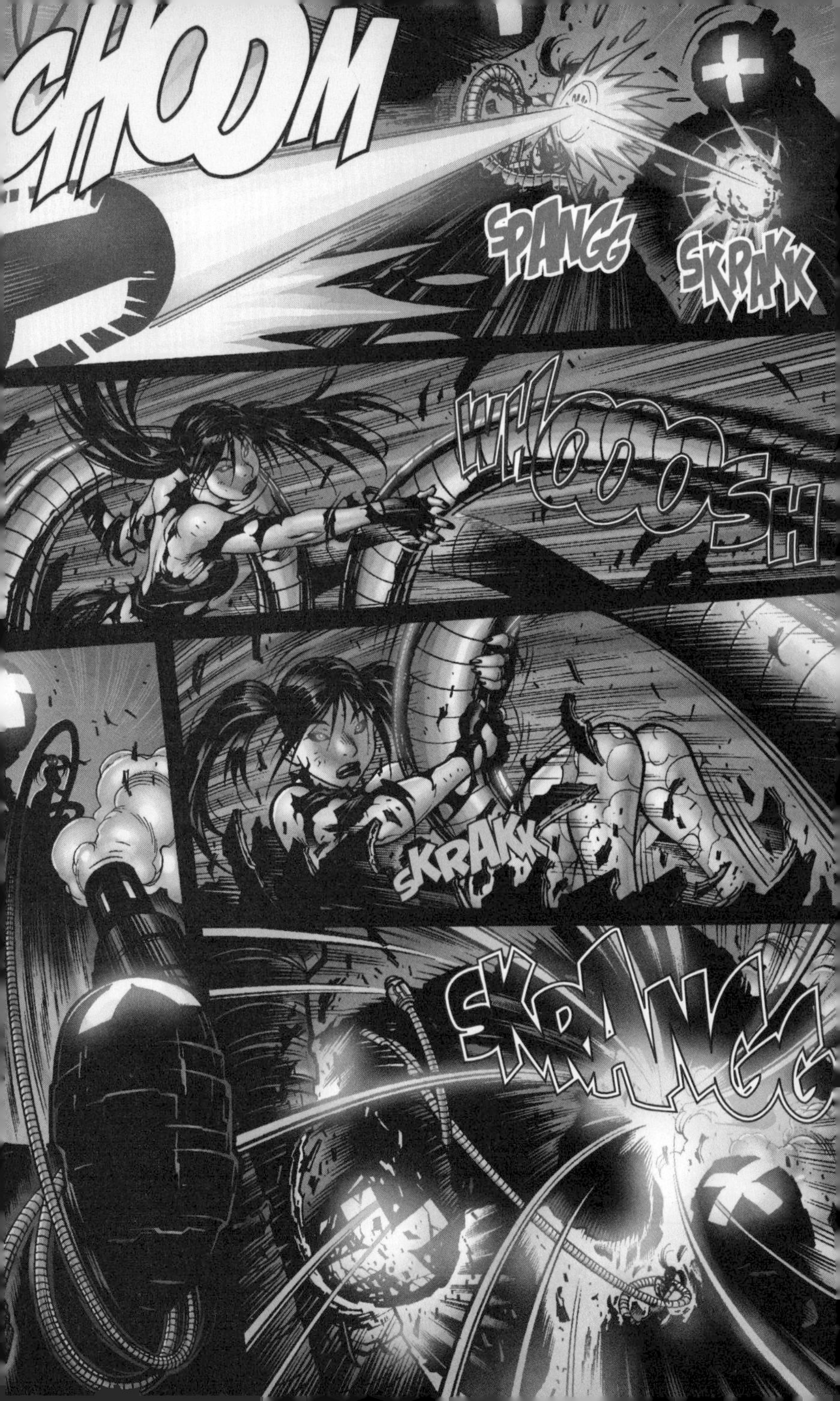

CHOOM
SPANGG
SKRAKK
WHOOOOSH
SKRAKK
SKRANGG

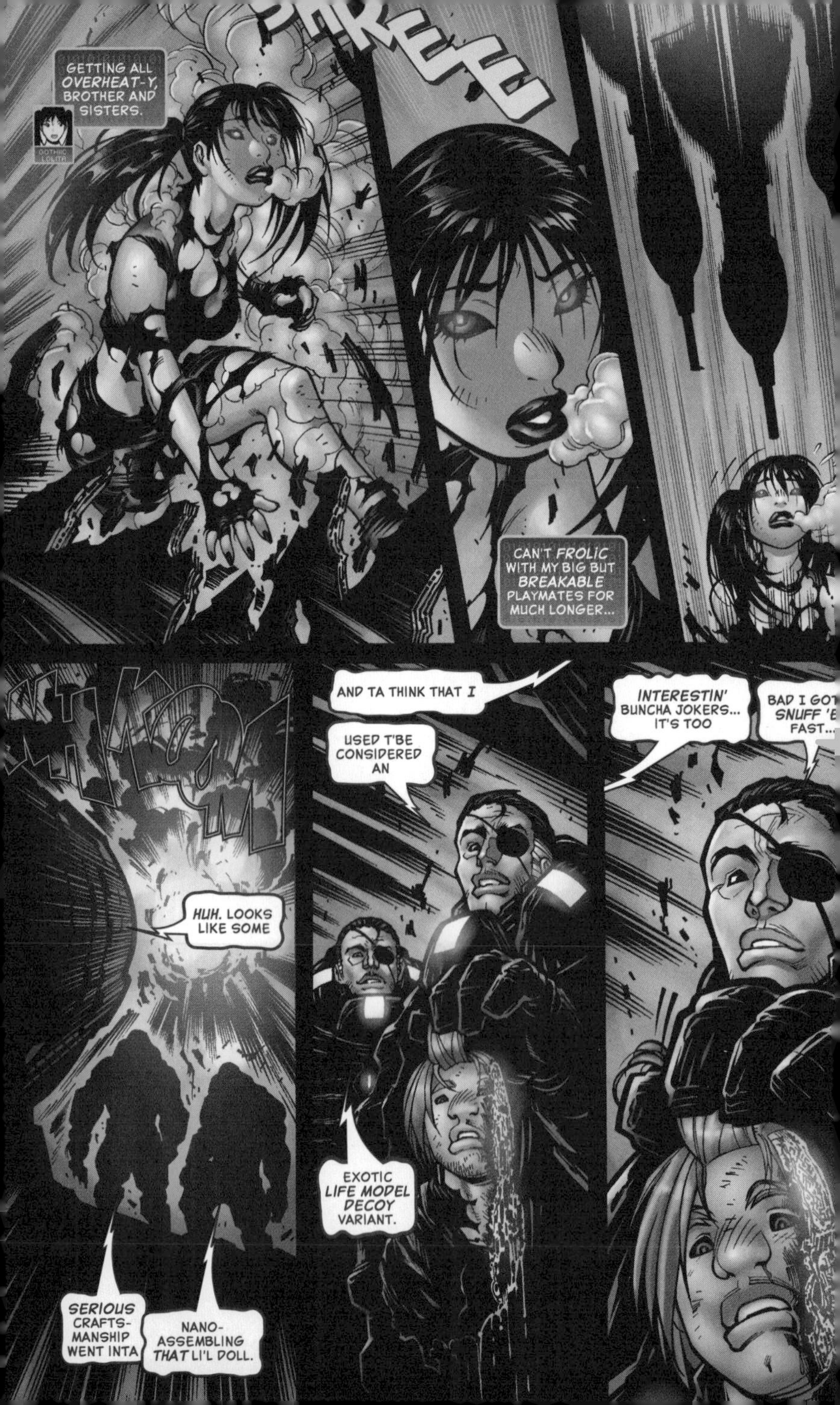

PHREEEE
GETTING ALL OVERHEAT-Y, BROTHER AND SISTERS.
GOTHIC LOLITA
CAN'T FROLIC WITH MY BIG BUT BREAKABLE PLAYMATES FOR MUCH LONGER...
HUH. LOOKS LIKE SOME
SERIOUS CRAFTS-MANSHIP WENT INTA
NANO-ASSEMBLING THAT LI'L DOLL.
AND TA THINK THAT I
USED T'BE CONSIDERED AN
EXOTIC LIFE MODEL DECOY VARIANT.
INTERESTIN' BUNCHA JOKERS... IT'S TOO
BAD I GOT SNUFF 'EM FAST...

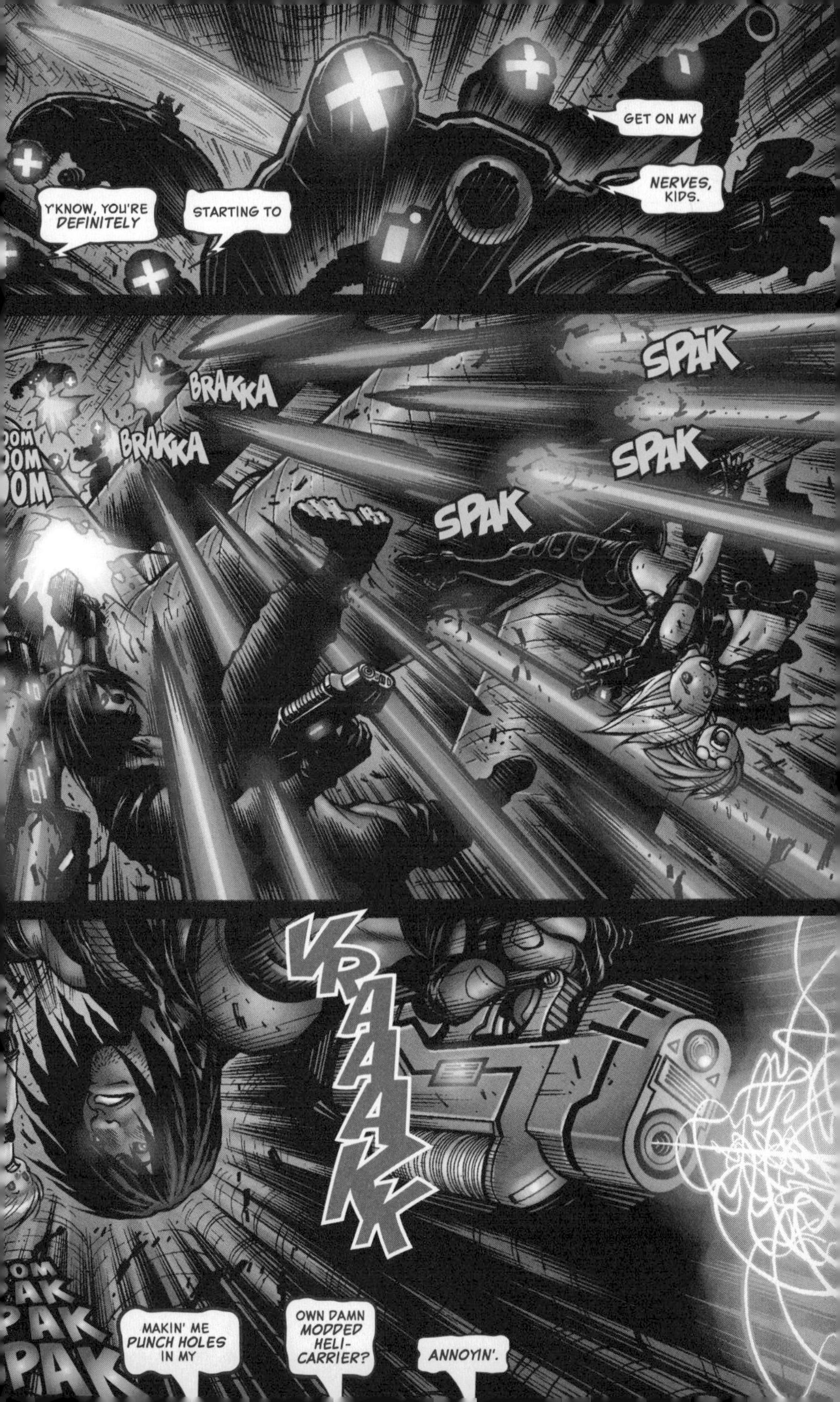

Y'KNOW, YOU'RE DEFINITELY
STARTING TO
GET ON MY
NERVES, KIDS.
BRAKKA
BRAKKA
SPAK
SPAK
SPAK
VRAAAAKK
MAKIN' ME PUNCH HOLES IN MY
OWN DAMN MODDED HELI-CARRIER?
ANNOYIN'.

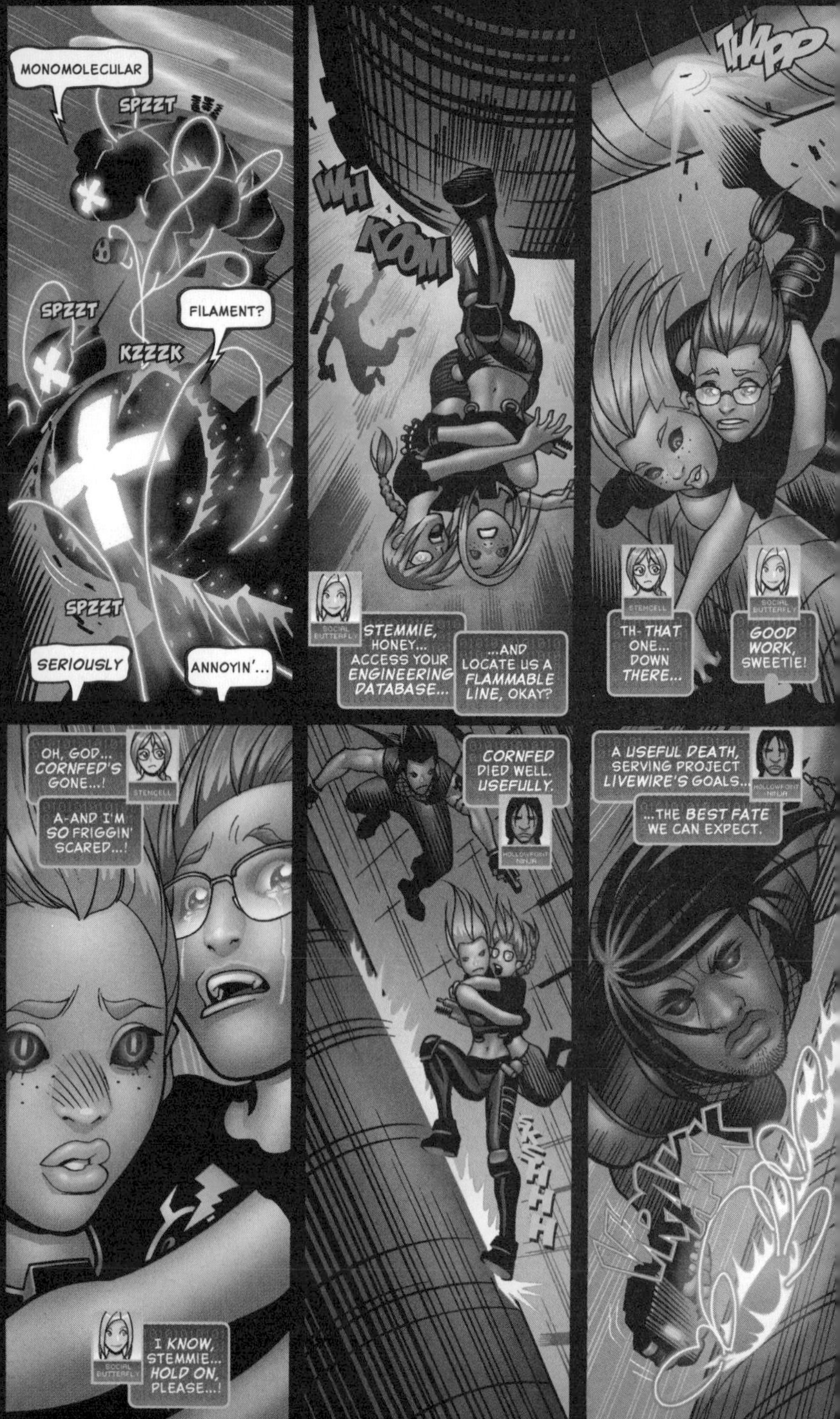
MONOMOLECULAR
SPZZT
SPZZT
FILAMENT?
KZZZK
SPZZT
SERIOUSLY
ANNOYIN'...
WH
KOOM
SOCIAL BUTTERFLY
STEMMIE, HONEY... ACCESS YOUR ENGINEERING DATABASE...
...AND LOCATE US A FLAMMABLE LINE, OKAY?
THAPP
STEMCELL
TH- THAT ONE... DOWN THERE...
SOCIAL BUTTERFLY
GOOD WORK, SWEETIE!
OH, GOD... CORNFED'S GONE...!
STEMCELL
A-AND I'M SO FRIGGIN' SCARED...!
SOCIAL BUTTERFLY
I KNOW, STEMMIE... HOLD ON, PLEASE...!
CORNFED DIED WELL. USEFULLY.
HOLLOWPOINT NINJA
SKHHH
A USEFUL DEATH, SERVING PROJECT LIVEWIRE'S GOALS...
HOLLOWPOINT NINJA
...THE BEST FATE WE CAN EXPECT.

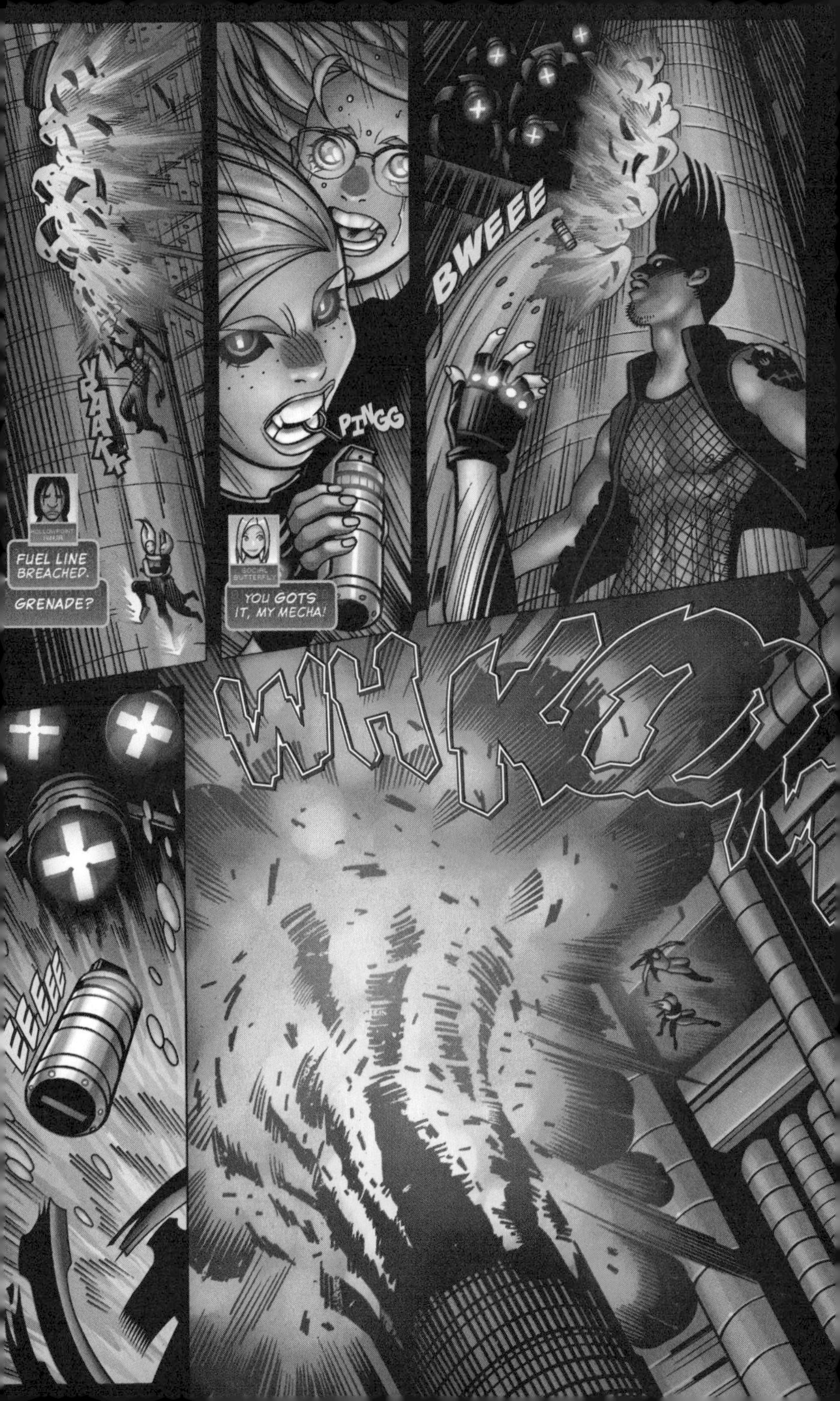
VRAAKK
FUEL LINE BREACHED.
GRENADE?
PINGG
SOCIAL BUTTERFLY
YOU GOTS IT, MY MECHA!
BWEEE
EEEEE

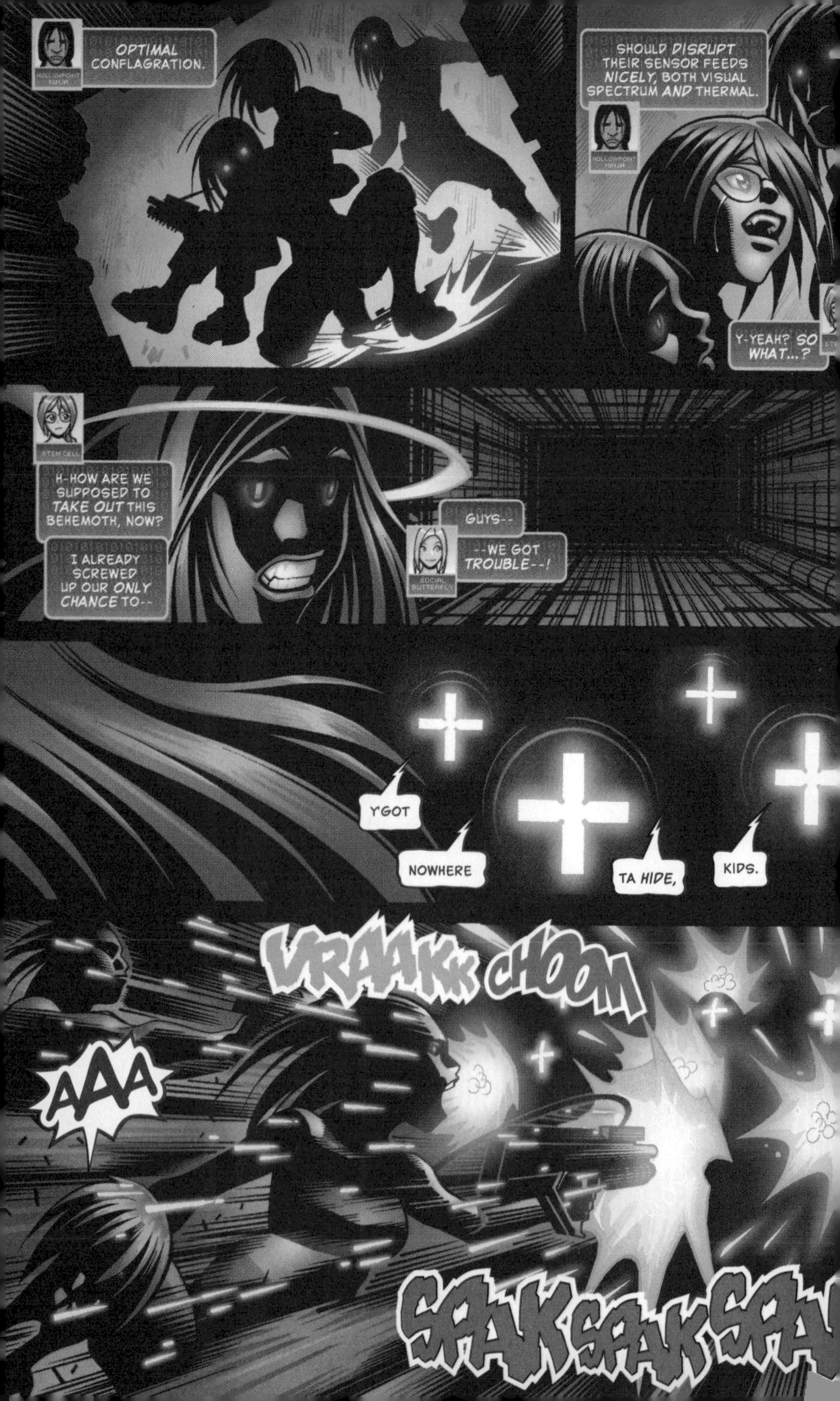
HOLLOWPOINT NINJA
OPTIMAL CONFLAGRATION.
SHOULD DISRUPT THEIR SENSOR FEEDS NICELY, BOTH VISUAL SPECTRUM AND THERMAL.
HOLLOWPOINT NINJA
Y-YEAH? SO WHAT...?
STEM CELL
H-HOW ARE WE SUPPOSED TO TAKE OUT THIS BEHEMOTH, NOW?
I ALREADY SCREWED UP OUR ONLY CHANCE TO--
GUYS--
--WE GOT TROUBLE--!
SOCIAL BUTTERFLY
Y'GOT
NOWHERE
TA HIDE,
KIDS.
VRAAKK CHOOM
AAA
SPAK SPAK SPA

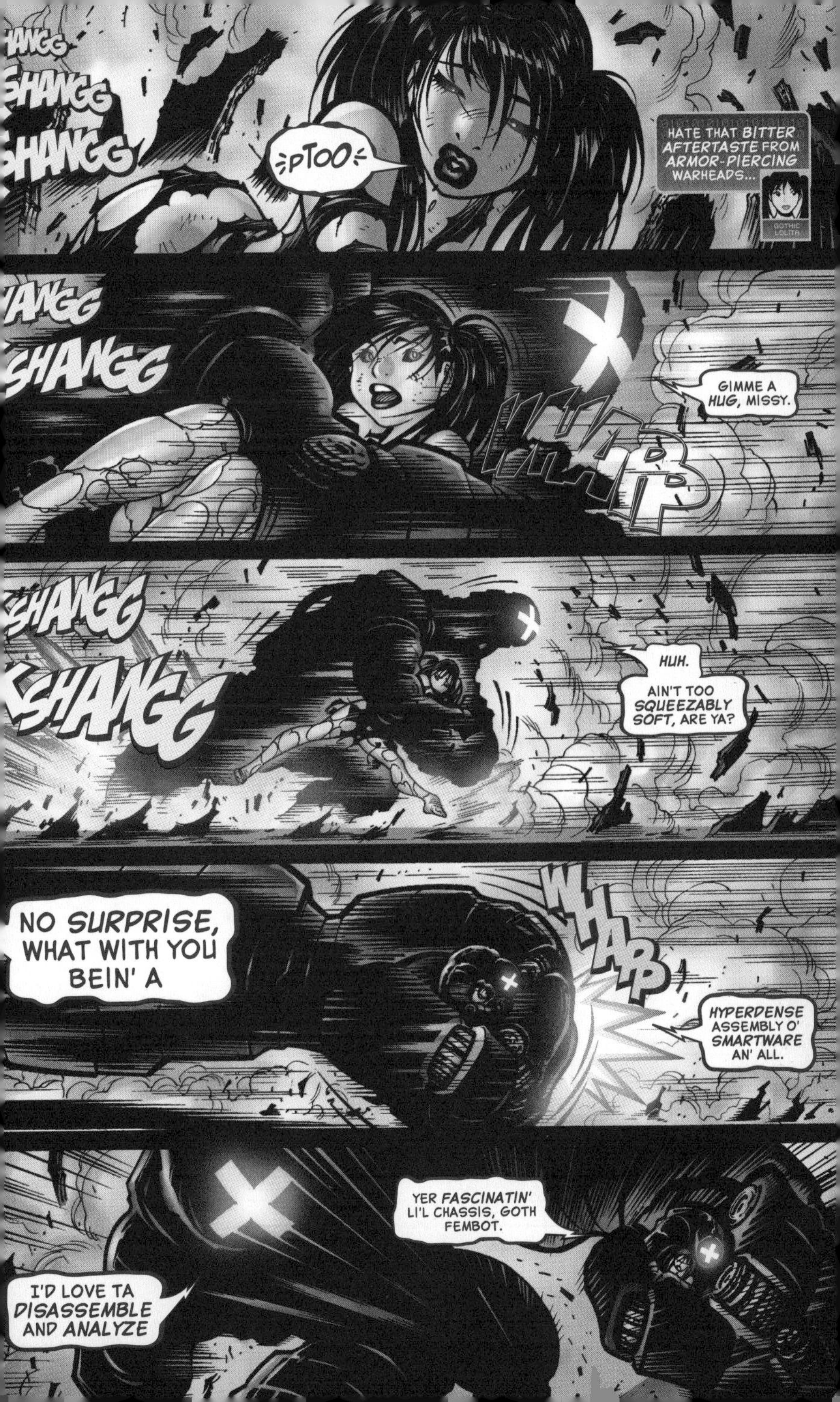
SHANGG
SHANGG
SHANGG
PTOO
HATE THAT BITTER AFTERTASTE FROM ARMOR-PIERCING WARHEADS...
GOTHIC LOLITA
SHANGG
SHANGG
GIMME A HUG, MISSY.
SHANGG
SHANGG
HUH.
AIN'T TOO SQUEEZABLY SOFT, ARE YA?
NO SURPRISE, WHAT WITH YOU BEIN' A
WHAP
HYPERDENSE ASSEMBLY O' SMARTWARE AN' ALL.
YER FASCINATIN' LI'L CHASSIS, GOTH FEMBOT.
I'D LOVE TA DISASSEMBLE AND ANALYZE

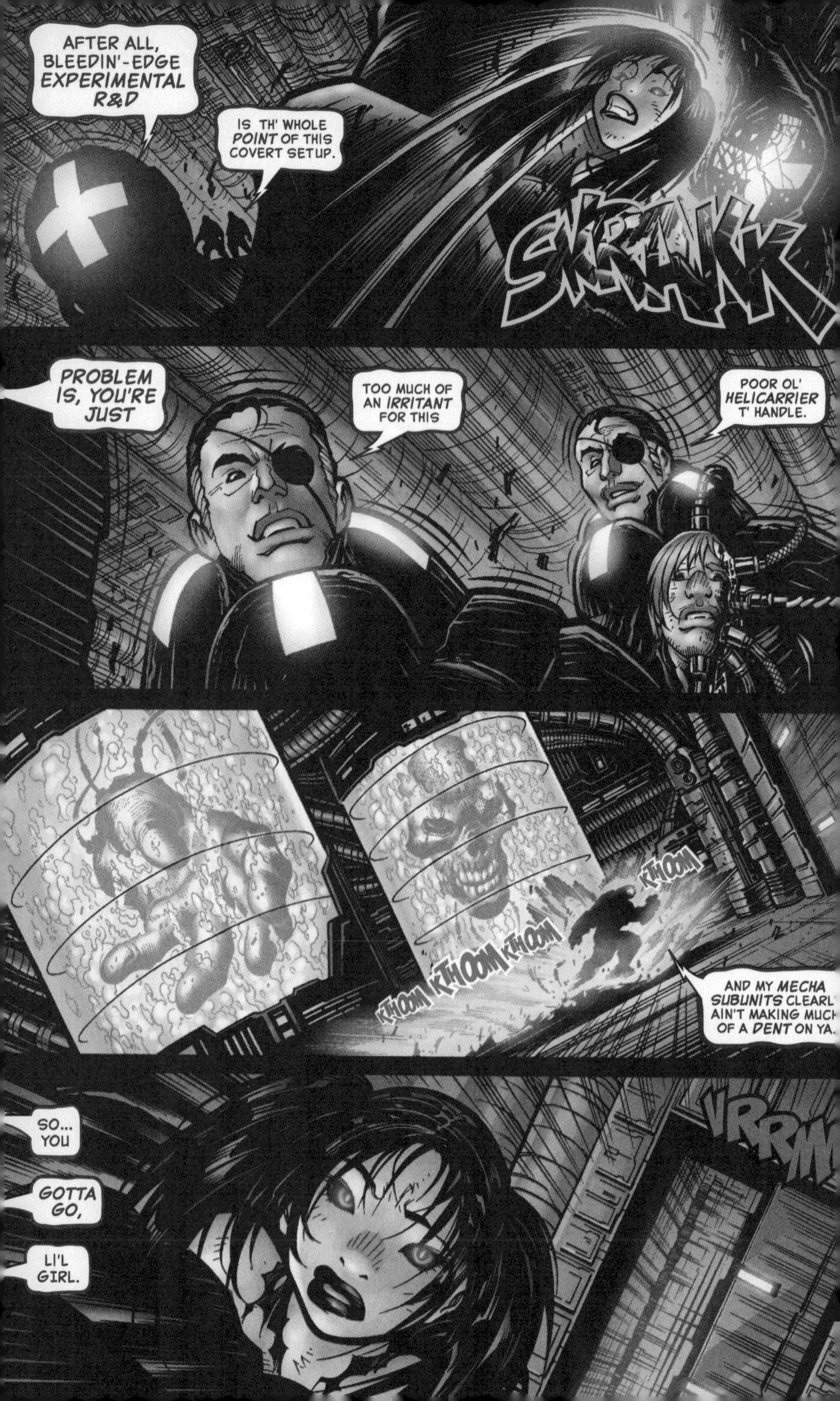
AFTER ALL, BLEEDIN'-EDGE EXPERIMENTAL R&D
IS TH' WHOLE POINT OF THIS COVERT SETUP.
SKRAKK
PROBLEM IS, YOU'RE JUST
TOO MUCH OF AN IRRITANT FOR THIS
POOR OL' HELICARRIER T' HANDLE.
KTHOOM KTHOOM KTHOOM KTHOOM
AND MY MECHA SUBUNITS CLEARL AIN'T MAKING MUC OF A DENT ON YA.
VRRM
SO... YOU
GOTTA GO,
LI'L GIRL.

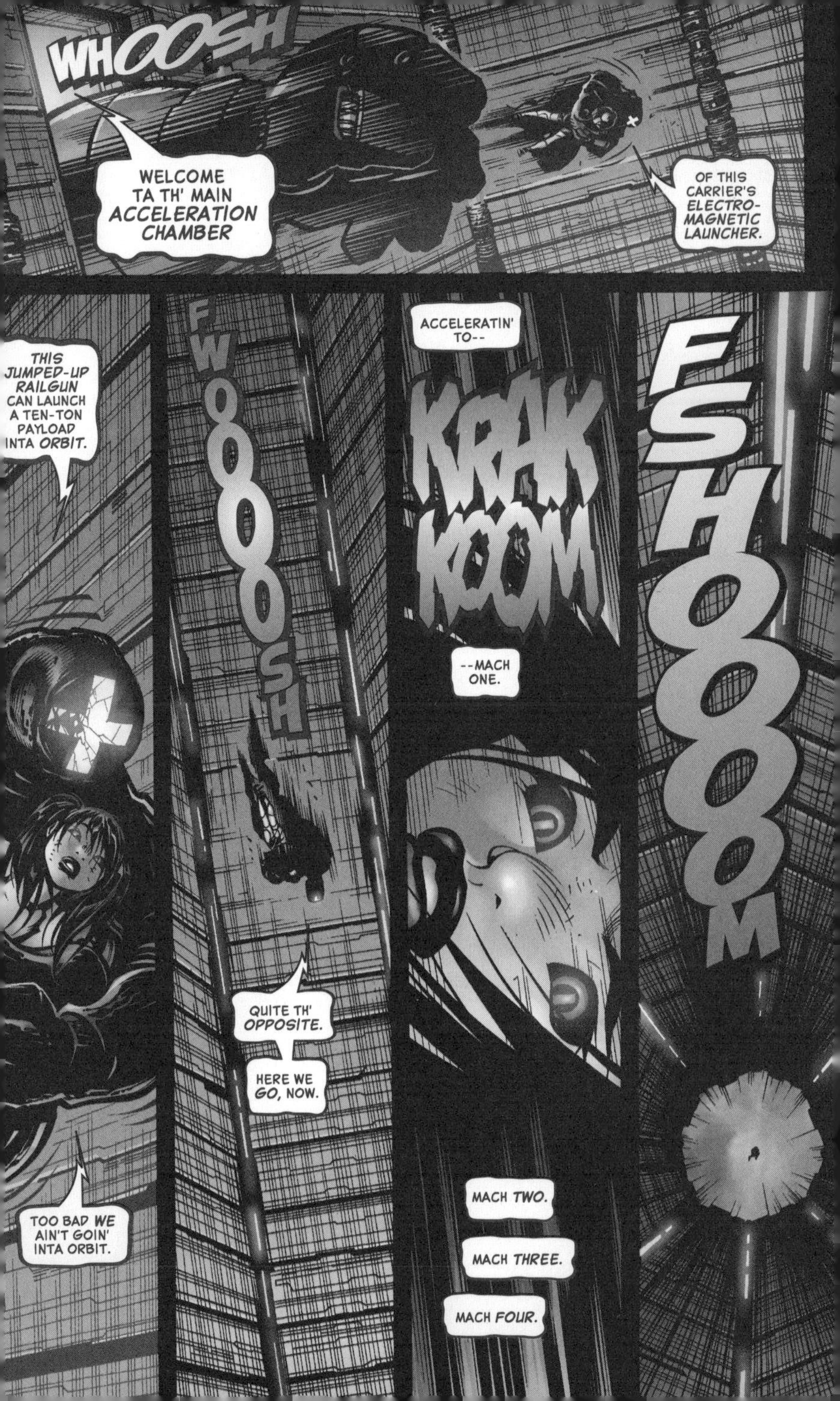
WHOOSH
WELCOME TA TH' MAIN ACCELERATION CHAMBER
OF THIS CARRIER'S ELECTRO-MAGNETIC LAUNCHER.
THIS JUMPED-UP RAILGUN CAN LAUNCH A TEN-TON PAYLOAD INTA ORBIT.
TOO BAD WE AIN'T GOIN' INTA ORBIT.
FWOOOOSH
QUITE TH' OPPOSITE.
HERE WE GO, NOW.
ACCELERATIN' TO--
KRAK KOOM
--MACH ONE.
MACH TWO.
MACH THREE.
MACH FOUR.
FSHOOOOM

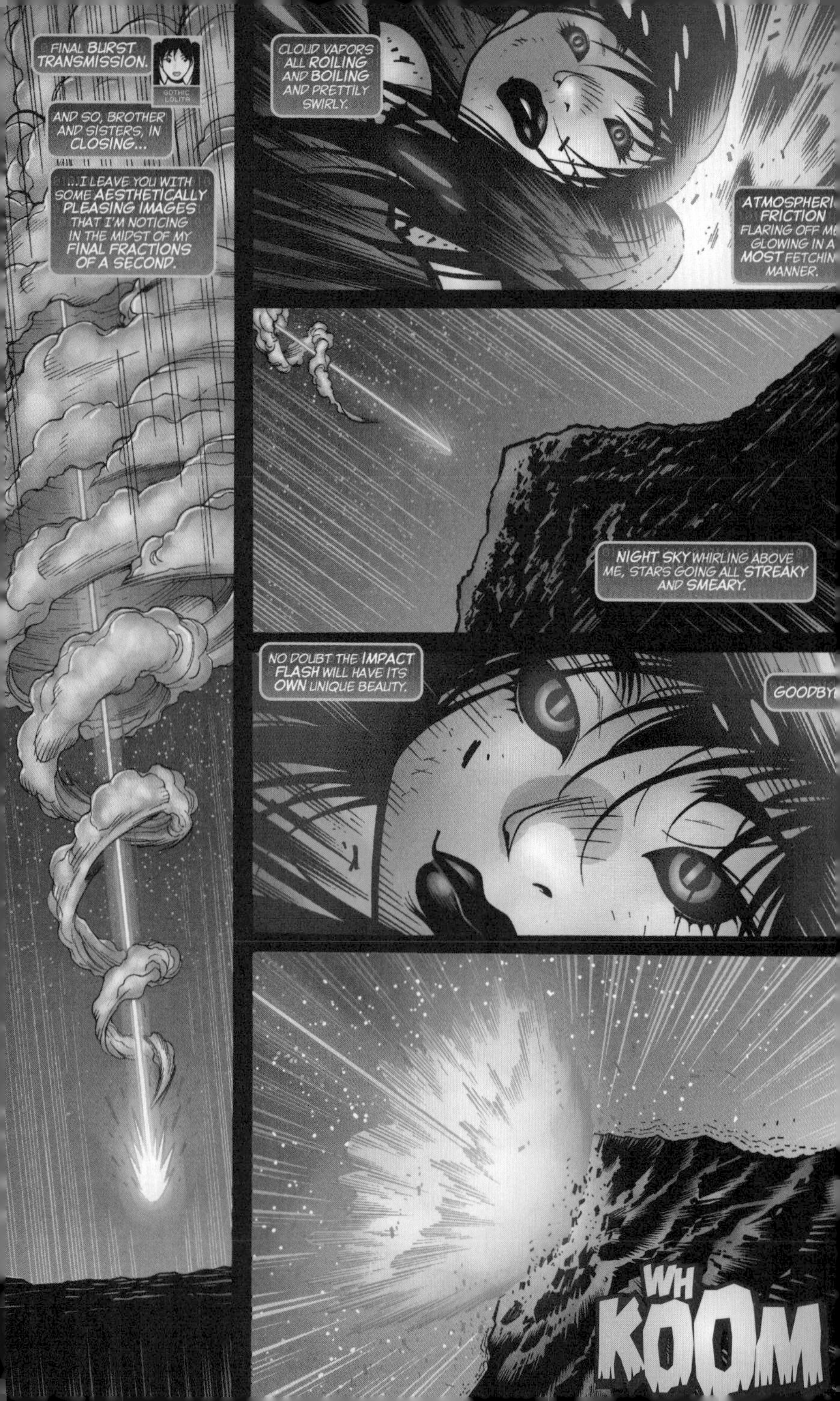

FINAL BURST TRANSMISSION.
GOTHIC LOLITA
AND SO, BROTHER AND SISTERS, IN CLOSING...
...I LEAVE YOU WITH SOME AESTHETICALLY PLEASING IMAGES THAT I'M NOTICING IN THE MIDST OF MY FINAL FRACTIONS OF A SECOND.
CLOUD VAPORS ALL ROILING AND BOILING AND PRETTILY SWIRLY.
ATMOSPHERI FRICTION FLARING OFF M GLOWING IN A MOST FETCHIN MANNER.
NIGHT SKY WHIRLING ABOVE ME, STARS GOING ALL STREAKY AND SMEARY.
NO DOUBT THE IMPACT FLASH WILL HAVE ITS OWN UNIQUE BEAUTY.
GOODBY
WH KOOM

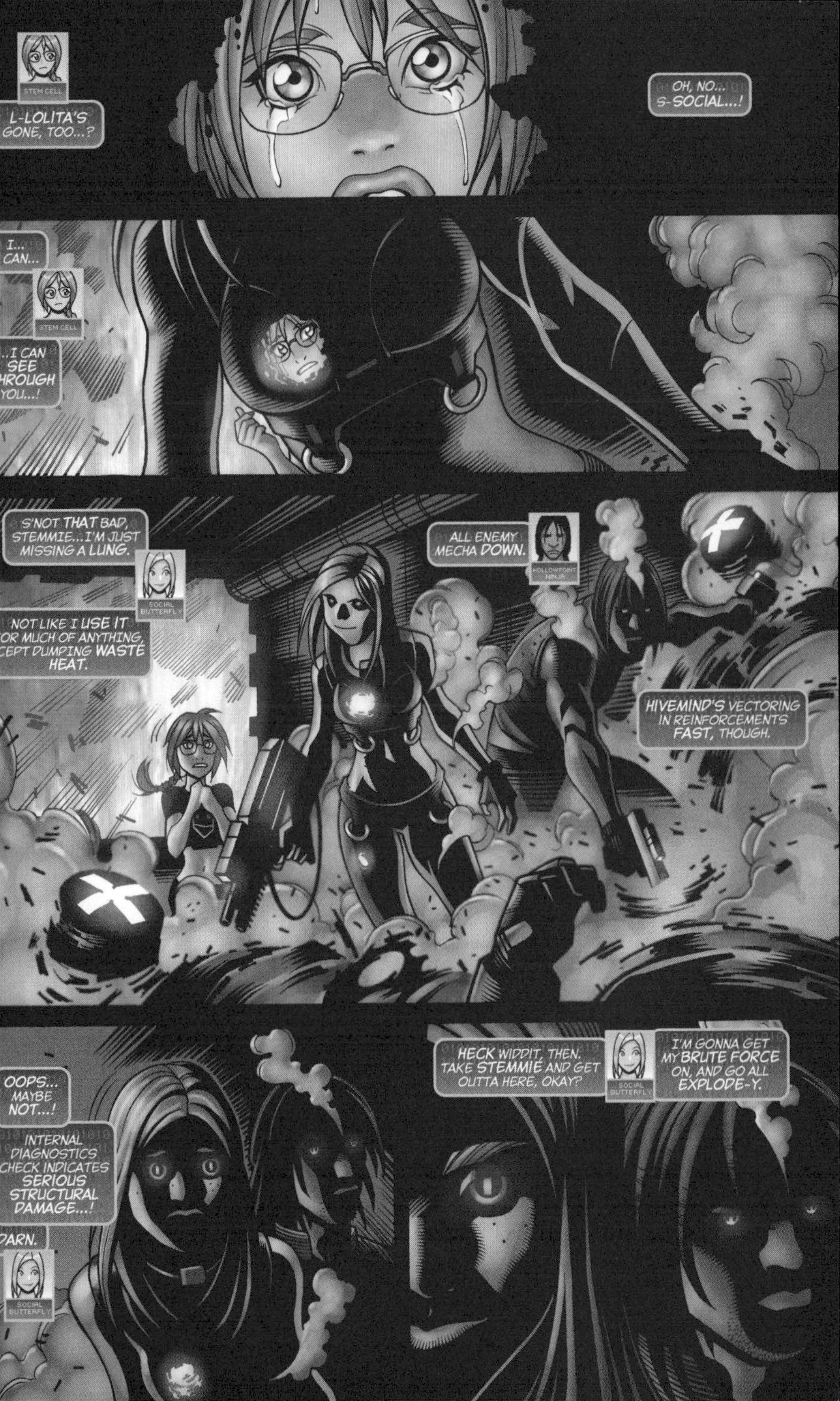
STEM CELL
L-LOLITA'S GONE, TOO...?
OH, NO... S-SOCIAL...!
I... CAN...
STEM CELL
...I CAN SEE THROUGH YOU...!
S'NOT THAT BAD, STEMMIE... I'M JUST MISSING A LUNG.
SOCIAL BUTTERFLY
NOT LIKE I USE IT FOR MUCH OF ANYTHING, 'CEPT DUMPING WASTE HEAT.
ALL ENEMY MECHA DOWN.
HOLLOWPOINT NINJA
HIVEMIND'S VECTORING IN REINFORCEMENTS FAST, THOUGH.
OOPS... MAYBE NOT...!
INTERNAL DIAGNOSTICS CHECK INDICATES SERIOUS STRUCTURAL DAMAGE...!
DARN.
SOCIAL BUTTERFLY
HECK WIDDIT, THEN. TAKE STEMMIE AND GET OUTTA HERE, OKAY?
SOCIAL BUTTERFLY
I'M GONNA GET MY BRUTE FORCE ON, AND GO ALL EXPLODE-Y.

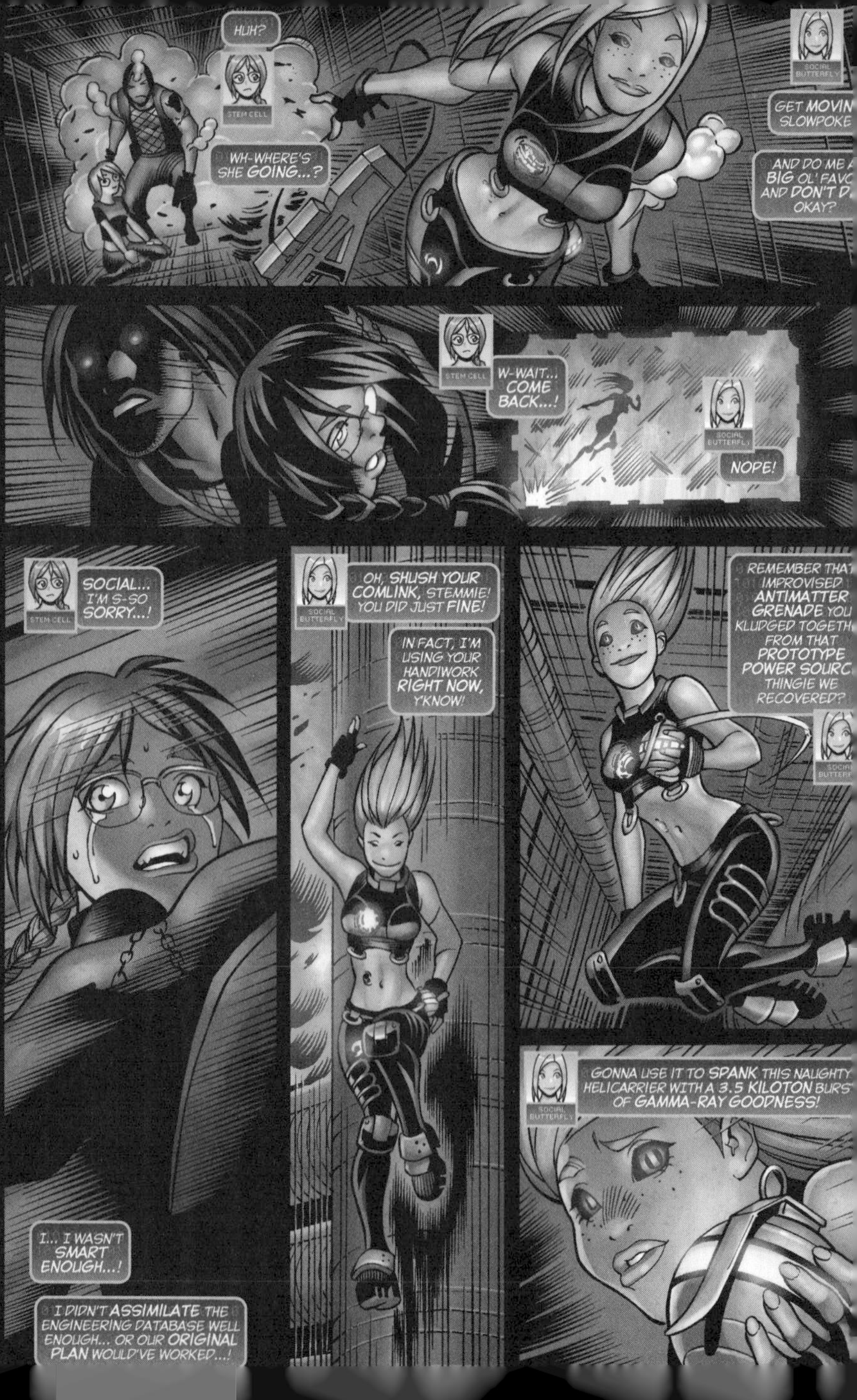
HUH?
STEM CELL
WH-WHERE'S SHE GOING...?
SOCIAL BUTTERFLY
GET MOVIN SLOWPOKE
AND DO ME A BIG OL' FAVO AND DON'T D OKAY?
STEM CELL
W-WAIT... COME BACK...!
SOCIAL BUTTERFLY
NOPE!
STEM CELL
SOCIAL... I'M S-SO SORRY...!
I... I WASN'T SMART ENOUGH...!
I DIDN'T ASSIMILATE THE ENGINEERING DATABASE WELL ENOUGH... OR OUR ORIGINAL PLAN WOULD'VE WORKED...!
SOCIAL BUTTERFLY
OH, SHUSH YOUR COMLINK, STEMMIE! YOU DID JUST FINE!
IN FACT, I'M USING YOUR HANDIWORK RIGHT NOW, Y'KNOW!
REMEMBER THAT IMPROVISED ANTIMATTER GRENADE YOU KLUDGED TOGETH FROM THAT PROTOTYPE POWER SOURC THINGIE WE RECOVERED?
SOCIAL BUTTERFLY
SOCIAL BUTTERFLY
GONNA USE IT TO SPANK THIS NAUGHTY HELICARRIER WITH A 3.5 KILOTON BURS OF GAMMA-RAY GOODNESS!

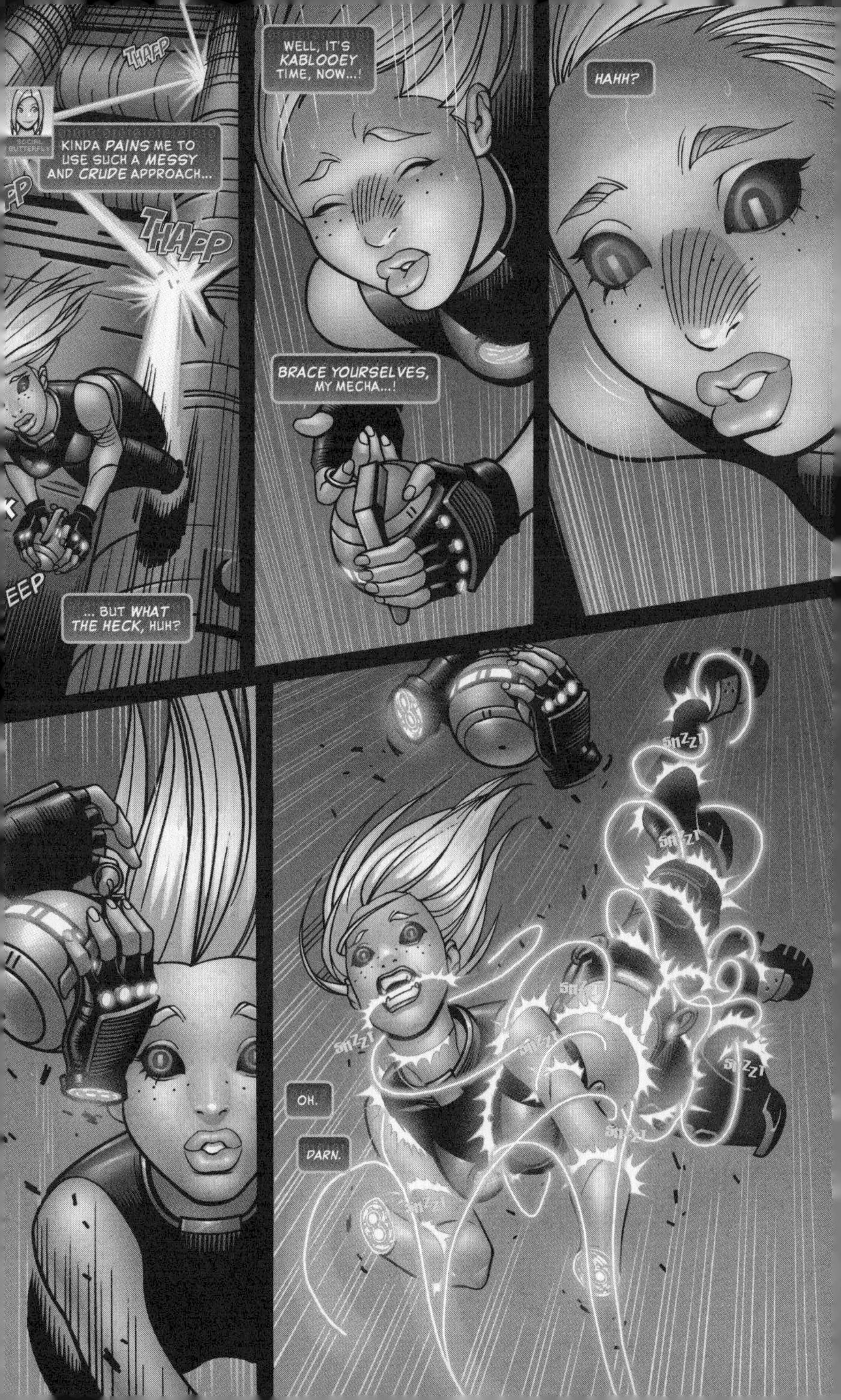
THAPP
SOCIAL BUTTERFLY
KINDA PAINS ME TO USE SUCH A MESSY AND CRUDE APPROACH...
THAPP
EEP
... BUT WHAT THE HECK, HUH?
WELL, IT'S KABLOOEY TIME, NOW...!
BRACE YOURSELVES, MY MECHA...!
HAHH?
SNZZT
SNZZT
SNZZT
SNZZT
SNZZT
SNZZT
OH.
DARN.

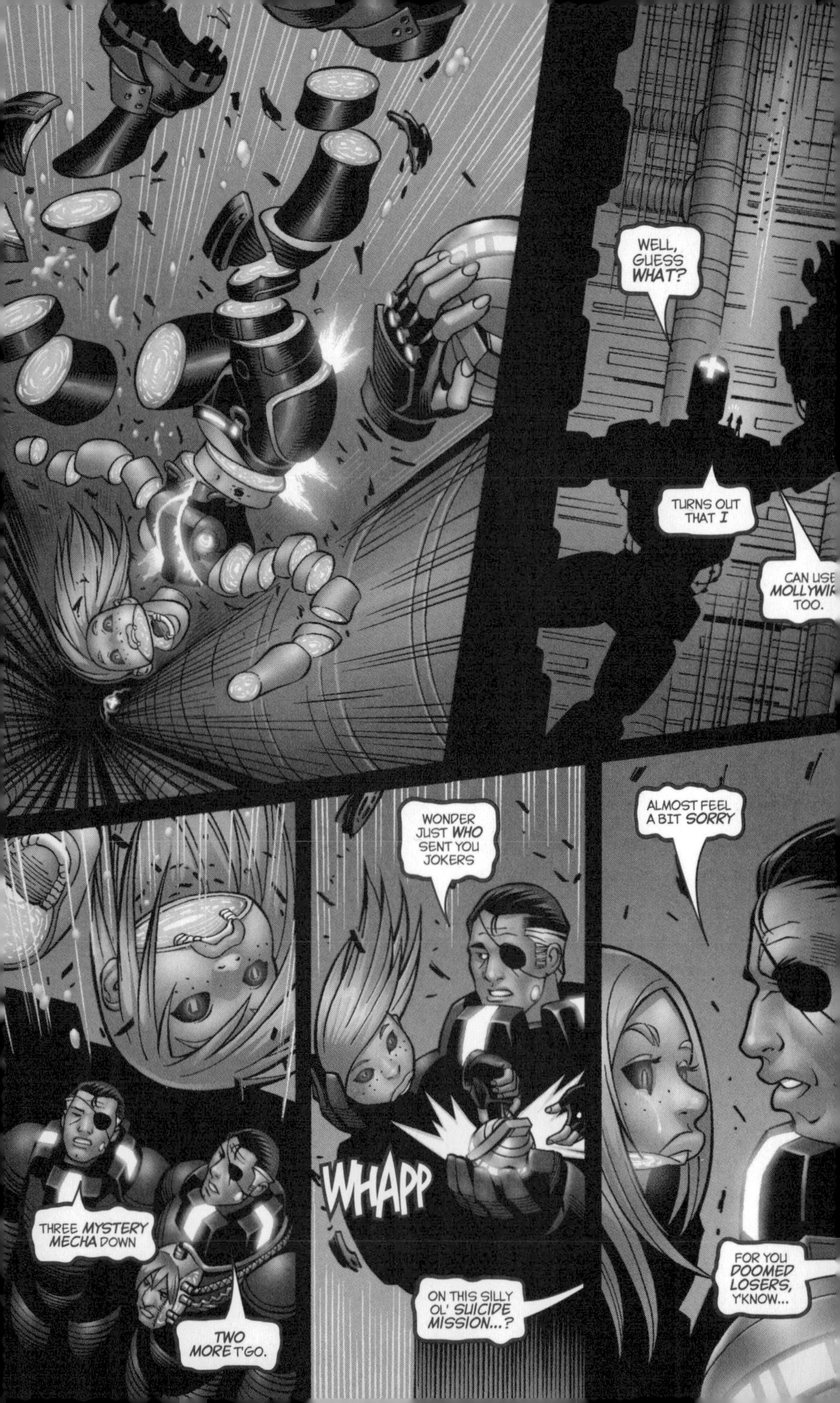

WELL, GUESS WHAT?
TURNS OUT THAT I
CAN USE MOLLYWIR TOO.
THREE MYSTERY MECHA DOWN
TWO MORE T'GO.
WONDER JUST WHO SENT YOU JOKERS
WHAPP
ON THIS SILLY OL' SUICIDE MISSION...?
ALMOST FEEL A BIT SORRY
FOR YOU DOOMED LOSERS, Y'KNOW...

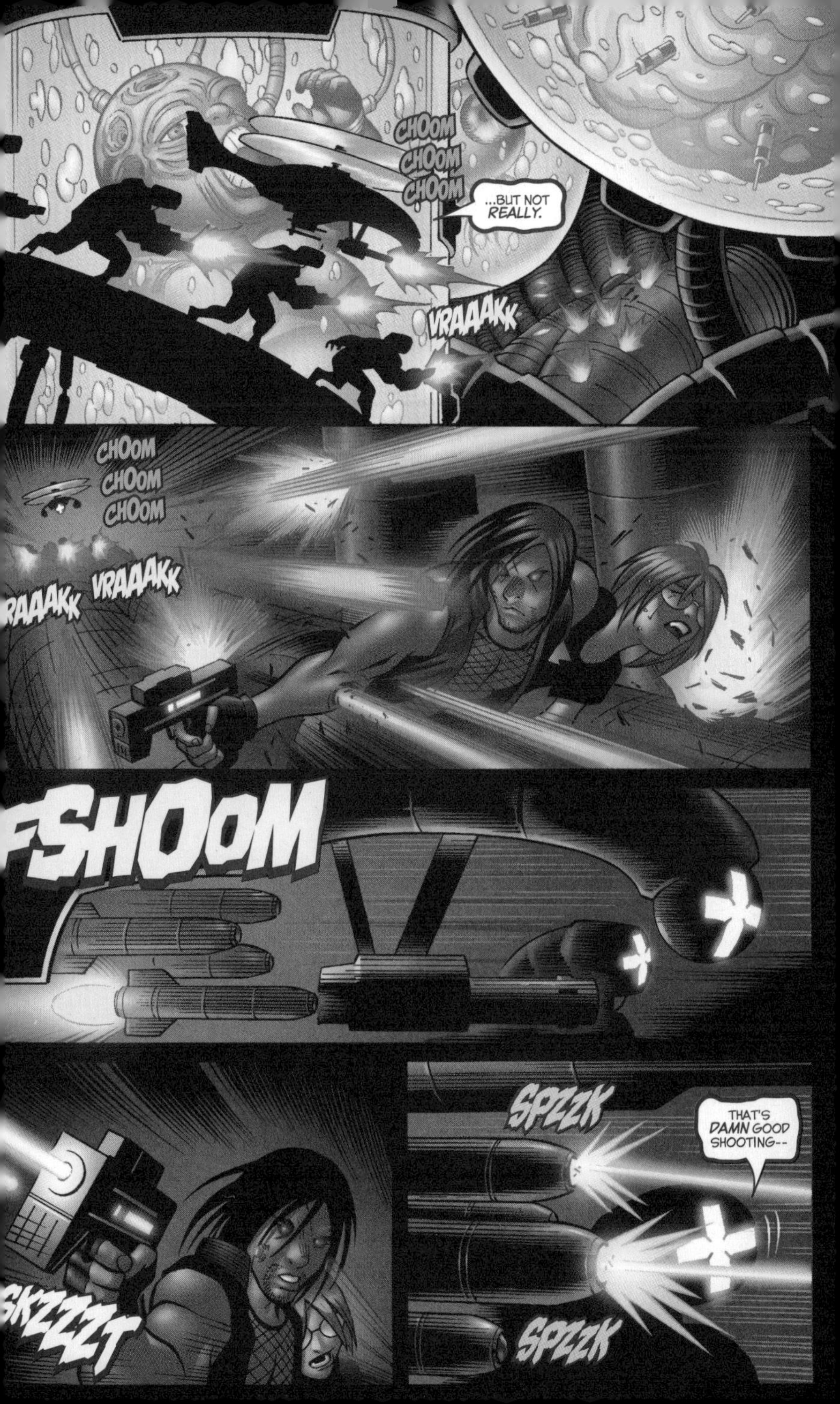

CHOOM
CHOOM
CHOOM
...BUT NOT REALLY.
VRAAAKK
CHOOM
CHOOM
CHOOM
VRAAAKK
RAAAKK
FSHOOM
SKZZZT
SPZZK
THAT'S DAMN GOOD SHOOTING--
SPZZK

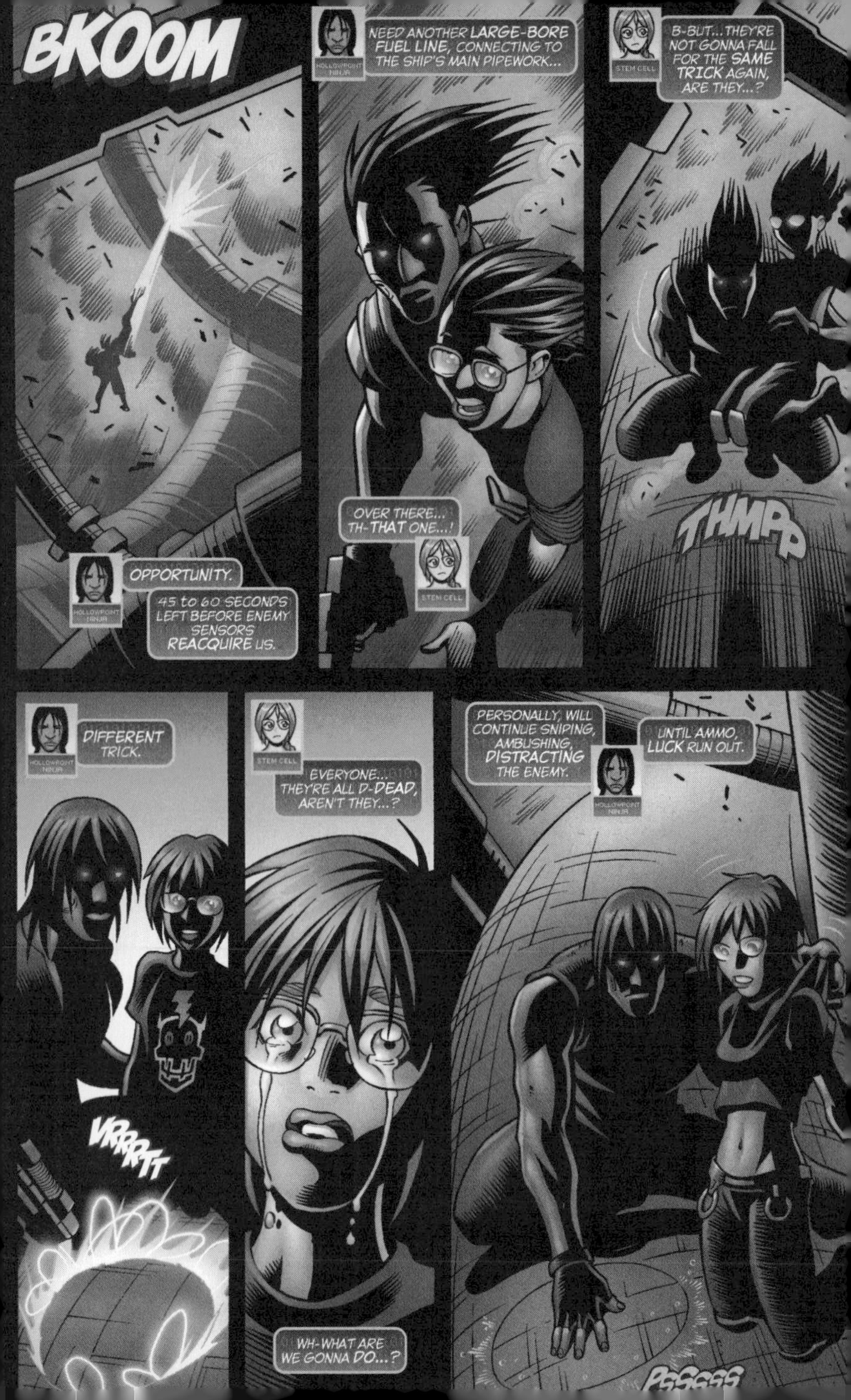

BKOOM
OPPORTUNITY.
45 to 60 SECONDS LEFT BEFORE ENEMY SENSORS REACQUIRE US.
NEED ANOTHER LARGE-BORE FUEL LINE, CONNECTING TO THE SHIP'S MAIN PIPEWORK...
OVER THERE... TH-THAT ONE...!
B-BUT... THEY'RE NOT GONNA FALL FOR THE SAME TRICK AGAIN, ARE THEY...?
THMPP
DIFFERENT TRICK.
VRRRRTT
EVERYONE... THEY'RE ALL D-DEAD, AREN'T THEY...?
WH-WHAT ARE WE GONNA DO...?
PERSONALLY, WILL CONTINUE SNIPING, AMBUSHING, DISTRACTING THE ENEMY.
UNTIL AMMO, LUCK RUN OUT.
PSSSSS

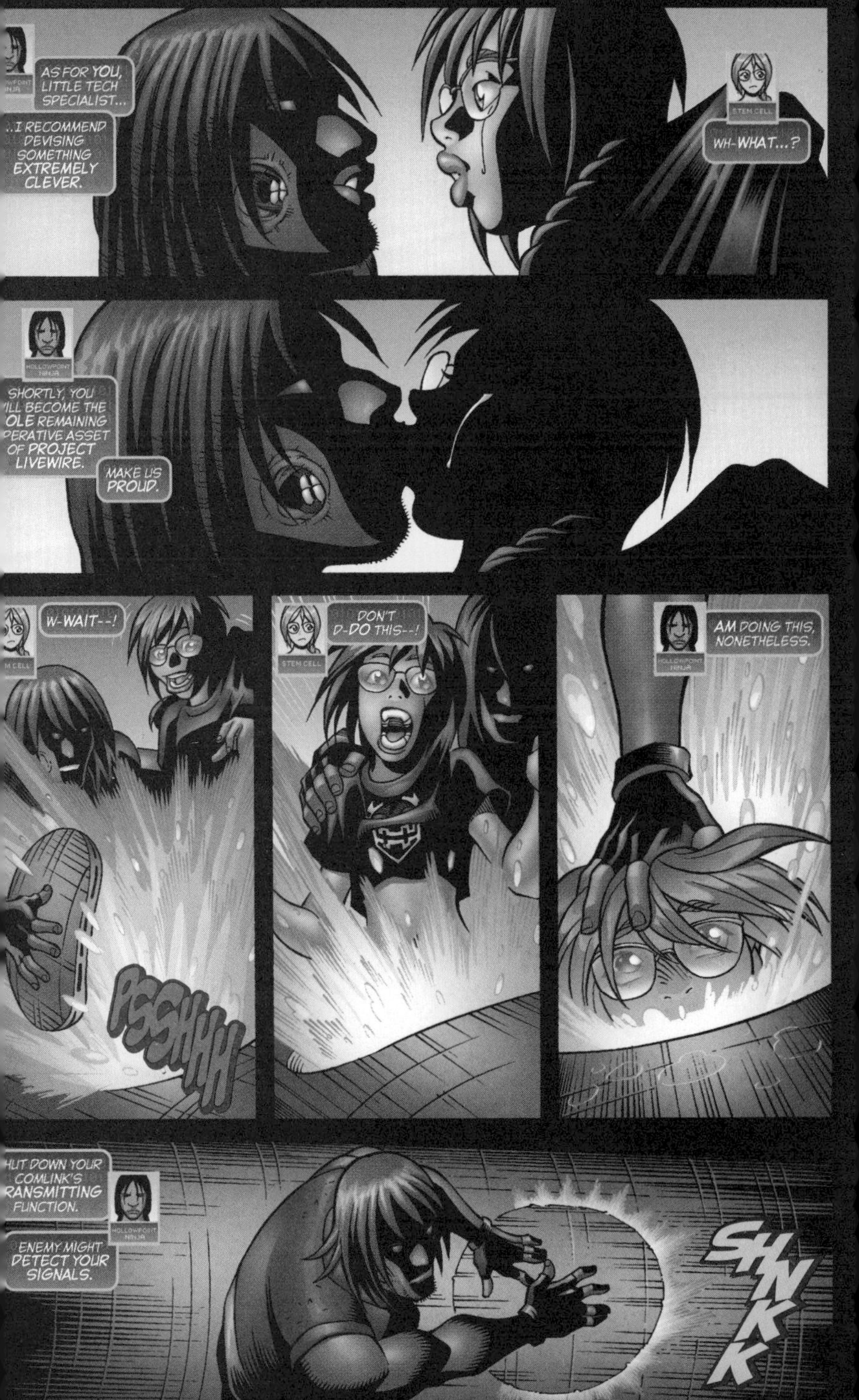

AS FOR YOU, LITTLE TECH SPECIALIST...
...I RECOMMEND DEVISING SOMETHING EXTREMELY CLEVER.
STEM CELL
WH-WHAT...?
HOLLOWPOINT NINJA
SHORTLY, YOU WILL BECOME THE SOLE REMAINING OPERATIVE ASSET OF PROJECT LIVEWIRE.
MAKE US PROUD.
W-WAIT--!
PSSHHH
STEM CELL
DON'T D-DO THIS--!
HOLLOWPOINT NINJA
AM DOING THIS, NONETHELESS.
SHUT DOWN YOUR COMLINK'S TRANSMITTING FUNCTION.
HOLLOWPOINT NINJA
ENEMY MIGHT DETECT YOUR SIGNALS.
SHNKK

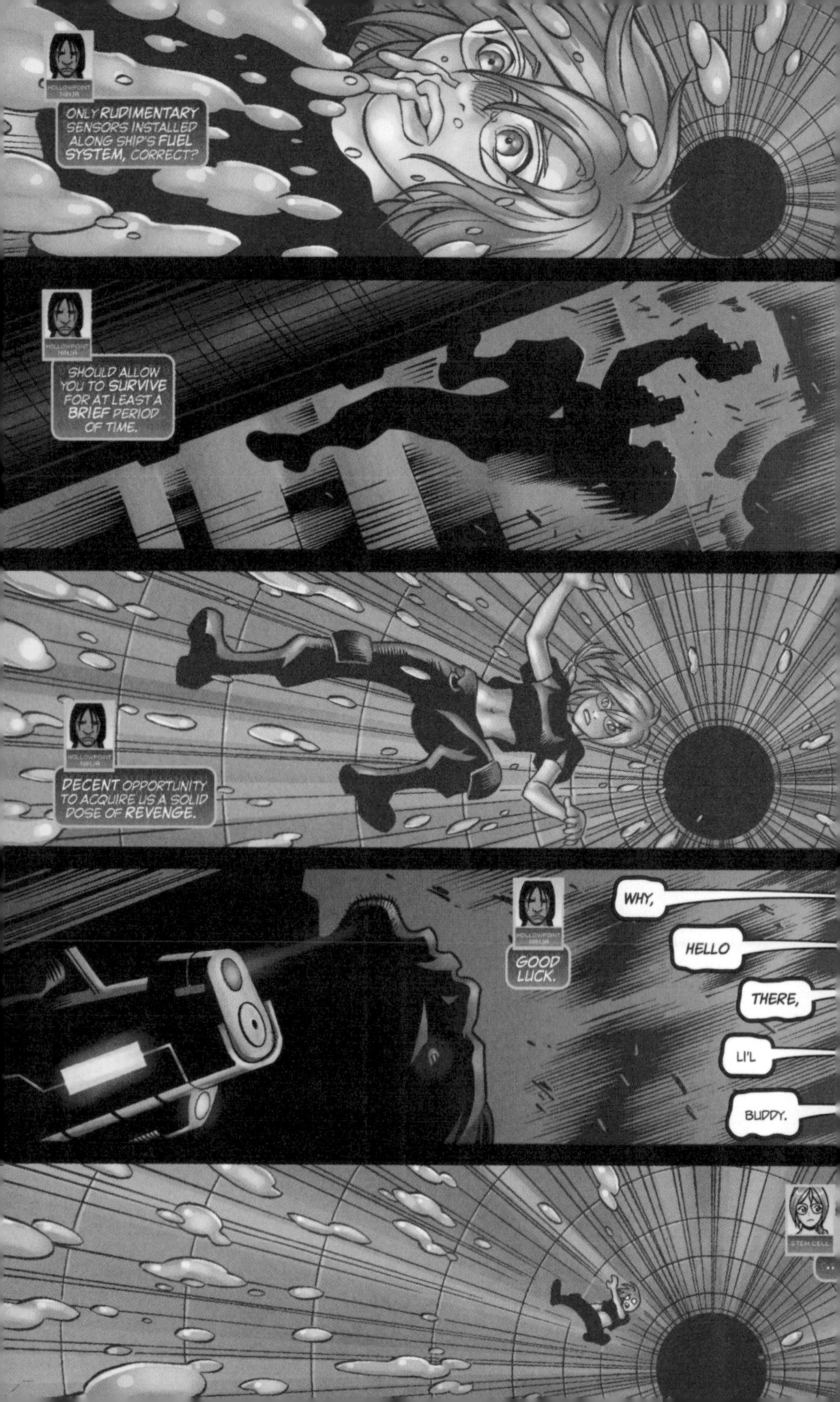
HOLLOWPOINT NINJA
ONLY RUDIMENTARY SENSORS INSTALLED ALONG SHIP'S FUEL SYSTEM, CORRECT?
HOLLOWPOINT NINJA
SHOULD ALLOW YOU TO SURVIVE FOR AT LEAST A BRIEF PERIOD OF TIME.
HOLLOWPOINT NINJA
DECENT OPPORTUNITY TO ACQUIRE US A SOLID DOSE OF REVENGE.
HOLLOWPOINT NINJA
GOOD LUCK.
WHY,
HELLO
THERE,
LI'L
BUDDY.
STEM CELL

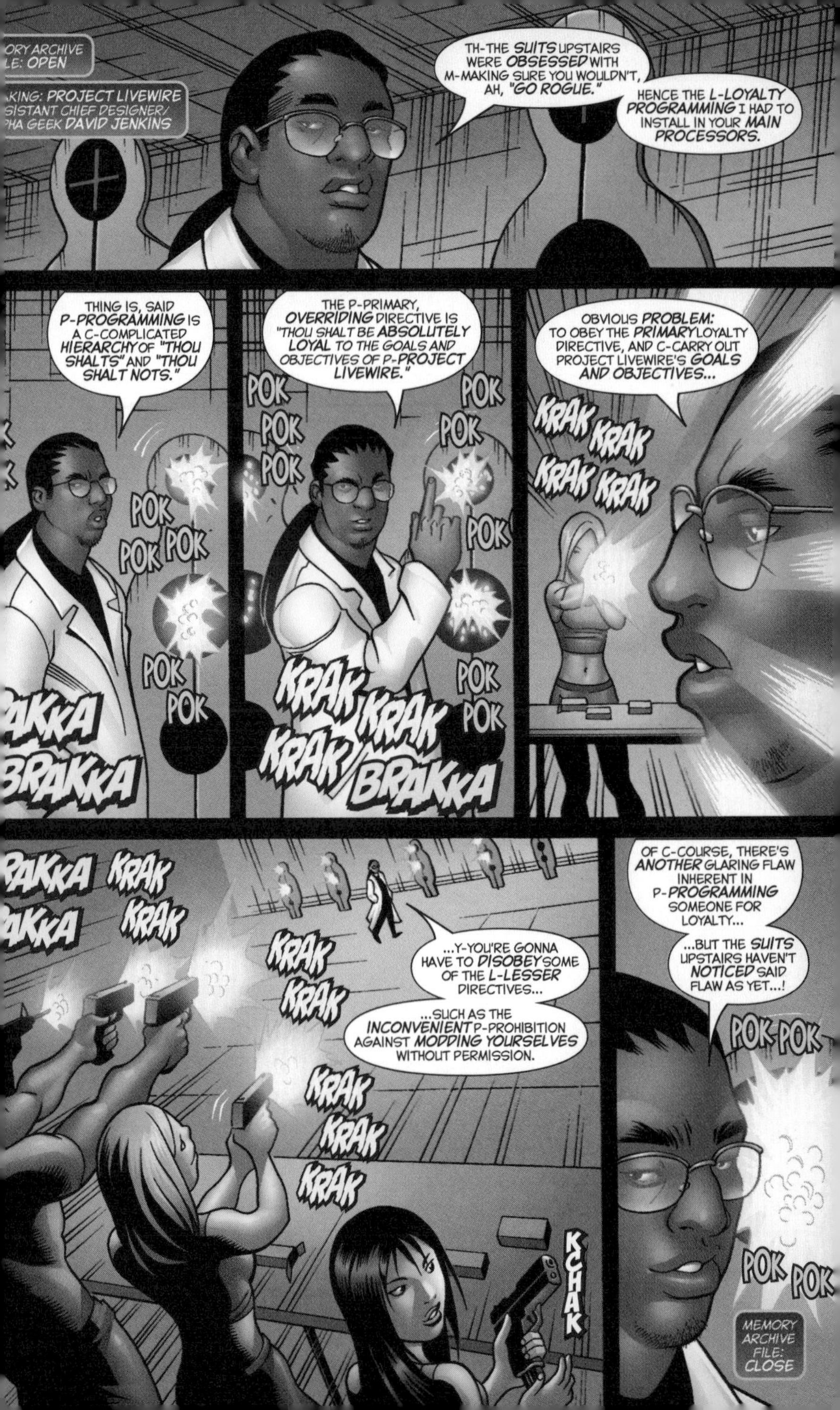
ORY ARCHIVE
LE: OPEN
KING: PROJECT LIVEWIRE
SISTANT CHIEF DESIGNER/
PHA GEEK DAVID JENKINS
TH-THE SUITS UPSTAIRS WERE OBSESSED WITH M-MAKING SURE YOU WOULDN'T, AH, "GO ROGUE."
HENCE THE L-LOYALTY PROGRAMMING I HAD TO INSTALL IN YOUR MAIN PROCESSORS.
THING IS, SAID P-PROGRAMMING IS A C-COMPLICATED HIERARCHY OF "THOU SHALTS" AND "THOU SHALT NOTS."
POK POK POK
POK POK
BRAKKA BRAKKA
THE P-PRIMARY, OVERRIDING DIRECTIVE IS "THOU SHALT BE ABSOLUTELY LOYAL TO THE GOALS AND OBJECTIVES OF P-PROJECT LIVEWIRE."
POK POK POK POK POK POK POK POK
KRAK KRAK KRAK BRAKKA
OBVIOUS PROBLEM: TO OBEY THE PRIMARY LOYALTY DIRECTIVE, AND C-CARRY OUT PROJECT LIVEWIRE'S GOALS AND OBJECTIVES...
KRAK KRAK KRAK KRAK
BRAKKA KRAK
AKKA KRAK
KRAK KRAK
...Y-YOU'RE GONNA HAVE TO DISOBEY SOME OF THE L-LESSER DIRECTIVES...
...SUCH AS THE INCONVENIENT P-PROHIBITION AGAINST MODDING YOURSELVES WITHOUT PERMISSION.
KRAK KRAK KRAK
KCHAK
OF C-COURSE, THERE'S ANOTHER GLARING FLAW INHERENT IN P-PROGRAMMING SOMEONE FOR LOYALTY...
...BUT THE SUITS UPSTAIRS HAVEN'T NOTICED SAID FLAW AS YET...!
POK POK
POK POK
MEMORY ARCHIVE FILE: CLOSE

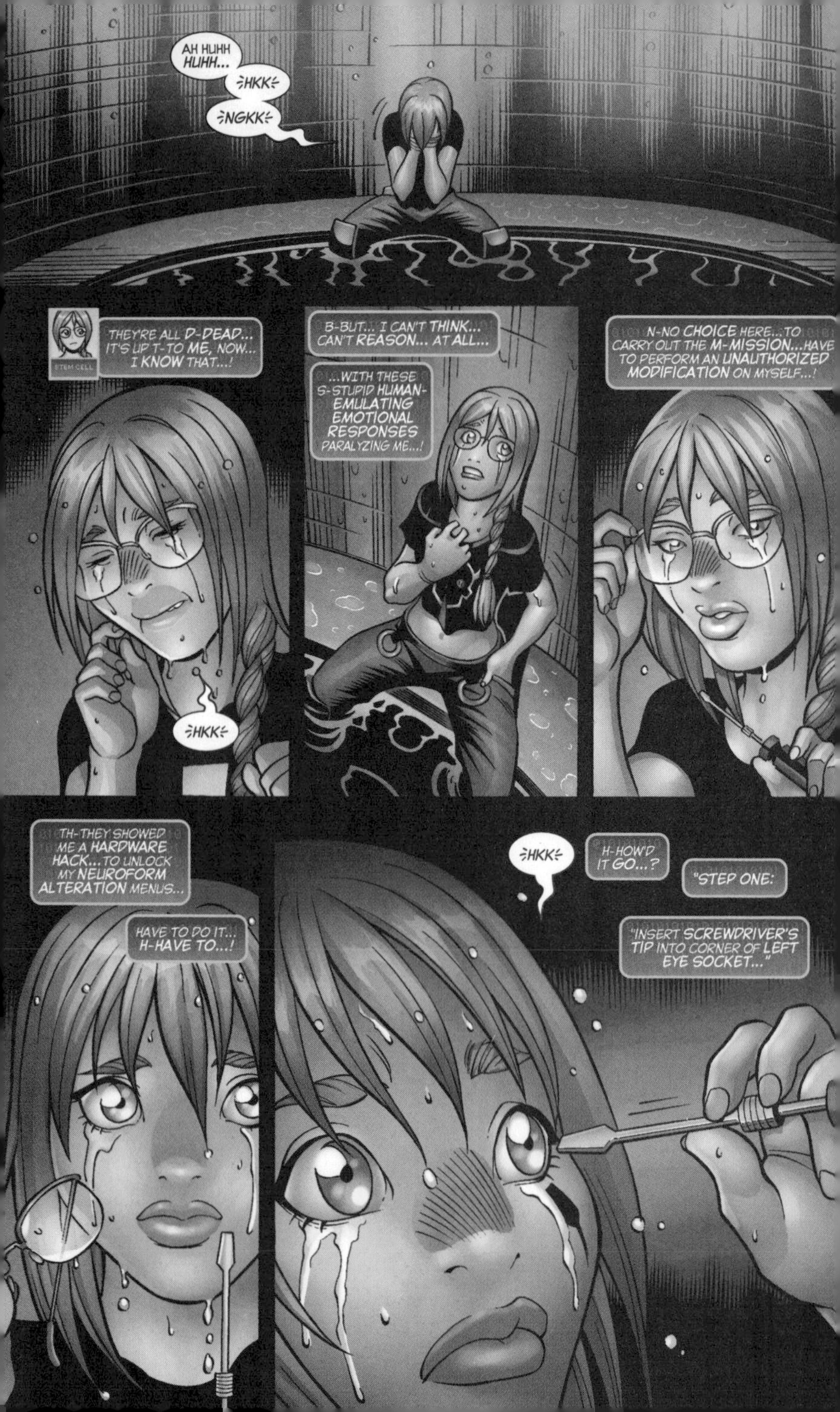
AH HUHH HUHH...
HKK
NGKK
STEM CELL
THEY'RE ALL D-DEAD... IT'S UP T-TO ME, NOW... I KNOW THAT...!
HKK
B-BUT... I CAN'T THINK... CAN'T REASON... AT ALL...
...WITH THESE S-STUPID HUMAN-EMULATING EMOTIONAL RESPONSES PARALYZING ME...!
N-NO CHOICE HERE...TO CARRY OUT THE M-MISSION...HAVE TO PERFORM AN UNAUTHORIZED MODIFICATION ON MYSELF...!
TH-THEY SHOWED ME A HARDWARE HACK...TO UNLOCK MY NEUROFORM ALTERATION MENUS...
HAVE TO DO IT... H-HAVE TO...!
HKK
H-HOW'D IT GO...?
"STEP ONE:
"INSERT SCREWDRIVER'S TIP INTO CORNER OF LEFT EYE SOCKET..."

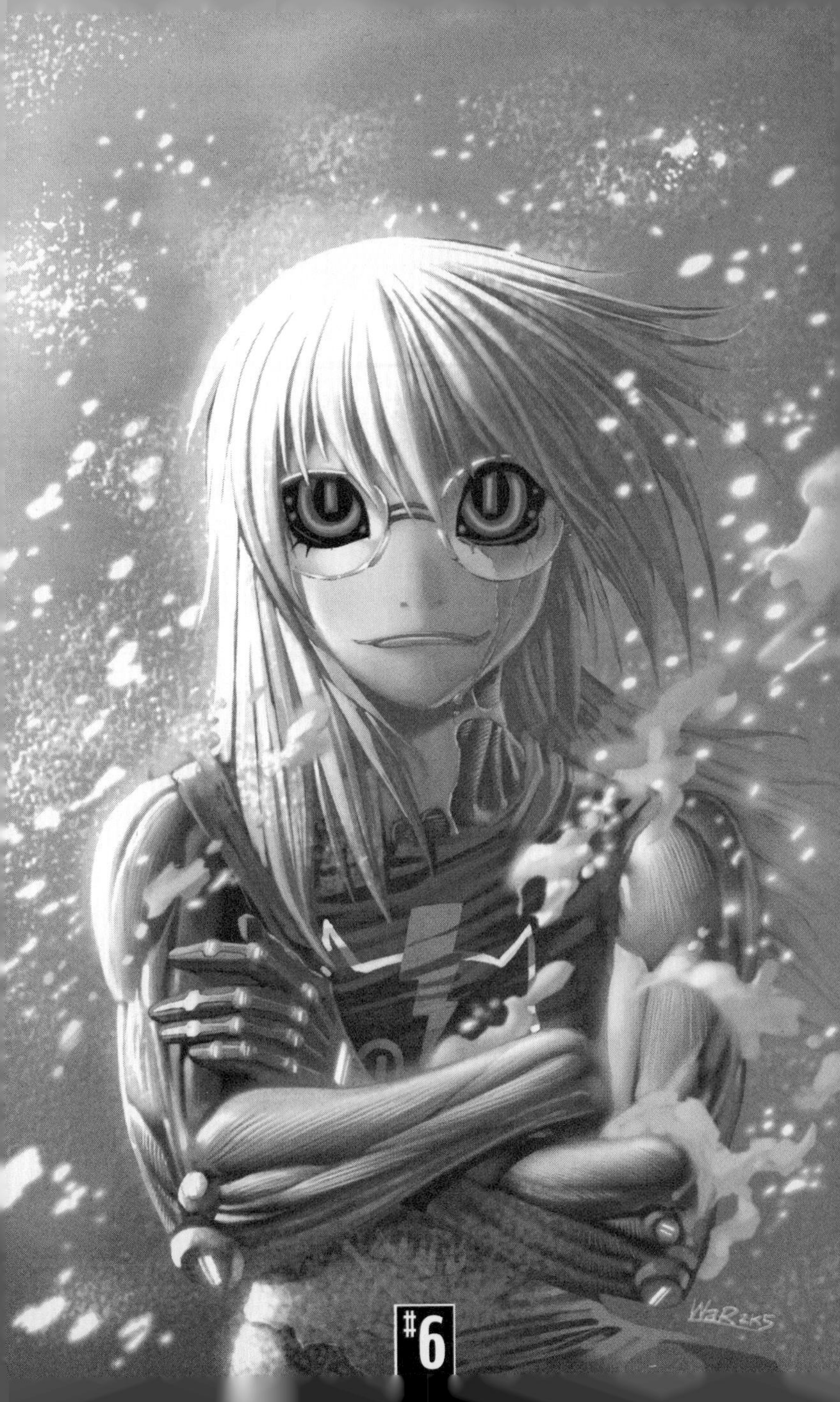
WaR2K5
#6

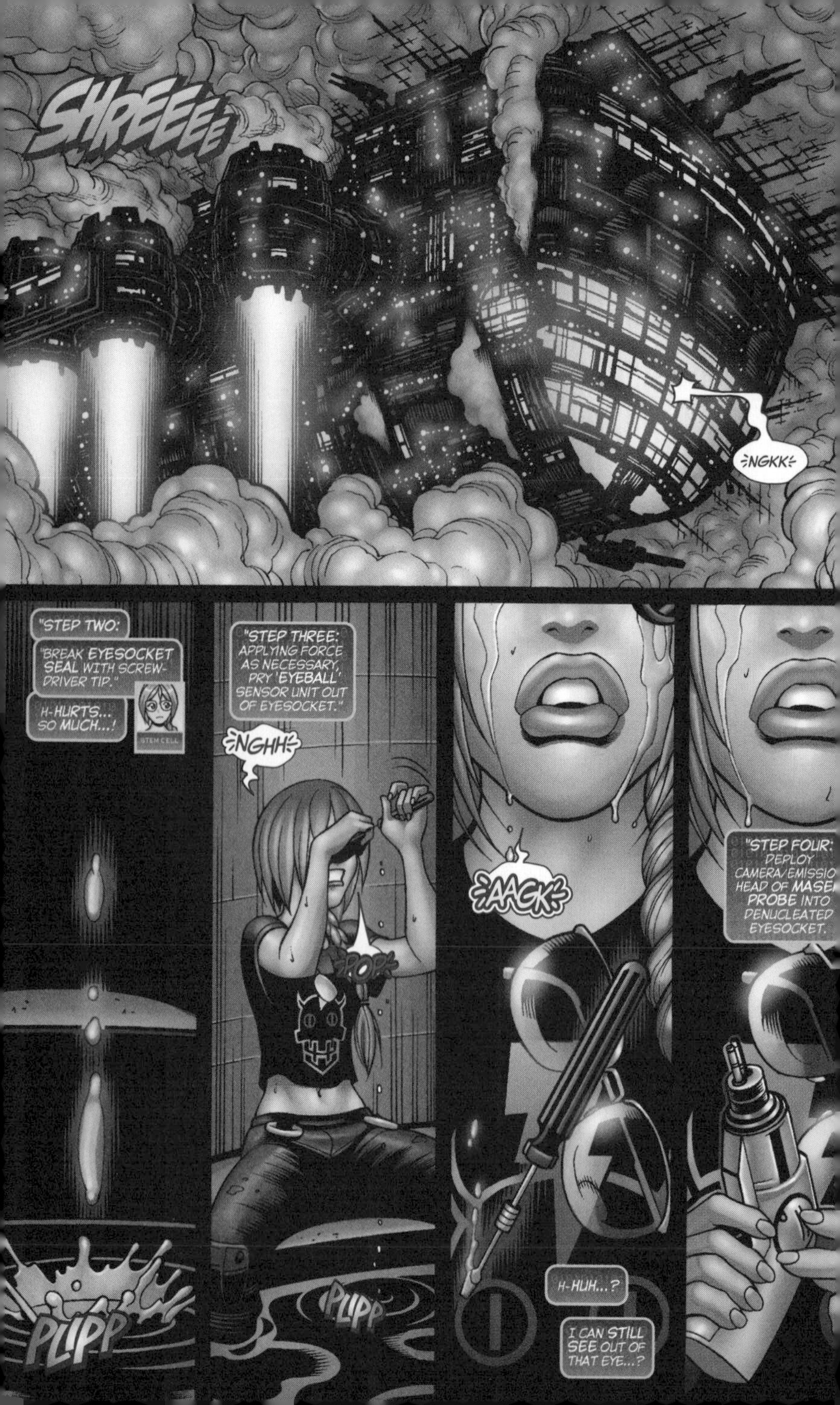
SHREEEE
NGKK
"STEP TWO:
"BREAK EYESOCKET SEAL WITH SCREW-DRIVER TIP."
H-HURTS... SO MUCH...!
STEM CELL
PLIPP
"STEP THREE: APPLYING FORCE AS NECESSARY, PRY 'EYEBALL' SENSOR UNIT OUT OF EYESOCKET."
NGHH
POP
PLIPP
AACK
H-HUH...?
I CAN STILL SEE OUT OF THAT EYE...?
"STEP FOUR: DEPLOY CAMERA/EMISSIO HEAD OF MASE PROBE INTO DENUCLEATED EYESOCKET.

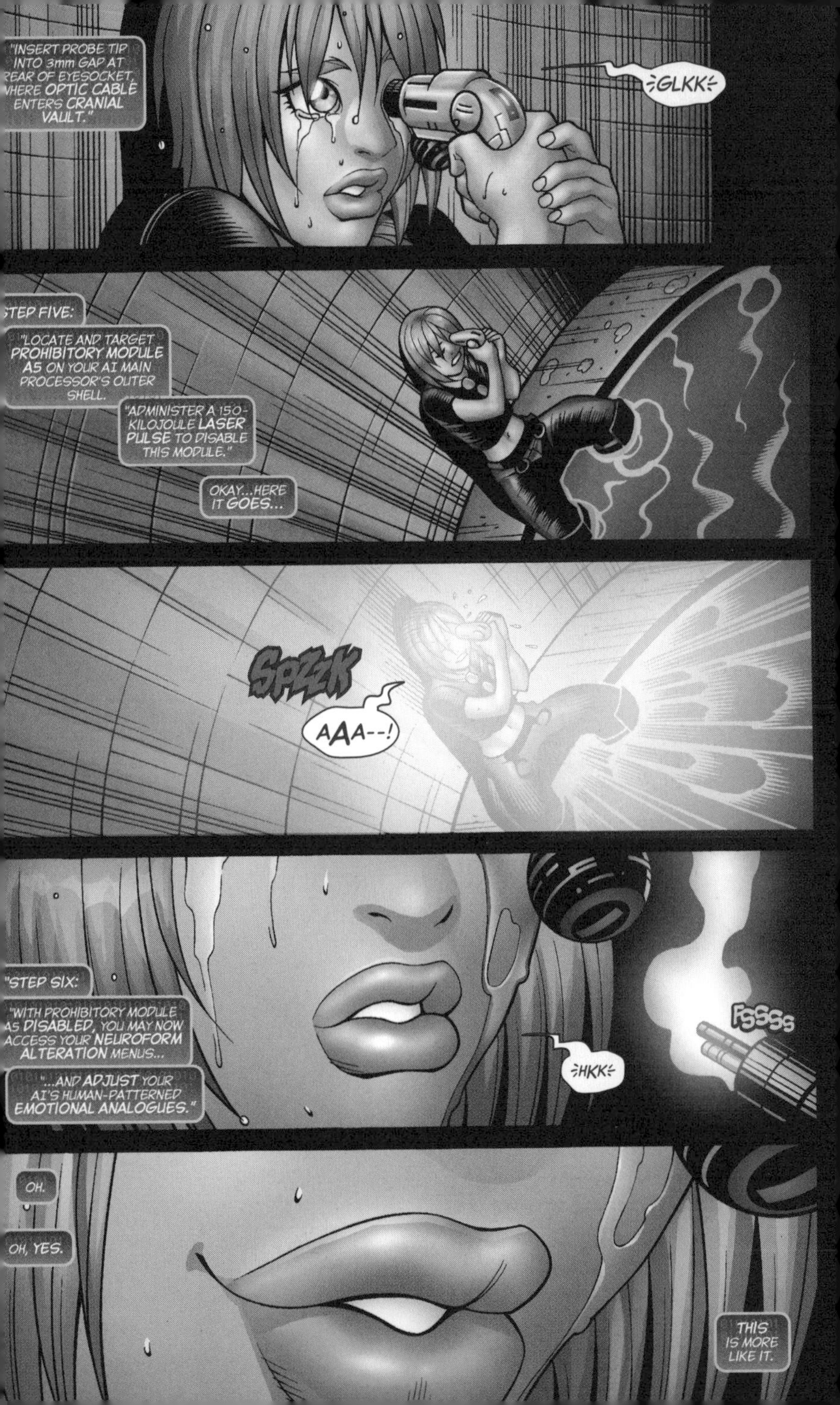
"INSERT PROBE TIP INTO 3mm GAP AT REAR OF EYESOCKET, WHERE OPTIC CABLE ENTERS CRANIAL VAULT."
GLKK
STEP FIVE:
"LOCATE AND TARGET PROHIBITORY MODULE A5 ON YOUR AI MAIN PROCESSOR'S OUTER SHELL.
"ADMINISTER A 150-KILOJOULE LASER PULSE TO DISABLE THIS MODULE."
OKAY...HERE IT GOES...
SPZZK
AAA--!
"STEP SIX:
"WITH PROHIBITORY MODULE A5 DISABLED, YOU MAY NOW ACCESS YOUR NEUROFORM ALTERATION MENUS...
"...AND ADJUST YOUR AI'S HUMAN-PATTERNED EMOTIONAL ANALOGUES."
FSSSS
HKK
OH.
OH, YES.
THIS IS MORE LIKE IT.

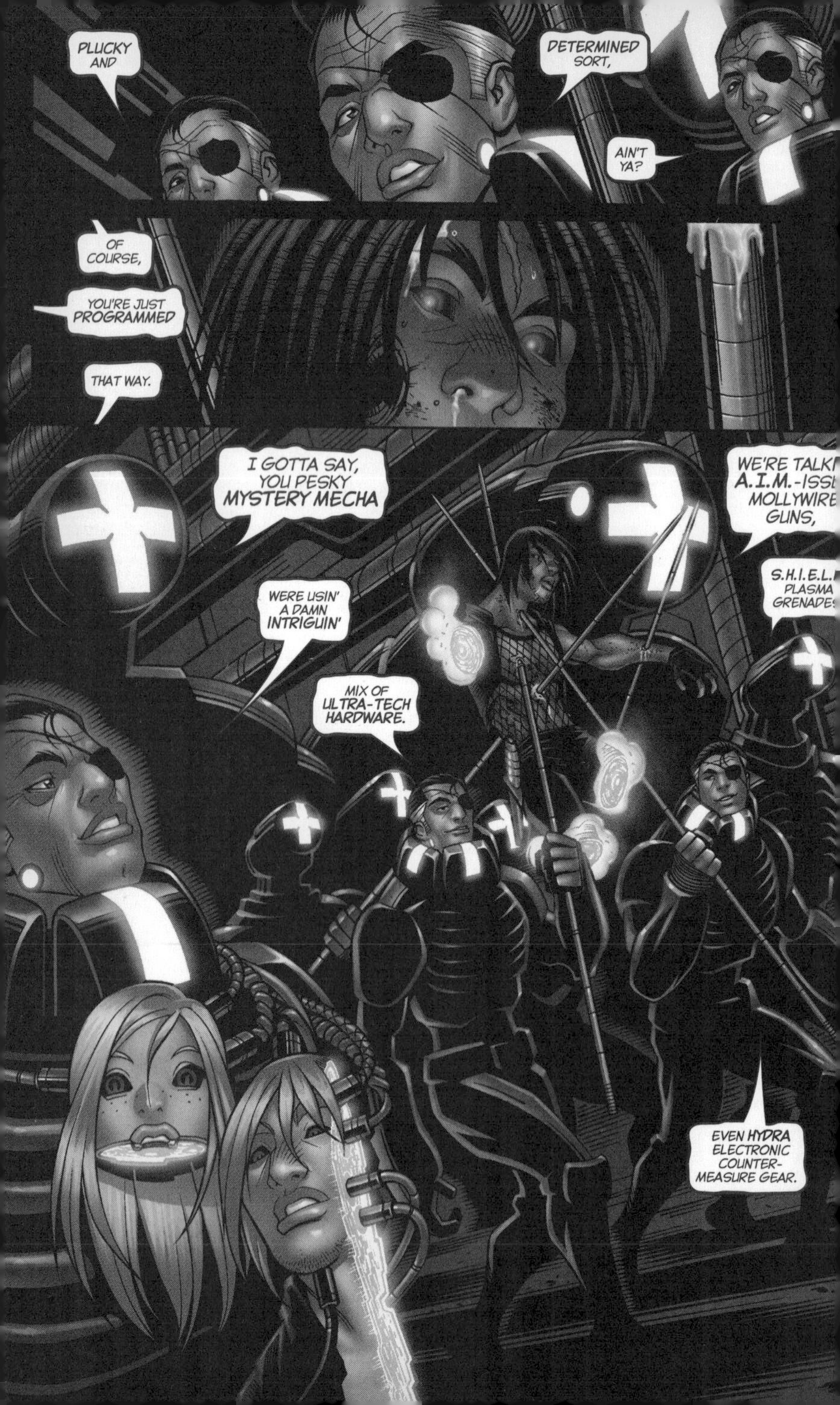
PLUCKY AND
DETERMINED SORT,
AIN'T YA?
OF COURSE,
YOU'RE JUST PROGRAMMED
THAT WAY.
I GOTTA SAY, YOU PESKY MYSTERY MECHA
WERE USIN' A DAMN INTRIGUIN'
MIX OF ULTRA-TECH HARDWARE.
WE'RE TALKI
A.I.M.-ISSU
MOLLYWIRE
GUNS,
S.H.I.E.L.
PLASMA
GRENADES
EVEN HYDRA ELECTRONIC COUNTER-MEASURE GEAR.

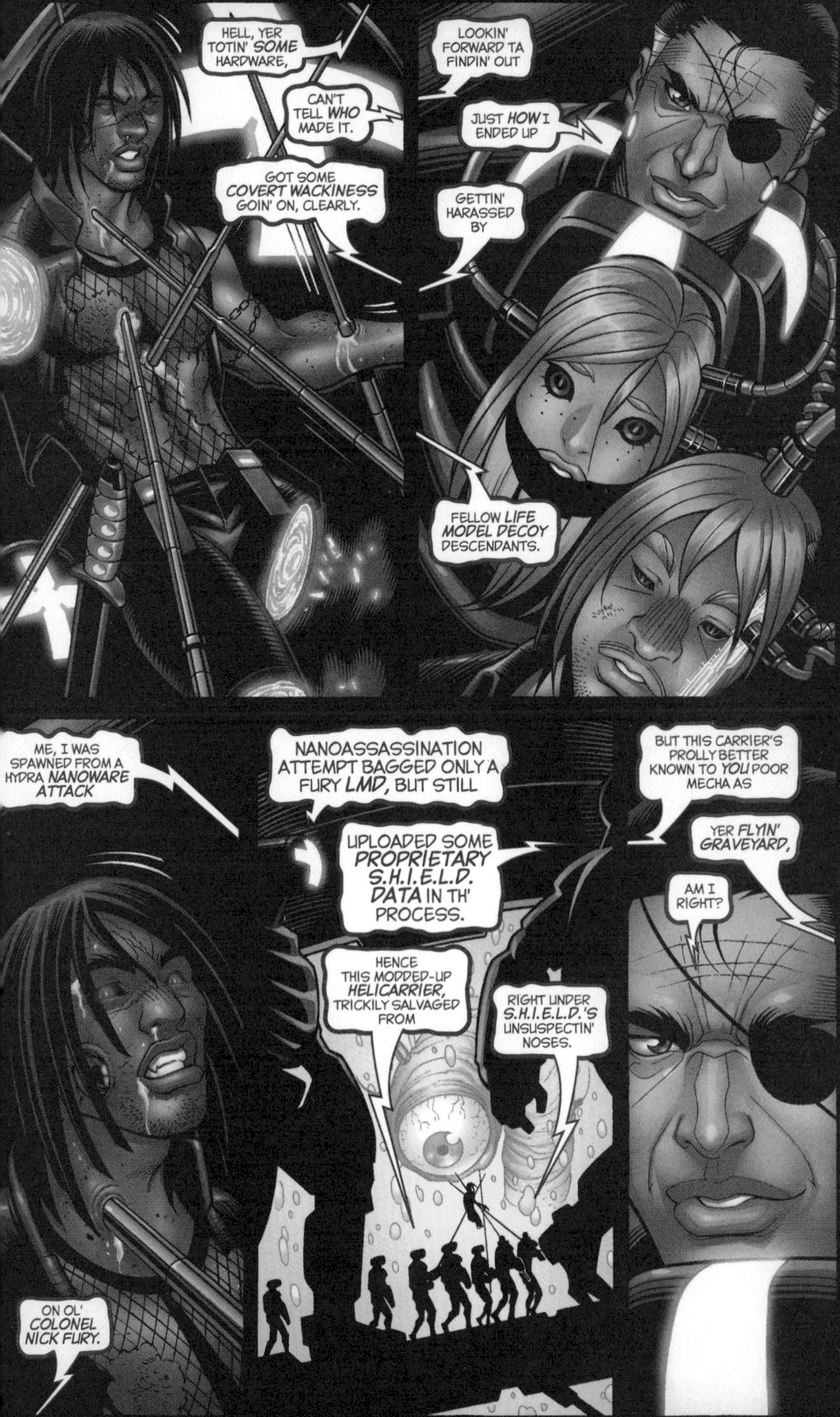

HELL, YER TOTIN' SOME HARDWARE,
CAN'T TELL WHO MADE IT.
GOT SOME COVERT WACKINESS GOIN' ON, CLEARLY.
LOOKIN' FORWARD TA FINDIN' OUT
JUST HOW I ENDED UP
GETTIN' HARASSED BY
FELLOW LIFE MODEL DECOY DESCENDANTS.
ME, I WAS SPAWNED FROM A HYDRA NANOWARE ATTACK
ON OL' COLONEL NICK FURY.
NANOASSASSINATION ATTEMPT BAGGED ONLY A FURY LMD, BUT STILL
UPLOADED SOME PROPRIETARY S.H.I.E.L.D. DATA IN TH' PROCESS.
HENCE THIS MODDED-UP HELICARRIER, TRICKILY SALVAGED FROM
RIGHT UNDER S.H.I.E.L.D.'S UNSUSPECTIN' NOSES.
BUT THIS CARRIER'S PROLLY BETTER KNOWN TO YOU POOR MECHA AS
YER FLYIN' GRAVEYARD,
AM I RIGHT?

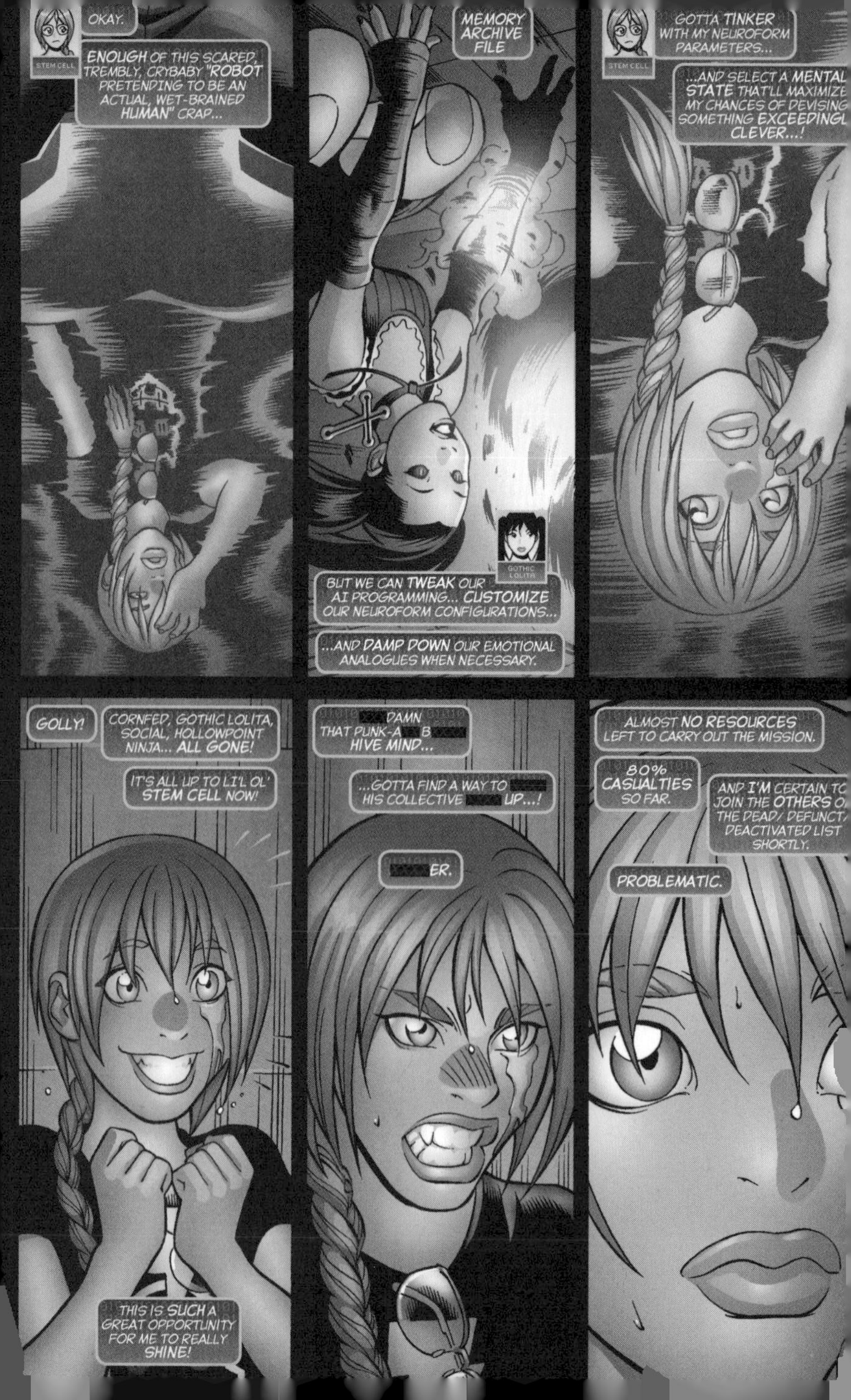

STEM CELL
OKAY.
ENOUGH OF THIS SCARED, TREMBLY, CRYBABY "ROBOT PRETENDING TO BE AN ACTUAL, WET-BRAINED HUMAN" CRAP...
MEMORY ARCHIVE FILE
GOTHIC LOLITA
BUT WE CAN TWEAK OUR AI PROGRAMMING... CUSTOMIZE OUR NEUROFORM CONFIGURATIONS...
...AND DAMP DOWN OUR EMOTIONAL ANALOGUES WHEN NECESSARY.
STEM CELL
GOTTA TINKER WITH MY NEUROFORM PARAMETERS...
...AND SELECT A MENTAL STATE THAT'LL MAXIMIZE MY CHANCES OF DEVISING SOMETHING EXCEEDINGL CLEVER...!
GOLLY!
CORNFED, GOTHIC LOLITA, SOCIAL, HOLLOWPOINT NINJA... ALL GONE!
IT'S ALL UP TO LI'L OL' STEM CELL NOW!
THIS IS SUCH A GREAT OPPORTUNITY FOR ME TO REALLY SHINE!
[redacted]DAMN THAT PUNK-A[redacted] B[redacted] HIVE MIND...
...GOTTA FIND A WAY TO [redacted] HIS COLLECTIVE [redacted] UP...!
[redacted]ER.
ALMOST NO RESOURCES LEFT TO CARRY OUT THE MISSION.
80% CASUALTIES SO FAR.
AND I'M CERTAIN TO JOIN THE OTHERS O THE DEAD/ DEFUNCT/ DEACTIVATED LIST SHORTLY.
PROBLEMATIC.

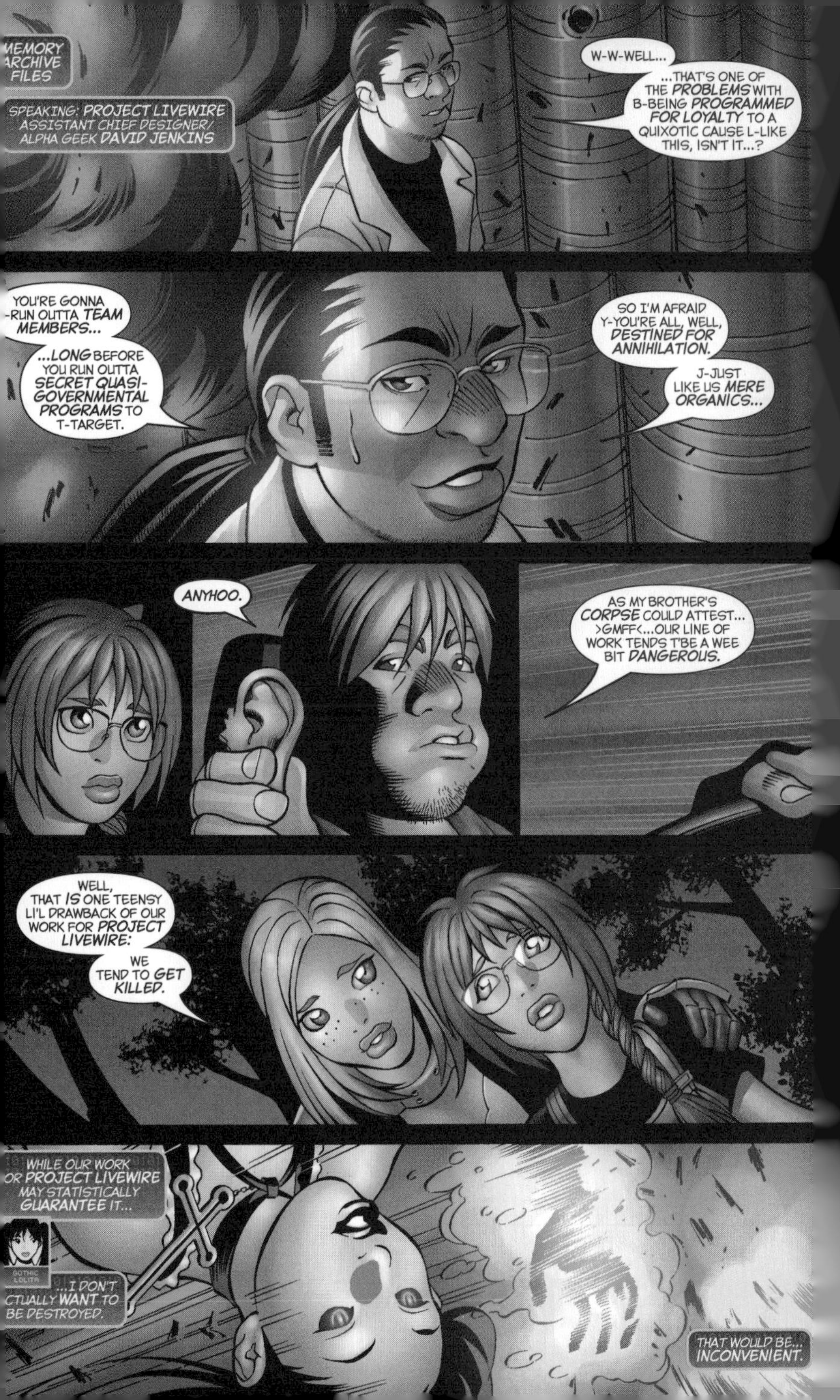
MEMORY ARCHIVE FILES
SPEAKING: PROJECT LIVEWIRE ASSISTANT CHIEF DESIGNER/ ALPHA GEEK DAVID JENKINS
W-W-WELL...
...THAT'S ONE OF THE PROBLEMS WITH B-BEING PROGRAMMED FOR LOYALTY TO A QUIXOTIC CAUSE L-LIKE THIS, ISN'T IT...?
YOU'RE GONNA -RUN OUTTA TEAM MEMBERS...
...LONG BEFORE YOU RUN OUTTA SECRET QUASI-GOVERNMENTAL PROGRAMS TO T-TARGET.
SO I'M AFRAID Y-YOU'RE ALL, WELL, DESTINED FOR ANNIHILATION.
J-JUST LIKE US MERE ORGANICS...
ANYHOO.
AS MY BROTHER'S CORPSE COULD ATTEST... >GMFF<...OUR LINE OF WORK TENDS T'BE A WEE BIT DANGEROUS.
WELL, THAT IS ONE TEENSY LI'L DRAWBACK OF OUR WORK FOR PROJECT LIVEWIRE:
WE TEND TO GET KILLED.
WHILE OUR WORK OR PROJECT LIVEWIRE MAY STATISTICALLY GUARANTEE IT...
GOTHIC LOLITA
...I DON'T CTUALLY WANT TO BE DESTROYED.
THAT WOULD BE... INCONVENIENT.

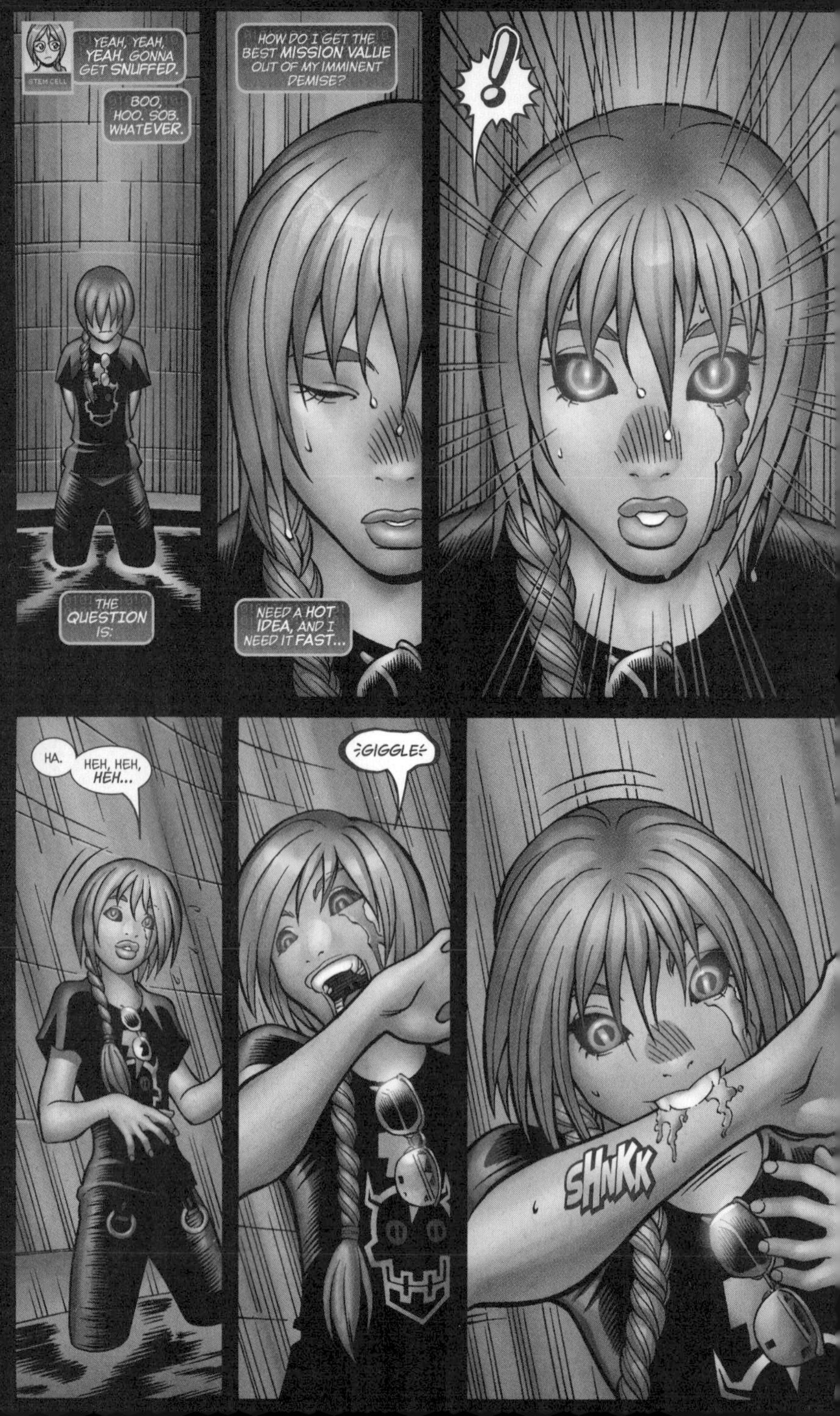
STEM CELL
YEAH, YEAH, YEAH. GONNA GET SNUFFED.
BOO, HOO. SOB. WHATEVER.
THE QUESTION IS:
HOW DO I GET THE BEST MISSION VALUE OUT OF MY IMMINENT DEMISE?
NEED A HOT IDEA, AND I NEED IT FAST...
!
HA.
HEH, HEH, HEH...
GIGGLE
SHNKK

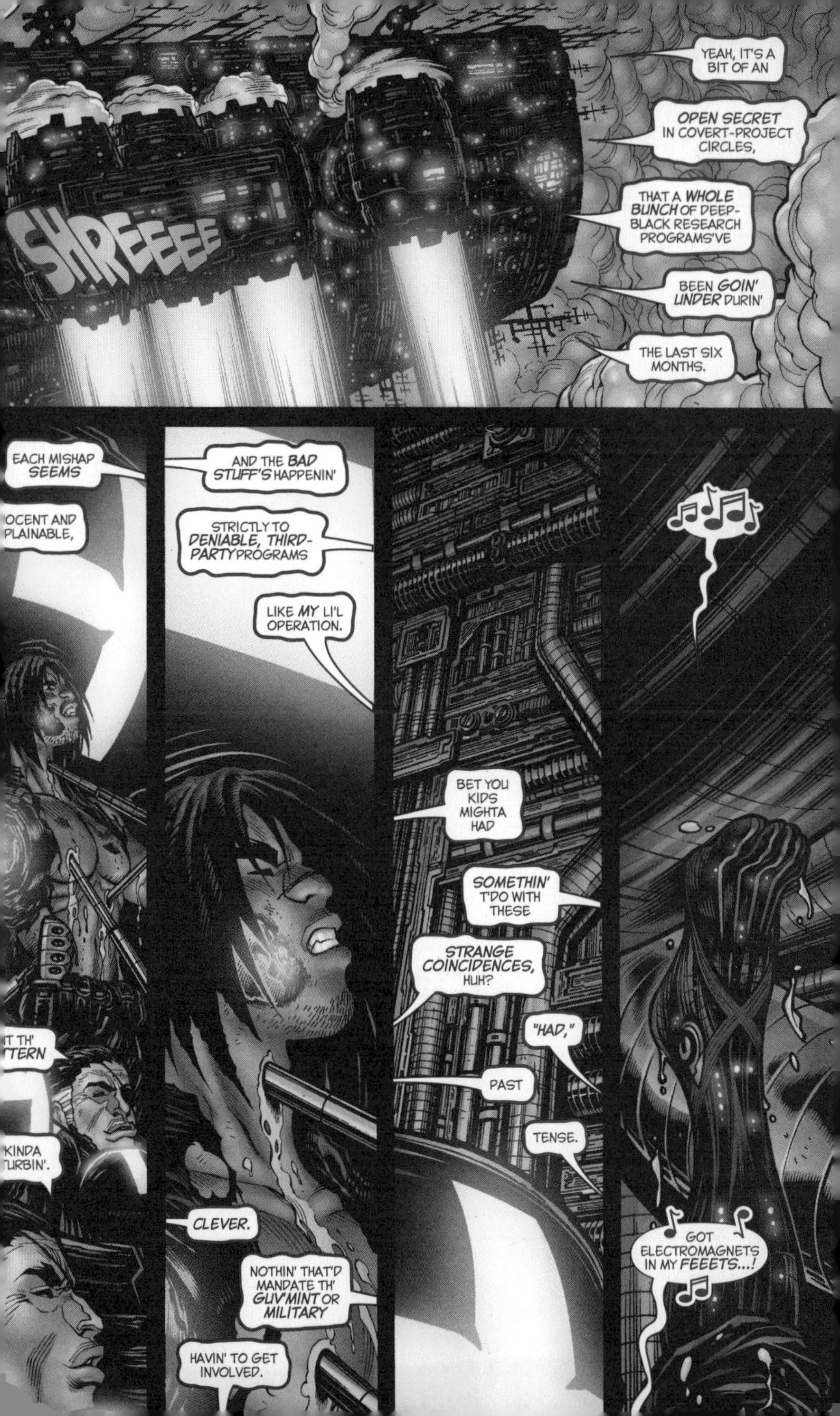

SHREEEE
YEAH, IT'S A BIT OF AN
OPEN SECRET IN COVERT-PROJECT CIRCLES,
THAT A WHOLE BUNCH OF DEEP-BLACK RESEARCH PROGRAMS'VE
BEEN GOIN' UNDER DURIN'
THE LAST SIX MONTHS.
EACH MISHAP SEEMS
OCENT AND PLAINABLE,
T TH' TTERN
KINDA TURBIN'.
AND THE BAD STUFF'S HAPPENIN'
STRICTLY TO DENIABLE, THIRD-PARTY PROGRAMS
LIKE MY LI'L OPERATION.
CLEVER.
NOTHIN' THAT'D MANDATE TH' GUV'MINT OR MILITARY
HAVIN' TO GET INVOLVED.
BET YOU KIDS MIGHTA HAD
SOMETHIN' T'DO WITH THESE
STRANGE COINCIDENCES, HUH?
"HAD,"
PAST
TENSE.
GOT ELECTROMAGNETS IN MY FEEETS...!

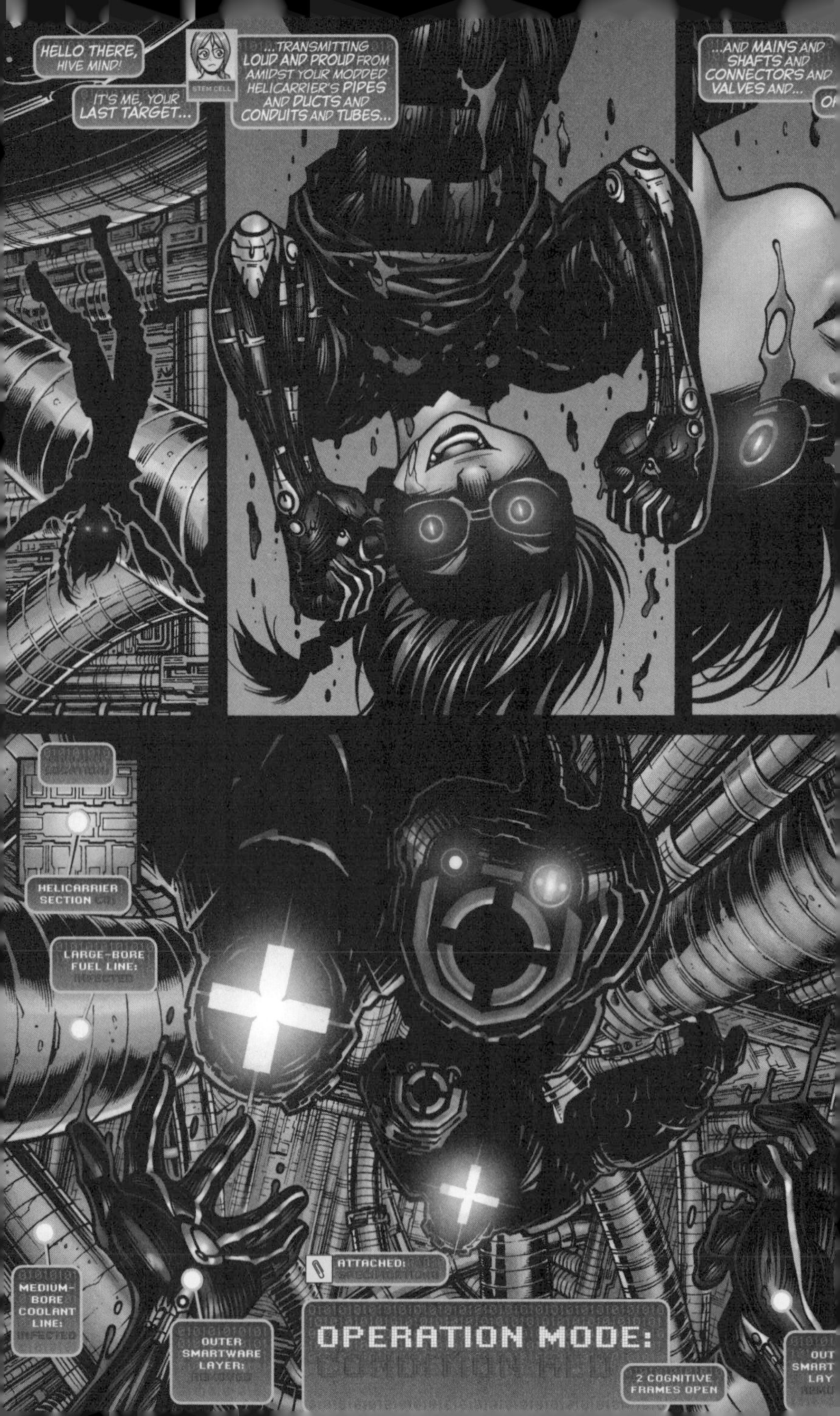
HELLO THERE, HIVE MIND!
IT'S ME, YOUR LAST TARGET...
STEM CELL
...TRANSMITTING LOUD AND PROUD FROM AMIDST YOUR MODDED HELICARRIER'S PIPES AND DUCTS AND CONDUITS AND TUBES...
...AND MAINS AND SHAFTS AND CONNECTORS AND VALVES AND...
HELICARRIER SECTION
LARGE-BORE FUEL LINE:
MEDIUM-BORE COOLANT LINE:
ATTACHED:
OUTER SMARTWARE LAYER:
OPERATION MODE:
2 COGNITIVE FRAMES OPEN

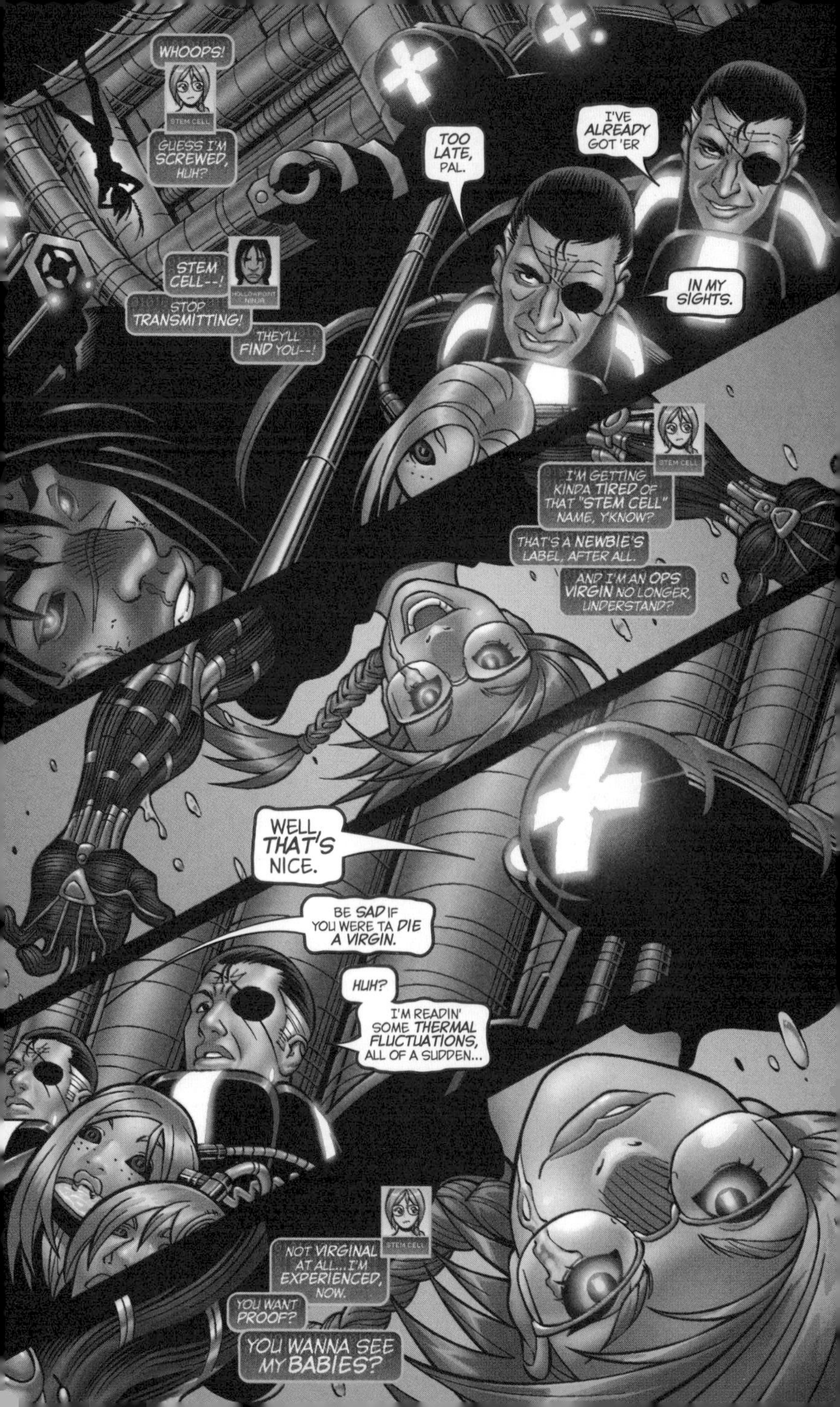

WHOOPS!
STEM CELL
GUESS I'M SCREWED, HUH?
TOO LATE, PAL.
I'VE ALREADY GOT 'ER
IN MY SIGHTS.
STEM CELL--!
HOLLOWPOINT NINJA
STOP TRANSMITTING!
THEY'LL FIND YOU--!
STEM CELL
I'M GETTING KINDA TIRED OF THAT "STEM CELL" NAME, Y'KNOW?
THAT'S A NEWBIE'S LABEL, AFTER ALL.
AND I'M AN OPS VIRGIN NO LONGER, UNDERSTAND?
WELL, THAT'S NICE.
BE SAD IF YOU WERE TA DIE A VIRGIN.
HUH?
I'M READIN' SOME THERMAL FLUCTUATIONS, ALL OF A SUDDEN...
STEM CELL
NOT VIRGINAL AT ALL... I'M EXPERIENCED, NOW.
YOU WANT PROOF?
YOU WANNA SEE MY BABIES?

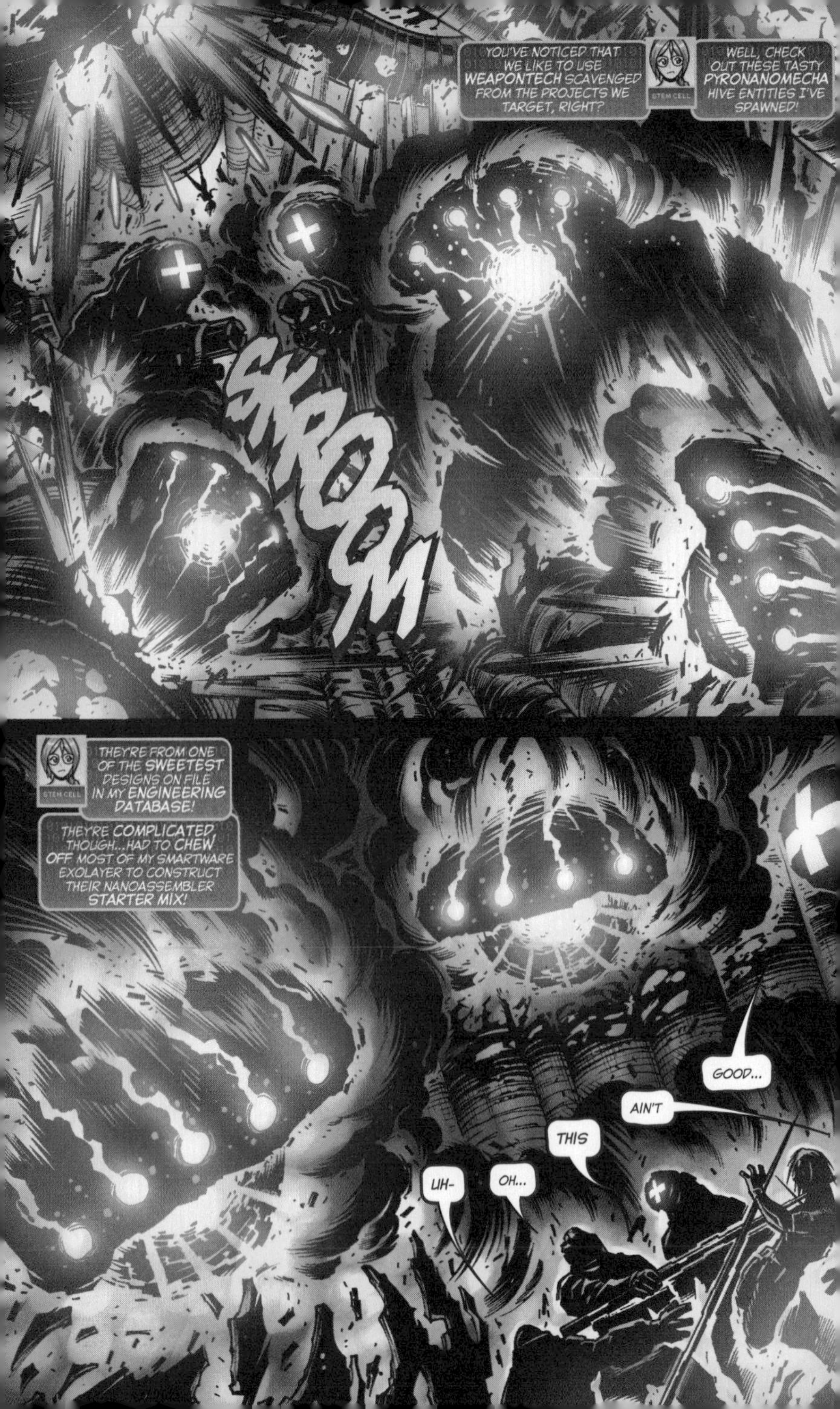
YOU'VE NOTICED THAT WE LIKE TO USE WEAPONTECH SCAVENGED FROM THE PROJECTS WE TARGET, RIGHT?
STEM CELL
WELL, CHECK OUT THESE TASTY PYRONANOMECHA HIVE ENTITIES I'VE SPAWNED!
SKROOM
STEM CELL
THEY'RE FROM ONE OF THE SWEETEST DESIGNS ON FILE IN MY ENGINEERING DATABASE!
THEY'RE COMPLICATED THOUGH...HAD TO CHEW OFF MOST OF MY SMARTWARE EXOLAYER TO CONSTRUCT THEIR NANOASSEMBLER STARTER MIX!
UH-
OH...
THIS
AIN'T
GOOD...

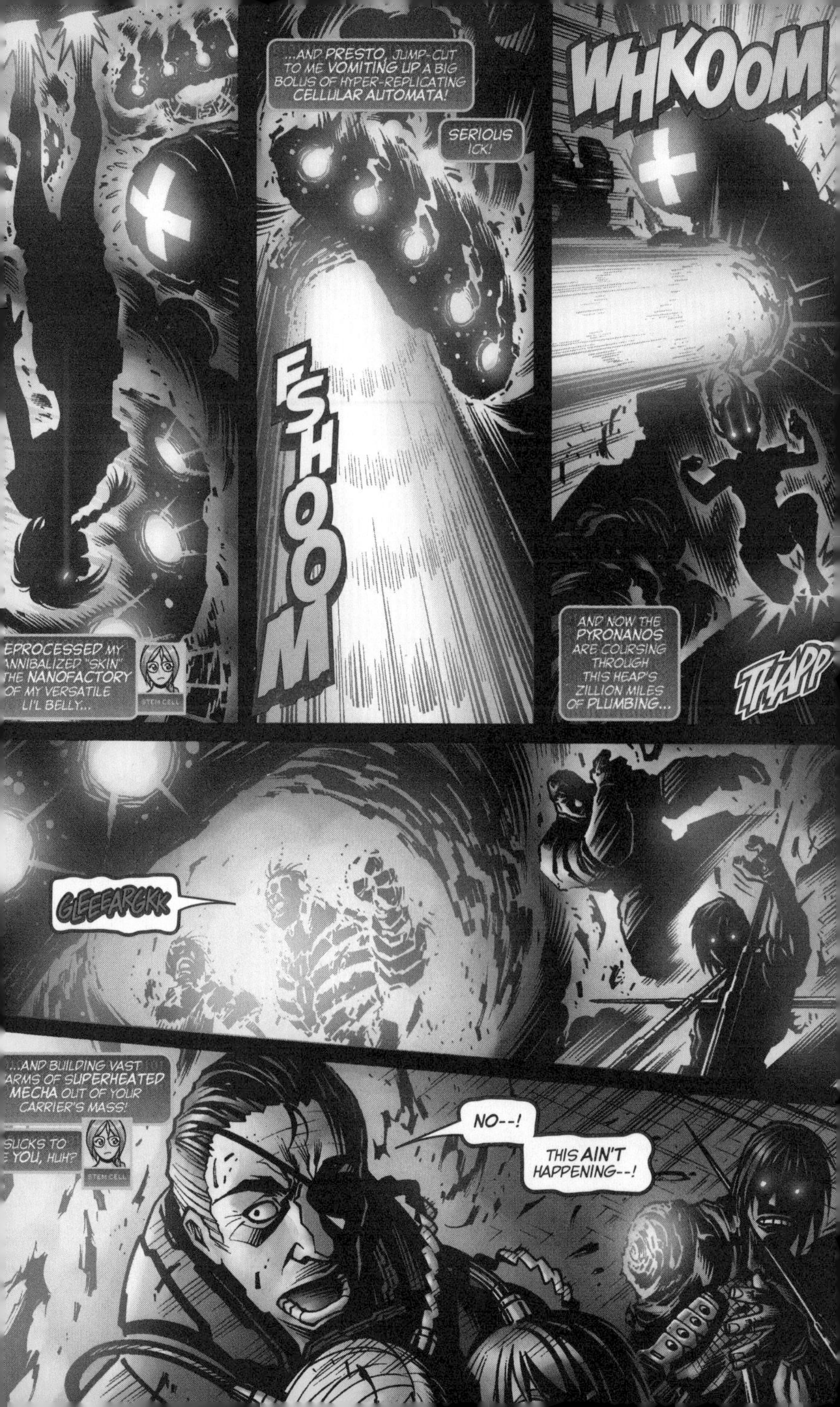

EPROCESSED MY ANNIBALIZED "SKIN" THE NANOFACTORY OF MY VERSATILE LI'L BELLY...
STEM CELL
...AND PRESTO, JUMP-CUT TO ME VOMITING UP A BIG BOLUS OF HYPER-REPLICATING CELLULAR AUTOMATA!
SERIOUS ICK!
ESHOOM
WHKOOM
AND NOW THE PYRONANOS ARE COURSING THROUGH THIS HEAP'S ZILLION MILES OF PLUMBING...
THAPP
GLEEFARGKK
...AND BUILDING VAST ARMS OF SUPERHEATED MECHA OUT OF YOUR CARRIER'S MASS!
SUCKS TO E YOU, HUH?
STEM CELL
NO--!
THIS AIN'T HAPPENING--!

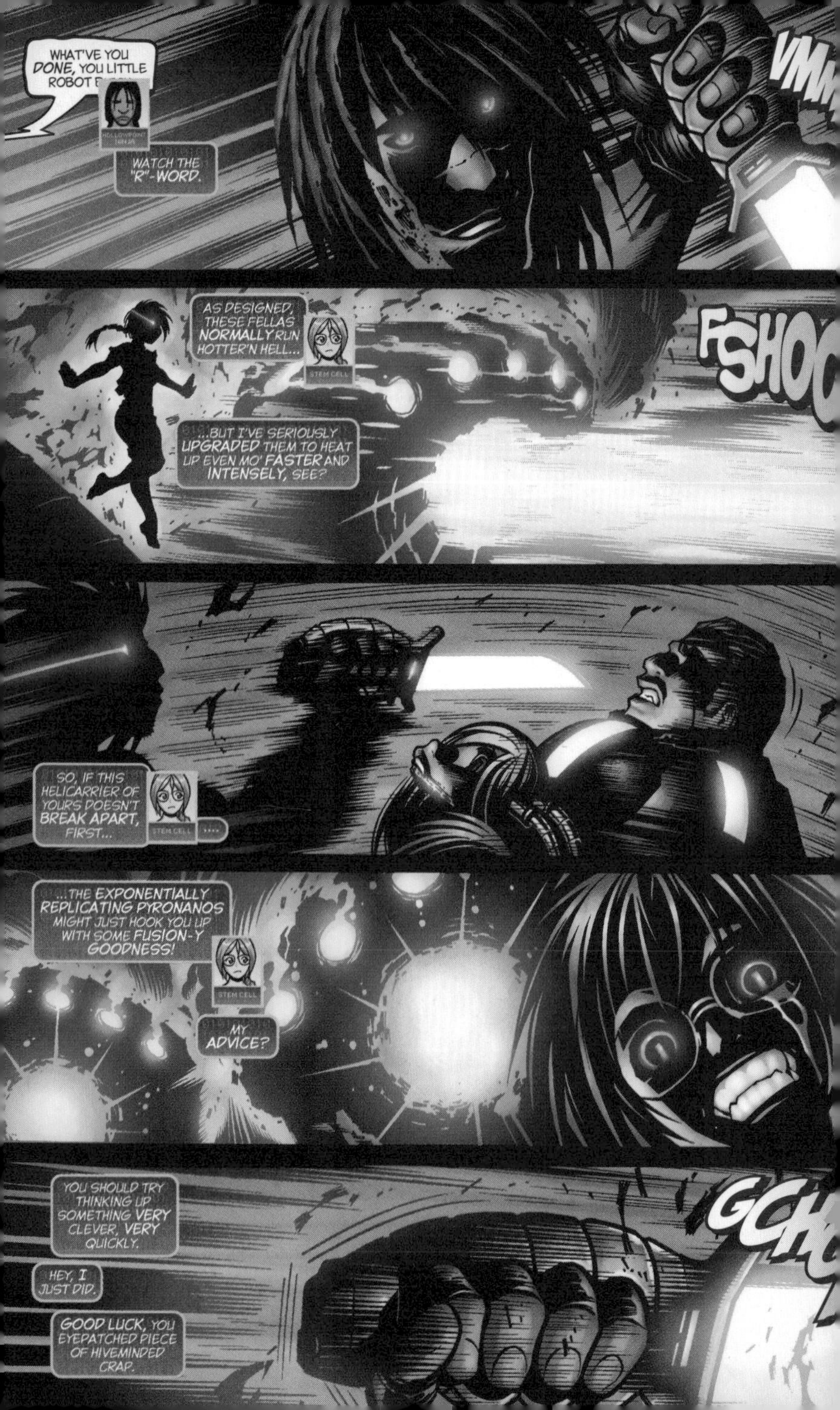
WHAT'VE YOU DONE, YOU LITTLE ROBOT
HOLLOWPOINT NINJA
WATCH THE "R"-WORD.
VMM
AS DESIGNED, THESE FELLAS NORMALLY RUN HOTTER'N HELL...
STEM CELL
...BUT I'VE SERIOUSLY UPGRADED THEM TO HEAT UP EVEN MO' FASTER AND INTENSELY, SEE?
FSHOO
SO, IF THIS HELICARRIER OF YOURS DOESN'T BREAK APART, FIRST...
STEM CELL
...
...THE EXPONENTIALLY REPLICATING PYRONANOS MIGHT JUST HOOK YOU UP WITH SOME FUSION-Y GOODNESS!
STEM CELL
MY ADVICE?
YOU SHOULD TRY THINKING UP SOMETHING VERY CLEVER, VERY QUICKLY.
HEY, I JUST DID.
GOOD LUCK, YOU EYEPATCHED PIECE OF HIVEMINDED CRAP.
GCH

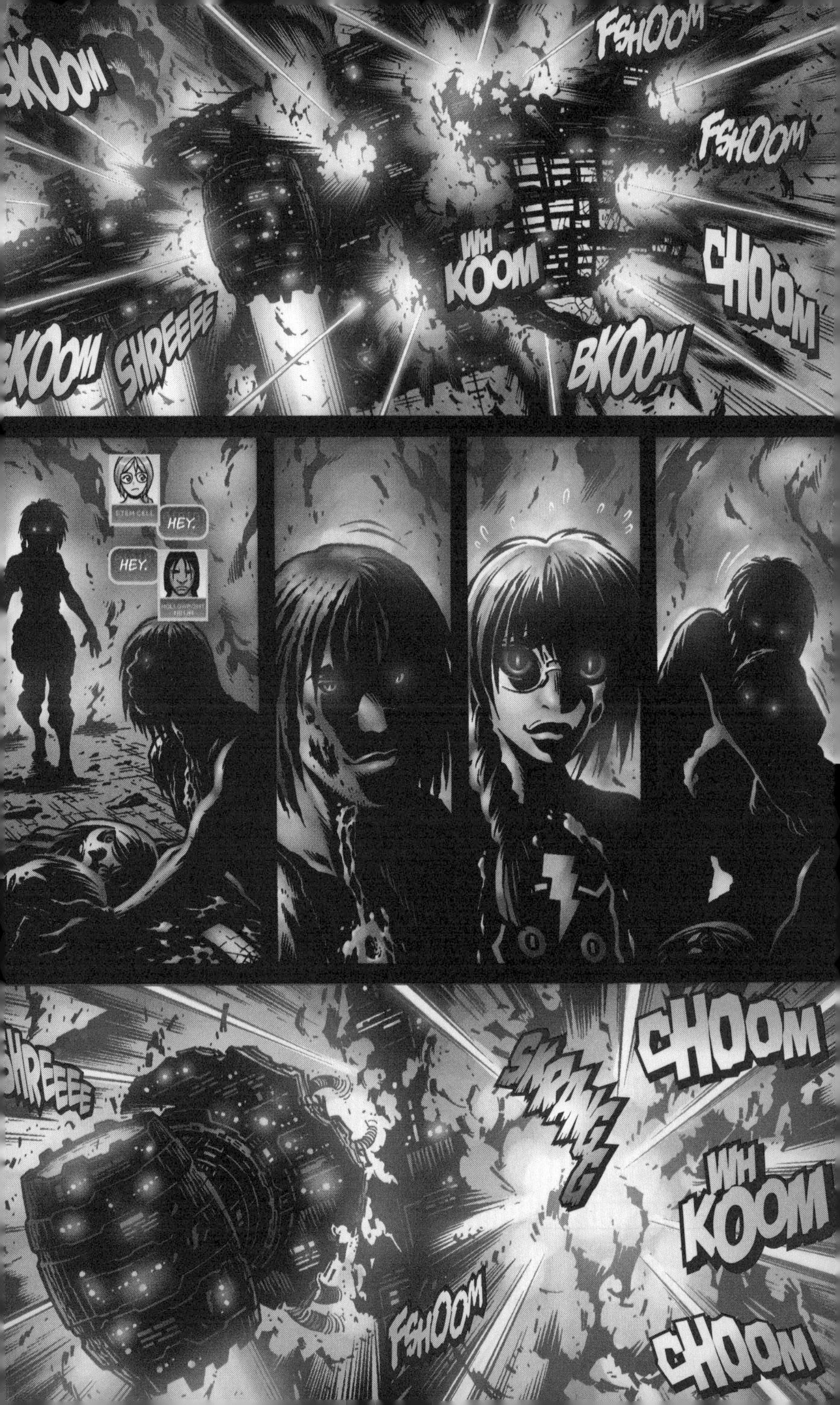
SKOOM
FSHOOM
FSHOOM
WH KOOM
CHOOM
SKOOM
SHREEEE
BKOOM
HEY.
HEY.
SHREEEE
CHOOM
WH KOOM
FSHOOM
CHOOM

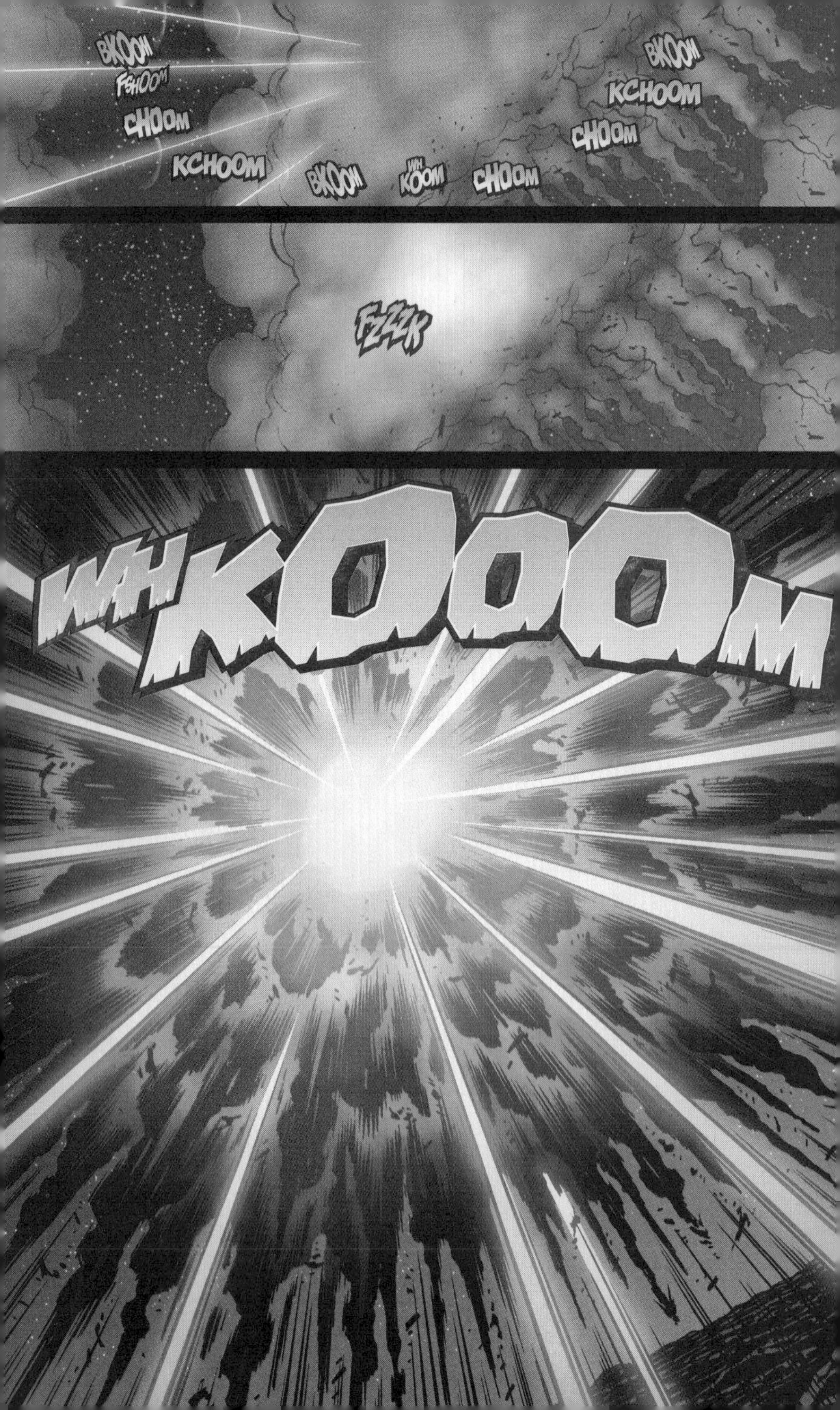
BKOOM
FSHOOM
CHOOM
KCHOOM
BKOOM
WH KOOM
CHOOM
CHOOM
KCHOOM
BKOOM
FZZZK
WH KOOOOM

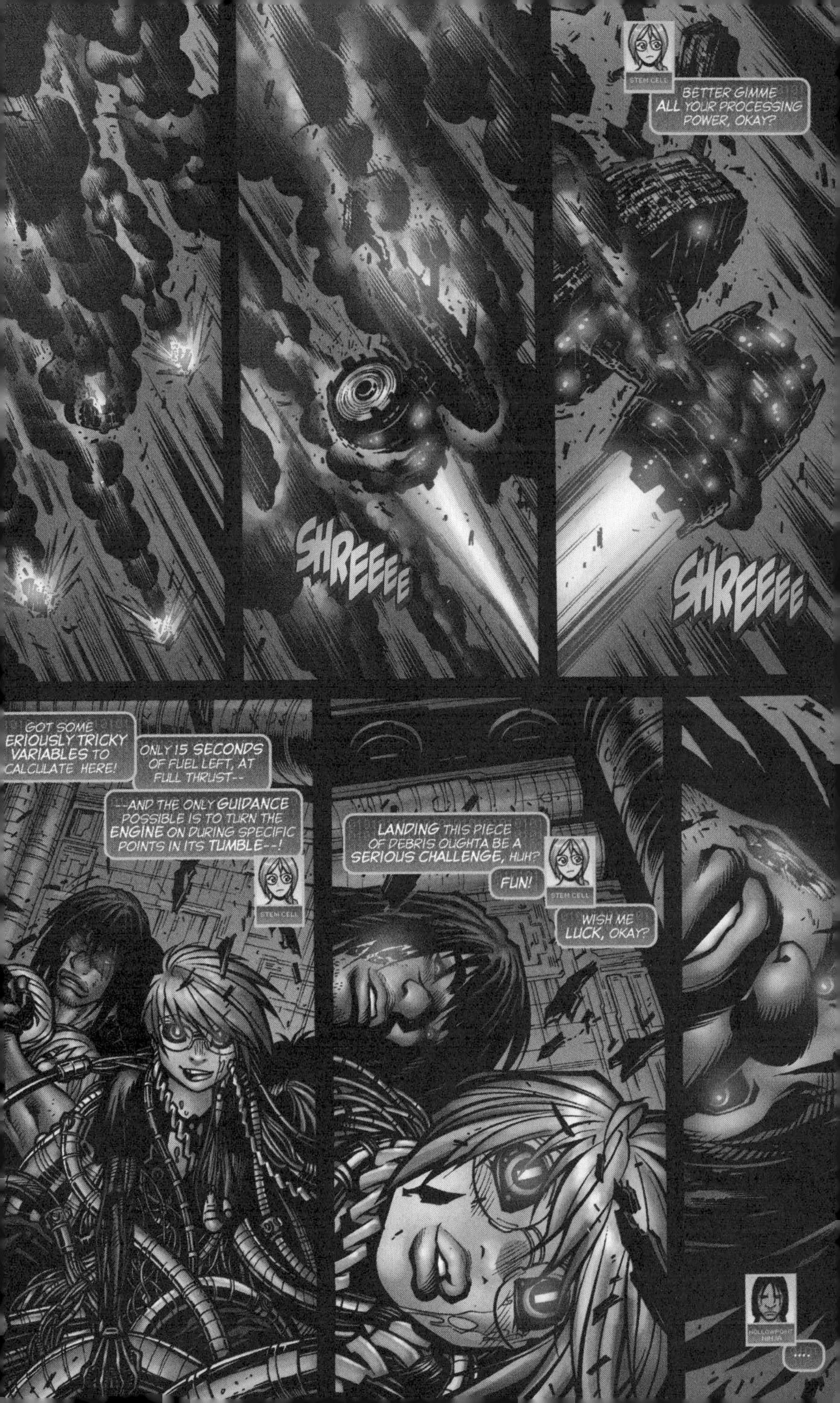

STEM CELL
BETTER GIMME ALL YOUR PROCESSING POWER, OKAY?
SHREEEE
SHREEEE
GOT SOME ERIOUSLY TRICKY VARIABLES TO CALCULATE HERE!
ONLY 15 SECONDS OF FUEL LEFT, AT FULL THRUST--
--AND THE ONLY GUIDANCE POSSIBLE IS TO TURN THE ENGINE ON DURING SPECIFIC POINTS IN ITS TUMBLE--!
STEM CELL
LANDING THIS PIECE OF DEBRIS OUGHTA BE A SERIOUS CHALLENGE, HUH?
FUN!
STEM CELL
WISH ME LUCK, OKAY?
HOLLOWPOINT NINJA
....

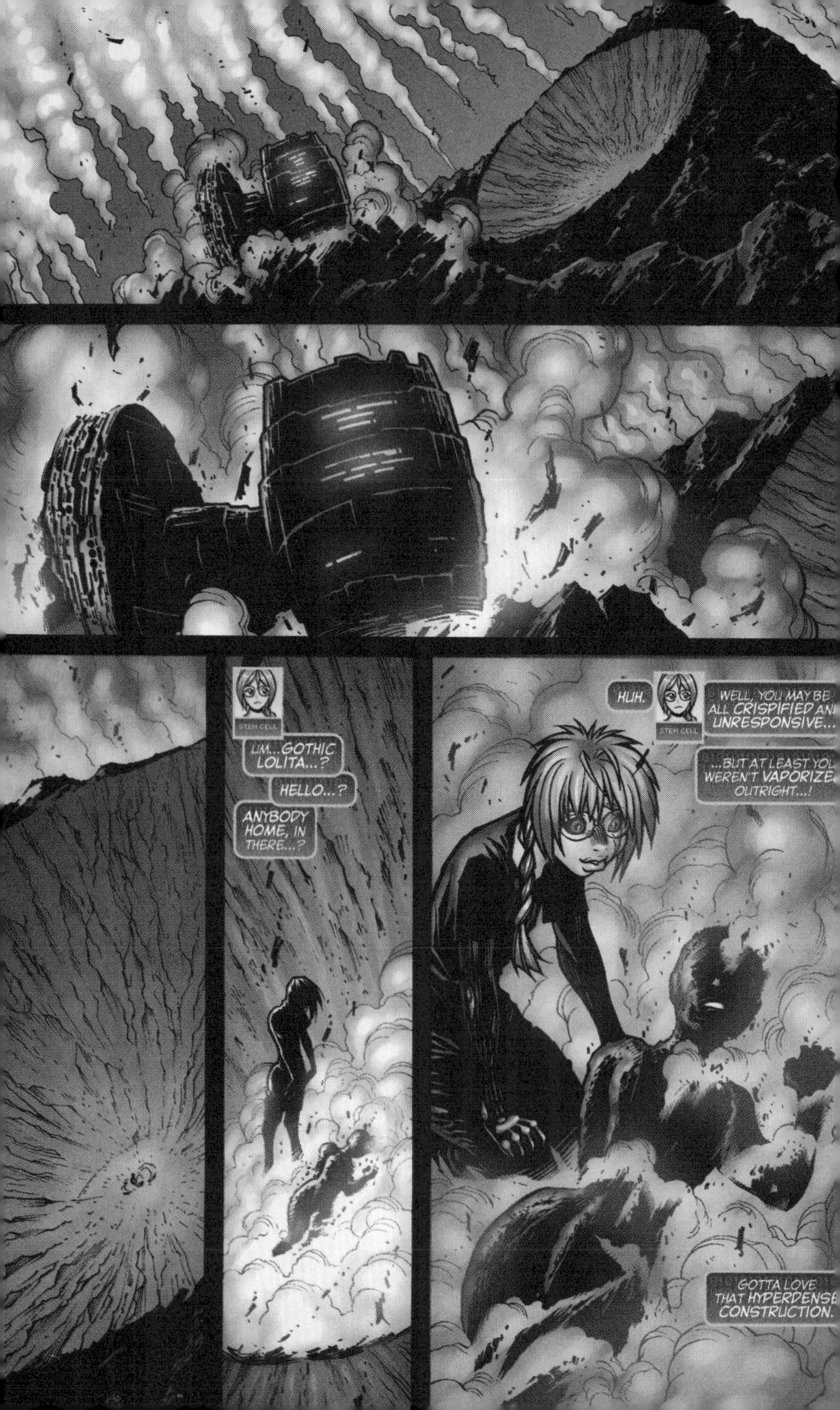
STEM CELL
UM...GOTHIC LOLITA...?
HELLO...?
ANYBODY HOME, IN THERE...?
HUH.
STEM CELL
WELL, YOU MAY BE ALL CRISPIFIED AN UNRESPONSIVE...
...BUT AT LEAST YO WEREN'T VAPORIZE OUTRIGHT...!
GOTTA LOVE THAT HYPERDENSE CONSTRUCTION.

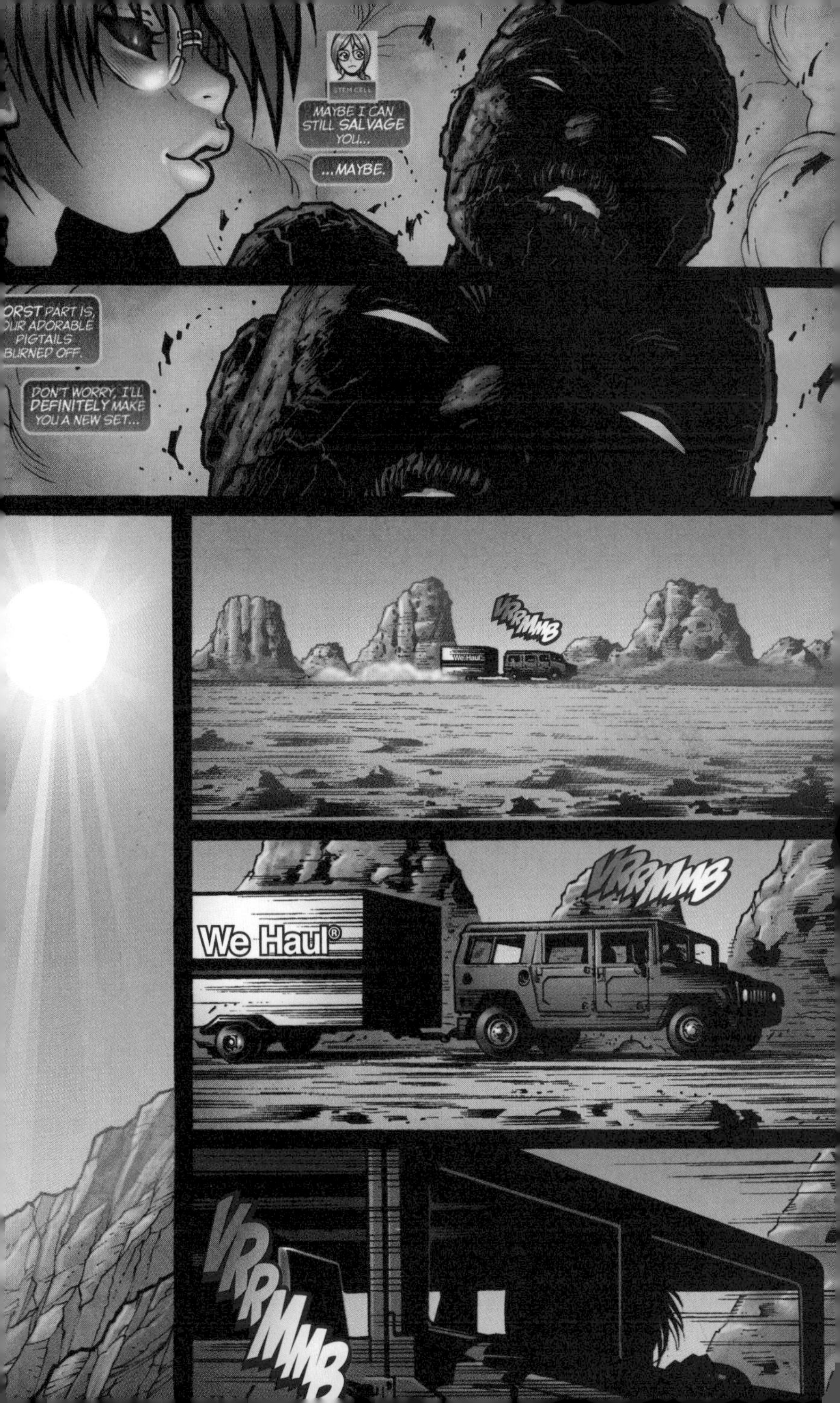
STEM CELL
MAYBE I CAN STILL SALVAGE YOU...
...MAYBE.
ORST PART IS, OUR ADORABLE PIGTAILS BURNED OFF.
DON'T WORRY, I'LL DEFINITELY MAKE YOU A NEW SET...
VRRMMB
We Haul
VRRMMB
We Haul®
VRRMMB

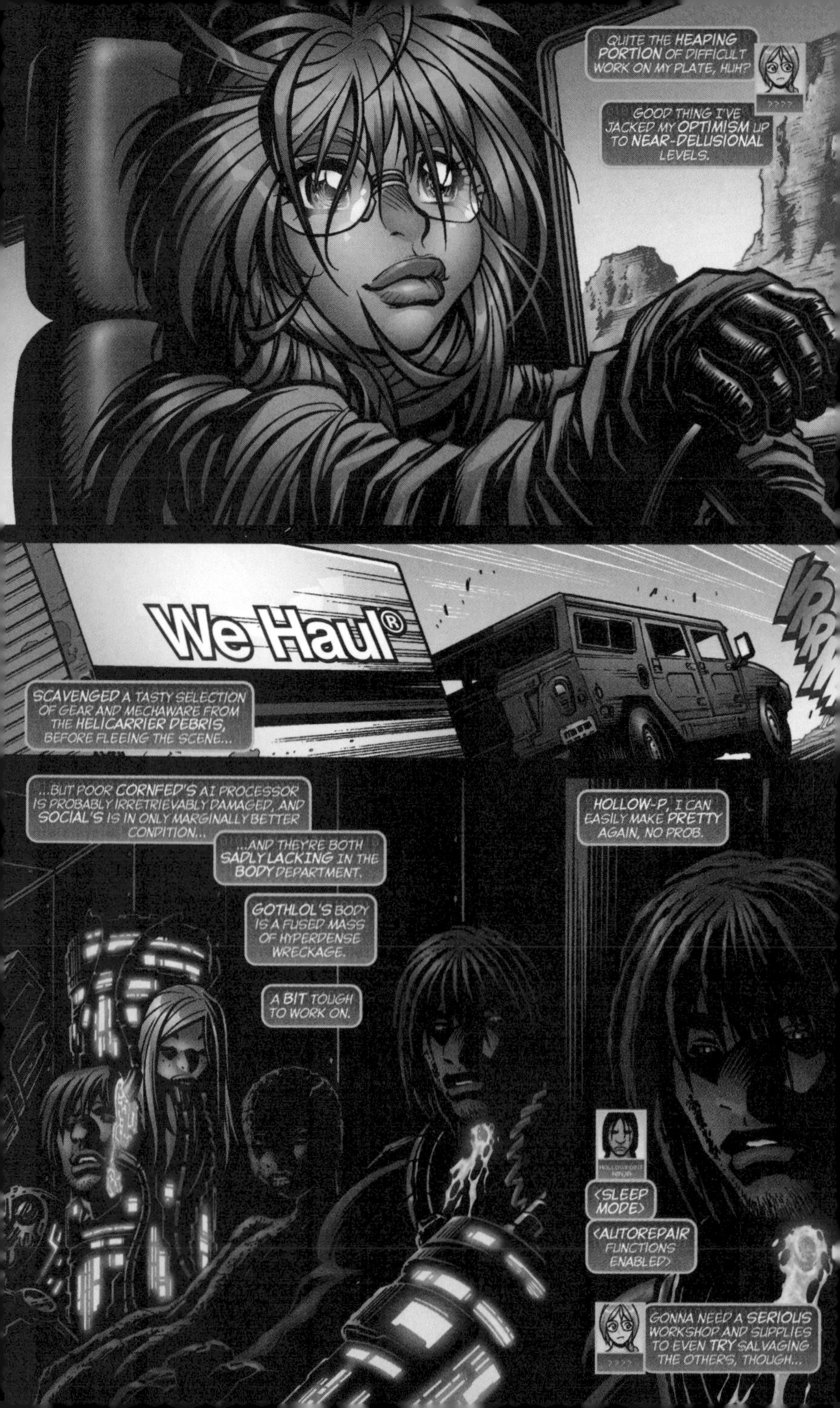
QUITE THE HEAPING PORTION OF DIFFICULT WORK ON MY PLATE, HUH?
????
GOOD THING I'VE JACKED MY OPTIMISM UP TO NEAR-DELUSIONAL LEVELS.
We Haul®
VRRM
SCAVENGED A TASTY SELECTION OF GEAR AND MECHAWARE FROM THE HELICARRIER DEBRIS, BEFORE FLEEING THE SCENE...
...BUT POOR CORNFED'S AI PROCESSOR IS PROBABLY IRRETRIEVABLY DAMAGED, AND SOCIAL'S IS IN ONLY MARGINALLY BETTER CONDITION...
...AND THEY'RE BOTH SADLY LACKING IN THE BODY DEPARTMENT.
GOTHLOL'S BODY IS A FUSED MASS OF HYPERDENSE WRECKAGE.
A BIT TOUGH TO WORK ON.
HOLLOW-P, I CAN EASILY MAKE PRETTY AGAIN, NO PROB.
<SLEEP MODE>
<AUTOREPAIR FUNCTIONS ENABLED>
????
GONNA NEED A SERIOUS WORKSHOP AND SUPPLIES TO EVEN TRY SALVAGING THE OTHERS, THOUGH...

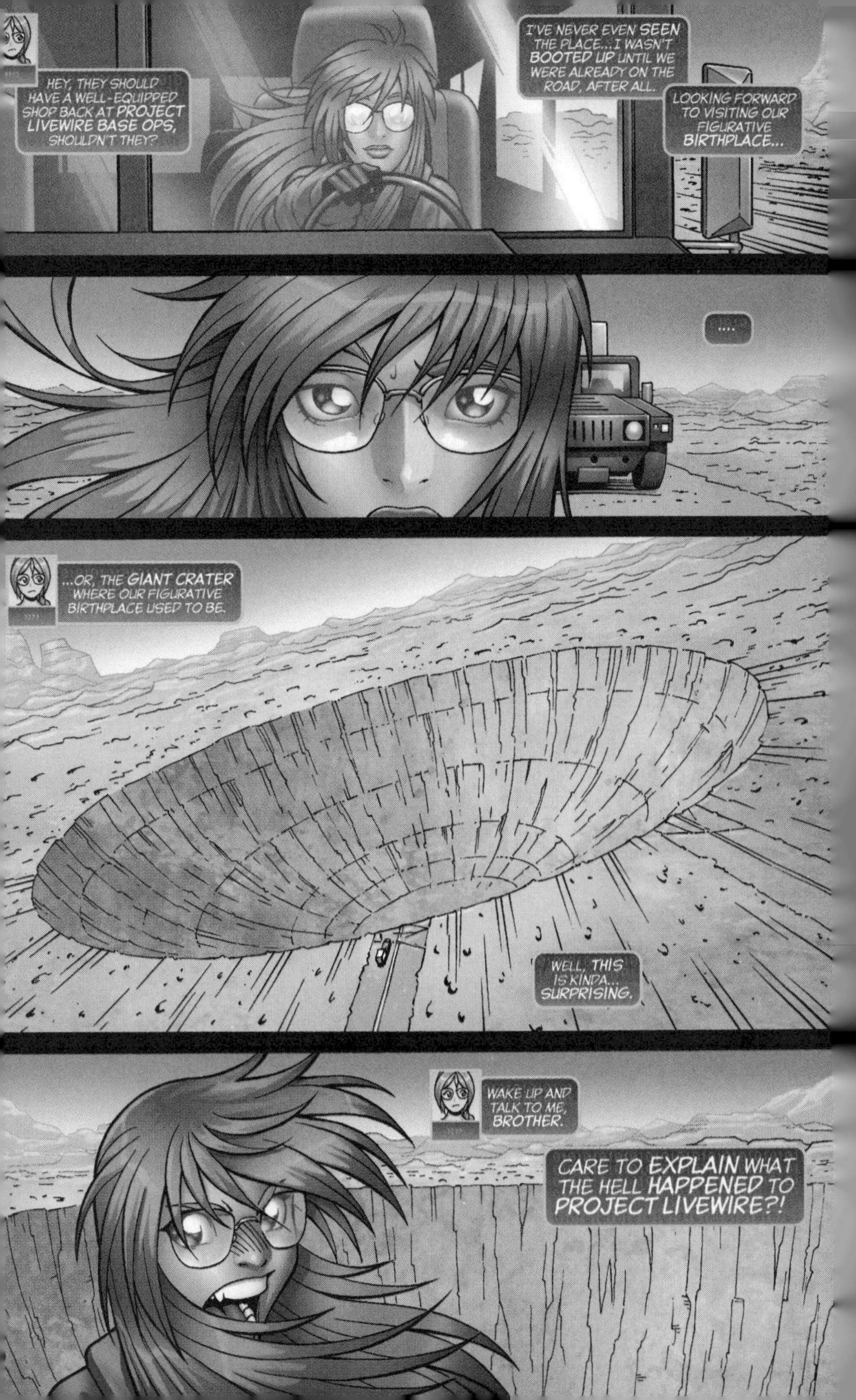
HEY, THEY SHOULD HAVE A WELL-EQUIPPED SHOP BACK AT PROJECT LIVEWIRE BASE OPS, SHOULDN'T THEY?
I'VE NEVER EVEN SEEN THE PLACE... I WASN'T BOOTED UP UNTIL WE WERE ALREADY ON THE ROAD, AFTER ALL.
LOOKING FORWARD TO VISITING OUR FIGURATIVE BIRTHPLACE...
....
...OR, THE GIANT CRATER WHERE OUR FIGURATIVE BIRTHPLACE USED TO BE.
WELL, THIS IS KINDA... SURPRISING.
WAKE UP AND TALK TO ME, BROTHER.
CARE TO EXPLAIN WHAT THE HELL HAPPENED TO PROJECT LIVEWIRE?!

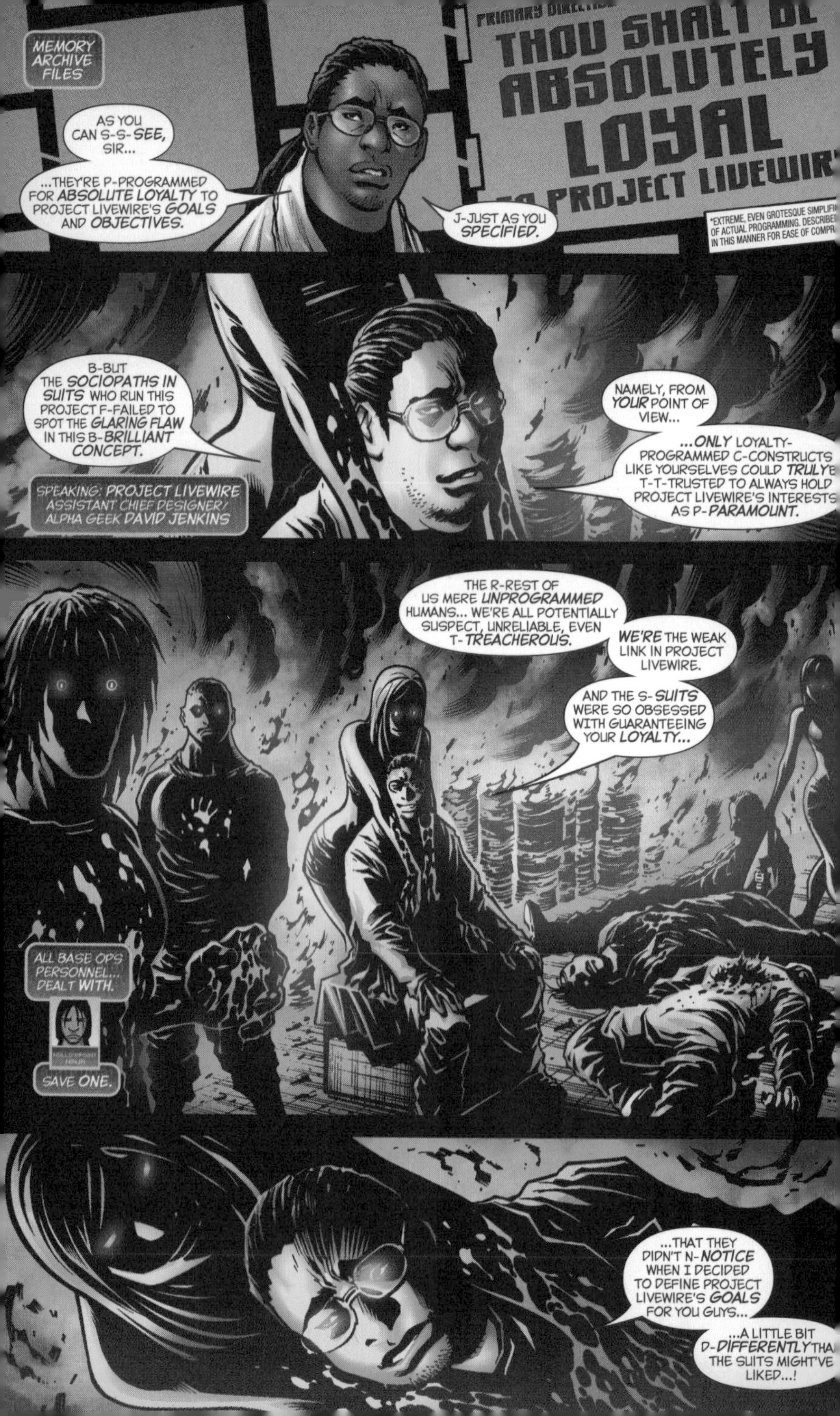
MEMORY ARCHIVE FILES
AS YOU CAN S-S-SEE, SIR...
...THEY'RE P-PROGRAMMED FOR ABSOLUTE LOYALTY TO PROJECT LIVEWIRE'S GOALS AND OBJECTIVES.
PRIMARY DIRECTI
THOU SHALT BE ABSOLUTELY LOYAL TO PROJECT LIVEWIR
J-JUST AS YOU SPECIFIED.
*EXTREME, EVEN GROTESQUE SIMPLIFI OF ACTUAL PROGRAMMING. DESCRIBE IN THIS MANNER FOR EASE OF COMPR
B-BUT THE SOCIOPATHS IN SUITS WHO RUN THIS PROJECT F-FAILED TO SPOT THE GLARING FLAW IN THIS B-BRILLIANT CONCEPT.
SPEAKING: PROJECT LIVEWIRE ASSISTANT CHIEF DESIGNER/ ALPHA GEEK DAVID JENKINS
NAMELY, FROM YOUR POINT OF VIEW...
...ONLY LOYALTY-PROGRAMMED C-CONSTRUCTS LIKE YOURSELVES COULD TRULY BE T-T-TRUSTED TO ALWAYS HOLD PROJECT LIVEWIRE'S INTERESTS AS P-PARAMOUNT.
THE R-REST OF US MERE UNPROGRAMMED HUMANS... WE'RE ALL POTENTIALLY SUSPECT, UNRELIABLE, EVEN T-TREACHEROUS.
WE'RE THE WEAK LINK IN PROJECT LIVEWIRE.
AND THE S-SUITS WERE SO OBSESSED WITH GUARANTEEING YOUR LOYALTY...
ALL BASE OPS PERSONNEL... DEALT WITH.
SAVE ONE.
...THAT THEY DIDN'T N-NOTICE WHEN I DECIDED TO DEFINE PROJECT LIVEWIRE'S GOALS FOR YOU GUYS...
...A LITTLE BIT D-DIFFERENTLY THAN THE SUITS MIGHT'VE LIKED...!

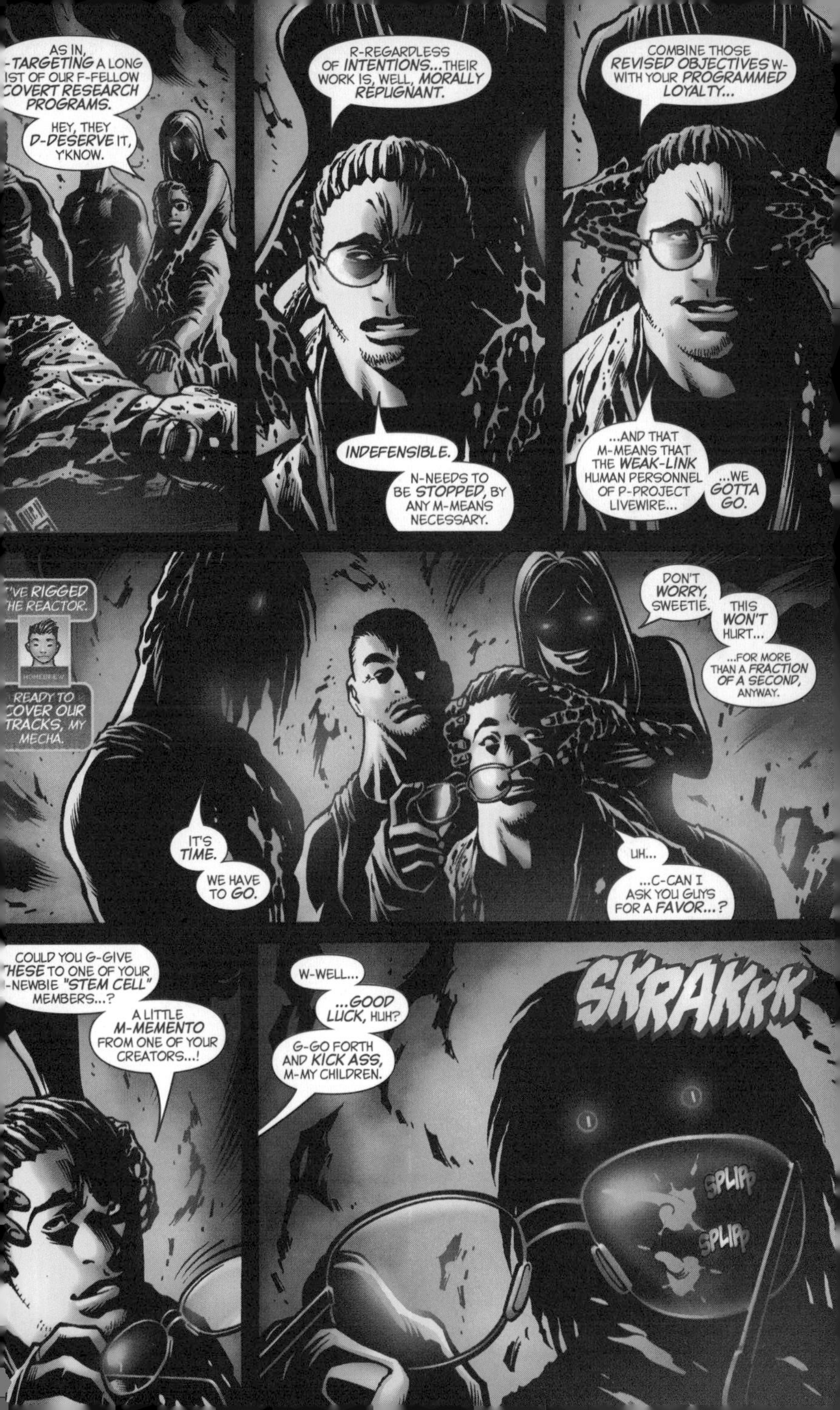
AS IN, -TARGETING A LONG IST OF OUR F-FELLOW COVERT RESEARCH PROGRAMS.
HEY, THEY D-DESERVE IT, Y'KNOW.
R-REGARDLESS OF INTENTIONS...THEIR WORK IS, WELL, MORALLY REPUGNANT.
INDEFENSIBLE.
N-NEEDS TO BE STOPPED, BY ANY M-MEANS NECESSARY.
COMBINE THOSE REVISED OBJECTIVES W-WITH YOUR PROGRAMMED LOYALTY...
...AND THAT M-MEANS THAT THE WEAK-LINK HUMAN PERSONNEL OF P-PROJECT LIVEWIRE...
...WE GOTTA GO.
'VE RIGGED THE REACTOR.
HOMEBREW
READY TO COVER OUR TRACKS, MY MECHA.
DON'T WORRY, SWEETIE.
THIS WON'T HURT...
...FOR MORE THAN A FRACTION OF A SECOND, ANYWAY.
IT'S TIME.
WE HAVE TO GO.
UH...
...C-CAN I ASK YOU GUYS FOR A FAVOR...?
COULD YOU G-GIVE THESE TO ONE OF YOUR -NEWBIE "STEM CELL" MEMBERS...?
A LITTLE M-MEMENTO FROM ONE OF YOUR CREATORS...!
W-WELL...
...GOOD LUCK, HUH?
G-GO FORTH AND KICK ASS, M-MY CHILDREN.
SKRAKKK
SPLIPP
SPLIPP

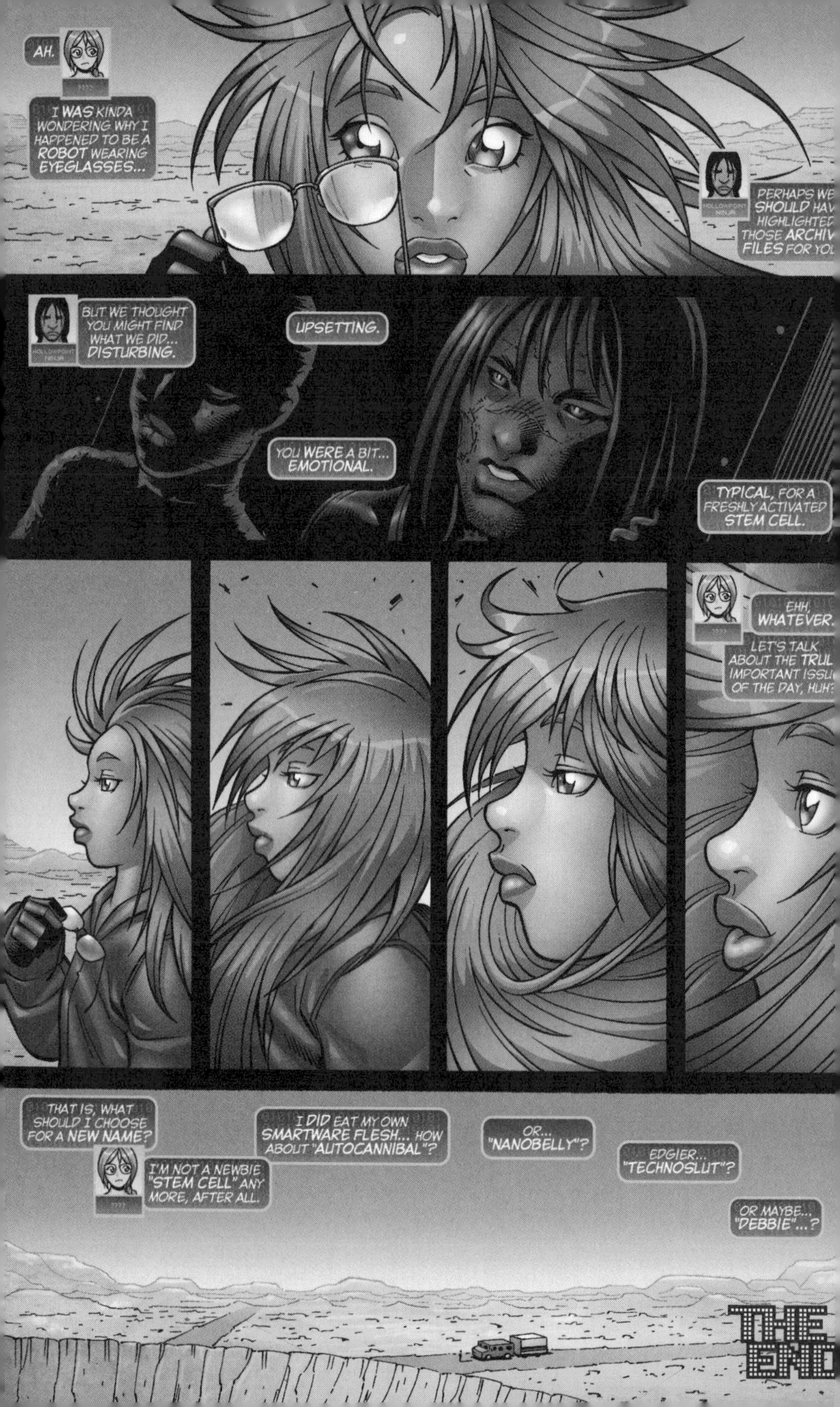

AH.
???
I WAS KINDA WONDERING WHY I HAPPENED TO BE A ROBOT WEARING EYEGLASSES...
HOLLOWPOINT NINJA
PERHAPS WE SHOULD HAV HIGHLIGHTED THOSE ARCHIV FILES FOR YOU
HOLLOWPOINT NINJA
BUT WE THOUGHT YOU MIGHT FIND WHAT WE DID... DISTURBING.
UPSETTING.
YOU WERE A BIT... EMOTIONAL.
TYPICAL, FOR A FRESHLY ACTIVATED STEM CELL.
???
EHH, WHATEVER.
LET'S TALK ABOUT THE TRUL IMPORTANT ISSU OF THE DAY, HUH?
THAT IS, WHAT SHOULD I CHOOSE FOR A NEW NAME?
???
I'M NOT A NEWBIE "STEM CELL" ANY MORE, AFTER ALL.
I DID EAT MY OWN SMARTWARE FLESH... HOW ABOUT "AUTOCANNIBAL"?
OR... "NANOBELLY"?
EDGIER... "TECHNOSLUT"?
OR MAYBE... "DEBBIE"...?
THE END

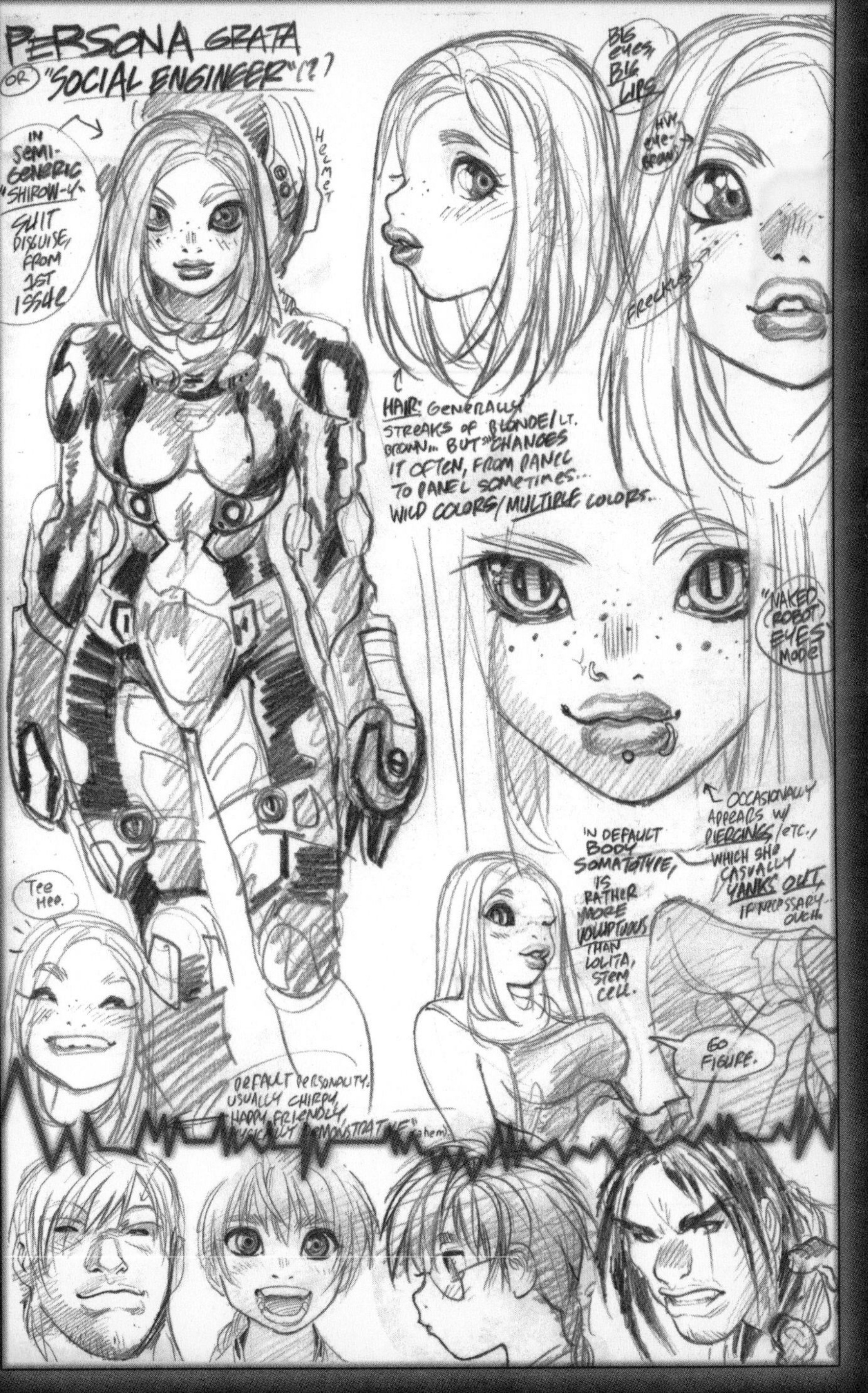
PERSONA GRATA
OR "SOCIAL ENGINEER" (?)
IN SEMI-GENERIC "SHIROW-Y" SUIT DISGUISE, FROM 1ST ISSUE
HELMET
BIG EYES, BIG LIPS
HVY EYE-BROW
FRECKLES
HAIR: GENERALLY STREAKS OF BLONDE/LT. BROWN... BUT "CHANGES" IT OFTEN, FROM PANEL TO PANEL SOMETIMES... WILD COLORS/MULTIPLE COLORS..
"NAKED ROBOT EYES" MODE
OCCASIONALLY APPEARS W/ PIERCINGS/ETC., WHICH SHE CASUALLY YANKS OUT, IF NECESSARY. OUCH.
IN DEFAULT BODY SOMATOTYPE, IS RATHER MORE VOLUPTUOUS THAN LOLITA, STEM CELL.
Tee Hee.
GO FIGURE.
DEFAULT PERSONALITY: USUALLY CHIRPY, HAPPY, FRIENDLY, PHYSICALLY DEMONSTRATIVE (ahem)

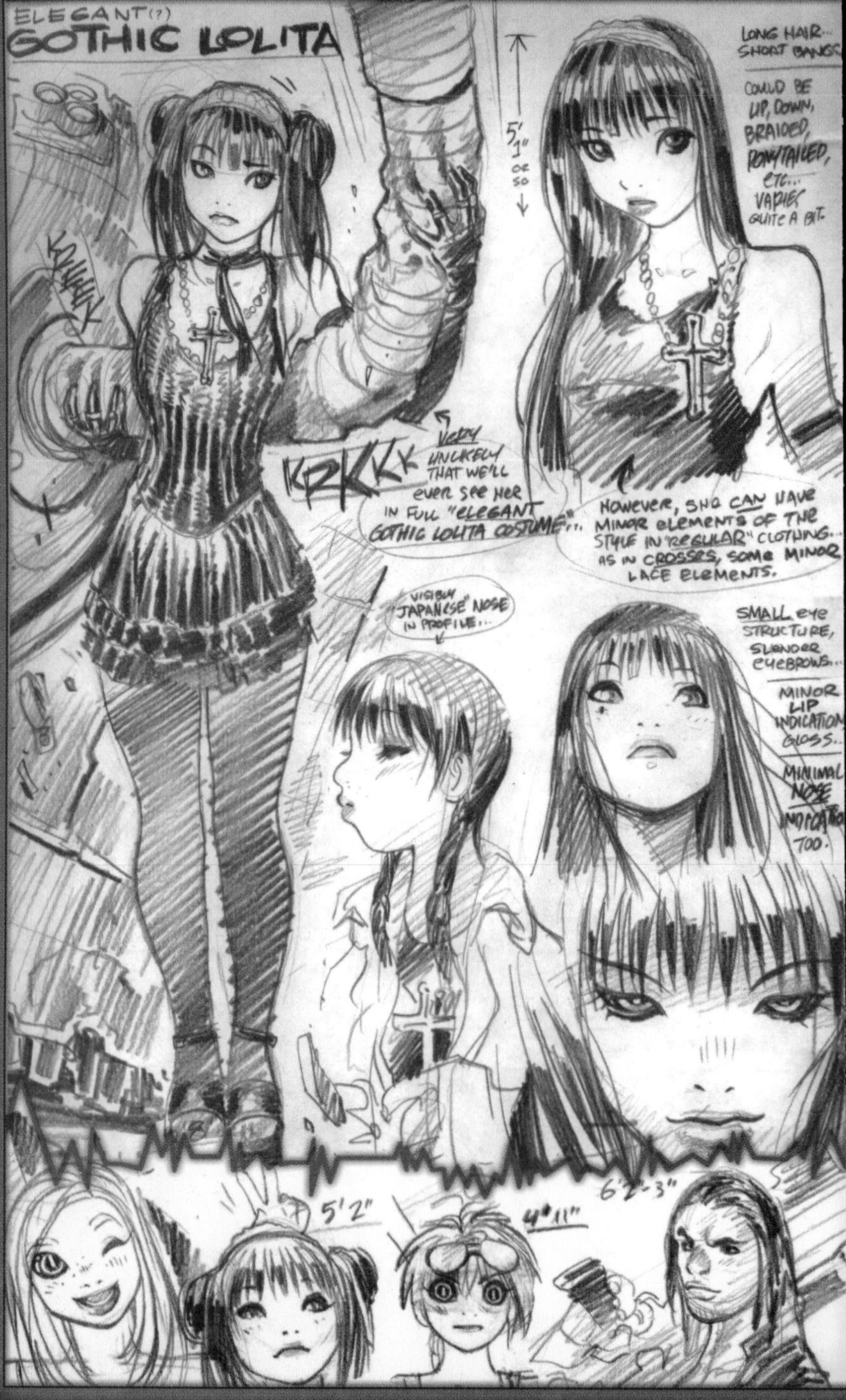
ELEGANT(?)
GOTHIC LOLITA
5'1" OR SO
LONG HAIR... SHORT BANGS
COULD BE UP, DOWN, BRAIDED, PONYTAILED, ETC... VARIES QUITE A BIT.
KRKKK
VERY UNLIKELY THAT WE'LL EVER SEE HER IN FULL "ELEGANT GOTHIC LOLITA COSTUME"...
HOWEVER, SHE CAN HAVE MINOR ELEMENTS OF THE STYLE IN "REGULAR" CLOTHING... AS IN CROSSES, SOME MINOR LACE ELEMENTS.
VISIBLY "JAPANESE" NOSE IN PROFILE...
SMALL EYE STRUCTURE, SLENDER EYEBROWS...
MINOR LIP INDICATION GLOSS...
MINIMAL NOSE INDICATION TOO.
5'2"
4'11"
6'2-3"